Suicidal Behaviour: Theories and Research Findings

Suicidal Behaviour

Theories and Research Findings

Edited by
D. De Leo, U. Bille-Brahe, A. Kerkhof, & A. Schmidtke

World Health Organization Regional Office for Europe

Hogrefe & Huber

Library of Congress Cataloguing-in-Publication Data

is available via the Library of Congress Marc Database
under the LC Control Number 2001111972

Library and Archives Canada Cataloguing-in-Publication

Suicidal behaviour: theories and research findings / D. De Leo . . . [et al.] (Eds.).
Includes bibliographical references and index.
ISBN 0-88937-267-5

1.Suicide—Prevention. 2.Suicidal behavior. 3.Suicide—Psychological aspects.
I.De Leo, Diego, 1951–
RC569.S84 2004   362.28'7   C2004-903647-5

PUBLISHING OFFICES
USA: Hogrefe & Huber Publishers, 875 Massachusetts Avenue, 7th Floor, Cambridge, MA 02139
          Tel. (866) 823-4726, Fax (617) 354-6875, E-mail info@hhpub.com
Europe: Hogrefe & Huber Publishers, Rohnsweg 25, 37085 Göttingen, Germany
          Tel. +49 551 49609-0, Fax +49 551 49609-88, E-mail hhpub@hogrefe.de

SALES AND DISTRIBUTION
USA: Hogrefe & Huber Publishers, Customer Service Department, 30 Amberwood Parkway,
          Ashland, OH 44805, Tel. (800) 228-3749, Fax (419) 281-6883
          E-mail custserv@hhpub.com
Europe: Hogrefe & Huber Publishers, Rohnsweg 25, 37085 Göttingen, Germany
          Tel. +49 551 49609-0, Fax +49 551 49609-88, E-mail hhpub@hogrefe.de

OTHER OFFICES
Canada: Hogrefe & Huber Publishers, 1543 Bayview Avenue, Toronto, Ontario, M4G 3B5
Switzerland: Hogrefe & Huber Publishers, Länggass-Strasse 76, CH-3000 Bern 9

Hogrefe & Huber Publishers
Incorporated and registered in the State of Washington, USA, and in Göttingen, Lower Saxony,
Germany

Printed and bound in Germany

ISBN 0-88937-267-5

Table of Contents

Part 4: Suicidal Behaviour in Special Interest Groups

Part 5: Clinical Aspects in Non-Fatal Suicidal Behaviour

Foreword

Even before suicide was clearly recognized as a major public health problem a few years ago, the WHO/EURO Multi-Centre Study on Suicidal Behaviour (originally the WHO/EURO Study on Parasuicide) initiated what was to become the largest multi-site source of information on suicide attempts.

For some 15 years, data were collected in up to 45 European cities – large- and medium-sized – and provided a wealth of knowledge on the epidemiology, demography, clinical aspects, associated factors (both risk and protective) and methods employed in a vast number of cases of suicide attempts. The use of a common methodology allowed reliable comparisons across sites and originated a kind of European atlas of suicide attempts. Numerous papers, dissertations, theses and books that used data collected by participants in this study attest to its scientific importance and created a sound basis for action that, from a public health perspective, should give priority to prevention.

And the time for action has arrived. The network of researchers, clinicians, public health officers, community leaders organized around this WHO/EURO study now has the possibility – as well as the moral obligation – to transform the knowledge amassed during all these years of the study's duration into concrete action to prevent suicidal behaviours and to improve the quality of the care for both those who are at greater or immediate risk and for those who have already engaged in suicidal acts.

It is our hope that the stamina that kept the WHO/EURO study alive and productive for so long will now fuel the same enthusiasm for the prevention of suicidal behaviours. WHO, at both Headquarters and the Regional Office for Europe, gives a high priority to suicide prevention and all well intentioned collaboration in this respect is welcome.

I wish readers of this book a fruitful and insightful reading, convinced that they will find in it lots of inspiration for their current or future work.

Dr Benedetto Saraceno
Director, Department of Mental Health and Substance Dependence
World Health Organization

Part 1

Introduction

Chapter 1
Suicide Prevention – Background, Problems, Strategies: Introductory Remarks

Wolfgang Rutz, M.D., Ph.D.

Regional Adviser, Mental Health, WHO Regional Office for Europe

Suicide is one of the most dramatic symptoms of mental illness. The diversity of suicide rates and populations in Europe is immense, and statistics can reveal up to a fifty-fold difference in the rates of suicidality between different countries and the populations at risk. Factors such as psychosocial determinants of mental health, biological and gender-related vulnerability, the quality, accessibility and acceptability of services, cultural influences as well as issues of social cohesion, existential meaning in life, helplessness and control, as well as dignity and identity, form intricate interrelated patterns in explaining the backgrounds of suicides. The countries of Eastern Europe, currently in dramatic transition, are illustrative examples here for the self-destructive consequences of change, transition, helplessness and unpredictability, as, in the same way, do Western Europe's at-risk populations – adolescents, farmers, elderly men and young women – reveal different factorial elements.

European countries show 300-fold differences in the national per capita income and an enormous variety in the provision and quality of care and support, including the development and implementation of suicide preventive strategies and national action plans against drugs and alcohol, a problem we know is related to suicide and suicide prevention.

From the wide diversity of suicide problems in Europe and worldwide and on the basis of the World Health Report 2001, the messages from the World Health Organization are:

– suicide is one of the most important public health problems, causing immense cost and suffering, both individually as well in the family and the society;

- it can be prevented;
- suicide prevention has to be comprehensive, multidisciplinary and involve different aspects of life as well as different sectors of society; and
- national strategies and policies have to be developed, addressing the specific problems as well as respecting the cultural patterns, value systems and societal structures of the individual country.

To cope with the problems of suicidal behaviour, to facilitate action and to raise awareness, a WHO European network on suicide prevention and research has recently evolved from the former WHO/EURO Multi-Centre Study on Suicidal Behaviour and is today established in most of the Members States of the Region. This network aims at:

- continuously assessing the suicide situation in Europe;
- creating, proposing and facilitating national mental health planning on suicide prevention, integrated in national master plans on mental health development;
- developing specific suicide preventive strategies; and
- continuously monitoring and evaluating the implementation of these.

The book presented here makes an important contribution to our knowledge of suicidal behaviour, illustrating the work already done by WHO and the former Multi-Centre Study, educating professionals and the public, raising awareness of this problem and facilitating the future work of this group and others. In over 20 chapters, European experts in the field of suicidology linked to the suicide prevention work of WHO, describe the current state of research, theory and practice.

Only accurate information, derived from reliable and valid data embedded in well-founded theory and practice – as presented in this volume – can originate effective prevention programs, which is the principle message of this book. I sincerely hope that the experiences matured by the scientists who have run the WHO/EURO study for nearly 15 years may guide European member states in the development of national and regional strategies of suicide prevention and the related research necessary monitoring and evaluation.

The present decrease of suicide in some European countries with nationally coordinated suicide prevention approaches is a sign of hope. The new consensus on focusing on comprehensive programmes that include sociological, psychological, existential as well as hereditary and psychopathological factors in the understanding and treatment of suicidal behaviour – as explored in detail in this book – permits the use of new tools that allow for concrete possibilities and new perspectives for powerful synergistic and comprehensive suicide prevention in Europe.

Chapter 2
The WHO/Euro Multi-Centre Study on Suicidal Behaviour: Its Background, History, Aims and Design

Unni Bille-Brahe[1], Armin Schmidtke[2], Ad Kerkhof[3] and Diego De Leo[4]

[1]*Suicide Research Centre, Odense, Denmark (retired),* [2]*Department of Clinical Psychology, University of Würzburg, Germany,* [3]*Department of Clinical Psychology, Vrije Universiteit, Amsterdam, The Netherlands,* [4]*Australian Institute for Suicide Research and Prevention, Griffith University, Brisbane, Australia*

Background, and the History in General

Lasting for many years, the WHO/EURO Multi-Centre Study on Suicidal Behaviour has been one of the few collaborative projects in the field of suicidological research. It is interesting to note that the endeavour began back in the beginning of the 1980s by one man having an idea. That man was Dr. John Henderson, Regional Officer of Mental Health at the WHO Regional Office for Europe in Copenhagen.

During the beginning of the 1980s, the World Health Assembly had worked out the common target "Health for All by the Year 2000" for all governments and the WHO. By that time, increasing rates of both completed and attempted suicide were causing concern in most European countries, and when the member countries of the European Region of WHO in 1984 wanted to specify the very broad goal of the Health for All programme into 32 concrete targets, one of these targets, namely Target 12, was to aim at the reduction of the problem of suicide: "By the year 2000, the current rising trends in suicides and attempted suicides in the Region should be reversed."

The Department of Mental Health at the WHO European Regional Office was, however, aware that to approach this target, there was a need for more valid and comparable information, especially on non-fatal suicidal acts. Some reports had been indicating that rates of attempted suicide were no longer increasing with the epidemic haste as in 1970s, but findings were not consistent, and more studies were obviously needed.

In May 1985, Dr. John Henderson therefore summoned a small group of experts to a brainstorm meeting. The group consisted of the late Prof. Niels Juel-Nielsen, Denmark, Professor Rene Diekstra, The Netherlands, Dr. Armin Schmidtke, Germany, and Dr. Peter Kennedy, England. The outcome of the meeting was that the group should act as a provisional planning group of advisers, and, with research fellow Stephen Platt as secretary, they should prepare a meeting for a Regional Office Working Group on Preventive Practices in Suicide and Attempted Suicide.

And thus the idea of a WHO/EURO Multi-Centre Study was launched in York in September, 1986. Through three days, 31 persons from 15 European countries discussed feasible structures for the project, and aims, designs, definitions, etc. In the end, a smaller working group was established, their task being to work out a strategy and then concrete plans for the project.

The group decided that the project should, at least for the time being, concentrate on non-fatal suicidal acts. As one of the main obstacles to epidemiological research had been the lack of common nomenclature, a term and a definition of non-fatal suicidal acts that were at the same time reasonable from a theoretical point of view, and operational in everyday praxis were therefore needed. The group agreed (following the previous suggestion made by Norman Kreitman and his colleagues, 1969) to introduce the term "parasuicide" to identify such acts, replacing the many other labels in use such as attempted suicide, deliberate self-harm, self-poisoning and the like, and a definition of the term was drafted:

An act with non-fatal outcome, in which an individual deliberately initiates a non-habitual behaviour that, without intervention from others, will cause self-harm, or deliberately ingests substance in excess of the described or generally recognized therapeutic dosage, and which is aimed at realizing changes which the subject desired via the actual or expected physical consequences.

The overall goal of the project was to enhance throughout Europe the awareness of the growing problem of suicidal behaviour, and to promote in general suicide research and prevention. The group decided that initially the Multicentre Study should concentrate on covering two broad areas of research, namely:

– monitoring of trends in the epidemiology of parasuicide, including the identification of risk factors (The Monitoring Study), and
– follow-up studies of parasuicide populations as special high risk group for further suicidal behaviour, with a view to identify social and personal characteristics predictive of future suicidal behaviour (The Repetition-Prediction Study).

A group of the leading researchers (Principal Investigators) from each individual participating centre was to be constituted, acting as a kind of General Assembly, while a steering group, appointed by WHO, was to be responsible for the detailed planning and the design of the instruments to be used. It was also to be the task of this steering group to "facilitate the progress, ensuring conformity and keeping in close control and supervision of the research in progress" (WHO, 1986).

The group of the Principal Investigators (PI), who planned to take part in the Multi-Centre Study, first met in London in November, 1986. At the meeting the following were appointed as members of the Steering Group (SG): Ass. Prof. Unni Bille-Brahe, Odense; Prof. Rene Diekstra, Leiden; Dr. Armin Schmidtke, Wuerzburg; and Ass. Prof. Stephen Platt, Edinburgh as technical coordinator. In March 1987, Rene Diekstra, due to other commitments, left the group and was replaced by Dr. Ad Kerkhof, also of Leiden.

The first task of the PI and SG was to outline the structure of the study. It was decided that a participating centre should cover a population of at least 200,000 adult inhabitants (15 years and older), and that the areas under study should be clearly defined both geographically and administratively to allow for comparison of information on the population of suicide attempters with the statistics on the total population in the area. All centres were asked to provide information on their area under study, including general background data such as the area's size and location, and the breakdown of its population according to age, sex, civil status, housing and urban/rural distribution. This background information was eventually presented in the publication *Facts and Figures* (Bille-Brahe et al., 1993, 1999), which also includes information on indicators of social stability/instability in the area (such as crime and violence), the general health situation (including the frequency of alcoholism and drug abuse), and on the local welfare and health care system including hospital facilities.

For the *Monitoring Study,* four targets were outlined:

- to assess the feasibility of using local case registers to monitor parasuicide in defined catchment areas
- to estimate the incidence of medically treated parasuicides and trends over time, using the standardized definition and case-finding criteria
- to identify socio-demographic risk factors significantly associated with parasuicide
- to ascertain variations in patterns of treatment following parasuicide in different cultural contexts with the aim of establishing more effective services for preventing this type of behaviour

The registration (or monitoring) of suicide attempts was to be carried out according to the same case finding criteria on consecutive episodes at all places within the health care system where suicide attempters were seen. A *Monitoring Form,* to be used by all centres, was to be worked out by the SG. The form should include questions about age, sex, the method(s) used, any previous suicide attempts, and about various socio-demographic characteristics such as civil status, usual and actual household composition, religion, education and economical activity and status. All monitoring data were to be transferred to the centre in Wuerzburg, where they were to be checked by Dr. Armin Schmidtke's group, being responsible for the quality of the Monitoring Study.

The *Repetition-Prediction Study* was to be a follow-up study with interviews to be carried out on random samples of suicide attempters. The aims were:

- to identify personal and social characteristics predictive of future suicidal behaviour
- to evaluate existing scales which have been designed to predict suicidal behaviour
- to estimate the social, the psychological, and the economic burden of repeated parasuicide on the individual, his/her close social milieu, and on society as a whole
- to assess the utilization of health and social services by the parasuicide population and the effectiveness of the various treatments offered
- to compare differences in personal characteristics (clinical, socio-demographical, psychological, etc.) among parasuicides in different cultural and socio-economic settings

The initial interview (EPSIS I) was to be carried out within one week after the attempt (or after regaining consciousness), the second interview one year later. All data were to be collected and corrected by the centre in Odense under the leadership of Unni Bille-Brahe.

When drafting the interview schedules for the follow-up study, the SG took point of departure in empirical research findings and theoretically based hypothesis about predictors of suicidal behaviour. The schedules therefore came to include instruments already well known such as the *Beck Depression Inventory* and the *Hopelessness Scale*, as well as instruments constructed especially for the study, such as the *Life Event and History Scale*, and the *Social Support Scale*. In addition to detailed medical and socio-demographic information, the schedules were to cover, by observer-rated or self-rated instruments, constructs such as motives for the suicide attempt, suicidal transmission, life events, social integration. While drafting the instruments, the SG was in regular contact with the participating centres, and drafts were discussed with the PI, who during this period met 2–3 times a year. In 1989, a draft for the schedules was sent to all participating centres for field testing, and based on the comments received, the SG worked out the final versions of *The European Parasuicide Study Interview Schedules (EPSIS I and II)* which were accepted in May 1989 (Kerkhof et al., 1993a, 1993b). The schedules were worked out in standard English versions, which were translated into the various languages and then back-translated for the sake of control. The standard English version of the schedules were presented in the 1st edition of *Facts and Figures*.

In 1988, Dr. Henderson stepped down from his official position at WHO, but he continued to act as administrator and chairperson of the PI meetings until Dr.Jose Sampaio Faria was appointed as the new Mental Health Officer later that year.

Due to other commitments, Stephen Platt had to leave the SG in 1991, and he was replaced by Diego De Leo. It can be added that for the last ten years of the study, the SG has had regular telephone meetings, usually once a month.

From the beginning, the working group and the WHO had stressed the importance of a close collaboration between centres, and it was decided that representatives from the centres participating in the Multicentre Study should meet regularly. Usually such meetings were arranged in connection with relevant European or international conferences or other events, but soon a tradition also developed for having annual technical meetings in Wuerzburg. No doubt these meetings, with their free discussions on theoretical, methodological and practical problems between trusted colleagues and experts in the field, have been contributional to the high quality of the Multicentre Study.

During these meetings, it became gradually clear that some publication rules for the Multicentre Study were needed, and a group, consisting of Armin Schmidtke, Unni Bille-Brahe, Ad Kerkhof, Diego De Leo and Juoko Lönnqvist (chairman), was commissioned by the PI to work out a set of such rules. In 1993, a set of *Publication Rules* was accepted by the PI and WHO, and a Publication Group was established. Armin Schmidtke, Unni Bille-Brahe and Ad Kerkhof were to be members ex officio, the chairman and a representative of the PI were to be elected by the PI for a two-year period. The provisional group was officially elected as the Publication Group (PG) in 1996. In 1998, Juoko Lönnqvist resigned from his task as chairman and, at the same time, Diego De Leo had served his term of two years. As new members Cees van Heeringen and Keith Hawton were then elected as chairman and PI representative, respectively. Since 2000, the Publication Group has consisted of Unni Bille-Brahe (chair), Heidi Hjelmeland (co-chair), Diego De Leo, Keith Hawton, Ad Kerkhof, Armin Schmidtke and Danuta Wasserman.

The first results from the Multi-Centre Study were released at a conference held by The Netherlands Institute for Advanced Study in the Humanities and Social Sciences, at Wassenaar in November, 1993 (later to be published in the book *Attempted Suicide in Europe. Findings from the Multicentre Study on Parasuicide by the WHO Regional Office for Europe* (Kerkhof et al., 1994).

In the same year, the centre in Odense entered, on behalf of the Multi-Centre Study, in negotiations with EC about financing the cost connected with dealing with the huge amount of data collected by the Repetition-Prediction Study. Funding was eventually granted for the project in cooperation with the EC Concerted Action on Attempted Suicide.

Gradually, the scope of the Multi-Centre Study had broadened to encompass both non-fatal and fatal suicidal acts (Bille-Brahe, 1998), and in 1999, the name was changed to *The WHO/Euro Multicentre Study on Suicidal Behaviour*.

In the mean time, the Mental Health Office at the WHO Regional Office for

Europe had been closed down. Dr. Jose Sampaio Faria had left office and was not to be replaced. Formally, however, the Multi-Centre Study continued to be under the auspices of the WHO Regional Office for Europe under the direction of Dr. Marc Danzon, Head of the Department for Lifestyle and Health. In 1998, it was decided by the WHO General Assembly that the topic of mental health was to be back on the priority list, and a new Mental Health Officer at the WHO Regional Office in Copenhagen was to be appointed. In 1999, the position was given to Dr. Wolfgang Rutz.

In 2000, a suggestion of establishing a task force for suicide prevention was launched at the meeting of PI in Bled, and at the annual meeting in Wuerzburg later that year, Dr Wolfgang Rutz presented the concrete plan for transforming the Multi-Centre Study into a *WHO/Euro Network for Suicide Prevention*. The establishment of the Network was confirmed at a special meeting in Copenhagen in May, 2001. According to the Terms of Reference, the network is to be "a tool for action of the WHO Regional Office for Europe and a pool of resources for the improvement of the situation regarding suicidality in Europe." The Network is going to consist of national centres of excellence (national "focal points"), and its tasks are listed as:

- to collect evidence-based knowledge on suicide prevention
- to collect information needed for the continuous monitoring of the suicidal in the country
- to coordinate national activities on suicide prevention
- to link internationally to national activities of other countries
- to facilitate development of guidelines on comprehensive suicide prevention
- to assist in starting national suicide prevention planning
- to monitor and evaluate this planning
- to produce position papers, scientific literature, books and information on suicidality in individual countries and Europe as a whole
- to offer peer review and peer support to members of the Network
- to function as a pool of resources for WHO and its member states
- to prepare an action plan on suicide prevention to be presented and adopted at this workshop
- to contribute to the European ministerial conference on mental health planned to be held in 2004, covering the field of suicidality

The SG of the Network is composed of Dr. Wolfgang Rutz (Chair), Prof. Armin Schmidtke (Secretary), Ass. Prof. Unni Bille-Brahe, Dr. Alexander Botsis, Prof. Diego De Leo, Dr. Margaret Kelleher, Prof. Ad Kerkhof, Prof. Airi Varnik and Prof. Danuta Wasserman. The Publication Group is consisting of Unni Bille-Brahe (Chair), Heidi Hjelmeland (Co-Chair), Diego De Leo, Keith Hawton, Ad Kerkhof, Armin Schmidtke and Danuta Wasserman. It should be added that after a meeting in Copenhagen in December, 2001,the name of the Network was changed into WHO/Euro Network for Suicide Prevention and Research.

The Progress of the Monitoring Study

The Monitoring Study started in 1989 with the following participating centres:

Berne, Switzerland (Dr. Konrad Michel)
Bordeaux, France (Dr. Xavier Pommerau)
Emilia-Romagna, Italy (Dr. Paolo Crepet)
Guipuzcoa, Spain (Dr. Imanol Querejeta)
Helsinki, Finland (Prof. Juoko Lönnqvist)
Innsbruck, Austria (Dr. Christian Haring)
Leiden, The Netherlands (Dr. Ad Kerkhof)
Odense, Denmark (Ass. Prof. Unni Bille-Brahe)
Oxford, England (Dr. Keith Hawton)
Padua, Italy (Dr. Diego De Leo)
Pontoise, France (Dr. A. Philippe)
Stockholm, Sweden (Ass. Prof. Danuta Wasserman)
Szeged, Hungary (Dr. Beata Temesvary)
Sør-Trøndelag, Norway (Prof. Tore Bjerke)
Umeå, Sweden (Dr. Ellinor Salander Renberg)
Würzburg, Germany (Dr. Armin Schmidtke).

The first report from the Multi-Centre Study was published in 1992 (Platt et al., 1992) and then a full report covering the years 1989–1992 was published in 1994 (Kerkhof et al., 1994).

Unfortunately, after a few years, six centres (Bordeaux, Emilia-Romagna, Guipuzcoa, Pontoise and Szeged, and later Leiden) had to drop out of the study – mainly because of lack of funds (it should be noted that for the first years, WHO covered the cost connected with the meetings of PG and SG. Each centre has always had to provide its own funding, and subsequently for covering costs of attending meetings).

On the other hand, new centres kept joining the Monitoring Study, which at the end comprised 21 active centres, including:

Cork, Ireland (Dr. Margaret Kelleher)
Gent, Belgium (Prof. Cees van Heeringen)
Rennes, France (Dr. Agnes Batt)
Leiden, The Netherlands, re-entered the study in 2001 (Ella Arensman)
Ljubljana, Slovenia (Prof. Onja Grad)
Novi Sad, The Federal Republic of Yugoslavia (Dr. Slavica Selacovic-Bursic)
Odessa, Ukraine (Dr. Alexander Mokhovikov)
Pecs, Hungary (Dr. Sandor Fekete)
Tallinn, Estonia (Prof. Airi Varnik)

Athens, Greece (Dr. Alexander Botsis)
Mamak, Turkey (Prof. Isik Sayil)
Holon-Batt, Israel (Prof. Alan Apter)

The new centres started monitoring in 1995. Reports from all centres, and also analyses of rates and trends based on data from the 10 centres that have provided data for the full period 1989–1997/1998, is presented in the book *Suicidal Behaviour in Europe: Results from the WHO/Euro Multi-Centre Study on Suicidal Behaviour* [Schmidtke, Bille-Brahe, De Leo, & Kerkhof, 2004).

About the Repetition-Prediction Study

Both the interview schedules include detailed instructions as to how to contact and inform the patient. Furthermore, to ensure inter-rater reliability, all interviewers attended a three-day intensive training at St. Andrews Hospital in Northampton, UK before the study started. At most centres, the first wave of interviews started in 1990.

Table 1 Numbers of interviews carried out in the period 1990–1993.

Centre	EPSIS I	EPSIS II
Berne	66	48
Emilia Romagna	56	–
Helsinki	224	115
Leiden	141	106
Odense	139	92
Padova	106	35
Stockholm	202	133
Sør Trøndelag	89	23
Umeå	122	49
Wuerzburg	124	–
In all	1269	601

In 1996, a second wave of the Repetition-Prediction Study was started, and a new training session was arranged by the centre in Odense, November, 1996. In the end, six new centres joined the study, but unfortunately, the funding from EU stopped in 1998, and consequently the controlling procedure could not be completed.

In December 2001, Dr. Christian Haring and his group volunteered to go through the control procedure for the EPSIS I and II interviews not yet corrected.

Table 2 Numbers of interviews carried out during the second period (1996–1998).

Centre	Controlled		Not controlled	
	EPSIS I	EPSIS II	EPSIS I	EPSIS II
Cork	–	–	146	?
Gent	112			28
Hall	70	–	–	?
Oxford	150			150
Pecs	101			31
Slovenia	62	–	–	–
In all	495	–	146	209

References

Bille-Brahe, U. et al. (1993, 1999). *Facts and figures*. Copenhagen: WHO Regional Office for Europe (1st and 2nd ed.).

Bille-Brahe, U. (1998). *Suicidal behaviour in Europe. The situation in the 1990s*. Copenhagen: WHO Regional Office for Europe.

Bille-Brahe, U. (2004). Definitions and terminology used in the WHO/Euro Multicentre Study. In A. Schmidtke et al. (Eds.), *Suicidal behaviour in Europe. Results from the WHO/ Euro Multicentre Study on Suicidal Behaviour*. Göttingen: Hogrefe & Huber.

Kerkhof, A. J. F. M., Schmidtke, A., Bille-Brahe, U., De Leo, D., & Lönnqvist, J. (Eds.). (1994). *Attempted suicide in Europe. Findings from the Multicentre Study on Parasuicide by the WHO Regional Office for Europe*. Leiden: DSWO Press.

Kerkhof, A. J. F. M., Bernasco, W., Bille-Brahe, U., Platt, S., & Schmidtke, A. (1993). European Parasuicide Study Interview Schedule (EPSIS I), Version 5.1. In U. Bille-Brahe et al. (Eds.), *Facts and figures*. Copenhagen: WHO/EUR/ICP/PSF018.

Kerkhof, A. J. F. M., van Egmond, M., Bille-Brahe, U., Platt, S., & Schmidtke A. (1993). European Parasuicide Study Interview Schedule (EPSIS II). In U. Bille-Brahe et al. (Eds.), *Facts and figures*. Copenhagen: WHO/EUR/ICP/PSF018.

Kreitman, N. et al. (1969). Parasuicide. *British Journal of Psychiatry, 115*, 746–747.

Platt, S., Bille-Brahe, U., Kerkhof, A. J. F. M., Schmidtke, A., Bjerke, T., Crepet, P., De Leo, D., Haring, C., Konnqvist, J., Michel, K., Phillippe, A., Pommerau, X., Querejeta, I., Salander Renberg, E., Temesvary, B., Wasserman, D., & Sampaio Faria, J. (1992). Parasuicide in Europe: The WHO/Euro Multicentre Study on Parasuicide I. Introduction and preliminary analysis for 1989. *Acta Psychiatrica Scandinavica, 85*, 97–104.

Schmidtke, A., Bille-Brahe, U., De Leo, D., & Kerkhof, A. J. F. M. (Eds.). (2004). *Suicidal behaviour in Europe. Results from the WHO/Euro Multicentre Study on Suicidal Behaviour*. Göttingen: Hogrefe & Huber.

WHO Regional Office for Europe (1986). *Summary report*. Working Group on Preventive Practices in Suicide and Attempted Suicide, York 22–26 September 1986. ICP/PSF 017. Copenhagen: Author.

Part 2

Theoretical Aspects

Chapter 3
Definitions of Suicidal Behaviour

Diego De Leo[1], Shelley Burgis[1], José M. Bertolote[2], Ad Kerkhof[3] and Unni Bille-Brahe[4]

[1]*Australian Institute for Suicide Research and Prevention, Griffith University, Brisbane, Australia,* [2]*World Health Organisation, Geneva, Switzerland,* [3]*Department of Clinical Psychology, Vrije Universiteit, Amsterdam, The Netherlands,* [4]*Suicide Research Centre, Odense, Denmark (retired)*

Introduction

Since 1903, when the first "International Classification of Diseases and Causes of Death" was adopted, suicide has been included in the section dealing with morbidity and mortality due to external causes. Reading through the proceedings of the various international conferences to update that classification (roughly every 10 years, until 1994), as discussed by Shneidman (1984), it becomes clear that suicide is a "residual mode," to be used when the other ones could not be confirmed. The other modes are: natural, accidental and homicidal, constituting together the NASH system,

In 1910, amidst complaints that there were too many categories for suicide and too few for accidents, there was also a proposal by Bertillon (the Chief Statistician from the City of Paris who drafted the "ICD-1") that the information on suicides and homicides should be left to justice, rather than to medicine. In his own words:

> "Indeed, justice has all the time needed to conduct a thorough enquiry in each case of violent death. Doctors, on the contrary, cannot do that. A doctor will usually hesitate before certifying that a given case is a suicide (and even more so a homicide) if it is not at all evident. He will always prefer to state what he actually sees, that is, that there was a crushing or a shot, or injury to such and such organ, without venturing to say that it was a suicide or a crime, since quite frequently he does not know at all, and would complicate his life with such a statement." (Bertillon, 1910)

From 1903 until 1948, all pertinent categories were classified under "Conditions produced by external causes" by the means used and phrased as "suicide due to . . ." From 1948 onwards (ICD-6) and until 1965 (ICD-8), the section was named "Accidents, poisoning and violence" and the pertinent category was renamed "Suicide and self-inflicted injury." ICD-9, in 1975, named the section "Injury and poisoning" and the category was named "Suicide"; a note explained that it included "suicide attempts; and purposefully self-inflicted injuries." ICD-10 (1992) created a category of "intentional self-harm" explaining that it included "purposefully self-inflicted poisoning or injury; and suicide (attempted)."

In 1964, Stengel proposed that suicide and suicide attempt referred to two distinct populations. However, strictly speaking, a "true" suicide attempt should refer only to those who failed to die, after having tried to kill themselves, and survived. A tentative step to overcome this semantic and conceptual snag was the introduction of the expression "suicidal behavior." This expression, which clearly stems from the behavioural approach predominant in the USA psychology, was a "politically correct" move brought forward by feminist scholars who objected to the supposed bias conveyed by the use of "attempt," mostly seen among women, and implying that women were less competent than men (among which "completed" suicide was more frequent) in "completing" that act (Lester, 1994).

From a logic perspective, the crucial elements to differentiate between suicidal, accidental or homicidal acts (as possible external causes of death, distinct from those due to natural causes) are actually two: (a) the locus of origin (self initiated) and (b) the intention (to cause or not cause death). The outcome, death or injury or nothing, is clearly the result of that, the visible phenomenon of a more immediate interest to health staff, particularly those working in emergency care settings.

In practice, suicide attempts, when serious enough to need medical attention (and the majority of these acts are *not*, and remain unknown to medical authorities) are mostly cared for at emergency rooms. In those places staff are ordinarily much more concerned with the nature of the injury or intoxication than with the eventual intention at the origin (or cause) of that injury or intoxication. The medical or surgical need is tended for and once this has cleared, the patient is either discharged (in the majority of the cases) or referred for further assessment and follow-up (which, in a minority of cases, involves mental health staff). Under these circumstances, the diagnosis recorded will reflect the nature of the injury or intoxication, as medical staff do not investigate the intention behind the act. Depending on the jurisdiction, in all cases of non-natural death, an investigation is conducted by the justice or police, thus fulfilling the wishes of Bertillon of more than 90 years ago.

As a consequence of these practices, most countries have national systems to record, collect and process information related to suicides (mortality registers) on a permanent basis, but so far no country has an equivalent system specific for suicide attempts (morbidity registers). In a few cases, there are similar registers for injuries and for intoxications, however, in most of them without reference to intentionality, which would allow for a distinction between accidental, criminal or self-inflicted injuries or intoxication.

The current public health approach, as indicated by ICD-10, is to group all intentional self-harm activities, and use this broad category in the context of both morbidity and mortality. It has the great advantage of being rather descriptive and of avoiding value-loaded terms such as suicide and suicide attempt. However, the assessment of intentionality remains a crucial issue that not only impacts heavily on sanitary matters but has also legal and criminological implications.

In this chapter, we will accompany the reader through the many existing problems that are endemic to the field of suicide and attempted suicide nomenclature, trying to explain why these render perennially dissatisfied researchers and clinicians. Supported by the experience matured within fifteen years of the WHO/EURO Multi-Centre Study on Parasuicide (Kerkhof et al., 1994), we will examine a number of definitional issues that normally complicate the understanding of suicidal behaviours, and eventually hinder the progress of suicide research and its logical outcome: suicide prevention.

Suicide mortality was not the main focus of the WHO/EURO study. The priority was instead suicide morbidity (attempted suicides), and this was due to the alarmingly increasing trends that were affecting Europe during the Eighties. The possible role of attempts as precursor/predictor of subsequent completed suicides was of course the ultimate justification for performing the study.

Although of common use and routinely accepted by WHO, in suicidology, "mortality/morbidity" emphasizes in an inappropriate way the disease model that is implicit in the use of this terminology. Suicide is a behaviour and not an illness; in addition, in most cases suicide attempts represent a kind of "spurious" morbidity, their actors having no intention to die at all, but just wanting to manipulate their environment. Once more, the role of intention(s) is of critical importance in the clinical/scientific appraisal of suicidal and suicided persons. In this light, it will be of interest to know how the WHO/EURO study group dealt with these issues and what are the outcomes of such a long, cooperative effort in the definitional domain.

The Importance of Consistent Definitions to Different Professional Domains

Adequate definitions form the backbone of any field of interest, and this is especially true for suicidology. In order to mount effective prevention efforts, suicidal behaviour must be understood, and in order to be understood suicidal behaviour, it must first be defined. Each person intuitively knows what he or she means when the topic of suicide arises in everyday conversation. However, the definition of suicide is inherently more complex than the simple words "killing oneself." Although it is doubtful that we will ever be able to construct universally unambiguous criteria to comprehensively characterise suicidal behaviours (and, overall, firmly establish the intention behind them), for scientific clarity it would be highly desirable that the set of definitions and the associated terminology be explicit and generalizable.

A large part of the difficulty in defining suicidal behaviour comes from the broad spectrum of outcomes that this term is currently used to describe. Fatal suicidal behaviour tends to have societal, clinical and demographic characteristics that are quite distinct from those of non-fatal suicidal behaviour, and this has led to the adoption of a range of different terms to try to encompass these differences. As it will be demonstrated later in this chapter, the intention to die constitutes an important distinction in many cases and this has prompted the use of alternative terminology, such as in the case of "parasuicide" adopted in the WHO/EURO study.

Terminology and definitions are the two elements that constitute a standard nomenclature (O'Carroll et al., 1996), and it is within both of these areas that suicidology is currently confusing. A satisfactory nomenclature of suicide should be applicable and usable both within and across all domains in which it is to be employed, whether the focus is research, clinical practice, public health, politics or law.

It is argued that inconsistent definitions of variables pose real world problems. For suicide, these problems emerge in three principal areas: (1) public health (certification of death and calculation of mortality rates), (2) research, and (3) clinical practice. As detailed below, each of these domains has different reasons for needing a standard definition of suicide and, consequently, differing applications for the definition.

Discussions regarding a lack of consistency in terminology and definitions for suicidology have predominantly centred on the possibility that suicide mortality rates are over- or underestimated regionally, nationally and internationally (Barraclough et al., 1976; O'Carroll, 1989). Cultural and socio-demographic differences provide important clues regarding the propensity to suicide in different populations. In terms of quantifying these trends, the accuracy of the information gathered is crucial. Prior to making governmental decisions, such as the allocation of resources to preventative programs, policy makers must be certain that relative differences in rates are true, and not attributable to systematic biases in reporting or identifying suicides.

The process of death certification has been flagged as one area in which biases can influence mortality rates. It is often unclear as to whether the death was self-inflicted, and it is even more complicated to determine post-hoc what was intended (O'Carroll, 1989). Cases of suicide are therefore not always clear-cut; there is often assumption and guesswork involved, and, without a consistent set of criteria for determining suicides versus what should be classified as accidental or homicidal, the guesswork involved is magnified.

In addition, there are numerous pressures on professionals that may influence appraisals, including societal and religious prejudices, and the expected impact of a suicide verdict on the victim's family (Barraclough et al., 1976; Schneidman, 1981). Alleviating the distress and feelings of guilt for survivors, allowing widows to collect their husband's life insurance money, the possibility of the suicide not being buried with full religious rites, and religious beliefs that suicide is a sin leading the family of a suicide victim to be shunned from the community, may each be seen as good reasons for not arriving at a true verdict (De Leo et al., 2002). Consequently, much research effort has been devoted to examining the consistency with which coroners, pathologists and other officials involved in cause of death identification make their decisions.

One of the very few international comparisons on death certification procedures specifically in relation to suicide was concluded in 1974 under the auspices of the WHO, and looked at both the variations between countries and between certifying authorities (Brooke & Atkinson, 1974). Results of the questionnaire, which was completed by officials in 24 participating countries, suggested that as elements of the classification process differ, so too will suicide statistics. The main areas of variation between countries were found in the qualifications of the officials involved, level of appointment and supervision, the additional inquiries undertaken, examinations and autopsies conducted, tools available in the fact-finding process, and the way in which the decision is recorded and information subsequently stored. All of these differences summated to the conclusion that there is considerable international variation in classifying a death as suicide. Just as standard definitions of diseases are effective in improving the consistency of diagnoses and comparability of incidence rates for that disease, the authors recommended that a standard definition would contribute to homogenising the classification of suicides and to reducing biases evident in mortality rates.

Other researchers have focused on international comparisons of suicide rates. For example, Sainsbury and Barraclough (1968) measured the suicide rates of immigrants to the United States and demonstrated that these were in the same rank order as the rates reported in their country of origin. More recently, Lester (1992) conducted a comparison of the suicide rates of 15 countries with the rates for undetermined and accidental deaths, to establish whether discrepancies could account for between country differences in rates. This analysis revealed few differences and Lester concluded that although miscounting may occur, it is unlikely to constitute a problem of a magnitude that would impact rates adversely.

To further investigate the accuracy of suicide mortality rates, country or within country comparisons of suicide classifications have been conducted. These studies tend to evidence a consistency in verdicts despite the lack of a common definition, and this persists both across regions and countries (Barraclough et al., 1976; Sainsbury & Jenkins, 1982). For example, Farberow and colleagues (1977) examined coroners' offices in 191 counties in the United States to determine whether the between region variation in suicide rates was resultant from characteristics of the coroners offices rather than real differences in rates. They found that in the larger counties biases introduced by officials had less impact than for the smaller counties. Taken together, these findings suggest that despite fears that suicide mortality rates are, at least partially, socially manufactured, this is not so far-reaching as to invalidate official statistics.

A WHO working group convened in 1981 to determine the validity and reliability of studying trends in suicidal behaviour. After examining the findings cited above and other similar studies, they concluded that there are true differences operating, and that continuing to collate official suicide data and examine relative differences between rates is worthwhile. Though they expressed a sufficient degree of confidence in mortality statistics, the group recommended persistence in considering and analysing suspected biases, and advocated the benefits that a standard nomenclature for suicide would have for this area (WHO, 1982).

Overall, the existing research paints a generally promising picture regarding the validity and reliability of suicide statistics. This said, we must remember that however small the effect, any bias is potentially damaging. Adopting a standard definition of suicide and suicidal behaviours will have a clear positive impact for the legal domain, reducing error and increasing the accuracy of suicide mortality rates. In turn, the correct determination of suicide deaths contributes to an understanding of the risk factors surrounding suicide through the direction of research and targeting high-risk groups (Rosenberg et al., 1988).

Even more so than for fatal behaviours, morbidity statistics counting non-fatal suicidal behaviours are seen as inherently containing error and only as estimates of the real situation. Unlike suicidal behaviour that ends in death, there are numerous physical outcomes and degrees (and types) of intention that are associated with non-fatal suicidal behaviour. This adds to the complexity of calculating incidence rates and heightens the importance of consistent definitions. In compiling statistical information, the following categories have usually been adopted:

- *Admissions* – The number of times a case is admitted to a heath care unit, regardless of the number of admissions of the same case in a single year.
- *Patients* – Each case is counted once only, regardless of how many admissions there were in that given year.
- *First ever attempts* – Cases are counted once only at the time of their first attempt (WHO, 1982).

However, whether or not a case is counted depends on whether or not they present to a health care professional following their attempt.

Research in suicidology is a second area plagued by existing definitional obfuscation (Smith & Maris, 1995). In a recent review, Santa Mina and Gallop (1998) highlighted the pervasive absence of definitional consistency and the impact of this deficiency on research, reporting that the majority of studies lack clear definitions of terminology used. Other reviewers have reported similar findings; for example, in each study reviewed by Ivanoff (1989) an idiosyncratic definition was employed. Most notably, this lack of consistent definitions contributes to a lack of comparability between studies (Linehan, 1997). Therefore, because suicidal behaviour is a complex phenomenon, and there are numerous subtypes of suicidal acts, an additional element of complexity is added to the problem.

Thirdly, in a clinical setting, clarity of terminology is essential to precise assessment, documentation of symptomatology and communication regarding patients between professionals. Measures of suicidality cannot be valid or reliable if they are not appropriately or consistently defined (Muehrer, 1995; O'Carroll et al., 1996). A lack of standard nomenclature is therefore detrimental to clinical practice in the application of studies on treatment effectiveness and risk assessment (Rudd, 1997). The treatment chosen may not prove effective or relevant for a particular patient if their characteristics differ in a significant way from those of the sample utilised in development of the treatment. This leaves open the dangerous likelihood of relapse into the suicidal crisis. Similar, and perhaps more serious, is the importance of a consistent set of terms and definitions to risk assessment. In this case, it is possible that a client will be wrongly assessed at a low level of risk, and such clinical misjudgements may end fatally.

In terms of the outcomes of interventions, realising the aims of effective clinical intervention and preventative campaigns is impossible without a solid definitional foundation. Silverman and Maris (1995) identify that for interventions to be successful the extent of the problem must first be clarified, as well as the target group, and then treatment and delivery strategies must be developed. Overall, consistent and clear definitions provide a strong basis for the development and provision of effective clinical care (Rudd, 1997).

* * *

In sum, there are clear definitional obstacles facing the field of suicidology. These obstacles manifest predominantly in three key areas: public health, academy and clinical domains. The acceptance of a common definition for suicidal behaviour would contribute significantly to resolving these issues. This was also the perspective taken in 1986 by the Working Group in Preventative Practices in Suicide and Attempted Suicide (WHO, 1986). The group aimed to take into account, learn from and progress beyond the mistakes evident in the historical progression of the terminology and meanings surrounding suicide. There are a number of advantages that accompany placing such considerations at the forefront of constructing a definition of suicidal behaviour. The aims of the definitional process are concretised, the definition is placed in context, and greater detail and understanding is gained regarding the language and associated meanings. We will now trace the progression of historical learning that culminated in the definition adopted for the WHO/EURO Multi-centre Study on Suicidal Behaviour.

Historical Definitions of Suicide*

The word suicide was firstly introduced in the 17th century, said to be derived from the Latin words *sui* (of oneself) and *caedere* (to kill). Apparently, Sir Thomas

---

* This covers only European and North American countries and literature, and not other cultural-geographic areas.

Browne – a physician and a philosopher – was the first to coin the term suicide in his Religio Medici (1642). The new word reflected a desire to distinguish between the homicide of oneself and the killing of another (Minois, 1999).

The conceptualisation of suicide has changed throughout history with popular perception, and this has shaped what is currently defined as suicide. In antiquity and the early Roman culture *mors voluntaris* was not only accepted but at times recommended. It has to be noted, however, that especially in Rome, the rules were in force only for free citizens – i.e. slaves were not allowed to kill themselves (if a newly bought slave killed himself, the new owner was entitled to have his money back!).

A first important cultural shift happened with the upcoming of the new Christianity and the increasing numbers of martyrs (the so-called "Donatists"), which turned out to be a more serious threat to the young Christian community than the cruellest persecution by the Romans. As Alvarez wrote ". . . *It culminated in the genuine lunacy of the Donatists, whose lust for martyrdom was so extreme that the Church eventually declared them heretics.*" (Alvarez, 1972). In fact, in 348, the Council of Carthage condemned for the first time in history voluntary death, for the very reason of the Donatism, which praised the practice (Minois, 1999). After the Council of Arles, in 452, the Church also condemned the suicide of all *famuli* (slaves and domestic servants), giving ground to procedures such as the confiscation of all goods of the suicided person.

This negative view continued, spurred by both law and religious influence, and the Councils of Braga (563) and Auxerre (578) ended by condemning all types of suicide, forbidding commemorative offerings and masses for suicides (Minois, 1999). Harsh penalties for suicides and their families existed during the middle ages. Suicide was viewed as a criminal act and actors were placed on trial. Courts of the time distinguished between two verdicts, *non compos mentis* for the innocent madman, and *felo de se* for those felons of themselves judged to be in violation of the laws of God and man (MacDonald, 1989). However, the popular conception of suicide shifted progressively away from criminality. The work of influential thinkers such as Emile Durkheim and Sigmund Freud led to an emphasis on the impact of external influences and the embracement of a more sociological and psychological concept of suicide. Since then, there have been many attempts to reach a consensus on the definition of suicide (see Table 1), yet, thus far, there is little agreement on what aspects are important for inclusion in a definition of suicide.

A number of common key aspects emerge from these definitions: the outcome of the behaviour, the agency of the act, the intention to die or stop living in order to achieve a different status, the consciousness/awareness of the outcomes. In addition, two important conceptual issues emerged, namely, the impact of a theoretical orientation and the place of cultural influences. The cross-cultural design of the WHO/EURO Multi-Centre Study heightened the importance of these characteristics of the definition. Numerous suicidologists from varied backgrounds constituted the group responsible for implementing this project; therefore, the definition settled on must have reflected and allowed for this diversity. In the same

Table 1 Frequently reported definitions of suicide.

"All cases of death resulting directly or indirectly from a positive or negative act of the victim himself, which he knows will produce this result" (Durkheim, 1897/1951).

"All behaviour that seeks and finds the solution to an existential problem by making an attempt on the life of the subject" (Baechler, 1980).

"Suicide is a conscious act of self-induced annihilation, best understood as a multidimensional malaise in a needful individual who defines an issue for which suicide is perceived as the best solution" (Shneidman, 1985).

"Death arising from an act inflicted upon oneself with the intention to kill oneself" (Rosenberg et al., 1988)

"Self-initiated, intentional death" (Ivanoff, 1989).

"The definition of suicide has four elements: 1) a suicide has taken place if death occurs; 2) it must be of one's own doing; 3) the agency of suicide can be active or passive; 4) it implies intentionally ending one's own life" (Mayo, 1992).

"Suicide is, by definition, not a disease, but a death that is caused by a self-inflicted intentional action or behaviour" (Silverman & Maris, 1995).

"The act of killing oneself deliberately initiated and performed by the person concerned in the full knowledge or expectation of its fatal outcome" (WHO, 1998).

vein, retaining a culturally neutral definition served to facilitate the intended international comparisons.

Some of the differences in the definitions outlined in Table 1 stem from the distinct theoretical approaches of the authors. For example, Durkheim's (1897/1951) characterisation of suicide is sociological, which is distinct from that of Shneidman (1985), who focuses on the psychological dimension, and Baechler (1980) who emphasises the existential one (Maris et al., 2000). The theoretical perspective explains the basis of the behaviour. However, definitions are a description of the concept rather than an explanation, and thus should not be guided by theory (Maris et al., 2000). A similar approach guided the choices of the WHO Working Group: a theoretical basis for the definition of suicide should have not been the driving force, as it could have actually hindered the goal of communication for at least two reasons. Firstly, those not adhering to the particular theoretical perspective would have been less likely to assume the definition. In fact, for a nomenclature to be useable, it must be applicable across all theoretical perspectives. Second, if the theory is superseded or lessens in popularity, then the definition too becomes obsolete and the desired definitional consistency is disrupted. The most valuable definition is thus one that is theory neutral.

Similarly, a definition for suicide should also be free of value judgement and remain culturally normative. Both of these characteristics serve to facilitate effective and precise communication. Exemplary of such value judgements is, for example, the German word for suicide, *selbstmord,* which translates literally to "self-murder" (the same holds true for Scandinavian countries). If suicide is defined as a crime, or as immoral, then the way toward unbiased discussion and research practice is impeded (Mayo, 1992). Cultural differences can also imbue a definition of suicide with a value judgement. For example, Stack (1996) explains that in the Japanese culture, suicidal behaviour is generally accepted, particularly in the face of shame. Such cultural differences in the attitudes towards suicidal acts clearly question the adequacy of a universal definition. A workable solution is retaining a culturally normative definition for suicide. This should be broad enough so as to be applicable to a range of belief systems, and, concurrently, specific enough to give an adequate description of the characteristics involved.

The WHO Working Group proposed to adopt a standard definition to be implemented in each site for the study in an attempt to take these issues into consideration. The definition of suicide adopted was as follows:

"Suicide is an act with a fatal outcome which the deceased, knowing or expecting a fatal outcome, had initiated and carried out with the purpose of provoking the changes he desired." (WHO/EURO, 1986)

As said in the Introduction, the central focus of the WHO/EURO Multi-Centre Study on Parasuicide (the initial name of the study) was the incidence of non-fatal suicidal behaviour. The task of the group was now to expand the definition to include non-lethal counterpart behaviours while retaining the link between fatal and non-fatal suicidal acts and the characteristics established in this definition of suicide. The primary difficulty in successfully achieving this goal revolved around the intentions behind the act. That is, not all attempts to commit suicide are failed suicides; there are probably many more cases that are manipulative or an attempt to seek attention (Bille-Brahe et al., 1995). The way that intentions were dealt with is a unique characteristic of the working group's definition of "parasuicide," a term firstly introduced by Kreitman in 1969. For the purposes of the study, parasuicide was delineated as:

"An act with a non-fatal outcome in which an individual deliberately initiates a non-habitual behaviour that, without intervention from others, will cause self-harm, or deliberately ingests a substance in excess of the prescribed or generally recognised therapeutic dosage, and which is aimed at realising changes which the subject desired, via the actual or expected physical consequences." (WHO/EURO, 1986)

There were a number of advantages and disadvantages associated with acceptance of the term parasuicide. As Bille-Brahe et al. (1994) describe, there are at least four ways in which the term has been used in practice:

1. Parasuicide is a subcategory of attempted suicide characterised by low levels of intention to die. This perspective is favoured in America.

2. Attempted suicide is a more specific subcategory of parasuicide characterised by a strong intention to die. This perspective is favoured in Europe.

3. Parasuicide and attempted suicide are mutually exclusive, the former describing cases with low suicidal intent, and the latter used to label cases where the intent to die is clearly evident.

4. Parasuicide and attempted suicide are used interchangeably, recognising the difficulties inherent in ascertaining intent.

The WHO/EURO Group favoured the fourth interpretation of the term, and expected that this would go a long way towards solving the definitional problems that were currently facing the area. This was appealing for three reasons: firstly, due to the lack of implication regarding intent, it remained easy to operationalise; secondly, it did not restrict the classification of cases on the basis of physical consequences; and thirdly, it retained the link between non-fatal suicidal behaviour and suicide (Bille Brahe et al., 1994).

As the study progressed, the disadvantages of the term became more apparent. In addition to the confusion it created in both research and clinical practice, the term parasuicide appeared to be plagued by semantic difficulties, not being easily translatable into other languages (Bille-Brahe et al., 1994). To begin with, the prefix "para" causes problems: in several languages it means "similar to" or "resembling to," but also means "mimicking," "pretending," a fact that is not true of all non-fatal suicidal behaviours. The nature of this term seems to address quite well those acts with no intention to die, but so well what is commonly known as "failed suicide," where the intention to die was present but, for reasons outside the control of the individual, the attempt at death was thwarted.

In choosing and defining a term, desirable and undesirable connotations must be considered. For example, the verbs "commit" and "attempt" are often paired with "suicide," adding a value judgment of wrongdoing or failure to the act. Such connotations impede the path of unbiased discussion and research practice (Egel, 1999). Substitute terminology that labels the act by the method, such as "self-poisoning" or "self-cutting," represents the official international approach since 1903, well before WHO was created, and applies to both suicide and attempted suicide. However, habitual or self-mutilating behaviours encompassed in this terminology are distinct from suicidal acts, and it would be desirable for this to be reflected in definitions and terms used to depict suicidal behaviour (Suyemoto, 1998).

The more generic "self-harm" (particularly popular in UK, South Africa, Australia and New Zealand) does not seem appropriate because it has been broadened in common usage to cover other behaviour patterns that have nothing to do with suicidal behaviour, thus inevitably ending to imply the absence of an intention to die (Linehan, 1997). In addition, in the words of Kreitman:

"Terms such as deliberate self-harm, self-injury or self-poisoning . . . neglect the very

real association that exists between attempted suicide and completed suicide." (Kreitman et al., 1969)

By 1994, the WHO Group had realised the extent of the problems associated with the term parasuicide, and this coincided with the publication of the first book on the study with attempted suicide rather than parasuicide in the title (Kerkhof et al., 1994). Actually the sub-title of the volume contained also the term parasuicide, and this was a way of both acknowledging the inherent difficulties in adopting a standardised terminology and also promoting the interchangeability of the two terms, as suggested by the Steering Group of the study. A few years later, in 1999, the group embraced an outcome-based orientation to the definitions as a solution to these problems, proposing the use of the terms "fatal" and "non-fatal" suicidal behaviour (De Leo et al., 1999). This encompasses the act while also respecting that intention is not necessarily always present. In acknowledgment of the increasingly evident difficulties related to the term parasuicide, the WHO/EURO Multi-Centre Study on Parasuicide was formally renamed to the WHO/EURO Multi-Centre Study on Suicidal Behaviour. The assembly of principal investigators of the study ratified the change on 11th November 1999, immediately after the 20th world congress of the International Association for Suicide Prevention in Athens.

Constructing a Definition of Suicide

As underlined by Mayo (1992, pp. 92), *"a suicide has taken place if death occurs."* A dead body, that is, the fatal outcome of the action or behaviour, is the first element that incontrovertibly qualifies all definitions of suicide. At the same time, this kind of outcome creates a neat separation from all other behaviours not ending in death, the outcome of which is thus non-fatal. The WHO/EURO definition of suicide reported above started with this essential element: *"Suicide is an act with fatal outcome."*

Agency of the act resulting in suicide is also an element common to many definitions. For example, all definitions listed in Table 1 specify that the subject instigated the act resulting in the end of his or her own life. This tends to be worded in two distinct ways: that the act is either self-initiated or self-inflicted. The first implies that the subject instigated but not necessarily carried out the behaviour, while the second suggests that the subject both initiated and conducted the act. This is an important distinction, because expressions of the second type exclude cases of what has been termed "hetero-suicide," in which the suicide victim dies by another's hand (Mohandie & Meloy, 2000). Although it is more frequently the case that the suicidal subject is also the one who engages in the suicidal act, this is not the aspect of agency that is most relevant to a definition of suicide.

As Durkheim's (1897/1951) definition specifies (see Table 1), the act undertaken by the subject to achieve death may be direct or indirect, active or passive. A direct or active act is one in which the deceased was also the agent of their death, the one who, for example, swallowed the pills or pulled the trigger. An indirect or passive suicide would involve some inaction on the victim's part, such as failing to move out of the path of an oncoming vehicle, or failing to comply with police instructions in order to avoid the use of deadly force ("suicide by cop"). Hence, it seems that the most important element of agency in relation to suicidal acts is the responsibility for the outcome, not the performance of the behaviour, and we can conclude that suicide should be defined as an act that is self-initiated.

However, responsibility for the act is not sufficient to distinguish suicide from other behaviours. There are many other acts that are self-initiated and potentially fatal, such as self-harm and habitual behaviours, which are clearly distinct from suicide. In particular, self-harm is a broad category, often used to describe situations ranging from substance abuse, eating disorders and reckless behaviour to mutilation and non-fatal suicidal acts (Santa Mina & Gallop, 1998). In addition, self-mutilation is often repetitive and habitual. Such behaviours are minus the intentions of the suicidal behaviours and thus are qualitatively different (Bille Brahe et al., 1995). Self-harm may also be differentiated from suicidal acts in terms of the way in which the individual perceives the act, and the function that the act serves for the individual (Suyemoto, 1998). These would not potentially lead to eventual suicide, and death as a result of these behaviours would be classed as accidental, not suicidal. For these reasons self-harming acts that are habitual should be excluded from a definition of suicide and suicidal acts.

Intent to die or stop living is a characteristic that distinguishes suicide from habitual and manipulative behaviours, and thus should be considered for inclusion in a definition of suicidal behaviour. Without consideration of the individual's intention, suicide cannot be easily distinguished from an accident. Suicidal intent, or intent to die, constitutes the second criteria for determination of death by suicide according to the Operational Criteria for the Determination of Suicide (OCDS: Rosenberg et al., 1988), and is also a key element in many other definitions for suicide (see Table 1). This is perhaps the most contentious aspect of the definitional debate on suicide and non-fatal suicidal behaviours. The inclusion of intent to die can determine the scope and applicability of a definition for suicide. If intent is judged to be important, the definition risks being too narrow: not everyone who suicides seeks death. On the other hand, if intent is absent from a definition then it is too broad and does not exclude self-injurious and repetitive behaviours (Allen, 2000). The fact that intention is included in definitions such as those in Table 1 has received much criticism, and the interpretive nature of this construct has lead to numerous problems, including operational and assessment difficulties.

In particular, definitions of suicide that include intent have been criticised for being non-scientific. Egel outlines the criteria for scientific definitions and claims that suicide, at present, does not meet these:

"The bedrock of scientific method is that (1) what there is can be experienced, (2) what there is can be described in a hypothetical form sentence, and (3) whatever is the consequent of an event hypothesis must be observable." (Egel, 1999, p. 393)

The intentions of the suicidal individual do not meet the third criteria because they are not directly observable (Egel, 1999). In addition, they can be falsified. What is intended by a suicidal act remains in the mind of the actor. If the act has a fatal outcome, then we are left to infer what was intended, unless a suicide note is found. If the act has a non-fatal outcome, we may ask the individual what they meant, but this is associated with pitfalls too. Memory is not infallible and is filtered through one's interpretation. This is especially true of those emotionally charged memories often connected with a suicidal crisis. Furthermore, suicide attempters may deliberately deny or minimize their previous intentions.

Given that assessment of suicidal intent requires interpretation, which is often from an outsider's perspective, it has been labelled vague and thus not easily measurable (Mayo, 1992). There are a number of additional reasons why "intentional" may represent an unsatisfactory term. Firstly, it entails an element of degree, and thus remains to be qualified (Mayo, 1992). It relates to the ever-prevalent ambivalence surrounding death by suicide (Maris et al. 2000). Shneidman (1981, p. 206) argues that the *"prototypical psychological picture of a person on the brink of suicide is one who wants to and does not want to."* This is also in line with Freudian theory, which suggests that within an individual, life and death wishes co-exist to varying degrees. In this context, the question should be raised regarding how much more must the suicidal subject wish for death rather than life in order for their death to be classified as a suicide. For example, if quantification were possible, do we distinguish between a suicide who wished for death 51% of the time and life 49% of the time, and another whose wishes balanced at 99% to 1% (Maris et al., 2000)? The suicidal individual is rarely 100% intent on dying, therefore it would be more accurate to assert that he or she does not *want* to die, but death is just a more appealing option than living.

The corresponding fact that there is not simply one type of intention, that there may be any number and quality of intentions within a single person at any time (Mayo, 1992), is a second reason that "intentional" has been criticised as vague and imprecise terminology. Definitions of suicidal phenomena typically do not include a specification of what intentions are being spoken of, simply stating that the act was intentional. On other occasions, they may focus on the subject's intent to die; yet both of these may be somewhat misleading. Intent relates to the goals that an individual has in using a certain method to achieve a particular result (Maris et al., 2000). Thus, although the action is intentional, it needs not to be interpreted as the goal. Suicidal intent is also not equivalent to the physical outcome of suicidal acts. That is, not all suicide survivors desired to live and not all suicidal deaths were intended. From a psychological perspective, the most important aspect of suicide is not death. Shneidman (1985) defines the intention at the core of suicide as the intent to cease, noting that suicide is more about ending suffering than death. From this perspective suicide is associated with the intention to achieve cessation of suffering using death as the means. The ultimate goal is to stop future consciousness of ongoing suffering.

In many cases, intention "to cease suffering" distinguishes more acceptably between suicidal acts and non-suicidal acts than the mere "intention to die" does. This might be the case of martyrs, for example. In them, death is certainly intentional but cessation of suffering seems to overcome the intention to die. In fact, martyrs may want to provoke the cessation of suffering of the group of individuals to which they belong (and of themselves or both). In addition, martyrs may intend to achieve some greater good by saving other lives.

Similarly, though death may be intentional, in some suicides this is not necessarily the case. Often, suicidal acts are a frantic attempt at improving one's life, not ending it (Mayo, 1992; Shneidman, 1981). It is particularly non-fatal suicidal acts that highlight the irrelevance of intent to die, though we argue here that these acts should still be classified as suicidal. For example, suicidal acts/gestures and attempts are undertaken with the intention to stop some unbearable situation. Death is not usually intended, but may be a consequence of the action. If intent to die was the criteria for determining suicide, then this would make such deaths accidental; this is not, however, in line with the common usage of the term suicide (Mayo, 1992).

Suicidal intent included as a definitional element of suicide makes conceptual and theoretical sense, and is perhaps regarded as the defining factor of suicidal acts. To remain useful, however, the constituents of a definition must be operationalisable. Intentions have proven difficult to concretise or quantify as a consequence of their interpretive nature and vagueness (Devries, 1968). Determining the intentions behind suicidal action requires a psychological assessment, which officials involved in certifying death are not typically trained to conduct. Furthermore, other parties, such as relatives or friends, are not always willing or available to provide the required information (O'Carroll, 1989). Correlates such as the lethality of the act or the method employed are frequently used to imply intent to die, in the absence of appropriate measures. Since these are not always reliably associated or highly correlated with intent, these often prove inadequate and this practice of assumption compounds the error (Linehan, 1997).

In the context of the overt characteristics only, the meaning of the behaviour often remains unclear. Intention thus places suicidologists in a quandary: it is a necessary element of suicide, without which the behaviour would be classified as accidental, but the problems that realising this concept bring seem insurmountable. Despite this, an "absence of evidence is not evidence of absence" (Rosenberg et al., 1988, p. 1446), and to omit intent from a definition of suicide is to leave out a crucial part of the definition. Such an omission would have dire consequences, for example, in a research setting, an omission of assessment of suicidal intent can lead to unacceptable levels of heterogeneity amongst subjects (Linehan, 1997).

For suicide to be intentional, it implies an awareness (or at least the expectation)

of the potentially lethal consequences (Rosenberg et al., 1988). It is this consciousness that distinguishes between a person who deliberately jumps off a bridge knowing that it will most likely end fatally, and another who flings themselves off a bridge
in the midst of a psychotic episode. The definitions used in the WHO/EURO Multi-Centre Study (see above) include a number of important elements, particularly
that the action is deliberate and the individual is consciously aware of their behaviour (Bille-Brahe et al., 1995). The rationalist perspective of a conscious act is also
included in the definitions proposed by Durkheim (1897/1951) and Shneidman
(1985). This awareness and understanding of potential death excludes cases such as
the mentally retarded, many of those affected by psychosis, and others who do not
fully comprehend the consequences of their actions.

Taken together, the arguments supporting the inclusion of intent in a definition
of suicide are strong and the problems of operationalisation are outweighed by the
importance of the concept. This measurement difficulty may be alleviated by the
use of established measurement techniques and scales. These include Beck's Suicide
Intent Scale for assessing intent in non-fatal suicidal behaviour (Beck et al., 1974),
and employing retrospective indexes (e.g. Jobes et al., 1987) or, in the case of fatal
suicidal acts, by psychological autopsies. For researchers and clinicians, it is also
important to take into account the intention to cease suffering in addition to the
traditionally measured intention to die, and to measure other interrelated factors
such as awareness of potential death, and previous suicidal ideation, which can provide further clues to the presence of intent. Thus, intentions can be accepted as a
central aspect of suicide.

Suicide may represent the solution to a problem, or a way to achieving a particular outcome. For example, amongst the definitions cited in Table 1, Baechler (1980,
p. 74) states that suicide *"seeks and finds the solution to an existential problem,"*
Shneidman (1985, p. 203) asserts that the suicidal individual *"defines an issue for
which suicide is perceived as the best solution,"* while the Working Group for the
WHO/EURO Multi-Centre Study (1986) defines parasuicide as *"aimed at realising
changes which the subject desired"* (but the same concept is expressed in the suicide
definition).

The death attained by suicide is a means to an end, not necessarily an end in itself.
As eloquently outlined by Baechler (1980), death is not viewed by the potential
suicide as a voluntary choice, but as the only option available that would provide a
change to the current, unaffordable situation. It is thus not appropriate to define
the act as wilful or as desired. Had the individual perceived other available solutions,
the situation would not have resulted in an attempt on the life of the individual, or
in their death. Clearly, these considerations need to be seen in the perspective of the
actor of the suicidal action, who feels that a choice has to be made among (almost)
equally unwanted alternatives.

The definitions of parasuicide and suicide proposed by the WHO Working
Group have been criticised because of their use of the wording "desired changes".
In light of what was discussed above, we might then propose a partial rephrasing of

it by substituting "wanted" to "desired" (see below), which is both semantically and conceptually more adhering to most interpretations.

This minor adaptation seems to be quite close to the Shneidman's concept of *"best solution"* (1985), and, at the same time, it better emphasises the situation of coercion that suicidal individuals face in their fatal dilemma. However, after more than 15 years from its initial formulation (1986), the WHO/EURO definition of suicide still retains its validity by possessing all fundamental requirements of a modern enunciation: responsibility, awareness of the potential lethality of the act, intention to die/provoke those changes that the subject is taken to prefer to living conditions otherwise perceived as unbearable.

In conclusion, after reconstructing all developmental stages and rational that guided the choices made in the building up of the definition of suicide, we are incline to re-propose – slightly modified – a quite similar enunciation:

> *"Suicide is an act with a fatal outcome which the deceased, knowing or expecting a potentially fatal outcome, has initiated and carried out with the purpose of bringing about wanted changes."*

The addition of *"potentially"* (fatal outcome) is another difference from the 1986 WHO/EURO definition. It is intended to encompass those cases in which an individual, with ambivalence or wanting to influence others, takes the risk of death in a suicide attempt and dies. His/her intention to die was not strong, and the attempt might have ended in survival as well, depending on coincidental factors, but death is instead the outcome. Similar cases are actual suicides, but a proper categorisation through the previous definition can be quite problematic. The case of risk-taking in extreme sports or stunts remains excluded from this definition, because this behaviour is not aimed at bringing about changes.

Heading Towards a Nomenclature for Suicidal Behaviour

The first step in expanding our definition to form a working nomenclature for suicidal behaviour is to clarify precisely what the role and characteristics of a successful set of terms and definitions is. Addressing the intricacies of an area is not the role of a nomenclature for suicide. As outlined by O'Carroll et al. (1996), a nomenclature forms the basis for, but is distinct from, appropriate classification. This is an important distinction because unlike a classification system, a nomenclature for suicide does not aim to be exhaustive or to precisely mirror reality; the aim is communication, utility and understanding.

Table 2 summarises the nomenclature we are proposing. The key terms are written in bold and become more specific as more elements are introduced. This pro-

Table 2 Fatal and non-fatal suicidal behaviour: Flow chart.

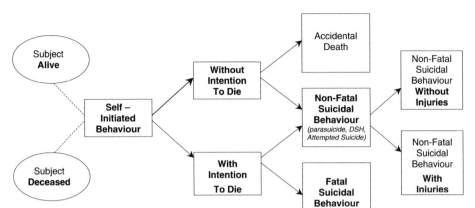

gression of specificity can be traced visually, from left to right. Similar to the process followed in arriving at our definition for fatal suicidal behaviour, the most logical starting point is the observation of the main outcome, that is, if the subject is alive or dead. Then, we need to establish that the behaviour was self-initiated, and, finally, intention to die or stop living is introduced to complete the set of terms.

Consistent with the more recent outcome-based orientation of the WHO/EURO Multi-Centre Study (De Leo et al., 1999), our proposed nomenclature considers the physical outcome of the suicidal act. Lethality may be defined as the medical probability that a behaviour, state or means will end fatally (Maris et al., 2000). In relation to suicidal behaviour, lethality or the physical outcome of the act relates to the probability of suicidal death or, what Shneidman (1981) terms, the "deathfulness" of the act.

There are a number of important limitations in the physical outcome approach that should be considered before we apply this as a criterion for the expansion of our definition. Firstly, the medical seriousness of suicidal acts does not necessarily relate to the definition or meaning of the behaviours. This implies that irrespective of differences in the physical consequences, or the dangerousness of the behaviour, fatal and non-fatal suicidal behaviour are closely related. The core concepts introduced above, that is, responsibility, awareness and intention, are definitive across the entire spectrum of suicidality; in this sense, the outcome of the suicidal behaviour (death vs. life) may be irrelevant. Exemplary of this, and in this case de-emphasising the centrality of physical consequences, is the inclusion of "aborted suicide attempts" as a category of non-fatal suicidal behaviour. Aborted suicide attempts are those in which an individual comes close to enacting a suicidal behaviour but does not complete the act and hence sustains no injury (Barber et al., 1998). Suicidal acts where the individual suffers injury and those where the individual aborts the act prior to implementation may be highly associated, particularly in terms of the intent to die (Barber et al., 1998). It thus appears that the main characteristics of suicidality remain, despite the outcome of the act.

Secondly, outcome is often positioned as synonymous with the intentions associated with suicide, most notably the suicidal individual's intention to die. The asserted premise of including lethality of the act in our definitions of suicidal behaviour is typically that we can infer some kind of meaning based on these overt characteristics, but this is not necessarily appropriate. For example, can more intent be ascribed to an individual who jumped of a 2nd floor balcony and sustained injuries that were not life-threatening, compared to an individual who escaped an attempt unscathed, having been coaxed off a 20th storey building ledge prior to jumping? Intent is only one associated factor and there are a number of varied characteristics that lethality may depend on, including gender, preparation, and knowledge about and access to means. Hence it is not necessarily true that fatality of attempts correlate with an intent to die (Arffa, 1983; Silverman & Maris, 1995). Rather than defining the meaning of lethality to suicidal behaviour, the confusion of outcome and intent instead serves to undermine the importance of the outcome of the act. As a result, it is important to recognise that outcome and intent are not perfectly associated.

There are two arms to any working nomenclature, definitions and terminology (O'Carroll et al., 1996). Through the combination of these two elements, this nomenclature appears to marry each of the key aspects that define suicide. The remaining terms in Table 2 expand on this definition through the specification of the possible presence of injuries that, for taxonomic purposes, might be further distinguished in external/visible or internal/non-visible (e.g. intoxication).

The proposed nomenclature encompasses the entire spectrum of suicidal behaviours. As a matter of fact, three broad outcomes may be identifiable: fatal suicidal behaviour, non-fatal suicidal behaviour with injuries, and non-fatal suicidal behaviour without injuries.

Following the suggestion of O'Carroll et al. (1996), intention to die or stop living is quantified here as any degree that is greater than zero. This acknowledges both the ambivalence in suicidal behaviour and the concurrent importance of other intentions to suicidal acts.

Simplicity is an advantage of this nomenclature. The set of terms used centres around the least possible number of distinguishing components, that is, outcome, responsibility, and intent. Furthermore, the progression of terms in the nomenclature is logically organised and consistent. This promotes effortless and, therefore, widespread use, hence going a long way towards meeting the aims of understanding and communication. Importantly, this simplicity also contributes to ensuring a culturally normative set of terms, one that is not grounded in a single theoretical perspective. This nomenclature meets the majority of practical needs, and a parsimonious use of terms and definitions may help to promote the interdisciplinary communication that is so crucial to suicidology.

As said in the introductory section, the staff of emergency wards will probably continue to be more interested in the physical consequences of a suicidal behaviour than in the ascertainment of the intention to die possibly involved in the act. On the other hand, intention(s) will remain (forever) exposed to deliberate denial or exaggeration. However, promoting the culture of investigating in deeper detail attempted suicide cases constitutes, in our view, a very worthwhile effort. Not only may it improve our understanding of suicidal behaviour, but it could also positively interfere with the entire aftercare process.

Conclusions

The acceptance of a consistent definition and terminology for suicide and suicidal behaviours appears to be the most applicable and usable solution to the definitional challenges facing suicidologists. Following detailed consideration of these problems, particularly as they manifested in the course of the WHO/EURO Multi-Centre Study on Suicidal Behaviour, we considered elements that are important to a usable definition for suicide. This definition was then expanded to form a more complete nomenclature for suicidal behaviour. This clearly implies the abandonment of the support given at the beginning of the WHO study to the term "parasuicide." The over-inclusive character of it has generated misleading interpretations and erroneous utilisations in different settings, nationally and internationally. Already in 1994 we suggested the interchangeability of the terms parasuicide and attempted suicide. Together with deliberate self-harm and deliberate self-poisoning, we are now proposing instead the comprehensive category of "non-fatal suicidal behaviour, with or without injuries." A consequent definition could be the following:

> *"A non-habitual act with non-fatal outcome that the individual, expecting to, or taking the risk, to die or to inflict bodily harm, initiated and carried out with the purpose of bringing about wanted changes."*

The acceptance and implementation of these terms and definitions may contribute to solve some of the problems that are associated with the assortment of terms and definitions currently used to describe suicide and related behaviours. We hope, too, that the proposed solution may advance the thoughtful and challenging debate that has thus far characterised this important and multidisciplinary field of interest. Beyond the Tower of Babel . . . or before?

References

Allen, F. (2000). Suicide: What is to be done? *Australian Psychologist, 35,* 29–31.
Alvarez, A. (1972). *The savage God: A study of suicide.* New York: Random House.

Arffa, S. (1983). Cognition and suicide: A methodological review. *Suicide and Life-Threatening Behavior, 13*, 109–122.

Baechler, J. (1980). A strategic theory. *Suicide and Life-Threatening Behavior, 10*, 70–99.

Barber, M. E., Marzuk, P. M., Leon, A. C., & Portera, L. (1998). Aborted suicide attempts: A new classification of suicidal behavior. *American Journal of Psychiatry, 155*, 385–389.

Barraclough, B., Holding, T., & Fayers, P. (1976). Influence of coroners' officers and pathologists on suicide verdicts. *British Journal of Psychiatry, 128*, 471–474.

Beck, A. T., Herman, I., & Schuyler, D. (1974). Development of suicidal intent scales. In A. T. Beck, H. L. P. Resnik, & D. Lettieri (Eds.), *Measurement of suicidal behaviours*. New York: Charles Press.

Bertillon, J. (1910). *Nomenclature Internationale des Maladies – Deuxième session – 1909 – Procès-verbaux* (p. 118). Paris: Service de Statistique de la Ville de Paris.

Bille-Brahe, U., Schmidtke, A., Kerkhof, A. J. F. M., De Leo, D., Lönnqvist, J., & Platt, S. (1994). Background and introduction to the study. In A. J. F. M Kerkhof, A. Schmidtke, U. Bille-Brahe, D. De Leo, & J. Lönnqvist (Eds.), *Attempted suicide in Europe. Findings from the Multicentre Study on Parasuicide by the WHO Regional Office for Europe* (pp. 3–15). Leiden: DSWO Press.

Bille-Brahe, U., Schmidtke, A., Kerkhof, A. J. F. M., De Leo, D., Lönnqvist, J., Platt, S., & Sampaio Faria, J. (1995). Background and introduction to the WHO/EURO Multicentre study on parasuicide. *Crisis, 16*, 72–84.

Dear, G. (2001). Further comments on the nomenclature for suicide-related thoughts and behavior. *Suicide and Life-Threatening Behavior, 31*, 234–235.

De Leo, D., Bertolote, J. M., Schmidtke, A., Bille-Brahe, U., & Kerkhof, A. J. F. M. (1999). Definitions in suicidology: The evidence-based and the public health approach. 20th World Congress of the International Association for Suicide Prevention, Athens. *Proceedings book* (p. 194).

De Leo. D, Bertolote, J. M., & Lester, D. (2002). Self-directed violence. In E. G. Krug, L. L. Dahlberg, J. A. Mercy, A. B. Zwi, & R. Lozano (Eds.), *World report on violence and health* (pp. 183–212). Geneva: World Health Organization.

Devries, A. G. (1968). Definition of suicidal behaviours. *Psychological Reports, 22*, 1093–1098.

Durkheim, E. (1951). *Suicide: A study in sociology* (J. A. Spaulding, & G. Simpson, Trans.). London, Glencoe: The Free Press. (Original work published 1897)

Egel, L. (1999). On the need for a new term for suicide. *Suicide and Life-Threatening Behavior, 29*, 393–394.

Farberow, N. L., MacKinnon, D. R., & Nelson, F. L. (1977). Suicide: Who's counting? *Public Health Reports, 92*, 223–232.

Ivanoff, A. (1989). Identifying psychological correlates of suicidal behavior in jail and detention facilities. *Psychiatric Quarterly, 60*, 73–84.

Jobes, D. A., Berman, A. L., & Josselson, A. R. (1987). Improving the validity and reliability of medical-legal certifications of suicide. *Suicide and Life-Threatening Behavior, 17*, 310–325.

Kaplan, S. J., & Schoeneberg, L. A. (1988). Defining suicide: Importance and implications for Judaism. *Journal of Religion and Health, 27*, 154–156.

Kerkhof, A. J. F. M., Schmidtke, A., Bille-Brahe, U., De Leo, D., & Lönnqvist, J. (Eds.). (1994). *Attempted suicide in Europe. Findings from the Multicentre Study on Parasuicide by the WHO Regional Office for Europe*. Leiden: DSWO Press.

Kreitman, N. (1977). *Parasuicide*. London: John Wiley.

Lester, D. (1992). Miscounting suicides. *Acta Psychiatrica Scandinavica, 85*, 15–16.

Lester, D. (1994). Suicide. In V. S. Ramachandran (Ed.), *Encyclopedia of human behavior* (Vol. 4, pp. 347–352). San Diego: Academic Press.

Linehan, M. M. (1997). Behavioral treatments of suicidal behaviours: Definitional obfuscation and treatment outcomes. In D. M. Stoff & Mann, J. J. (Eds.), The neurobiology of suicide: From the bench to the clinic. *Annals of the New York Academy of Sciences, 836,* 302–328. New York: New York Academy of Sciences.

MacDonald, M. (1989). The medicalization of suicide in England: Laymen, physicians, and cultural change, 1500–1870. *The Milbank Quarterly, 67,* 69–91.

Maris, R., Berman, A., & Silverman, M. (2000). The theoretical component in suicidology. In R. Maris, A. Berman, & M. Silverman (Eds.), *Comprehensive textbook of suicidology* (pp. 26–61). New York: Guilford Press.

Mayo, D. J. (1992). What is being predicted? The definition of "suicide." In R. Maris, A. Berman, J. Maltsberger, & R. Yufit (Eds.), *Assessment and prediction of suicide,* (pp. 88–101). New York: Guilford Press.

Minois, G. (1999). *History of suicide: voluntary death in western culture.* Baltimore, MD: Johns Hopkins University Press.

Mohandie, K., & Meloy, J. R. (2000). Clinical and forensic indicators of "suicide by cop." *Journal of Forensic Science, 45,* 384–389.

Muehrer, P. (1995). Suicide and sexual orientation: A critical summary of recent research and directions for future research. *Suicide and Life-Threatening Behavior, 25,* 72–81.

O'Carroll, P. W. (1989). A consideration of the validity and reliability of suicide mortality data. *Suicide and Life-Threatening Behavior, 19,* 1–16.

O'Carroll, P. W., Berman, A. L., Maris, R. W., Moscicki, E. K., Tanney, B. L., & Silverman, M. M. (1996). Beyond the tower of Babel: A nomenclature for suicidology. *Suicide and Life-Threatening Behavior, 26,* 237–252.

Rosenberg, M. L., Davidson, L. E., Smith, J. C., Berman, A. L., Buzbee, H., Gantner, G., Gay, G. A., Moore-Lewis, B., Mills, D. H., Murray, D., O'Carroll, P. W., & Jobes, D. (1988). Operational criteria for the determination of suicide. *Journal of Forensic Sciences, 33,* 1445–1456.

Rudd, M. D. (1997). What's in a name . . . *Suicide and Life-Threatening Behavior, 27,* 326–327.

Sainsbury, P., & Barraclough, B. M. (1968). Differences between suicide rates. *Nature, 220,* 1252.

Sainsbury, P., & Jenkins, J. S. (1982) The accuracy of officially reported suicide statistics for purposes of epidemiological research. *Journal of Epidemiology and Community Health, 36,* 43–48.

Santa Mina, E. E., & Gallop, R. M. (1998). Childhood sexual and physical abuse and adult self-harm and suicidal behaviour: A literature review. *Canadian Journal of Psychiatry, 43,* 793–800.

Shneidman, E. S. (1981). Suicide. *Suicide and Life-Threatening Behavior, 11,* 198–220.

Shneidman, E. S. (1984). Suicide. In R. Corsini (Ed.), *Encyclopedia of psychology* (Vol. 3, pp. 383–386), New York: Wiley.

Shneidman, E. S. (1985). *Definition of suicide.* New Jersey: Jason Aronson Incorporated.

Silverman, M. M., & Maris, R. W. (1995). The prevention of suicidal behaviours: An overview. *Suicide and Life-Threatening Behavior, 25,* 10–21.

Smith, K., & Maris, R. (1995). Suggested recommendations for the study of suicide and other life-threatening behaviours. *Suicide and Life-Threatening Behavior, 25,* 533–534.

Stack, S. (1996). The effect of the media on suicide: Evidence from Japan, 1955–1985. *Suicide and Life-Threatening Behavior, 26,* 132–142.

Stengel, E. (1964). *Suicide and attempted suicide.* Baltimore: Penguin.

Suyemoto, K. L (1998). The functions of self-mutilation. *Clinical Psychology Review, 18,* 531–554.

World Health Organisation (1974). *Suicide and attempted suicide*: Public Health Paper No. 58. Brooke, E. (Ed). Geneva: WHO.

World Health Organisation (1986). *Summary report, Working group in preventative practices in suicide and attempted suicide.* Copenhagen: WHO Regional Office for Europe.

World Health Organisation (1998). *Primary prevention of mental, neurological and psychosocial disorders. Suicide.* Geneva: WHO.

Chapter 4
Psychological Dimensions of Attempted Suicide: Theories and Data

Elena Chopin[1], Ad Kerkhof[1], and Ella Arensman[2]

[1]*Department of Clinical Psychology, Vrije Universiteit, Amsterdam, The Netherlands,*
[2]*National Suicide Research Foundation, Cork, Ireland*

Introduction

Why do people attempt suicide without fatal outcome? What are the psychological explanations of such strange behaviour? Although many studies were conducted identifying lists of factors related to attempted suicide, they almost entirely lack theoretical explanation. Yet, a sound theory is crucial for a proper understanding and adequate clinical care. Such theory should be based on empirical research and tested by it (Leenaars, 1990; Maris, 1981; Maris, Berman & Silverman 2000). However, all existing theoretical approaches to attempted suicide have limited empirical support and seem to deal only with parts of the spectrum. It is all the more difficult to shape agreeable theories as the term "attempted suicide" is ambiguous. This single term is used for a variety of self-destructive behaviours, which creates confusion. Therefore, to test the validity of theories of attempted suicide, one must first establish the different dimensions, or subsets, of attempted suicides. Then, one can see whether these dimensions do support any theory. We hypothesise that the theories of attempted suicide developed so far, only partially explain this behaviour, and that they are complementary to one another at best.

The aim of this study is to evaluate the theories of attempted suicides. We will, firstly, review the most important psychological theories as well as classification studies. Secondly, we will establish the different dimensions of attempted suicide within a large data set obtained from the Repetition-Prediction Study of the

WHO/Euro Multi-Centre Study on Suicidal Behaviour. Finally, we will test the relevant theories against the empirical findings of this study.

Background

Our thinking of attempted suicide gained momentum when we realised that attempted suicide and suicide were partly different phenomena. A few psychological models have been put forward, stressing different aspects of attempted suicide. However, all had to deal with the fact that attempted suicide and suicide are different, yet related concepts. Although theories of attempted suicide do result from theories of suicide, they also have to depart from these theories in order to explain the differences. These intellectual acrobatics resulted in a mix of theoretical notions that more or less successfully explained the overlap as well as the differences between suicide and attempted suicide. Therefore, in our conceptual analysis, whenever necessary, we will highlight theories on suicide in order to understand attempted suicide. As presented theories are not mutually exclusive, there is considerable overlap or similarity between them, yet differences are substantial.

Psychoanalytic Concepts of Attempted Suicide

Psychoanalytic theories usually did not distinguish suicide and attempted suicide as separate phenomena. Suicide attempts were merely seen as failure to commit suicide. Freud has never synthesised his ideas on suicide into organised theory (Litman, 1996). In 1917, Freud related suicide to a condition of melancholia. A melancholic person will identify with both the loved and the hated object, and by wishing to kill an introjected object, he will eventually commit suicide (Freud, 1963). According to Litman (1996), Freud did not think that this concept could be applied for all cases of suicide; he rather spoke about suicidal process in persons suffering from melancholia.

Later, in 1920, Freud argued that suicide is motivated by a death instinct. In the psyche of all persons, there are supposedly two opposite forces, the "libido," i.e., life force, and the "thanatos," i.e., death force. Suicide occurs when the balance between these two forces is disturbed and thanatos overpowers libido (Freud, 1955).

Another representative of psychoanalytic school, Menninger (1996), argued that there is a triad present in all suicides: the wish to die, the wish to kill and the wish to be killed, and that the suicidal act is an extreme manifestation of the death instinct directed against the self.

Although psychoanalytic thinking has been influential in clinical practice, the empirical support for the views on attempted suicide has not been convincing (Weinacker, 1999).

Attempted Suicide is a Form of Interpersonal Communication

From the nineteen sixties to the eighties, it was popular to believe that attempted suicide is a form of communication. Especially popular was the "cry for help" concept (Farberow & Shneidman, 1961; Stengel, 1962; Kreitman, 1977; France, 1982).

Stengel (1961, 1975) thought of attempted suicide as a conscious or subconscious act of communication addressed to others. It can be conceived as an alarm signal, showing distress and appealing for help. It is motivated by expected reactions from the suicide attempters' environment (such as showing of love and care). The danger of repetition depends on whether or not the attempted suicide has brought the desired changes.

Stengel noticed, however, that the population of persons who attempted suicide may be heterogeneous and may also include failed suicides of persons who genuinely wanted to die. Stengel (1973, 1975) also hypothesised that attempted suicide can have a mixed and ambivalent motivation, so that in many cases attempted suicide might be at the same time oriented towards death as well as towards life. Furthermore, an attempted suicide may serve a catharsis function, releasing aggression directed towards oneself and/or towards others (Stengel, 1962, 1975).

Similarly, Kreitman (1977) argued that suicide attempts predominantly have communicative and manipulative functions. However, he too noticed that among suicide attempters there are persons at maximum risk for eventual death from suicide. These are marked by long-standing and severe personality problems, social failures and interpersonal problems.

In the same line, Maris (1981) stated that the main goals of attempted suicides are manipulation, attention-seeking and catharsis of depressive affect. The author inferred that persons attempting suicide are primarily young females using low-lethality methods in their self-harm. Maris (1981) was one of the first authors to emphasise the process-like nature of suicidal behaviour. His "suicidal career" theory states that suicidality originates in childhood traumas and in the "multiproblem family of origin." As early life problems tend to be repeated in adolescence and adulthood, suicidal careers are marked by repeated stresses, failures, depression and relationships problems. Consequently, the personal biography always influences the persons' self-destructive reaction to crisis. Maris argued that the majority of those attempting suicide do not really want to die, but want to change something in their lives. Therefore, their first suicide attempt is usually manipulative, while the further development of suicidal behaviour depends on the reaction of significant others. If the reaction is positive, and the person is relieved, the need to perform self-destructive behaviour may diminish. If the problems are solved only temporarily, the person may repeat the suicidal act. Repetition of attempted suicide may become a conditioned reaction as a person learns to cope with stress and life events by repeated self-destructive behaviour (Maris, 1992).

Attempted Suicide is Reactive

The motives behind suicide attempts were better understood when researchers started to study reports provided by the suicide attempters themselves. Studies by Bancroft et al. (1979), and later Michel, Valach, and Waeber (1994) demonstrated that medically trained helpers may have been too quick in attributing manipulative or communicative motives to suicidal behaviour. Even the concept of a cry for help could be misleading. Bancroft et al. (1979) showed that only 15 percent of the suicide attempters had been motivated by the need for help. In the study by Michel et al. (1994), 52 percent of the respondents had not been expecting any help. Furthermore, 50 percent of the attempters indicated that they would not have accepted help, even if it had been offered (Michel et al., 1994).

With striking similarity, studies by Bancroft, Skrimshire and Simkin (1976), Bancroft et al. (1979) and Michel et al. (1994) showed that the main motive behind suicide attempts was a need to find relief from an unbearable state of mind or situation. To a somewhat lesser extent, the motive was a wish to die. Bancroft et al. (1979) explained these findings by suggesting that the attempters who were denying manipulative motives perhaps were less honest in their self-report. Michel et al. (1994), however, interpreted these findings differently, arguing that the mental state prior to the suicide attempt is characterised by an unbearable emotional state, which has to be distinguished from underlying, often long-lasting, interpersonal problems. The authors associated these findings with thoughts of Shneidman who stressed that the major reason for suicide is psychological pain or "psychache."

Although Shneidman (1992, 1993, 1996, 1998) addressed the issue of completed suicide, his ideas are useful to understand the aetiology of attempted suicide as well. Shneidman stated that suicide is an escape from unbearable psychological pain. This is the pain of negative emotions – guilt, fear, defeat, shame, humiliation, disgrace, grief, woe, loneliness, hopelessness, frustrated love, fractured needs, rage and hostility. A necessary condition for suicide is a lowered psychological pain threshold combined with the belief that cessation of the consciousness will bring relief from such pain.

Shneidman stressed the psychological nature of suicide. Attempts to relate suicide to non-psychological variables, such as sex, age, race, socio-economic status etc. are non-conclusive because they ignore the essence of suicide – intolerable psychological pain. The author posited the "ten commonalities of suicide." (1) The common *purpose* of suicide is to *seek a solution*. (2) The common *goal* of suicide is *cessation* of consciousness. (3) The common *stimulus* in suicide is *intolerable psychological pain*. (4) The common *stressor* in suicide is frustrated psychological *needs*. (5) The common *emotion* is *helplessness-hopelessness*. (6) The common *cognitive state* toward suicide is *ambivalence*. (7) The common *perceptual* state is *constriction*. (8) The common *action* in suicide is *escape*. (9) The common *interpersonal act* in suicide is *communication of intent*. (10) The common *consistency* in suicide is with lifelong *coping patterns*.

Shneidmans' theory probably is the most comprehensive theory on suicide. Unfortunately, he did not explicitly adapt this theory to attempted suicide, but the concept of psychological pain was fundamental for other authors.

Williams and Pollock (1997, 2000, 2001) elaborated on the cry-of-pain theoretical model. This model views suicidal behaviour (both suicides and attempted suicides) as an attempt to escape from a feeling of entrapment when an individual believes that there is no other rescue from an external situation or from inner turmoil. Suicidal ideation derives from a feeling of being both "defeated" and "closed in." Feelings of defeat can arise from external circumstances (poor relationships, unemployment, and job stress) or from intolerable inner turbulence. The essential feature of such stresses is that they are a cue for the individual that he is defeated in some meaningful area of life. However, the defeat alone is not a sufficient trigger for suicide; it should be combined with a lack of escape possibilities and the absence (whether real or imaginary) of rescue factors.

The cry-of-pain theory emphasises the reactive element of suicidal behaviour rather than the communicative element. Suicidal behaviour manifests when a person is feeling trapped and in pain. Only secondarily may the "cry" be an attempt to ask for help. Although cry for help may be an important factor, the self-destructive behaviour is not motivated by it. In learning theory terms, it is not an "operant." However, it may be that in some cases of repeated suicidal behaviour, the response comes to function as an operant (Williams & Pollock, 2000).

The cry-of-pain theoretical model recognises some differences between suicide and attempted suicide. When a person feels that there is no escape, he can react with a sequence of different behaviours, one of which is suicidal behaviour. At earlier stages of the sequence, when the escape possibility is threatened but not yet absent, escape attempts will be marked by high levels of activity, anger and protest. Thus, less serious suicidal behaviour is an attempt to re-establish escape routes following defeat or rejection. Lethal suicide attempts represent the psychological pain of the person who feels completely defeated, with no escape routes and no possibility for rescue. The intensity of suicidal behaviour also depends on other factors such as the severity of the events triggering defeat, temperament (e.g., affective instability), learning history and biological predisposition for impulsive and destructive behaviour.

Cognitive Theories on Suicidal Behaviour

Beck (1980) postulates that suicidal intent is a continuum. At the one end, there is a definite intention to die, at the other end, the intention is to go on living. Many different forms of suicide intent may be found along this continuum. When the intent is aimed at continuation of living, suicidal behaviour may be used to achieve some interpersonal changes or to make others realise that help is needed. At the other extreme, motives for suicidal behaviour can be to escape from life, to be relieved from intolerable emotional distress, to avoid feeling trapped. Sometimes the intent may even be ambiguous, resulting in a kind of gamble with life and death.

Thus, less serious suicide attempts are likely to be associated with manipulative motives as well as with lower levels of depression and hopelessness. In contrast, more serious attempts are likely to correspond with escape motives and to heightened levels depression and hopelessness. A study by Beck (1980) showed that while 56 percent of suicide attempts were motivated by a wish to escape, 13 percent wanted to produce changes in their social or family environment. The remaining 31 percent reported varying combinations of escape and manipulative motives.

Serious suicidal behaviour, according to Beck (1980), is strongly correlated to depression and hopelessness. However, hopelessness is crucial: it is the bridge between depression and suicidal intent. In their study, Beck, Kovacs and Weissman (1996) argued that suicidal behaviour in depressed persons derives from certain cognitive distortions. Suicide-prone persons have exaggerated negative views about the outside world, about themselves, and about their future. Not only do they tend to magnify their own problems, but also they do not believe in their own ability to solve them. Furthermore, such persons badly tolerate uncertainty, and they are prone to incorporate the idea that death will solve their problems. "In a sense, suicide serves as a kind of 'opiate' for this kind of person and, analogous to the drug-dependent person, the suicide-prone individual regards his own idiosyncratic form of 'relief' as highly desirable" (Beck, 1980, pp. 222–223).

The coincidental factors, such as a recent stressful life event, may affect the balance in favour of committing suicide. Life stresses influencing suicidal behaviour may be different amongst men and women. Attempted suicides by men may be related to failure to perform at school or at work, which in turn, associates with loss of self-esteem. By contrast, attempted suicides by women are more often preceded by relationship problems.

Two other representatives of the cognitive school, Hughes and Neimeyer (1990), presented a future-oriented "model of suicidal choice." This model is based on data from empirical research (on cognitive structures, problem-solving skills and future anticipations of suicidal persons) as well as on Kelly's (1955) psychology of personal constructs. Humans always seek prediction and hypothesise about the future. Suicidal behaviour may occur when the process of predicting the future is disrupted. Either the future seems totally predictable and negative or totally unpredictable. Both conditions are "anticipatory failures."

With the first anticipatory failure of predictable future, the negative outcome of life is obvious and there is no point to wait. Persons afflicted by such views are trapped in their own singular thinking patterns and their negative anticipations. Here, suicidal behaviour associates with depression and is likely to be well planned and lethal.

With the second anticipatory failure, the unpredictability of the future is associated with anxiety. Being unsure about the future, the person seeks to embrace any kind of certainty, may it even be suicidal behaviour. Here, suicide attempts tend to be impulsive and less dangerous than in the "predictable" condition.

The cognitive model of suicidal choice affirms that non-suicidal people have stable and positive views of themselves and the future. Lower levels of suicidal ideation might occur when a person fails in the important areas of life. As a consequence, negative elements may be integrated into the previously positive system of evaluation. As self-destruction is only considered to be one of many possible solutions, the suicidal ideation is likely to be short and problems are likely to be resolved.

Due to some people's rigid or constricted cognitive systems, their ability to cope adequately with stress is hampered. When moderate levels of invalidation occur, they incorporate more negative elements into the view of themselves. Suicidal ideation gains momentum as the individual's cognitive construct system looses its coherence and becomes disorganised. Consequently, the present and future seem uncertain and anxiety levels rise, causing impulsive low-lethality suicide attempts to occur. Such attempts represent a search for certainty and are aimed at bringing relief from tension. Nevertheless, suicide is still perceived as harmful.

As problem-solving continues to be ineffective and invalidation builds up, future anticipations become both stable and negative. Thinking about death becomes positive, while the future and the self are viewed as negative. Suicidal behaviour occurring at this point is likely to be well planned and highly lethal.

Hughes and Neimeyer observed that the progression from the positive view of the future to the negative one may not always be gradual. It is also important to note that suicide is not simply the result of problem-solving deficits or a disrupted construct system or other cognitive factors. Suicidal behaviour is the outcome of future-oriented cognitive factors combined with stressful life events. Other non-cognitive factors, such as threats to important relationships or a biologically induced depression, are therefore required before entering the path to suicide. In the absence of such stresses, a person's problem-solving abilities cannot be strained beyond coping limits. This future-oriented model uses a process approach to suicidal behaviour, which was further investigated by other authors.

Process-Oriented Theories of Attempted Suicide

As stated before, Maris (1981, 1992) was one of the first authors to introduce the concept of a "suicidal career," hypothesising that the suicidal process usually originates from childhood traumas and is characterised by repeated stresses and failures throughout life.

Social learning theory also can be considered to be a process-oriented theory. The literature on application of this theory to suicidal behaviour is surprisingly scarce. Lester (1994) posits that suicidal conduct may be learned. Suicidal behaviour finds its roots in childhood, as a suicidal person fails to integrate normal values, namely towards life and death. Early life experiences and a certain education shape the thinking patterns and associations of a suicidal person. Punishment, and its interpretation, has a primordial role. In particular, the repression of aggression, and turning it against oneself, is one of the drivers in the development of suicidal thought processes. As the self-destructive behaviour is reinforced by the person's environment, a set of expectations is assimilated. Suicide can become an act of manipulation, as a reaction is expected from self-inflicted harm. Depression, due for instance to lack of rewards or learned helplessness, is also recognised as a significant cause of suicidal conduct (Leenaars 1990; Lester 1994).

Michel (1997, 2001), spoke about the suicidal process in terms of an action theory. All human behaviour, including suicidal, is goal-oriented. In his/her life career, a person occasionally fails to achieve goals. Suicidal behaviour is often the result of career failures, such as occupational, relationships and identity (self-career). Suicide may temporarily occupy the top position in the hierarchy of goals, because it may be perceived as a possible solution to the subjectively felt unbearable situation. Suicidal behaviour may re-appear throughout life as an eventual goal in critical life moments. After a suicide attempt, life-oriented goals can win over again.

The psychological state prior to a suicide attempt is often characterised by a process of dissociation, which may be understood as a defence against pain, distress or humiliation, or against the threat of a collapse of the self-image. Suicidal conduct could therefore be a means of protecting one's self-esteem and reasserting a lost dignity (Michel, 1997, 2001).

Van Heeringen, Hawton and Williams (2000) combined contemporary empirical psychiatric, psychological and biological findings into a process-approach model. Attempted suicide and suicide are parts of a continuum of self-harming behaviours. Any suicidal act is preceded by a process that might start with fleeting suicidal thoughts, then progresses through more concrete plans to subsequent suicide attempts (which are often recurrent and tend to become more dangerous with time) and finally to completed suicide. In every suicidal pathway there is a threshold before which the suicidal process is not observable. Although suicidal processes have to be studied more in depth, research has shown that the early phases of such processes are associated with anger and anxiety, while later stages may be characterised by high levels of depression and especially hopelessness. Although stressful life events play an important role in triggering early depressive episodes, later, the role of events declines as the number of depressive episodes increases (Van Heeringen et al., 2000; Van Heeringen, 2001).

The development of a suicidal process depends upon an interaction between stress and diathesis (persistent vulnerability). Diathesis originates either in genetic features or in traumatic early life experiences. Such vulnerability consists of biological and psychological traits, which become apparent when specific stressors occur. Research shows that such stressors are primarily interpersonal. Upon meeting with stressful life events, the diathesis manifests through two components. The first – social component – influences the way life events are perceived. The second com-

Table 1 Features of the theories of attempted suicide.

Features	Psycho-analysis Freud, Menninger	Communication Stengel	Communication Kreitman	Suicidal career Maris	Psychache Shneidman	Cry of pain Williams & Pollock	Social learning Lester	Cognitive Beck	Cognitive Hughes & Neineyer	Goal-oriented Michel	Process Van Heeringen, Hawton & Williams
Intrapersonal	xx	x	x	xx	xx	xx	xx	xx	xx	xx	xx
Interpersonal		xx	xx	x	x	x	xx	xx	x		x
Heterogeneity		x	x			x	x	xx	xx		xx
Retroflexed hostility	xx	x					xx				
Communication		xx	xx	xx	xx	x	xx	xx			
Cry for help		xx	xx	x		x	x	xx			
Catharsis	x	x		x	xx				x		
Ambivalence	xx	x		x	xx			xx	x		
Childhood traumas				xx			xx		x	xx	x
Invalidation			x	xx			xx	xx	xx	xx	xx
Learned behaviour				xx			xx				xx
Relief from psycho-logical pain					xx	xx		xx	xx	xx	xx
Escape					xx	xx		xx	xx	xx	xx
Depression	x			x	xx	xx	xx	xx	xx	x	xx
Hopelessness					xx	xx	xx	xx	xx	x	xx
Defeat				x	xx	xx	xx	xx	xx	x	xx
Entrapment					xx	xx		xx	xx		xx
Cognitive distortion					xx	xx		xx	xx		xx
Impulsivity						x		xx	xx		
Process/suicidal career				xx			xx	xx	xx	xx	xx
Stress/vulnerability			x	xx	xx	x		xx	xx	xx	xx
Coping deficiency				x	xx	x	x	xx	xx	x	xx
Goal-/solution-oriented					xx			xx	xx	xx	xx

ponent – problem solving capacity – is responsible for the way the person acts in response to these events. As stress and diathesis are interrelated, the accumulation of negative life experiences may weaken the coping abilities, whilst the diathesis advances and suicidal process gains momentum. Consequently, less severe stressors may provoke suicidal reactions (Van Heeringen et al., 2000; Van Heeringen, 2001).

Empirical Classification Studies

The diversity of opinions presented above is likely to owe to the problem of terminology – the one single term "attempted suicide" is used to describe different types of self-destructive behaviour. Kreitman stated: "Much research on attempted suicide is handicapped by including under the single term a great range of psychological syndromes and social reactions. Yet within this diversity certain regularities can be observed, suggesting the possibility, as well desirability, of sub classification within the broad group" (Kreitman, 1977, p. 41). Below, we will present an overview of several relevant empirical classification studies. Firstly, we will present empirical works reflecting upon the distribution of motives of attempted suicides. Then, we will present an overview of empirical studies that included a larger number of social-demographic and psychological variables.

Empirical Studies into Motivation for Attempted Suicide

Bancroft et al. (1976) found that the majority of suicide attempts are motivated by the wish to find relief from an unbearable situation or state of mind. However, approximately one third of the suicide attempters had other goals than physical death. These goals were: appeal, manipulation and revenge. Later, Bancroft et al. (1979) pointed at certain dimensions distinguishing suicide attempters with high suicide risk or severe depression from those motivated by the need to impact significant others, or to gain social acceptability for the act. The authors classified their sample of suicide attempters into several subgroups, according to the most prominent motives behind the attempt: (1) to find relief from unbearable state of mind; (2) to seek help or to escape from an impossible situation; (3) to influence someone, to make others sorry, to frighten or take revenge, to show how much they love someone; (4) to make thing easy for others and to die.

Hjelmeland et al. (2002) used the same list of motives (Bancroft et al., 1976, 1979) to conduct a factor analysis on the WHO/EURO Multi-Centre Study on Suicidal Behaviour, Repetition-Prediction Study data. Four factors were extracted: care seeking (seeking attention or testing love); influencing others (revenge, punishment and manipulation); temporary escape and final exit (unbearable thoughts or situation, wish to die and to make things easier for others).

Other studies investigating the motives for attempted suicide repeatedly show that the population of attempted suicides consists of at least two major subgroups: those wanting to die or to find a relief from unbearable state of mind/situation and those who do not want to die but want to change something in their interpersonal situation.

Classification Studies Involving Social-Demographic and Psychological Variables

Arensman and Kerkhof (1996), reviewing attempted suicide classification studies published between 1963 and 1993, found that only few studies have classified the population of suicide attempters empirically without a priori assumptions. Despite several differences among these classifications, the studies partly agree on the existence of two subgroups having opposite characteristics, and at least one intermediate subgroup with mixed characteristics. They named the opposite subgroups as "mild" and "severe" suicide attempts. Mild suicide attempts were associated with young age, low lethality, interpersonal motivation, low suicide intent and lack of precautions against discovery. In contrast, severe attempts were associated with old age, many precautions to prevent discovery, high level of suicidal preoccupation, high suicide intent, self-directed motivation and hard methods used for the attempt. In between there appeared to be a mixed or ambivalent group with intermediate levels of suicidal intent, and both intra- and interpersonal motivation.

Method

The WHO/EURO Multi-Centre Study on Suicidal Behaviour, Repetition-Prediction Project conducted structural interviews with persons of 15 year and older, treated in medical facilities due to attempted suicide. They were interviewed within one week after their suicide attempt or after re-gaining consciousness. Sixteen centres from fourteen countries participated in the study, namely Switzerland (Bern), Italy (Emilia-Romagna and Padua), Finland (Helsinki), The Netherlands (Leiden), Denmark (Odense), United Kingdom (Oxford), Sweden (Stockholm and Umeå), Norway (Sør-Trøndelag), Germany (Würzburg), Belgium (Gent), Slovenia (Ljubljana), Austria (Hall), Ireland (Cork) and Hungary (Pecs). All data were collected concurrently according to a common standard procedure. In total, 1,910 persons were interviewed.

The instrument used was the *European Attempted Suicide Study Interview Schedule* (EPSIS1), which consists of a number of observer-rated and self-report instruments (Kerkhof et al., 1993). In this chapter, we are using information on: previous suicide attempts; stressful life events (*Stressful and Traumatic Events Questionnaire*, STEQ, Kerkhof et al., 1993); depression (*Beck Depression Inventory*, BDI, Beck et al., 1961); hopelessness (the *Hopelessness Scale*, HS, Beck et al., 1974); self-esteem (*Self-Esteem Scale*, SES, Rosenberg, 1965) and anger (*State-Trait Anger Scale*, STAS, Spielberger, 1988). This analysis further includes motives (Bancroft et al., 1979) and reasons for the attempt as well as suicide intent (*Suicide Intent Scale*, SIS, Beck et al., 1974).

Data Analysis

In order to find out the importance of the motives behind suicide attempts, we first analysed the frequency distribution of the motives. Then, a principal components analysis (varimax rotation) was carried out to investigate the major dimensions in our sample.

Results

Distribution of Attempted Suicide Motives

It appears that a majority of respondents assigned most importance to the motives signalling unbearable psychological pain and lack of escape possibilities. The most frequently reported motives were "the situation was so unbearable that I could not think of any other alternative" (73%); "my thoughts were so unbearable I could not endure them any longer" (66%) followed by "I wanted to die" (62%). Half of the interviewed persons (51%) assigned importance to the wish to get away from an unacceptable situation. Loss of control also appeared to be fairly important: 42% assigned major and 20% minor influence to this factor. Communicative motives (showing love or despair and asking for help) had had a major influence on the attempt in less than one third of the cases. Manipulative and revenge motives were reported rather rarely (see Table 2).

Principal Components Analysis

The sample was best represented by a four-factor solution. The total variance explained was 54.5%. There were two interpersonal motivation factors one of which relating to the cry for help/influencing others, and the other reflecting partnership problems (rejection or fear of rejection). And there were two self-directed motivation factors, one indicating the wish to die and the other implying long-term vulnerability characterised by experience of unbearable psychological pain, depression,

Table 2 Motives for attempted suicides.

Motive	Minor influence (%)	Major influence (%)
The situation was so unbearable that I could not think of any other alternative	13	73
My thoughts were so unbearable I could not endure them any longer	17	66
I wanted to die	15	62
I wanted to get away for a while from an unacceptable situation	15	51
It seemed that I lost control over myself, and I do not know why I did it	20	42
I wanted to get help from someone	19	31
I wanted others to know how desperate I felt	18	32
I wanted to sleep for a while	13	27
I wanted to make things easier for others	19	26
I wanted to know if someone really cared about me	15	20
I wanted to show someone how much I loved him/her	11	20
I wanted to persuade someone to change his/her mind	12	14
I wanted others to pay for the way they treated me	12	14
I wanted to make someone feel guilty	13	13

hopelessness, several negative events through life as well as recurring suicidal behaviour.

Factor 1. Self-directed: vulnerability
(eigenvalue = 3.1, variance explained = 21%)

Variables indicating a long-term vulnerability and emotional suffering clustered on these dimensions: depression (.79); low self-esteem (.79); hopelessness (.76); anger (.39); loneliness (.43); problems making friends (.54) and the large number of negative events throughout life (.53). The incidence of previous suicide attempts loaded .48 on this factor, suggesting a relationship between vulnerability and recurrent suicidal behaviour. The most prominent motives related to this factor were the experience of unbearable psychological pain/wish to die (.36). However the same motives had a higher loading on the Factor2.

Factor 2: Self-directed: the wish to die
(eigenvalue 1.8, variance explained = 12%)

The "wish-to-die factor" was distinguished by the highest loading on the *Suicide Intent Scale* (.84). It also loaded highest on death directed motives (.61). It is a bipolar factor, since the motives cry for help (–.48) and temporary escape (–.62) loaded highly negative.

Factor 3. Interpersonal: partnership problems
(eigenvalue 1.7, variance explained = 11%)

Here, partnership problems grouped together: a reason for the suicide attempt "problems with partner" loaded highest (.73) together with the reason "rejection by lover" (.81). Furthermore, "problems with loneliness" loaded (.52); "problems making friends" loaded (.35). The suicide attempts following rejection by the partner were associated with mixed motivation. However interpersonal motives, especially those referring to showing or testing love, were more prominent (.22). Factor 3 showed no association with long-term social or psychological problems, the suicide attempt was exclusively a reaction to a loss of partner.

Factor 4. Interpersonal: cry for help/influencing others
(eigenvalue 1.5, variance explained = 10%)

Interpersonal motives indicating an emotional appeal and cry for help (.61) as well an attempt to influence others (.80) were essential features of the Factor 4. These motives were associated with highest scores on the *State/Trait Anger Scale* (.47). This factor showed no association with long-term vulnerability or suicide intent.

Interrelation of Dimensions

This study has shown that there is a clear distinction between self-directed (unbearable psychological pain/dying) motivation and interpersonal (communication, cry for help, influencing others) motives for suicide attempt. Interpersonal motives seem to be incompatible with high suicide intent suggesting that those having interpersonal motives do not want to die, rather they want to change something in their social environment.

The further distinctions can be made within the interpersonal and self-directed domains. In the interpersonal domain, it seems sensible to distinguish between the persons whose suicide attempts are motivated by a cry for help and those influenced by the separation from the partner.

In the self-directed domain, vulnerability and wish-to-die factors are overlapping to a certain degree. In both factors, unbearable psychological pain plays a primordial role. However, an unbearable psychological pain is not necessarily tied-up with high suicide intent. For instance, chronic psychological problems and previous self-destructive behaviour may reflect a learned response in coping with difficulties in life. In such case, vulnerability dimension is not related to elevated suicide intent. This finding probably applies to the well known category of the chronic suicide attempts' repeaters who never actually commit suicide. In the same way, the wish-to-die dimension sometimes can be independent from a long-term vulnerability.

Reflections on the Theoretical Framework

1. Psycho-Analytic Explanations

In this study only the (state/trait) anger variable is indirectly related to psycho-analytic hostility concept. Problems handling anger showed a moderate association with the vulnerability dimension and strong association with the dimension represented by the cry for help/influencing others motives. Since we could evaluate only a level of outward-oriented anger, the validity of a psycho-analytic theory on self-directed anger cannot be fairly evaluated on the basis of our data.

2. Attempted Suicide is a Form of Interpersonal Communication

The presence of communicative motives (hereafter will be called "cry for help") is the best criterion discriminating between subsets of attempted suicides. When present, the cry-for-help motives are incompatible with a wish to die or with high suicide intent. The cry for help is, nevertheless, much less frequent than self-directed motives. Therefore, theories stressing the importance of the cry for help motive only deal with a part of the whole picture, that is, less than one third of the entire observed population. We did find support for the theoretical notions of Stengel, Kreitman, Maris, and many others, who emphasise the communicative nature of non-fatal suicidal behaviour, but it applied for a minority of the attempters in our sample, and among these, the level of importance varied. Our study also suggests that within the interpersonal communication domain, it is helpful to distinguish between attempters whose attempt is directly related to partnership problems and attempters whose cry for help is directed towards other significant persons.

3. Attempted Suicide is Reactive

Unbearable psychological pain and the thought that one can escape this pain by dying or by ceasing the flow of consciousness seems to be the most powerful explanation for many attempted suicides. Hence, the theory by Shneidman stating that the common stimulus in suicide is intolerable psychological pain and that the common emotion is helplessness-hopelessness can be relevant to most suicide attempts as well.

The "cry-of-pain" theory by Williams and Pollock, stating that suicidal behaviour occurs due to unbearable experiences combined with perceived absence of other escape possibilities or rescue factors, also covers most suicide attempts – but again not all.

4. Cognitive Theory on Attempted Suicide

The results of our study support the theory put forward by Beck, stating that there are several dimensions of attempted suicides. Some suicide attempts are related to depression, hopelessness and elevated suicide intent, and they are motivated by the wish to escape from life and intolerable mental or emotional distress, and by the feeling of being entrapped. On the other hand, there are also attempts devoid of any serious suicide intent, depression or hopelessness, and these attempts are usually interpersonally motivated, serving some communicative functions.

The model by Hughes and Neimeyer is also supported by our results. Attempts carried out with serious suicide intent are consistent with the final stage of their model of suicidal choice, being characterised by cumulative invalidation, severe depression, hopelessness and death-oriented motivation. Attempts carried out with other-than-death motives can be related to the earlier stages of their model of suicidal choice, which are characterised by low to moderate levels of invalidation, short suicidal ideation, less serious suicide intent and a negative view on death.

5. Process-Oriented Theories of Attempted Suicide

These theories affirm that attempted suicide is the result of life-long processes with vulnerable people. Such attempted suicides are associated with deficient coping patterns, accompanied by the experience of many stressful life events. Most of process-oriented theories, therefore, in differing degrees corresponded to the vulnerability dimension in our study.

The theory of suicidal career by Maris found solid support in the vulnerability dimension, demonstrating that attempted suicides may be associated with negative life events, with stresses and failures throughout life and with repetition of suicide attempts (which might be a conditioned reaction to life crises). However Maris' approach, whereby life-long vulnerability goes together with interpersonal motives for the act, was not verified by our findings. In contrary, the vulnerability factor was linked to self-directed motives (such as unbearable psychological pain and wish to die).

The social learning theory focuses on the learning aspect of suicidal behaviour. This theory states that learned self-harm behaviour might be associated with depression, learned helplessness (which could be indirectly related to the concepts of hopelessness and low self-esteem). Such features are compatible with our description of a long-term vulnerability dimension.

The goal-oriented action theory by Michel postulates that the immediate goal of suicidal action is to escape from an unbearable state of mind, which is a result of accumulated negative life experiences. His theory finds support in our dimension of vulnerability, although wish to die might have a dimension of its own, independent from vulnerability.

The process theory by Van Heeringen, Hawton and Williams states that attempted suicide and suicide are expressions of a continuum of self-harming behaviours. The early stages of the process are characterised by elevated anger/anxiety and the later stages are typified by high levels of invalidation, depression, hopelessness, suicide intent as well as by self-directed motivation and recurrent suicide attempts. Applying this theory to our data, we have assumed that less serious interpersonally oriented suicide attempts (Factor 4) represent an early stage of a suicidal process whereas Factor1 (vulnerability) correspond to a later stage of the process. In agreement with Van Heeringen, Hawton and Williams concept, our findings indeed have shown that Factor 4 (influencing others/cry for help) was associated with high scores on anger scale. Furthermore, in our study, Factor1 (vulnerability) largely resembled description of later stages of the suicidal process. This factor was related to depression, hopelessness, low self-esteem, social problems, accumulation of negative life events, self-directed motivation for self-harm and recurrent suicidal behaviour. However, our study has shown that the vulnerability dimension does not necessarily associate with high suicide intent. One may, therefore, doubt whether there is only one model of a suicidal process applicable to all suicidal behaviour. It seems that a person may have a strong wish to die and high suicide intent without following the expected vulnerability script.

Discussion

The theories of attempted suicide considered in this overview appear to be partially valid and complementary to one another rather than mutually exclusive. Process-oriented theories can explain more subtleties in the aetiology of attempted suicides, and our study supports these theories. However, there may be different processes or pathways leading to attempted suicide. The processes of the persons who are afraid to lose their partner might be different from the processes of those who considered themselves to be a life-long failure.

Theories that highlight the presence of multiple motives for attempted suicides perform better in explaining non-fatal suicidal behaviour than theories emphasising a single motivation. As is the case with much other human behaviour, attempted suicide can be triggered by a combination of motives, even when these appear to be conflicting. However, some motive combinations are more probable, and at least one is unlikely. For instance, those motivated by a cry for help do not have strong wishes to die nor do they have high suicide intent. In all the other combinations, the wish-to-die and suicide intent can be present in varying degrees.

Theories that regard suicidal behaviour as heterogeneous are more relevant since they can explain interpersonal as well as self-directed aspects of self-destructive behaviour. Therefore, the cognitive models, and especially the theory by Beck, appear to be valid and have the greatest descriptive power. In agreement with this theory, our findings show that there are at least two, perhaps even four (two interpersonal and two self-directed) dimensions of attempted suicides.

Although aimed at addressing completed suicide, the theory of psychache by Shneidman can explain many suicide attempts. The theory of cry of pain by Williams and Pollock deals with non-fatal suicidal behaviour, but falls short of explaining some suicide attempts, which are not motivated by unbearable psychological pain.

In view of the broad spectrum of motives behind suicide attempts, theories should recognise and address specific subsets or dimensions of this behaviour. This would not only help us to better understand the aetiology of attempted suicides, but also would enable us to devise optimal treatments targeting specific needs. Our data might, for example, suggest treating the desire to die with cognitive therapy, interpersonal problems with assertiveness training, fear of losing a partner with relationship counselling, and to treat life-long vulnerability with self-esteem enhancing therapies. A thorough psychological assessment and understanding of the aetiology of attempted suicide needs at least four dimensions and at least two complementary theories.

Acknowledgements

Special thanks to Prof. J. Neeleman for his valuable assistance with data analysis.

References

Arensman, E., & Kerkhof, A. J. F. M. (1996). Classification of attempted suicide: A review of empirical studies, 1963–1993. *Suicide and Life-Threatening Behavior, 26,* 46–67.

Bancroft, J.H. J., Skrimshire, A. M., & Simkin, S. (1976). The reasons people give for taking overdoses. *British Journal of Psychiatry, 128,* 538–548.

Bancroft, J., Hawton, K., Simkin, S., Kingston, B., Cumming, C., & Whitwell, D. (1979). The reasons people give for taking overdoses: A further inquiry. *British Journal of Medical Psychology, 52,* 353–365.

Bancroft, J., & Hawton, K. (1983). Why people take overdoses: A study of psychiatrists' judgements. *British Journal of Medical Psychology, 56,* 197–204.

Bancroft, J.H. J., & Marsack, P. (1977). The repetitiveness of self-poisoning and self-injury. *British Journal of Psychiatry, 131*, 394–399.

Beck, A. T., Ward, C. H., Mendelson, M., Mock, J., & Erbaugh, J. (1961). An inventory for measuring depression. *Archives of General Psychiatry, 4*, 561–571.

Beck, A. T., Schuyler, D., & Herman, J. (1974). Development of Suicidal Intent Scales. In A. T. Beck, H. L. P. Resnik, & D. J. Lettieri (Eds.), *The prediction of suicide* (pp. 45–56). Bowie, MD: Charles Press.

Beck, A. T., Weissman, A., Lester, D., & Trexler, L. (1974). The measurement of pessimism: the hopelessness scale. *Journal of Consulting and Clinical Psychology, 42*, 861–865.

Beck, A. T. (1980). *Cognitive therapy of depression.* Chichester, UK: Wiley.

Beck, A. T., Kovacs, M., & Weissman, A. (1996). Hopelessness and suicidal behaviour. In J. T. Maltsberger & M. J. Goldblatt (Eds), *Essential papers on suicide* (pp. 331–341). New York: University Press.

Heeringen van, K., Hawton, K., & Williams M. (2000). Pathways to suicide: an integrative approach. In. K. Hawton & K. Heeringen van (Eds.), *Suicide and attempted suicide* (pp. 223–234). Chichester, UK: Wiley.

Heeringen van, K. (2001) The suicidal process and related concepts. In K. Heeringen van (Ed.), *Understanding suicidal behaviour* (pp. 3–14). Chichester, UK: Wiley.

Heeringen van, K. (2001). Towards a psychobiological model of the suicidal behaviour. In K. Heeringen van (Ed.), *Understanding suicidal behaviour,* (pp. 136–159). Chichester, UK: Wiley.

Heeringen van, K. (2001). The process approach to suicidal behaviour: Future directions in research, treatment and prevention. In K. Heeringen van (Ed.),*Understanding suicidal behaviour* (pp. 288–304). Chichester, UK: Wiley.

Hjelmeland, H., Hawton, K., Nordvik, H., Bille-Brahe, U., De Leo, D., Fekete, S., Grad, O., Haring, K., Kerkhof, A. J. F. M., Lönnqvist, J., Michel, K., Salander-Renberg, E., Schmidtke, A., Van Heeringen, K., & Wasserman, D. (2002). Why people engage in parasuicide: A cross-cultural study of intentions. *Suicide and Life-Threatening Behavior, 32*(4), 380–393.

Hughes, S. L., & Neimeyer, R. A. (1990). A cognitive model of suicidal behavior. In D. Lester (Ed.), *Current concepts of suicide* (pp. 1–29). Philadelphia: The Charles Press Publishers.

Farberow, N. L., & Shneidman, E. S. (1961). *The cry for help.* New York: McGraw Hill.

France, K. (1982), *Crisis Intervention.* Springfield, IL: CC Thomas.

Freud, S. (1955). Beyond the pleasure principle. In J. Strachey (Ed. and Trans.), *The standard edition of the complete psychological works of Sigmund Freud (Vol. 18).* London: Hogarth Press. (Original work published in 1920).

Freud, S. (1963). Mourning and melancholia. In J. Strachey (Ed. and Trans.), *The standard edition of the complete psychological works of Sigmund Freud (Vol. 14).* London: Hogarth Press. (Original work published in 1917).

Kelly, G. A. (1955). *The psychology of personal constructs.* New York: Norton.

Kerkhof, A. J. F. M., Bernasco, W., Bille Brahe, U., Platt, S., & Schmidtke, A. (1989). *WHO/EURO Multicentre Study on Parasuicide Interview Schedule (EPSIS).* Leiden: Leiden University, Department of Clinical, Health and Personality Psychology.

Kerkhof, A. J. F. M., & Arensman, E. (2001). Pathways to suicide: The epidemiology of the suicidal process. In K. Heeringen van (Ed.), *Understanding suicidal behaviour* (pp. 15–39). Chichester, UK: Wiley and Sons.

Kreitman, N. (1977). *Parasuicide.* London: John Wiley.

Leenaars, A. A. (1990). Psychological perspectives on suicide. In D. Lester (Ed.), *Current concepts of suicide* (pp. 159–167). Philadelphia: The Charles Press Publishers.

Lester, D. (1994). A comparison of 15 theories of suicide. *Suicide and Life-Threatening Behavior, 24*, 80–88.

Litman, R. E. (1996). Sigmund Freud on suicide. In J. T. Maltsberger & M. J. Goldblatt (Eds), *Essential papers on suicide* (pp. 201–220). New York: New York University Press.

Maris, R. (1981). *Pathways to suicide: A survey of self-destructive behaviors*. Baltimore, MD: Johns Hopkins University Press.

Maris, R. W. (1992). How are suicides different? In R. W. Maris, A. L. Berman, J. T. Maltsberger, & R. I. Yufit (Eds.), *Assessment and prediction of suicide* (pp. 65–87). New York: The Guilford Press.

Maris, R., Berman, A. L., & Silverman, M. M. (2000). *Comprehensive textbook of suicidology*. New York: The Guilford Press.

Menninger, K. A. (1996). Psychoanalytic aspects of suicide. In J. T. Maltsberger & M. J. Goldblatt (Eds), *Essential papers on suicide* (pp. 20–35). New York: New York University Press.

Michel, K., Valach, L., & Waeber, V. (1994). Understanding deliberate self-harm: The patients' view. *Crisis, 15*, 172–179.

Michel, K., & Valach, L. (1997). Suicide as goal-directed action. *Archives of Suicide Research, 3*, 213–221.

Michel, K., & Valach, L. (2001). Suicide as goal-directed action. In K. Heeringen van (Ed.), *Understanding suicidal behaviour* (pp. 230–251). Chichester, UK: Wiley.

Rosenberg, M. (1965). *Society and the adolescent self-image*. Princeton, NJ: Princeton University Press.

Shneidman, E. S. (1992). What do suicides have in common? Summary of the psychological approach. In B. Bongar (Ed.), *Suicide: Guidelines for assessment, management & treatment* (pp. 3–15). Oxford: Oxford University Press.

Shneidman, E. S. (1993). *Suicide as a psychache. A clinical approach to self-destructive behavior*. Northvale, NJ: Jason Aronson Inc.

Shneidman, E. S. (1993). Suicide as a psychache. *Journal of Nervous and Mental Disease, 181*, 145–147.

Shneidman, E. S. (1996). Suicide as a psychache. In J. T. Maltsberger & M. J. Goldblatt (Eds.), *Essential papers on suicide* (pp. 633–639). New York: New York University Press.

Shneidman, E. S. (1998). Further reflections on suicide and psychache. *Suicide and Life-Threatening Behavior, 28*, 245–250.

Spielberger, C. D. (1988). *State-Trait Anger Expression Inventory. Professional manual*. Tampa: University of South Florida.

Stengel, E. (1962). Recent research into suicide and attempted suicide. *American Journal of psychiatry, 118*, 725–727.

Stengel, E. (1973). A matter of communication. In E. S. Shneidman (Ed.), *On the nature of suicide* (pp. 74–81). San Francisco: Jossey-Bass.

Stengel, E. (1975). *Suicide and attempted suicide*. UK: C. Niccols & Company Ltd.

Weinacker, B. (1999). *The role of anger experience and anger expression in the explanation of suicidal behaviour*. Ph.D. dissertation, Vrije Universiteit Amsterdam.

Williams, J. M. G. (1997). *Cry of pain: Understanding suicide and self-harm*. Harmondsworth: Penguin.

Williams, J. M. G., & Pollock L. R. (2000). The psychology of suicidal behaviour. In K. Hawton & K. Heeringen van (Eds.), *Suicide and attempted suicide* (pp. 79–95). Chichester, UK: Wiley.

Williams, J. M. G., & Pollock L. R. (2001). Psychological aspects of the suicidal process. In K. Heeringen van (Ed.), *Understanding suicidal behaviour* (pp. 76–94). Chichester, UK: Wiley.

Chapter 5
The Psychobiology of Suicidal Behaviour

Cornelis Van Heeringen, Gwendolyn Portzky and Kurt Audenaert

Department of Psychiatry, University of Gent, Belgium

Introduction

There is little doubt about the crucial role of depression in the development of suicidal behaviour, but the question why some depressed individual commit suicide, while others do not take their own lives, is still difficult to answer. From a clinical point of view this is an extremely important question, and many divergent approaches to the study of suicidal behaviour have contributed substantially to the identification of characteristics, which are associated with an increased risk of its occurrence.

These characteristics include, among others, hopelessness, impaired serotonergic functioning, problem solving deficiencies, sensitivity to social stimuli, personality disorder, temperament, (mainly interpersonal) life events, and noradrenergic dysfunction. Studies in the cognitive psychological and biological domains have in particular been fruitful in identifying factors that may increase the risk of suicidal behaviour (van Heeringen, 2001). Cognitive psychological studies have shown that, among depressed individuals, patients with an increased risk of suicidal behaviour are characterized by three characteristics, i.e., attentional biases towards being a loser, and by a perceived "no escape" and "no rescue" from stressful psychosocial circumstances (Williams and Pollock, 2001).

Biological research on the causes of suicidal behaviour has focused in particular on the role of serotonin (5-HT) (Van Praag, 2001). The association between impaired serotonergic function and suicidal behaviour probably is the most replicated finding in biological psychiatry.

A comprehensive framework, in which these characteristics and their mutual relationships are described, is currently lacking. Based on data, which were collected in the context of the WHO/EURO Multi-Centre Study on Suicidal Behaviour, this chapter will describe a psychobiological model of suicidal behaviour, describing the (relationship between) factors, which may increase or decrease the probability of occurrence of suicidal behaviour. These factors relate to a predisposition, or *diathesis*, for suicidal behaviour, by referring to persistent biological or psychological characteristics that may predispose individuals to suicidal behaviour. The term "probability" is used because of the fact that currently recognized risk factors for suicidal behaviour lack the specificity, based on which one could use a deterministic approach to the description of risk factors.

The psychobiological model described in this chapter thus reflects a probabilistic approach by identifying two clusters of characteristics. The co-occurrence of these clusters in depressed individuals is hypothesized to define their predisposition to suicidal behaviour. Risk factors, i.e., components of these clusters, are thus not described in a dichotomous "normal" versus "abnormal" sense, but rather in terms of variations in dimensions of human functioning.

Two main components can be discerned as constituting this predisposition for suicidal behaviour. Research in areas other than suicidology (including animal studies) has shown that the adequate functioning of both systems is essential for adequate coping with stressful events. Preceding a discussion of these two components of the psychobiological model the "social brain" concept will be described, which provides a useful framework for understanding the role of the two components in the development of suicidal behaviour.

The Social Brain

Deakin (1996) described the concept of the social brain, or the basolateral circuit, consisting of the brain's prefrontal and temporal cortices, executing their functions via feedback loops in close connection with the subcortical amygdala and hippocampus, respectively. Thus, a first subsystem of the basolateral circuit is thought to consist of the temporal cortex in conjunction with the hippocampus, and is thought to be involved in the processing of sensory information. From a neurobiological point of view, the function of this subsystem is mediated by the serotonin $(5\text{-HT})_{1a}$ system, in conjunction with the noradrenergic system. Deakin has postulated that adaptation or tolerance to stress is the main function of this system, and that dysfunction of the system may lead to subordinance, low self-esteem and depressive ideation. The second subsystem of the basolateral circuit is thought to consist of the (orbital) prefrontal cortex in connection with the amygdala, which mediates approach or avoidance behaviour through dopaminergic and serotonergic (5-HT_2) neuromodulation, respectively. Dysfunction of this system may become apparent through social anxiety and hopelessness.

Assessing the Probability of Suicidal Behaviour in Depression: A Psychobiological Approach

We have studied characteristics of these subsystems with regard to their role in the development of suicidal behaviour, using psychiatric, biological, neuropsychological and functional neuro-imaging assessments in patients with a history of suicidal behaviour, psychiatric patients without such a history and healthy controls. Based on the social brain concept and the findings of these studies, it appears that there are indeed, at least, two different clusters of characteristics, which we have called the "social interaction component" and the "behavioural inhibition component" (van Heeringen, 2001).

The Social Interaction Component

There is little doubt about an association between suicidal behaviour and the occurrence of particular life events. Epidemiological and cognitive-psychological studies have shown in particular a precipitating role of problems that threaten the integration or status of the individual in the system in which they live, and that commonly are of an interpersonal nature. In terms of personality, the perception of stimuli in the interpersonal domain is thought to be modulated by the (at least partially) heritable temperamental dimension "reward dependence."

From a neurobiological point of view, reward dependence is probably influenced by the noradrenergic and 5-HT_{1a} neurotransmission systems (Cloninger, 1998). We have found in different studies that attempted suicide patients are comparatively low in reward dependence, which may become apparent as being aloof and socially detached. Moreover, attempted suicide patients have higher levels of production of the stress hormone cortisol when compared to psychiatric controls, with levels of urinary cortisol excretion correlating significantly and negatively with reward dependence scores (van Heeringen et al., 2000). This means that low reward dependence is associated with an increased stress response in attempted suicide patients, or, in other words, that low reward dependence reflects a reduced resilience towards psychosocial stressors. It remains to be demonstrated whether low reward dependence actually reflects the attentional bias to perceive oneself as being a loser when confronted with psychosocial stress, which has been postulated to be one of the core cognitive psychological characteristics associated with suicidal behaviour. Based on these considerations it can be speculated that a decreased resilience among attempted suicide patients is associated with a personality characteristic, that is modulated by the noradrenergic and 5-HT_{1a} systems and may become manifest through a detached or aloof personality style, due to which the stress system is activated (leading to increased cortisol production) when confronted with particular adverse situations.

The Behavioural Inhibition Component

More evidence-based information is available regarding the involvement of this second component in the development of suicidal behaviour. For example, we have provided evidence of the role of this component in the development of suicidal behaviour by means of functional neuro-imaging studies using a highly selective 5-HT$_{2a}$ receptor ligand, showing a decreased 5-HT$_{2a}$ receptor binding potential in the prefrontal cortex when compared to healthy volunteers (Audenaert et al., 2000a). Particularly interesting was the finding of a correlation between prefrontal 5-HT$_{2a}$ receptor binding potential and levels of hopelessness and the temperamental dimension "harm avoidance" (van Heeringen et al., 2003). These findings indicate that attempted suicide patients are characterized by a cluster of reduced prefrontal 5-HT$_{2a}$ functioning, high levels of hopelessness and increased scores on harm avoidance, a hypothetically heritable temperamental dimension, which reflects biases in the regulation of anxiety, or in behavioural inhibition when confronted with adverse stimuli.

These findings thus suggest a role of the prefrontal serotonin system in emotional (i.e., feelings of hopelessness) and behavioural (i.e., behavioural inhibition) characteristics, which may, however, be secondary to cognitive functions. Cognitive psychologists have indeed demonstrated that, in addition to the attentional biases as described above, suicidal behaviour is associated with a perceived no escape and no rescue from psychosocial adversity. The no escape notion appears to be associated with overgeneral memory functions, leading to impaired problem-solving capacities and perceived entrapment, while it is becoming clear that the no rescue perception is related to deficiencies in the fluent generation of positive events to occur in the future, leading to feelings of hopelessness (Williams & Pollock, 2001). Our group has recently studied the role of the prefrontal cortex in verbal fluency tasks by means of functional neuro-imaging techniques, and shown that fluency-related activation indeed occurs in the prefrontal cortex (Audenaert et al., 2000b). Taking into account the localisation of working memory in the prefrontal cortex, and the role of the serotonergic system in the process of memory and learning, we suggest that the crucial dysfunction in the motor-expressive part of the basolateral circuit in association with suicidal behaviour consists of a serotonergically mediated disturbance in memory functions, which underlies a deficit in the retrieval of appropriate problem-solving strategies and in the prospective cognitive functions, which are typically related to the prefrontal cortex.

Conclusions

The research findings, as described above, indicate that interrelated psychological and biological characteristics constitute the sensitivity to stress and determine the behavioural reaction to psychosocial stressors among depressed individuals, thus contributing to the occurrence of suicide among these individuals. Table 1 summa-

Table 1 Two components of a diathesis for suicidal behaviour.

Approach	Social interaction component	Behavioural inhibition component
Psychiatric	depressive ideation	anxiety/hopelessness
Cognitive psycho-logical	sensitivity to signals of defeat (re-silience)	deficient problem-solving (no escape) deficient generation of positive future events (no rescue)
Neurobiological	$5\text{-}HT_{1a}$/noradrenaline	$5\text{-}HT_2$/dopamine
Neuropsychological	attention	autobiographical memory fluency
Neuro-anatomical	(fronto-)temporal lobe hippocampus	prefrontal lobe amygdala
Temperament	reward dependence	harm avoidance

rizes the main ingredients of the two components of a diathesis for suicidal behaviour, as they were described in this chapter.

It appears that many of these ingredients actually describe the same underlying mechanisms. While many aspects of this model clearly need further study, the proposed model may provide a comprehensive framework for organising our current knowledge with regard to characteristics that may increase or reduce the probability of occurrence of suicidal behaviour. More particularly, the model may, for example, explain why not all depressed individuals (dysfunction of the first component) engage in suicidal behaviour (dysfunction of the two systems), or why dysfunction of the serotonergic system (i.e., the second component) does not automatically lead to suicidal behaviour, particularly when resilience (the first component) is not impaired.

This model may also provide guidelines to the prediction, treatment and prevention of suicide in depressed individuals. As many of the described factors, which may influence the occurrence of suicidal behaviour, can be described in psychological and biological terms, efficacious treatment can be based on psychological and biological approaches. The psychobiological model, as described in this chapter, suggests that a combination of pharmacological and psychotherapeutic treatments is required to influence the probability of occurrence of suicidal behaviour. Little is actually known about the actual function of identified biological factors, such as the serotonin system, in the prefrontal cortex, but research in other than the suicidological area has indicated that these factors may be involved in processes of memory and learning. It can thus be suggested that the psychopharmacological component of treatment (e.g., antidepressants with an effect on the serotonergic system) actually is necessary to provide or enhance the functional substrate for the process of learning, which is the focus of the psychotherapeutic component. Such a combined treatment approach may well have the effect on the occurrence of suicidal behaviour that currently used approaches are clearly lacking (Hawton, 2001).

References

Audenaert, K., Van Laere, K., Dumont, F., Slegers, G., Mertens, J., van Heeringen, C., & Dierckx, R. A. (2000a). Decreased prefrontal serotonin 5-HT$_{2a}$ receptor binding potential in deliberate self-harm patients. *European Journal of Nuclear Medicine, 28*, 175–182.

Audenaert, K., Brans, B., Van Laere, K., Lahorte, P., Versijpt, J., Van Heeringen, C., Dierckx, R. A. (2000b). Verbal fluency as a prefrontal activation probe: a validation study using ^{99m}Tc-ECD brain SPET. *European Journal of Nuclear Medicine, 27*,1800–1808.

Cloninger, C. R. (1998). The genetics and psychobiology of the seven-factor model of personality. In K. R. Silk (Ed.), *Biology of personality disorders.* Washington DC: American Psychiatric Press.

Deakin, J.F. W. (1996). 5-HT, antidepressant drugs and the psychosocial origins of depression. *Journal of Psychopharmacology, 10*, 31–38.

Hawton, K. (2001). The treatment of suicidal behaviour in the context of the suicidal process. In C. van Heeringen (Ed.), *Understanding suicidal behaviour: The suicidal process approach to research, treatment and prevention* (pp. 212–230). Chichester, UK: Wiley.

Van Heeringen, C. (2001). *Understanding suicidal behaviour: The suicidal process approach to research, treatment and prevention.* Chichester, UK: Wiley.

Van Heeringen, C., Audenaert, K., van de Wiele, L., & Verstraete, A. (2000). Cortisol in violent suicidal behavior: association with personality and monoaminergic activity. *Journal of Affective Disorders, 60*, 181–189.

Van Heeringen, C., Audenaert, K., Van Laere, K., & Dierckx, R. A. (2003). Prefrontal 5-HT2a receptor binding index, hopelessness and personality characteristics in attempted suicide. *Journal of Affective Disorders, 74*, 149–158.

Williams, J. M. G., & Pollock, L. (2001). Psychological aspects of the suicidal process. In C. van Heeringen (Ed.), *Understanding suicidal behaviour: The suicidal process approach to research, treatment and prevention* (pp. 76–94). Chichester, UK: Wiley.

Chapter 6
Intentional Aspects of Non-Fatal Suicidal Behaviour

Heidi Hjelmeland[1] and Keith Hawton[2]

[1]Department of Psychology, Norwegian University of Science and Technology, Trondheim, Norway, [2]Centre for Suicide Research, University of Oxford, England

An important issue in research on nonfatal suicidal behaviour concerns the intentions associated with it. The important question is: "*Why* do people engage in deliberate self-harming behaviour not resulting in death?" or, more specifically, "What do they want to *achieve* by their acts?" Two aspects of intent have been focused in research, namely the level of suicidal intent and various motives, reasons or intentions. This chapter addresses both these aspects.

One major problem of comparing results from different previous studies has been the variation in the terms used for non-fatal suicidal behaviour; for example, attempted suicide, parasuicide, self-injury, self-poisoning, deliberate self-harm or non-fatal suicidal behaviour (e.g., O'Carroll et al., 1996; Leenaars et al., 1997). Moreover, the definitions of these terms have varied from one study to another within the same country and between different countries, resulting in considerable variation between the samples of patients studied. This has significant implications for interpretation of the results of studies of intentional aspects of non-fatal suicidal behaviour. Cross-cultural studies employing the same definition of the behaviour, the same assessment instruments, and the same method of data collection are scarce. The fact that the WHO/EURO Multi-Centre Study on Suicidal Behaviour encompasses all these important methodological factors is one of the major strengths of the project. When the issues of level of suicidal intent and various intentions involved in non-fatal suicidal behaviour are discussed in this chapter, we first summarise previous research within the area and then present the contributions of the WHO Study and discuss these within the framework of previous findings. Before that, however, it is necessary to consider the rather confusing and inconsistent terminology involved in this field.

Terminology

A review of the suicidological research literature shows that the concepts motive, reason, aim, purpose, and intention are employed somewhat inconsistently and confusingly in this field. The following are some examples.

Birtchnell and Alarcon (1971) employed the terms "intentions" and "motivations" for attempting suicide without differentiating between the concepts. As an example of a motive/intention of attempted suicide they suggested "frighten or get your own back on someone." Bancroft and co-workers (1976, 1979) used the terms "reasons" and "motives" of the suicidal act, meaning, for instance, seeking help from someone, escaping for a while from an impossible situation or a terrible state of mind, or influencing someone to change their mind. Hawton and colleagues (1982) and James and Hawton (1985) employed the terms "motivational aspects" of, and "reasons" for self-poisoning, and by that meant the same as Bancroft and co-workers (1979). They also used the term "suicidal intent" meaning whether the patients had wanted to die or not. Michel and colleagues (1994) used the term "motives for attempting suicide," meaning, for instance, "I wanted to get help from someone" and "I wanted to persuade someone to change his/her mind."

Lukianowicz (1972) juxtaposed "motives" with "aims," i.e., something in the future that patients had wanted to achieve by the suicidal act. However, under the term "motives" he also listed marital problems and mental illness, i.e., factors leading up to the suicidal behaviour. Kovacs and co-workers (1975) categorised various reasons into the item "purpose of the attempt" from the *Suicide Intent Scale* (SIS; Beck et al., 1974). This contains the categories (a) to manipulate others, to effect a change in the environment, to get attention, revenge, (b) components of a and c, and (c) to escape from life, to seek surcease; an irreversible solution to problems. Velamoor and Cernovsky (1992) used both the terms "motive to die" or "not to die" and "intent to die" or "not to die." Hettiarachchi and Kodituwakku (1989) used the term "motive" meaning, for instance, wishing to die or to manipulate a situation.

As can be seen from this brief summary, a certain amount of disagreement and confusion reigns within this research field with regard to the use of such basic concepts as reason, motive and intention. They are most often (almost always) used as synonyms regarding something the patient wanted to happen in the future, something they wanted to achieve by their act, e.g., to influence someone to change their mind, to get help, to escape from life temporarily, to die, etc. Moreover, the term suicidal *intent* is employed when the extent to which a person wanted to die is assessed. This inconsistency is probably due to inherent different paradigmatic bases. Failure to discuss such paradigmatic differences leads to rather diffuse employment of these terms. Since searching for answers to the question of why some people engage in nonfatal suicidal behaviour is a central issue in research in this area, clarification of terminology is important.

In 1999, Hjelmeland and Knizek made an attempt to clarify what would be the proper use of these various terms. This discussion was based on the assumption that the suicidal act is rooted in, and communicates a message about, the ongoing dialogue between the individual and their social milieu. In psychological research fields outside that of suicidal behaviour, it has been common to distinguish more clearly between motives and intentions. For instance, Trevarthen (1982) distinguished between the two concepts by claiming that intentions originate from motives and that intentional acts satisfy motives, i.e., motives gain active expression through intentions. Hoffman (1984) also distinguished between motives and intentions, and claimed that: "*a motive is a forward-looking reason for acting, i.e., that state of mind which makes a particular result attractive enough to the agent for him to want to effect it.*" Moreover, he suggested that *intention* can be viewed both as a state of mind that exists prior to an act causing the intended result (and if so, according to Hoffman, it is often, although wrongly, equated with motive), and as "*a kind of action rather than an inner mental antecedent of action.*" Heckhausen and Kuhl (1985) claimed that motivations start as wishes and must become intentions before they can result in an act. Alicke and colleagues (1990) claimed that: "*Whereas intentions specify an actor's wants and desires, motives supply the reason for the desire.*"

So, both for the non-suicidologists Hoffman (1984) and Alicke (1990), and also for some researchers on suicidal behaviour, e.g., Bancroft and colleagues (1976; 1979), Hawton and colleagues (1982), and Michel and colleagues (1994), motives and reasons seem to be synonymous. However, for suicide researchers these terms seem to mean something different than what they do for researchers from other fields of psychology. If motives and intentions are to be distinguished, it seems from the examples cited above that intentions are more directly related to the actual act than are motives. Or as Hoffman (1984) claimed, intention can be a kind of action in itself as well. The act, in turn, is carried out to achieve something; for example, to influence someone to change their mind. Thus the intention goes both before the act and is expressed by the act. In other words, when the suicidal act is explained in terms of something the subject wanted to achieve (aims or goals), the term intention seems more appropriate than the term motive (Hjelmeland & Knizek, 1999).

Hjelmeland and Knizek elaborated further on this: In a dictionary of psychology (Reber, 1985) the term motive is defined as: "*(1) A state of arousal that impels an organism to action, and (2) a rationalization, justification or excuse that a person gives as the reason for his or her behaviour. . . . it provides a characterization of the cause of the behaviour.*" Intention is in the same dictionary defined as: "*Generally, any desire, plan, purpose, aim or belief that is oriented toward some goal, some end state.*"

Using theory of science terminology, motives are associated with causal explanations, while intentions are associated with teleological explanations of the suicidal acts. Causal explanations imply that the explanation of the act lies in the past, whereas teleological explanations imply that the explanation of the act lies in the future, that the subject is trying to achieve something by the act.

The dictionary definition of motive quoted above includes both the terms reason and cause. However, Buss (1978) has emphasised the necessity of distinguishing between causes and reasons by arguing from an actor's perspective. According to Buss: *"Causes are that which brings about a change"* while *"Reasons are that for which the change is brought about (e.g., goals, purposes, etc.)."* Buss elaborated: *"Behaviour that is done by a person – that is intended, that has a goal or purpose – is an action and is explained by the actor with reasons."* Stated somewhat differently, Buss claimed that the subjects or actors would always explain their intended behaviour in terms of *reasons*, not in terms of *causes*. Later, however, Buss (1979) modified his view slightly by stating that although it was *possible* for actors to use causal explanations, they would *mainly* explain their behaviour in terms of reasons. The philosophical distinction between reasons and causes was supported by Locke and Pennington (1982), when they suggested that reasons are forms of internal causes, i.e., what are usually referred to as personal or subjective reasons. A study by Hinkle and Schmidt (1984) supported Buss' hypothesis in that it confirmed that actors mainly explain their actions in terms of reasons and not in terms of causes.

Based on these arguments, Hjelmeland and Knizek (1999) concluded that not only does a distinction between motives and intentions seem appropriate and necessary, moreover reasons should be associated with intentions rather than with motives. According to Gilje and Grimen (1993) (and also Buss 1978; 1979) there are some problems with causal explanations in human behaviour, and thus teleological explanations should be preferred. Since the scientific psychological literature links motives to causality and intentions to teleological explanations, and, since intentions are more closely connected to acts than are motives, the concept of intention is preferable in explaining suicidal behaviour from the actor's perspective. Thus, according to Hjelmeland and Knizek (1999), intention is the appropriate notion to address the question of what the patients wanted to achieve by suicidal acts, whether it was to die or to influence some significant other, and it is in this sense the term intention is used in this chapter. When the degree to which a person wanted to die is reported, the term *"level* of suicidal intent" is used. We will now turn to considering this aspect of suicidal behaviour.

Level of Suicidal Intent

The main instrument in assessing the level of suicidal intent has been the *Suicide Intent Scale* (SIS) developed by Beck and co-workers (1974). They defined suicidal intent as *"the seriousness or intensity of the wish of a patient to terminate his life."* The SIS comprises 15 items that are scored 0, 1, or 2, yielding a possible range of sum scores from 0 to 30. The first eight items consist of questions regarding the objective circumstances of the suicidal act. These items deal with the following issues: (1) isolation, (2) timing, (3) precautions against discovery/intervention, (4) action to gain help after the act, (5) final act in anticipation of death, (6) degree of planning, (7) suicide note (farewell letter) and (8) communication of intent before the act.

The remaining seven items consist of questions regarding the patients' subjective report of the intent of the act: (9) purpose of the act, (10) expectations regarding fatality of the act, (11) conceptions of the method's lethality, (12) seriousness of the act, (13) ambivalence towards living, (14) conception of reversibility, and (15) degree of premeditation.

The average level of suicidal intent of patients engaging in nonfatal suicidal behaviour has consistently been reported to be rather low when assessed by the SIS (e.g., Hawton et al., 1982; James & Hawton, 1982; Pallikkathayil & McBride, 1986; O'Brien et al., 1987; Hamdi et al., 1991; Strosahl et al., 1992; Kingsbury, 1993; Nielsen et al., 1993). However, the actual level has varied between studies, from a mean of 8.1 ($SD = 4.8$) in a study of adolescent self-poisoners (Hawton et al., 1982) to a mean of 13.9 (no measure of SD reported) in a study of all age groups (Strosahl et al., 1992).

Several authors have also pointed to the frequent failure to take account of gender in studies of suicidal behaviour (e.g., Jack, 1992; Canetto & Lester, 1995). Yet there are obvious gender differences in the incidence of suicidal behaviour, i.e., more men than women commit suicide, while more women than men engage in non-fatal suicidal behaviour. Based on these gender differences in the epidemiology of fatal and non-fatal suicidal behaviour, it could be hypothesised that men engaging in non-fatal suicidal acts would generally have a higher level of suicidal intent than women. This might indicate that non-fatal suicidal behaviour by men could more often be classified as failed suicide, while for women the behaviour may more often involve non-fatal intentions (e.g., communicating distress and the need for help).

The results of the few studies of possible gender differences in levels of suicidal intent have varied. In some, all using the SIS (Beck et al., 1974), no overall difference in suicidal intent has been found between the genders (O'Brien et al., 1987; Strosahl et al., 1992; Nielsen et al., 1993), whereas in a study in which a shortened version of this scale (only including 12 of the 15 items) was used, male patients had a higher mean level of suicidal intent than female patients (Pierce, 1977). Probably the general conclusion at this point is that there is, surprisingly, no *major* difference in level of suicidal intent between men and women engaging in non-fatal suicidal behaviour.

Suicide rates usually increase with age (with some exceptions; for instance, in Norway, suicide rates do not differ much between age groups), while the highest rates of non-fatal suicidal behaviour are among younger people. There is little information on whether level of suicidal intent in non-fatal suicidal behaviour increases with age. Hamdi and co-workers (1991) found gender differences in level of suicidal intent for adolescents, but not for other age-groups; young females had a significantly higher level of suicidal intent than young males. The fact that this study was carried out in a non-Western country (United Arab Emirates) and this result is contrary to what one might expect in Western settings suggests that it might reflect local circumstances. Nevertheless, it suggests that age, and age-gender interactions should be considered when studying suicidal intent.

One aim of the Multi-Centre Study in relation to suicidal intent was to compare the level of suicidal intent in female and male parasuicide patients in groups across different regions in several European countries and according to age group (Hjelmeland et al., 2000). Data from nine European regions participating in the first wave of the Repetition-Prediction part of the Multi-Centre Study were included in these analyses. The regions were Sør-Trøndelag (Norway), Stockholm and Umeå (Sweden), Helsinki (Finland), Odense (Denmark), Leiden (The Netherlands), Würzburg (Germany), Bern (Switzerland) and Padova (Italy). A total of 1,212 patients (752 females, 62%, and 460 males, 38%) aged 15 years and over were included in the analyses.

The mean level of suicidal intent ($M = 12.8$, $SD = 6.8$) was similar to that in other studies (e.g., Hawton et al., 1982; James & Hawton, 1982; Pallikkathayil & McBride, 1986; O'Brien et al., 1987; Hamdi et al., 1991; Strosahl et al., 1992; Kingsbury, 1993; Nielsen et al., 1993). However, statistically significant differences were found for both region and gender in the total suicidal intent scores. The lowest total mean value was found in Sør-Trøndelag ($M = 11.0$, $SD = 6.3$) and the highest in Bern ($M = 14.8$, $SD = 7.0$). The lowest mean value for women was also found in Sør-Trøndelag ($M = 10.7$, $SD = 5.9$) and the highest in Bern ($M = 15.0$, $SD = 7.3$). For men, the lowest mean value was found in Helsinki ($M = 9.8$, $SD = 6.8$) and the highest in Stockholm ($M = 15.2$, $SD = 7.4$). However, only a minimal proportion of the variance in overall scores was accounted for by region and gender (see Hjelmeland et al., 2000, for more details).

When the objective (circumstances) and subjective (self-report) parts of the SIS were analysed separately as dependent variables, statistically significant effects of region were found. However, again only minimal proportions of the overall variance were accounted for by region. Taking age into consideration did not change these results. This clearly indicates that the large sample size resulting in a very high statistical power caused small effects to become statistically significant. Thus, although statistically reliable, the effects of region and gender on SIS scores were so small that they have neither theoretical nor practical significance.

The effect of gender was so small that it provides little support for the hypothesis that men engaging in non-fatal suicidal behaviour have a higher level of suicidal intent than do women. This was also supported by the absence of gender differences in relation to the objective circumstances of the suicidal act and in whether the purpose of the act (SIS, item 9) had been to commit suicide, to obtain a temporary rest or to manipulate some significant other(s). Also, absence of a gender difference in scores regarding premeditation before the act (SIS, item 15) is in contrast to the common assumption that men, especially the young, are more impulsive with regard to suicidal behaviour than are women.

Various Intentions Involved in Non-Fatal Suicidal Behaviour

As mentioned previously, research has shown that acts of deliberate self-poisoning and self-injury often involve a variety of different intentions and that these often include non-suicidal purposes (e.g., Birtchnell & Alarcon, 1971; Lukianowicz, 1972; Bancroft et al., 1976, 1979; Hawton et al., 1982; James & Hawton, 1985; Varadaraj et al., 1986; Velamoor & Cernovsky, 1992; Michel et al., 1994; Hjelmeland, 1995; Holden et al., 1998). Examples of the types of intentions that have been identified include, for example, a temporary escape from unbearable circumstances, an attempt to influence some significant other(s), and a signal that a person needs help.

Many of the previous studies of intentions underlying nonfatal suicidal behaviour have been conducted in the United Kingdom (Birtchnell & Alarcon, 1971; Lukianowicz, 1972; Bancroft et al., 1976, 1979; Hawton et al., 1982; James & Hawton, 1985; Varadaraj et al., 1986; Velamoor & Cernovsky, 1992). Michel and colleagues (1994) used similar methodology as in some of these earlier studies (Bancroft et al., 1979; Hawton et al., 1982; James & Hawton, 1985) in an investigation of parasuicide patients in Switzerland and found some differences in the proportions of Swiss patients choosing various intentions compared to those in the British studies. For instance, a very large proportion of the patients in the Swiss study (91%) claimed that the intention had been to escape from an unbearable/terrible situation compared to those in the British studies (56% in Bancroft et al., 1979; 42% in Hawton et al., 1982; 44% in James & Hawton, 1985). Another example was the intention "to make things easier for someone," which was chosen by 33% in the Swiss but only by 7% in one of the British samples (Bancroft et al., 1979). Boergers and colleagues (1998) compared the frequencies of various reasons for suicidal behaviour among American adolescents with data reported from the Netherlands and the UK, and also found some differences. This raised the question of possible cross-national or cross-cultural differences in the intentions involved in nonfatal suicidal behaviour. The WHO Study provided a unique opportunity to examine this issue.

An important question is whether nonfatal suicidal behaviour involves different non-suicidal intentions for men and women. The potential significance of gender was neglected in most of the earlier studies. Even where results have been reported separately for men and women, it is unclear whether they were subjected to statistical testing, although major differences were not apparent. This is perhaps surprising given the gender differences in prevalence of non-fatal suicidal behaviour. The same applies to age. For example, do young men tend to communicate different things through non-fatal suicidal behaviour than do elderly men?

Thus one aim of the Repetition-Prediction part of the Multi-Centre Study was to study self-reported intentions involved in non-fatal suicidal behaviour, or in other words, what the behaviour *meant* to the patients themselves (Hjelmeland et al., in press). Data from 14 regions in 13 different European countries participating in both the first and second wave of the Repetition-Prediction part of the Multi-Centre Study were included in the analyses. These regions were Sør-Trøndelag (Norway), Umeå and Stockholm (Sweden), Helsinki (Finland), Odense (Denmark), Oxford (United Kingdom), Leiden (The Netherlands), Gent (Belgium), Würzburg (Germany), Hall/Innsbruck (Austria), Bern (Switzerland), Pecs (Hungary), Ljubljana (Slovenia) and Padova (Italy). The data analysed were based on a total of 1,646 patients, 1,003 (61%) women and 643 (39%) men aged 15 years and over.

The instrument used in this study was a well-tested questionnaire containing a number of intentions involved in nonfatal suicidal behaviour which had been identified in a series of previous investigations (e.g., Bancroft et al., 1979; Hawton et al., 1982; James & Hawton, 1985).

The questionnaire consists of 14 possible intentions people might have for engaging in suicidal behaviour (Table 1). In the WHO Study each item was scored according to the relevance the patient said it had to why they carried out the suicidal act: major influence (score of 3), minor influence (2), or no influence (1). The patients could indicate more than one intention as having influenced the act.

The intentions were grouped by means of a factor analysis. This resulted in four factors which were used to construct sub-scales labelled *care seeking* (items 2, 6, 8 and 9), *influencing others* (items 10–12), *temporary escape* (items 5 and 14), and *final exit* (items 1, 4, 7 and 13), while "loss of control" was retained and analysed as a single item (see Table 1 for the list of items).

Statistically significant differences between the regions were found for three of the sub-scales and in the item loss of control, but only minimal proportions of the variance were accounted for by region. When the pooled data set was analysed, a statistically significant difference between men and women was found, but again only a very small proportion of the variance was explained by gender. Moreover, when gender was en-

---

Table 1 The list of possible intentions on the questionnaire.

1. My thoughts were so unbearable, I could not endure them any longer.
2. I wanted to show someone how much I loved him/her.
3. It seemed that I lost control of myself, and I do not know why I did it.
4. The situation was so unbearable that I could not think of any other alternative.
5. I wanted to get away for a while from an unacceptable situation.
6. I wanted others to know how desperate I felt.
7. I wanted to die.
8. I wanted to get help from someone.
9. I wanted to know if someone really cared about me.
10. I wanted others to pay for the way they treated me.
11. I wanted to make someone feel guilty.
12. I wanted to persuade someone to change his/her mind.
13. I wanted to make things easier for others.
14. I wanted to sleep for a while.

tered into two-way analyses together with region, the gender difference disappeared. Some age differences were found in women, but here too the effect sizes were very low. No age differences were found in men. Small, but statistically significant differences were probably due to the large sample size resulting in very high statistical power. Thus the main finding from this study was that people engaging in non-fatal suicidal behaviour in different countries tend to indicate specific intentions for their acts at a similar rate, and that the actual intentions do not vary greatly with gender or age (see Hjelmeland et al., in press, for further details).

Rates of suicide and nonfatal suicidal behaviour vary between countries and regions (Schmidtke et al., 1996; 1999). One possible explanation might be the extent to which nonfatal suicidal behaviour involves suicidal or non-suicidal intentions. Thus, where suicidal intention is frequent, one might expect suicide rates to be higher than in regions where it is less frequent. On the other hand, where suicidal intention is less commonly implicated in non-fatal suicidal behaviour, one might expect rates of such behaviour to be higher. It was also possible to investigate this issue in the Multi-Centre Study. To our knowledge, this has never been addressed before.

The hypothesis that there would be a positive correlation between the suicide rates, both national and regional, and the frequency of choice of the intention "wanted to die" was supported only for women (and only when national suicide rates were used). The hypothesis that there would be a negative correlation between rates of non-fatal suicidal behaviour and "wanted to die" was not supported, although the result almost reached the level of statistical significance, especially for men (Hjelmeland et al., in press).

The use of an intention questionnaire, like that in this study, is likely to be helpful in assessment in clinical practice. The questionnaire could, for example, be completed by both the patient and the therapist, separately, and thus serve as a valuable basis to develop an understanding of the intention(s) underlying the act. The instrument may also be useful in treatment; understanding why the suicidal act occurred is important when deciding what should be focused on in therapy, including the possible prevention of future episodes. This notion was supported by the findings of Holden et al. (1998) that patient-attributed reasons for non-fatal suicidal behaviour predicted a number of suicide criteria, namely a wish to die as stated by the patients themselves, and suicidal desire, suicide preparation and overall suicide risk as estimated by their clinicians. Furthermore, these authors found that some of the patient-attributed reasons ("internal perturbations") were just as good predictors for suicide risk as hopelessness has previously been found to be (e.g., Beck et al., 1985). Knowledge and understanding of the intentions involved in non-fatal suicidal behaviour are thus relevant factors to consider when deciding on appropriate treatment of suicidal individuals and prevention of future suicidal behaviour.

There are several differences between the regions participating in the Multi-Centre Study both in the prevalence of suicidal behaviour and in the characteristics of the patients (Schmidtke et al., 1996; Bille-Brahe et al., 1996a; Bille-Brahe et al., 1996b; Bille-Brahe et al., 1997). The patterns of level of suicidal intent and of various intentions involved in non-fatal suicidal behaviour was, however, quite consistent across regions, genders and age groups. Thus the findings from different regions and countries using these types of instruments are probably generalisable to other settings.

The report from the Multi-Centre Study regarding level of suicide intent (Hjelmeland et al., 2000) was the first step in examining the meaning of the suicidal act ascribed by patients from different regions and countries. The report of a range of intentions has been the second step (Hjelmeland et al., in press). Quantitative methodology has been used in both these reports. One possible next step will be to use qualitative methodology to examine explanations at the individual level. Methods based on the phenomenological perspective, in which the central issue is to consider the meaning of phenomena in relation to each individual's personal circumstances, could be fruitful.

References

Alicke, M. D., Weigold, M. F., & Rogers, S. L. (1990). Inferring intentions and responsibility from motives and outcomes: evidential and extra-evidential judgements. *Social Cognition*, 8, 286–305.

Bancroft, J., Hawton, K., Simkin, S., Kingston, B., Cumming, C., & Whitwell, D. (1979). The reasons people give for taking overdoses: A further inquiry. *British Journal of Medical Psychology*, 52, 353–365.

Bancroft, J.H. J., Skrimshire, A. M., & Simkin, S. (1976). The reasons people give for taking overdoses. *British Journal of Psychiatry*, 128, 538–548.

Beck, A. T., Schuyler, D., & Herman, I. (1974). Development of suicidal intent scales. In: A. T. Beck, H. L. P. Resnik, & D. J. Letieri (Eds.), *The prediction of suicide*. Philadelphia, PA: The Charles Press.

Beck., A. T., Steer, R. A., Kovacs, M., & Garrison, B. (1985). Hopelessness and eventual suicide: A 10-year prospective study of patients hospitalized with suicidal ideation. *American Journal of Psychiatry*, 142, 559–563.

Bille-Brahe, U., Andersen, K., Wasserman, D., Schmidtke, A., Bjerke, T., Crepet, P., De Leo, D., Haring, C., Hawton, K., Kerkhof, A. J. F. M., Lönnqvist, J., Michel, P., Phillippe, I., Querejeta, I., Salander-Renberg, E., & Temesváry, B. (1996a). The WHO-EURO Multicentre Study: Risk of parasuicide and the comparability of the areas under study. *Crisis*, 17, 32–42.

Bille-Brahe, U., Kerkhof, A. J. F. M., De Leo, D., Schmidtke, A., Crepet, P., Lönnqvist, J., Michel, K., Salander-Renberg, E., Stiles, T. C., Wasserman, D., & Egebo, H. (1996b). A repetition-prediction study on European parasuicide populations. Part II of the WHO/EURO Multicentre Study on Parasuicide in cooperation with the EC concerted action on attempted suicide. *Crisis*, 17, 22–31.

Bille-Brahe, U., Kerkhof, A. J. F. M., De Leo, D., Schmidtke, A., Crepet, P., Lönnqvist, J., Michel, K., Salander-Renberg, E., Stiles, T. C., Wasserman, D., Aagaard, B., Egebo, H., & Jensen, B. (1997). A repetition-prediction study of European parasuicide populations: a summary of the first report from part II of the WHO/EURO Multicentre Study on Parasuicide in cooperation with the EC concerted action on attempted suicide. *Acta Psychiatrica Scandinavica*, 95, 81–86.

Birtchnell, J., & Alarcon, J. (1971). The motivation and emotional state of 91 cases of attempted suicide. *British Journal of Medical Psychology*, 44, 45–52.

Boergers, J., Spirito, A., & Donaldson, D. (1998). Reasons for adolescent suicide attempts: Associations with psychological functioning. *Journal of American Academy of Child and Adolescent Psychiatry, 37,* 1287–1293.

Buss, A. R. (1978). Causes and reasons in attribution theory: a conceptual critique. *Journal of Personality and Social Psychology, 36,* 1311–1321.

Buss, A. R. (1979). On the relationship between causes and reasons. *Journal of Personality and Social Psychology, 37,* 1458–1461.

Canetto, S. S., & Lester, D. (Eds.). (1995). *Women and suicidal behavior.* New York: Springer.

Gilje, N., & Grimen, H. (1993). *Samfunnsvitenskapenes forutsetninger* [The presuppositions of the social sciences]. Oslo: Universitetsforlaget.

Hamdi, E., Amin, Y., & Mattar, T. (1991). Clinical correlates of intent in attempted suicide. *Acta Psychiatrica Scandinavica, 83,* 406–411.

Hawton, K., Cole, D., O'Grady, J., & Osborn, M. (1982). Motivational aspects of deliberate self-poisoning in adolescents. *British Journal of Psychiatry, 141,* 286–291.

Heckhausen, H., & Kuhl, J. (1985). From wishes to action: the dead ends and short cuts on the long way to action. In M. Frese & J. Sabini (Eds.), *Goal directed behavior: The concept of action in psychology* (pp. 134–159). Hillsdale, NJ: Erlbaum.

Hettiarachchi, J., & Kodituwakku, G. C. S. (1989). Self poisoning in Sri Lanka: motivational aspects. *The International Journal of Social Psychiatry, 35,* 204–208.

Hinkle, S., & Schmidt, D. F. (1984). The Buss cause/reason hypotheses: an empirical investigation. *Social Psychology Quarterly, 47,* 358–364.

Hjelmeland, H. (1995). Verbally expressed intentions of parasuicide: I. Characteristics of patients with various intentions. *Crisis, 16,* 176–181.

Hjelmeland, H., Hawton, K., Nordvik, H., Bille-Brahe, U., De Leo, D., Fekete, S., Grad, O., Haring, C., Kerkhof, A. J. F. M., Lönnqvist, J., Michel, K., Salander Renberg, E., Schmidtke, A., Van Heeringen, K., & Wasserman, D. (2002) Why people engage in parasuicide: A cross-cultural study of intentions. *Suicide and Life-Threatening Behavior, 32,* 380–393.

Hjelmeland, H., & Knizek, B. L. (1999). Conceptual confusion about intentions and motives of nonfatal suicidal behavior: A discussion of terms employed in the literature of suicidology. *Archives of Suicide Research, 5,* 275–281.

Hjelmeland, H., Nordvik, H., Bille-Brahe, U., De Leo, D., Kerkhof, A. J.F. M., Lönnqvist, J., Michel, K., Salander-Renberg, E., Schmidtke, A., & Wasserman, D. (2000). A cross-cultural study of suicide intent in parasuicide patients. *Suicide and Life-Threatening Behavior, 30,* 295–303.

Holden, R. R., Kerr, P. S., Mendonca, J. D., & Velamoor, V. R. (1998). Are some motives more linked to suicide proneness than others. *Journal of Clinical Psychology, 54,* 569–576.

Hoffman, R. (1984). Intention, double effect, and single result. *Philosophy and Phenomenological Research, XLIV,* 389–393.

Jack, R. (1992). *Women and attempted suicide.* Hove, UK: Erlbaum.

James, D., & Hawton, K. (1985). Overdoses: explanations and attitudes in self-poisoners and significant others. *British Journal of Psychiatry, 146,* 481–5.

Kingsbury, S. J. (1993). Clinical components of suicidal intent in adolescent overdose. *Journal of the American Academy of Children and Adolescent Psychiatry, 32,* 518–520.

Kovacs, M., Beck, A. T., & Weissman, A. (1975). The use of suicidal motives in the psychotherapy of attempted suicides. *American Journal of Psychotherapy, 29,* 363–368.

Leenaars, A. A., De Leo, D., Diekstra, R.F. W., Goldney, R. D., Kelleher, M. J., Lester, D., & Nordstrom, P. (1997). Consultations for research in suicidology. *Archives of Suicide Research, 3,* 139–151.

Locke, D., & Pennington, D. (1982). Reasons and other causes: Their role in attribution processes. *Journal of Personality and Social Psychology, 42,* 212–223.

Lukianowicz, N. (1972). Suicidal behaviour: an attempt to modify the environment. *British Journal of Psychiatry, 121,* 387–390.

Michel, K., Valach, L., & Waeber, V. (1994). Understanding deliberate self-harm: The patients' views. *Crisis, 15,* 172–178, 186.

Nielsen, A. S., Stenager, E., & Bille-Brahe, U. (1993). Attempted suicide, suicidal intent, and alcohol. *Crisis, 14,* 32–38.

O'Brien, G., Holton, A. R., Hurren, K., Watt, L., & Hassanyeh, F. (1987). Deliberate self-harm – Correlates of suicidal intent and severity of depression. *Acta Psychiatrica Scandinavica, 75,* 474–477.

O'Carroll, P. W., Berman, A., Maris, R., Moscicki, E. K., Tanney, B. L., & Silverman, M. M. (1996). Beyond the Tower of Babel: A nomenclature for suicidology. *Suicide and Life-Threatening Behavior, 26,* 237–52.

Pallikkathayil, L., & McBride, A. B. (1986). Suicide attempts. *Journal of Psychosocial Nursing, 24,* 13–8.

Pierce, D. W. (1977). Suicidal intent and self-injury. *British Journal of Psychiatry, 130,* 377–85.

Reber, A. S. (1985). *The Penguin dictionary of psychology.* London: Penguin.

Schmidtke, A., Bille-Brahe, U., De Leo, D., Kerkhof, A. J. F. M., Bjerke, T., Crepet, P., Haring, C., Hawton, K., Lönnqvist, J., Michel, K., Pommereau, X., Querejeta, I., Phillipe, I., Salander Renberg, E., Temesváry, B., Wasserman, D., Fricke, S., Weinacker, B., & Sampaio-Faria, J. G. (1996). Attempted suicide in Europe: rates, trends and sociodemographic characteristics of suicide attempters during the period 1989–1992. Results of the WHO/EURO Multicentre Study on Parasuicide. *Acta Psychiatrica Scandinavica, 93,* 327–338.

Schmidtke, A., Weinacker, B., Apter, A., Batt, A., Berman, A., Bille-Brahe, U., Botsis, A., De Leo, D., Doneux, R., Goldney, R., Grad, O., Haring, C., Hawton, K., Hjelmeland, H., Kelleher, M., Kerkhof, A. J. F. M., Leenaars, A., Lönnqvist, J., Michel, K., Ostamo, A., Salander Renberg, E., Sayil, I., Takahashi, C., Van Heeringen C., Värnik, A., & Wasserman, D. (1999). Suicide rates in the world: Update. *Archives of Suicide Research, 5,* 81–89.

Strosahl, K., Chiles, J. A., & Linehan, M. (1992). Prediction of suicide intent in hospitalized parasuicides: reasons for living, hopelessness, and depression. *Comprehensive Psychiatry, 33,* 366–373.

Trevarthen, C. (1982). The primary motives for cooperative understanding. In: G. Butterworth & P. Light (Eds.), *Social cognition: Studies of the development of understanding* (pp. 77–109). Brighton, UK: Harvester Press,.

Varadaraj, R., Mendonca, J. D., & Rauchenberg, P. M. (1986). Motives and intent: A comparison of views of overdose patients and their key relatives/friends. *Canadian Journal of Psychiatry, 31,* 621–624.

Velamoor, V. R., & Cernovsky, Z. Z. (1992). Suicide with the motive "to die" or "not to die" and its socioanamnestic correlates. *Social Behavior and Personality, 20,* 193–198.

Part 3

Research Findings

Chapter 7
Socio-Demographic Variables of Suicide Attempters

Armin Schmidtke and Cordula Löhr

Department of Clinical Psychology, University of Würzburg, Germany

Introduction

Despite the common burden, the suicide situation in Europe differs between the various countries. In recent years, especially in Eastern Europe, the rank order of suicide rates among the various countries has changed dramatically. In some of the nations, very high suicide figures can be found; however, intra-nationally, rates for different regions may vary significantly. In some countries, suicide figures are decreasing by co-varying with a stable social situation and a good economic status. In other countries suicidality is increasing by co-varying with social changes and instability, unemployment and increasing prevalence of psychiatric illnesses. The burden due to years of life lost is immense. Every suicide also affects on average at least 5–6 other persons (Diekstra et al., 1995).

However, until now, it has proven almost impossible to make valid comparisons about various aspects of suicidal behaviour among different European countries. In the absence of national data, researchers have been forced to rely on local surveys, which vary markedly in terms of their nominal and operational definitions of suicide attempts, representativeness of the sample, time span covered, amount of information gathered, etc. In addition, local studies have not always been adequate from an epidemiological standpoint (e.g., failing to identify risk factors for suicide attempts) or from the perspective of health-service referral (e.g., failing to identify patterns of treatment following suicide attempt). Therefore, previous examinations on the epidemiology of suicide attempts in Europe (Diekstra, 1982, 1996) were restricted to information gathered in different centres with neither uniform definitions nor standardized case-finding criteria. In the WHO/EURO Multi-Centre Study on Suicidal Behaviour, therefore, one aim was to generate an epidemiological picture of suicide attempters in the European Region as well as to gather information about special risk groups. The study tried to overcome some difficulties of previous studies with a common definition ("para-suicide") and common case finding criteria. Information was collected about various socio-demographic variables, such as current marital status, household composition, religious denomination, level of education (based on appropriate national standards), level of vocational training, economic situation at the time of the suicide attempt, change of address during the past year, and the treatment offered after the suicide attempt (Platt et al., 1992; Schmidtke et al., 1993).

Of course the reliability of these social variables varies. However, one can be reasonably confident that the data collected are valid and, therefore, also comparisons between centres and countries are valid. As Platt et al. (1992, p. 102) stated ". . . *like is being compared with like.*"

Findings

The age distribution of suicide attempts is quite different from the age distribution of suicides in most countries. The highest person-based rates for men were mostly found among the 25–34 year-olds. The highest person-based rates for females were found in the age groups 15–34 years. The rates in the age groups 55+ years were mostly the lowest. These results were stable over the entire investigation period.

Generally, the methods used in the suicide attempt were mostly "soft." For these methods, a slight increase over time was detectable. Results showed that "alcohol" (X65) alone as a method of attempted suicide and "car accident" (X82) should not be overlooked.

The frequencies of the different methods of attempted suicide in the various centres were more or less comparable; however, exceptions were found. The method car accident seems to be common in German-speaking countries, while, according to data, it is not used in the southern part of Europe. On the contrary, there are surprisingly high rates of using herbicides and pesticides in Hungary and in Rennes, France (Michel et al., 2000).

Methods used for suicide attempts did not co-vary significantly with age. Soft methods were prevalent in all age groups.

Religion in suicide attempters, as far as it could be assessed across the individual centres, did not differ from that of the general populations.

The analysis according to marital status showed that the category with the highest average percentage was that of single persons. This finding seems to be stable over time. Considering the hypothesis that the probability of being married and consequently being divorced is less among younger age groups, a separate analysis for persons older than 25 years was performed. This analysis showed that the general results were age dependent and that an interaction effect exists (see Chapter 10).

For the first time, the usual, formal living situation and household composition, and the situation existing at the time of the suicidal act were differentiated. Nearly a quarter of the males and 20% of the females were usually living alone. Social integration, as indicated by the usual living situation, relatively often differed from the living situation shortly before the suicide attempt. Some of the suicide attempters changed their living conditions before the suicidal act. The most frequent change shortly before the suicidal act was a move from a socially stable situation to living alone, in an unstable situation, or in an institution.

More than half of all suicide attempters have only a low level of formal education. The formal education of this group, in general, does not match the distribution in the general population, with people of lower educational status being over-represented among attempters.

The picture is similar with regard to vocational training. A high percentage of both male and female suicide attempters had received no vocational training. Therefore, also the rate of unemployment is very high, up to a fifth of all suicide attempters, and a high percentage (up to a third) are economically inactive (in those who were able to work). This changed over time with an increase in rates of unemployment. Due to these facts, nearly half of all suicide attempters belong to the lowest social class.

The most prevalent diagnosis for males and females was "adjustment disorder" (ICD 9: 309; males: 26%, females: 29%). For males, the second condition in terms of prevalence was "addiction and alcohol and substance abuse" (ICD 9: 303, 304, and 305; 24%), followed by affective disorders (21%). For females, the second most frequent diagnosis was affective disorder (29%), followed by "personality disorder" (13%). However, in reference to Lester (1972), adjustment disorder (as well as "abnormal reaction to stress") could possibly represent a so-called "contaminated" diagnosis.

The type of aftercare most often recommended to males was "in-patient treatment" (53%). "Out-patient treatment" was recommended in 19% of cases, and "non-hospital based treatment" in 14%.

In females, no further treatment was recommended after the suicide attempt in 14% of cases. The type of aftercare most often recommended was in-patient treatment (50%). Out-patient treatment was recommended in 22% of cases, and non-hospital based treatment in 16%.

A high percentage of previous suicide attempts were found in both males (42%) and females (45%). Of males, 18% repeated the act within 12 months, whereas this was the case for 22% of the females.

Comparisons between the persons who had made only one suicide attempt and those who made two and more suicide attempts (independently of time period) showed that the mean age did not differ. However, repeaters were more often divorced or separated and unemployed. The methods used in suicide attempts were generally not significantly different. However, females who made only one suicide attempt used the method "poisoning" more often than repeaters did.

The types of psychiatric diagnoses in repeaters were different from those in the "first-evers." More male repeaters had addiction diagnoses, neuroses and personality disorders and fewer had adjustment disorders and acute reactions to stress.

In female repeaters a diagnosis of "neuroses and personality disorder" (without neurotic depression) was more common than in non-repeaters. The recommended aftercare did not differ between repeaters and non-repeaters.

Discussion

The results show that perhaps some of the long-standing hypotheses and opinions about suicide attempters should be modified. For example, the first results indicate that for some samples the female to male ratio is not as disproportionately different as indicated in many previous epidemiological studies on suicidal behaviour (e.g., Böcker, 1973; Diekstra, 1982).

With regard to the socio-demographic variables, results clearly show that compared with the general population, suicide attempters belong more often to those social categories indicating social destabilization and poverty. Thus, this study has also provided additional evidence of a co-variation of certain socio-demographic or socio-economic conditions and occurrence of attempted suicide (Welz, 1980, 1983; Platt & Kreitman, 1985; Platt, 1986; Mösler, et al., 1990; Petronis et al., 1990; Rygnestad & Hauge, 1991).

However, for international comparisons, further analyses are needed, especially with regard to the base rates of the different variables in the general population, and a cross-cultural framework to account for the data (cf. Leenaars, 1994). The results also clearly show that for future research the differentiation of the usual living conditions and household composition and living conditions immediately preceding the suicidal act would be useful.

If the rates of repetition of suicide attempts are computed, results give the impression that the rate of repetition is increasing over time, especially for men. Results lead to the hypothesis that suicide attempters could be quickly separated into two groups: a group with only one or two attempts, and another with three or more attempts. In comparison to findings from the 1980s, it seems that rates of repetition of suicide attempts within 12 months from previous act are increasing (Schmidtke et al., 1988).

It also seems that the recommendations for aftercare have changed over time. In recent years, less aftercare and inpatient treatment was recommended. How far this may reflect a better network of outpatient treatment or an improved knowledge about suicide attempters has to be tested in further analyses.

In comparing the various countries, it could be hypothesised that differences are due to differences in death certification and classification of suicide attempters. However, since several studies have shown that differences in the rank order of suicide rates in the native countries co-vary with differences of the same cultural groups in other countries (Sainsbury & Barraclough, 1968; Lester, 1972; Schmidtke et al., 1994), the difference in ascertainment procedures do not explain all differences in the suicide rates between the various European countries (e.g., Diekstra, 1996). Other proof for this assumption is that Hungary or Saxony and Thuringia, regardless of their government, have had consistently higher suicide rates than the rest of Europe or Germany.

Historically, some authors have hypothesised that suicide rates in areas with a higher percentage of Germans are higher than in regions with a more Roman or Slavic population (e.g., Morselli, 1881). These hypotheses were also used to explain, for example, the constant differences of suicide rates within Germany. Still, in 1960, Winkler explained this with the *"known tendency of the Saxonian-Thuringian population towards suicide"* and, he added, *"since other factors can be excluded, this must be due to their 'character'"* (Winkler, 1960, p. 144).

Today, the hypotheses regarding these ethnic differences are numerous, ranging from biology to nutritional and attitudinal factors. However, biological differences do not seem to provide sufficient explanation for these differences. Attitudinal factors are perhaps more relevant (Fekete & Schmidtke, 1995, Fekete et al., 2001). These factors perhaps also affect suicide rates of immigrants. Even in European countries that regard themselves as most tolerant, immigrants are often considered as rural and "primitive" individuals.

Methodologically rigorous studies have shown that differences in suicide rates between countries are not equally distributed across all age groups. Most differences are only significant for the older age groups (Moksony, 1995; Schmidtke, 1995).

Despite the fact that many studies (including the Multi-Centre one) show a co-variation of certain primarily negative socio-demographic or socio-economic conditions and the occurrence of at least attempted suicide (Platt & Kreitman, 1985; Platt, 1986; Rygnestad & Hauge, 1991; Schmidtke et al., 1996), simple socio-demographic explanations (e.g., different unemployment rates, different participation of women in the labour force, and social security systems) do not explain the variations in European suicide and suicide attempt rates either. Whereas unemployment rates were increasing in UK in the 70s, suicide rates decreased. Although unemployment rates in the Eastern parts of Germany have increased and are now significantly higher than before (officially, GDR did not have unemployed citizens), suicide rates are decreasing (Schmidtke, 1995). Also, in the WHO/EURO Multi-Centre Study on Suicidal Behaviour, there is no significant co-variation between socio-economic factors, e.g., unemployment rates and suicide attempt rates within the various centres. Only the frequency of divorce and the number of persons receiving public assistance showed significant correlations (Bille-Brahe et al., 1996). Studies also show that teenage suicide rates, in particular, are not related to the quality of life (Lester, 1988). However, time series analyses on data from 1911 to 1990 in Norway showed that alcohol consumption and divorce were independently and significantly associated with male suicide rates, but not with female suicide rates (Rossow, 1993).

Geographical differences between European countries are also confounded by differences in religious variables. European countries differ with regard to the prevalence of main religions. Previous studies show, for example, significant co-variations between rates of suicide and of undetermined deaths and religious affiliation even within the same country. In more Catholic regions, suicide rates are mostly lower and rates of undetermined death higher, whereas suicide rates are higher in more Protestant regions (Bojanovsky, 1979, 1981). One reason for this might be the different reactions of the religions to funeral ceremonies. Until recently, in some Catholic regions, suicide victims were not buried with religious ceremonies, therefore, increasing the probability of the under-reporting of suicide. However, the results of the WHO/EURO Multi-Centre Study on Suicidal Behaviour show that this hypothesis today cannot explain any great part of the variances. For example, in Würzburg, Germany, an area with a primarily Catholic population, the religious affiliation of suicide attempters shows no difference with that of the general population (Schmidtke et al., 1994). The reason for the decrease of the co-variation between religion and suicidal behaviour on a macro level may be that a gap is slowly growing between personal and institutional religious experience, even in such countries as Italy, which are normally regarded as more religiously oriented. The results of the European Value Study show, for example, that ritual participation and membership in a particular denomination is no longer a significant indicator for religiousness and for areas such as family, partnership, children, goals of life, and moral values (Zulehner & Denz, 1993; Capraro, 1994).

If a behaviour is culturally sanctioned, the probability for such behaviour to occur is lower. Thus, an important target for the explanation of differences and primary prevention may be of local nature, perhaps influenced by age and gender specific cultures of suicidal behaviour itself (Andriolo, 1984; Platt, 1989, 1993; Retterstol, 1993; Draguns, 1994; Canetto & Lester, 1995; Leenaars, 1995). Socio-cultural attitudes and the role of elderly people in society have, for example, a significant relevance for the incidence of suicide in the elderly (De Leo et al., 2001). Variations in European countries may therefore explain the significant differences among suicide rates of the elderly (Bron, 1989). Cultural attitudes towards individual suicide methods also play an important role in how often they will be used for suicide (Snowdon, 1978).

Different attitudes and values in general seem to have no great influence on suicidal behaviour. Results of the European Value Study (a study assessing various values as the underlying motivation for desires and preferences in different European countries, for example, religious values, tolerance against immigrants, ecological values, work values, values towards unemployment, participation of females in the labour force, leisure behaviour, criminal behaviour, etc.) (Ashford & Timms, 1992; Zulehner & Denz, 1993; World Values Study Group, 1994) do not co-vary with the results of the WHO/EURO Multi-Centre Study on Parasuicide (Aish-van Vaerenberg, 1996). This study also revealed that there is no co-variation between an increasing leniency and permissiveness and the acceptance of deviant behaviour (Halman, 1995).

When attitudes seem to be relevant, these attitudes reflect more special attitudes towards suicidal behaviour. The most striking finding within Europe in the last decade is the different and changing attitude towards suicide (Diekstra & Garnefski,

1995). European countries differ significantly, for example, regarding the number of headlines containing suicide themes. For the year 1981, there was a significant difference between Eastern and Western countries, with nearly no reports in Eastern countries. With regard to the content, there were also significant differences between Eastern and Western countries. Whereas, for example, the rate of suicide reports of "positive" prominent celebrities was highest in Hungary, suicide reports of "negative" celebrities were significantly more frequent in German headlines. Reports containing positive consequences of suicidal behaviour were also more frequent in Hungary and Lithuania, whereas negative consequences of suicidal behaviour are more often described in German and Austrian headlines (Schmidtke & Fekete, 1996; Fekete et al., 2001). Diekstra & Garnefski (1995), therefore, see the more frequent presentation of suicide models as being a reason for the increase of suicidal behaviour among adolescents.

Some survey studies also show different attitudes towards suicidal behaviour. One hypothesis for the explanation of the high suicide rates in the former GDR is that different attitudes towards psychological aspects in politics enhance suicidal behaviour (Belau, 1991). Swedish adolescents have more liberal attitudes towards suicide than Turkish adolescents. However, Turkish adolescents show greater acceptance of a suicidal peer than Swedish adolescents (Eskin, 1995a). Attitudes towards life and death are also different (Weiss & Perry, 1975). However, the differences in attitudes are not reflected in suicide notes. A recent comparison between German and US suicide notes revealed no major differences with regard to several aspects (Leenaars et al., 1994).

Cultural characteristics and attitudes of a population may also affect the relevant importance of the various factors involved in suicidal attempts. For example, findings indicate that suppression of personal freedom by parents is a major risk factor for suicidal attempts in Greek female adolescents (Beratis, 1990, 1991).

There exist some hypotheses that the various European countries differ with regard to differences in personalities of their individuals. They assume differences in the level of introversion-extraversion, impulsivity, and the coping strategies with stress. For example, comparing Turkish adolescents making suicide attempts to Swedish adolescents making suicide attempts, less positive assertive skills were found for the Swedish adolescents (Eskin, 1995b). Robertson & Cochrane (1976) assume that a change has occurred in the world-view of young people, and that this has been responsible for the differential increase in attempted suicide. The elements of this change were seen in an emphasis on the importance of "self-fulfilment," a belief that society, rather than the individual, should be responsible for providing the means to personal fulfilment; and a resulting tendency to regard social and material deprivations as obstacles to self-fulfilment. It was postulated that individuals who possess these values, and who live in objectively deprived circumstances, would be less willing to tolerate stress than would their older counterparts, who were seen as emphasizing personal fulfilment and more personal responsibility. However, results of some studies suggest that no clear link between attitudes and actual suicidal behaviour at the societal level seem to exist (Kerkhof & Nathawat, 1989), and that personality correlates of those with suicidal tendencies are rather similar despite differences in age and cultural background (Irfani, 1978).

Perhaps based on different attitudes, European countries also differ widely with regard to their prevention strategies. Whereas organizations like the Samaritans were founded relatively early in the United Kingdom (the primary goal of these organizations is suicide prevention), no such organizations were present until 1989 in Eastern countries. Also, the date of foundation of the different national suicide prevention organizations differs widely, with Austria having one of the first (international) organizations – perhaps due to their high suicide rate – and Switzerland funding such an organization relatively late. In some countries even the various local organizations do not share the same names (as in Germany). The various nations also differ with regard to national suicide prevention programs and funds for such programs. However, these variations partially depend on the structure and constitution of a given country.

References

Aish-van Vaerenbergh, A.-M. (1996). *The European Value Study (EVS): Theoretical and methodological issues in cross-national or cross-cultural research.* Paper presented at the WHO Meeting "Cross-cultural analysis: Theoretical, methodological and practical issues," Stockholm, Sweden.

Andriolo, K. R. (1984). Selbstmord als Krise der Gemeinschaft – Zur gesellschaftlichen Bewertung der Selbsttötung im transkulturellen Vergleich [Suicide as a community crisis [The transcultural comparison of societal judgements of suicide]. *Psychosozial, 23,* 56–67.

Ashford, S., & Timms, N. (1992) *What Europe thinks: A study of European values.* Dartmouth, UK: Aldershot Publishers.

Belau, D. (1991). Interpretation der Selbsttötung auf dem Hintergrund der DDR-Kultur [Interpreting suicide against the background of DDR culture]. *Suizidprophylaxe, 18,* 271–285.

Beratis, S. (1990). Factors associated with adolescent suicidal attempts in Greece. *Psychopathology, 23,* 161–168.

Beratis, S. (1991). Suicide attempts and suicides in Greek adolescents. In D. Papadatou & C. Papadatos (Eds.), *Children and death: Series in death education, aging, and health care* (pp. 77 – 84). New York: Hemisphere.

Bille-Brahe, U., Andersen, K., Wasserman, D., Schmidtke, A., Bjerke, T., Crepet, P., DeLeo, D., Haring, C., Hawton, K., Kerkhof, A. J. F. M., Lönnqvist, J., Michel, K., Philippe, A., Querejeta, I., Salander-Renberg, E., & Temesvary, B. (1996). The WHO-EURO Multicentre Study: Risk of parasuicide and the comparability of the areas under study. *Crisis, 17,* 32–42.

Böcker, F. (1973). *Suizide und Suizidversuche in der Großstadt, dargestellt am Beispiel der Stadt Köln* [Suicide and suicide attempts in the city based on the example of Cologne]. Stuttgart, Germany: Thieme.

Bojanovsky, J. (1979). Leben Protestanten länger? [Do protestants live longer?]. *Medizin, Mensch, Gesellschaft, 4,* 120–123.

Bojanovsky, J. (1981). Religion und Lebenserwartung [Religion and life expectations]. *Lebensversicherungsmedizin, 33*, 141–142.

Bron, B. (1989). Suizidalitat im Alter [Suicide in old age]. *Fortschritte der Medizin, 107*, 266–270.

Canetto, S. S., & Lester, D. (1995). Gender and the primary prevention of suicide mortality. *Suicide and Life-Threatening Behavior, 25*, 58–69.

Capraro, G. (1994). La religiosita degli italiani tra esperienza personale e appartenenza instituzionale: elementi per una tipologia [Religiosity of Italians between personal experience and the institutional affiliations: Elements for typology]. *Studi di Sociologia, 32*, 37–57.

De Leo, D., Bille-Brahe, U., Arensman, E., Hjelmeland, H., Haring, C., Hawton, K., Lönnqvist, J., Michel, K., Salander Renberg, E., Schmidtke, A., & Wasserman, D. (2001). Suicidal behavior in elderly Europeans. In D. Deleo, (Ed.), *Suicide and euthanasia in older adults* (pp. 21–35). Göttingen: Hogrefe & Huber.

Diekstra, R.F. W. (1982). Epidemiology of attempted suicide in the EEC. In J. Wilmotte & J. Mendlewicz (Eds.), *New trends in suicide prevention* (pp. 1–16). Basel: Karger.

Diekstra, R.F. W. (1996). The epidemiology of suicide and parasuicide. *Archives of Suicide Research, 2*, 1–29.

Diekstra, R.F. W., & Garnefski, N. (1995). On the nature, magnitude, and causality of suicidal behaviors: an international perspective. *Suicide and Life-Threatening Behavior, 25*, 36–57.

Diekstra, R.F. W., Gulbinat, W., Kienhorst, I., & De Leo, D. (1995). *Preventing strategies on suicide.* Leiden: E. J.Brill/WHO-Geneva.

Draguns, J. G. (1994). Pathological and clinical aspects. In L. Loeb Adler & U. P. Gielen (Eds.), *Cross-cultural topics in psychology* (pp. 165–177). Greenwood, Westport: Praeger.

Eskin, M. (1995a). Adolescents' attitudes towards suicide, and a suicidal peer: a comparison between Swedish and Turkish high school students. *Scandinavian Journal of Psychology, 36*, 201–207.

Eskin, M. (1995b). Suicidal behavior as related to social support and assertiveness among Swedish and Turkish high school students: a cross-cultural investigation. *Journal of Clinical Psychology, 51*, 158–172.

Fekete, S., & Schmidtke, A. (1996). The impact of mass-media reports on suicide and the reflected attitudes conveyed towards self-destruction: Previous studies and some new data from Hungary and Germany. In Mishara B. (Ed.), *The impact of suicide* (pp. 156–172). New York: Springer.

Fekete, S., Schmidtke, A., Takahashi, Y., Etzersdorfer, E., Upanne, M., & Osvath, P. (2001). Mass media, cultural attitudes, and suicide: Results of an international comparative study. *Crisis, 22*, 170–172.

Gulbinat, W. (1996). The epidemiology of suicide in old age. *Archives of Suicide Research, 2*, 31–42.

Halman, L. (1995). Is there a moral decline? A cross-national inquiry into morality in contemporary society. *International Social Science Journal, 47*, 419–439.

Irfani, S. (1978). Personality correlates of suicidal tendency among Iranian and Turkish students. *Journal of Psychology, 99*, 151–153.

Kerkhof, A. J. F. M., & Nathawat, S. S. (1989). Suicidal behavior and attitudes towards suicide among students in India and the Netherlands: A cross-cultural comparison. In R.F.W. Dieckstra, R. Moris, S. Platt, A. Schmidtke, & G. Sonneck (Eds.), *Suicide and its prevention: The role of attitude and imitation* (Advances in suicidology, Vol. 1, pp. 144–159). Leiden: Brill.

Leenaars, A. (1994). Conference report: Attempted suicide in Europe. *Crisis, 15*, 90

Leenaars, A. (1995). Suicide. In H. Wass & R. A. Neimeyer (Eds.), *Dying: Facing the facts: Series in death education, aging, and health care* (3rd ed., pp. 347–383). Philadelphia: Taylor & Francis.

Leenaars, A., Lester, D., Wenckstern, S., & Heim, N. (1994). Suizid-Abschiedsbriefe – Ein Vergleich deutscher und amerikanischer Abschiedsbriefe von Suizidenten [Suicide notes – A comparison of German and American suicide notes]. *Suizidprophylaxe, 21,* 99–101.

Lester, D. (1972). *Why people kill themselves.* Springfield, IL: Thomas.

Lester, D. (1988). Youth suicide: A cross-cultural perspective. *Adolescence, 23,* 955–958.

Michel, K., Ballinari, P., Bille-Brahe, U., Bjerke, T., Crepet, P., De Leo, D., Haring, C., Hawton, K., Kerkhof, A. D. J. F., Lönnqvist, J., Querejeta, I., Salander-Renberg, E., Schmidtke, A., Temesvary, B., & Wasserman, D. (2000). Methods used for parasuicide: Results of the WHO/EURO Multicentre Study on Parasuicide. *Social Psychiatry and Psychiatric Epidemiology, 35,* 156–163.

Moksony, F. (1995) The age pattern of suicide in Hungary. *Archives of Suicide Research, 1,* 217–222.

Morselli, H. (1881). *Der Selbstmord* [Suicide]. Leipzig: Brockhaus.

Mösler, T. A., Pontzen, W., & Rummler, W. (1990). The relationship between suicidal acts and unemployment. In G. Ferrari, M. Bellini, & P. Crepet (Eds.), *Suicidal behavior and risk factors.* Bologna: Monduzzi.

Petronis, K. R., Samuels, J. F., Moscicki, E. K., & Anthony, J. C. (1990). An epidemiologic investigation of potential risk factors for suicide attempts. *Social Psychiatry and Psychiatric Epidemiology, 25,* 193–199.

Platt, S. (1986). Parasuicide and unemployment. *British Journal of Psychiatry, 149,* 401–405.

Platt, S., & Kreitman, N. (1985). Is unemployment a cause of parasuicide? *British Medical Journal, 290,* 161.

Platt, S., Bille-Brahe, U., Kerkhof, A. F. J. D., Schmidtke, A., Bjerke, T., Crepet, P., De Leo, D., Haring, C., Hawton, K., Lönnqvist, J., Michel, K., Philippe, A., Querejeta, I., Salander-Renberg, E., Temesvary, B., Wasserman, D., & Sampaio-Faria, J. (1992). Parasuicide in Europe: The WHO/EURO Multicentre Study on Parasuicide. I. Introduction and preliminary analysis for 1989. *Acta Psychiatrica Scandinavica, 85,* 97–104.

Retterstol, N. (1993). *Suicide: A European perspective.* Cambridge, UK: Cambridge University Press.

Robertson, A., & Cochrane, R, (1976). Attempted suicide and cultural change: An empirical investigation. *Human Relations, 29,* 863–883.

Rossow, I. (1993). Suicide, alcohol, and divorce; aspects of gender and family integration. *Addiction, 88,* 1659–1665.

Rygnestad, T., & Hauge, L. (1991). Epidemiological, social and psychiatric aspects in self-poisoned patients. A prospective comparative study from Trondheim, Norway between 1978 and 1987. *Social Psychiatry and Psychiatric Epidemiology, 26,* 53–62.

Sainsbury, P., & Barraclough, B. M. (1968). Differences between suicide rates. *Nature, 220,* 1252.

Schmidtke, A. (1989). *WHO (Euro) Multicentre Study of Parasuicide.* Working paper for the WHO Consultation on Strategies for reducing suicidal behaviour in the European Region, Szeged, Hungary, ICP/PSF 024/18.

Schmidtke, A. (1995). Suizid- und Suizidversuchsraten in Deutschland [Suicide and suicide attempt rates in Germany]. In M. Wolfersdorf & W. Kaschka (Eds.). *Suizidalität – Die biologische Dimension* (pp. 17– 32). Heidelberg, Germany: Springer.

Schmidtke, A., & Fekete, S. (1996, April). *The international study on newspaper headlines about suicidal behaviour: Design and preliminary results.* Paper presented at the Meeting of the International Academy for Suicide Research, St. Louis, MO.

Schmidtke, A., Häfner, H., Möller, H. J., Wedler, H., & Böhme, K. (1988). Häufigkeiten und Trends von Suizidversuchen in der Bundesrepublik Deutschland: eine methodische Studie [Frequency and trends of suicide attempts in the Republic of Germany: A methodological study]. *Öffentliches Gesundheitswesen, 50,* 272–277.

Schmidtke, A., Bille-Brahe, U., Kerkhof, A. J. F. M., De Leo, D., Platt, S., Sampaio-Faria, J., Henderson, J., & Pototzky, W. (1993). The WHO/EURO Multicentre Project on Parasuicide – State of the art. *Italian Journal of Suicidology, 3,* 83–95.

Schmidtke, A., Fricke, S., & Weinacker, B. (1994). The epidemiology of attempted suicide in the Würzburg area, Germany 1989–1992. In A. J. F. M. Kerkhof, A. Schmidtke, U. Bille-Brahe, D. DeLeo, & J. Lönnqvist (Eds.). *Attempted suicide in Europe* (pp. 159–174). Leiden: DSWO Press.

Schmidtke, A., Bille-Brahe, U., D. DeLeo, D., Kerkhof, A. J. F. M., Bjerke, T., Crepet, P., Haring, C., Hawton, K., Lönnqvist, J., Michel, K., Philippe, A., Pommereau, X., Querejeta, I., Salander-Renberg, E., Temesvary, B., Wasserman, D., Fricke, S., Weinacker, B., & Sampaio-Faria, J. G. (1996). Attempted suicide in Europe: Rates, trends and sociodemographic characteristics of suicide attempters, 1989–1992. Results of the WHO/EURO Multicentre Study on Parasuicide. *Acta Psychiatrica Scandinavica, 93,* 327–338.

Snowdon, J. (1978). Suicide in Australia – A comparison with suicide in England and Wales. *Australian and New Zealand-Journal of Psychiatry, 13,* 301–307.

Weiss, J. M., & Perry, M. E. (1975). Transcultural attitudes towards homicide and suicide. *Suicide, 5,* 223–227.

Welz, R. (1980). Suicidal areas: Cluster analysis profiles of urban environments. *Acta Psychiatrica Scandinavica, 62*(Suppl. 285).

Welz, R. (1983). *Drogen, Alkohol und Suizid* [Drugs, alcohol and suicide]. Stuttgart: Enke.

Winkler, W. F. (1960). Über den Wandel in Häufigkeit, Bedingungen und Beurteilung des Suicids in der Nachkriegszeit [The change in frequency, conditions and assessment of suicide after the war]. *Der Öffentliche Gesundheitsdienst, 22,* 135–145.

World Values Study Group. (1994). *World Values Survey, 1981–1984 and 1990–1993.* Interuniversity Consortium for Political and Social Research, Ann Arbor, MI.

Zulehner, P. M., & Denz H. (1993). *Wie Europa lebt und glaubt* [How Europe lives and believes]. Düsseldorf: Patmos.

Chapter 8
Negative Life Events and Non-Fatal Suicidal Behaviour

Ella Arensman[1] and Ad Kerkhof[2]

[1]National Suicide Research Foundation, Cork, Ireland, [2]Department of Clinical Psychology, Vrije Universiteit, Amsterdam, The Netherlands

Introduction

Research among various patient populations has shown that stressful and traumatic life events play an important role in the aetiology of psychological and psychiatric disorders, such as posttraumatic stress disorder (PTSD), other anxiety disorders and depression (Kessler, 1997; Miller, 1997; Dohrenwend, 1998). However, there is still insufficient agreement among authors about how stressful and traumatic life events are related to different types of psychopathology, and whether there is a relationship between specific life events and specific psychological and psychiatric disorders.

So far, research findings point at a non-specific stress reaction. However, there are indications for a relationship between the specific features of an event, such as type, duration and circumstances under which the event occurred, and the intensity and duration of the stress reaction and symptomatology (Herman, 1992; Draijer & Boon, 1993; Van der Kolk et al., 1996). In addition, it appears that personal and social factors contribute as mediating factors to the way in which people cope with stressful and traumatic events. As such, these factors have an influence on both the short-term and the long-term risk of developing a psychological or psychiatric disorder (Saxe et al., 1993; Van der Kolk & Fisler, 1994).

In addition to psychopathology in general, an important part of the literature has focused on the role of stressful and traumatic life events in the development of suicidal behaviour, in which the major focus has been on the relationship between recent stressful or traumatic events and non-fatal suicidal behaviour. In general, it appears that attempted suicide patients report more stressful and traumatic life events than those who do not exhibit this behaviour. Moreover, there appears to be a relationship between having repeatedly experienced stressful or traumatic events and an increased risk of repeated suicidal behaviour. It seems important to differentiate between subgroups of patients, e.g., young versus older suicide attempters, which may have implications for the development of treatment and prevention strategies.

In the first part of this chapter, a brief overview of the findings of previous studies on the relationship between life events and suicidal behaviour will be presented. The second part will focus on important findings of the WHO/EURO Multicentre Study on Suicidal Behaviour with regard to the assessment of life events and the role of life events in the prediction of suicidal behaviour. In the last part, implications of the findings for theory, research and clinical practice will be discussed.

Overview of Studies on the Relationship Between Negative Life Events and Non-Fatal Suicidal Behaviour

Methodological Issues

Although a large number of studies have focused on the relationship between life events and suicidal behaviour, the study findings are not always comparable, mainly due to differences in study design, operationalisation of concepts, method of data collection, and period over which life events were examined. For these reasons, it has not been possible to draw any conclusions on causality with regard to the relationships between life events and suicidal behaviour.

In a number of studies, operationalisations of stressful and traumatic life events were absent and no distinctions were made between events occurring occasionally, traumatic experiences, and long-term or chronic stressful situations. However, research has indicated that the consequences of occasional events and chronic experiences can be different in terms of type and duration of psychological and psychiatric symptoms (Terr, 1994; Dohrenwend, 1998).

Most studies use a retrospective design, which has some major disadvantages, such as the risk of obtaining incomplete information or distortion of information due to problems of recollection. Moreover, no predictions can be made of the value of life events for future suicidal behaviour merely on the basis of a retrospective design. With regard to the method of data collection, most studies have been using open-ended questions, often resulting in a wide range of life events, which makes it difficult to compare the findings. Studies using a self-report questionnaire or structured interview often fail to provide information on the development and psychometric properties of the instrument.

A final issue concerns the period over which life events were examined, which varies from the entire life up to six months prior to the index suicide attempt. Previously, in studies focusing on the relationship between life events and suicidal behaviour, only life events during a period of two years or less prior to the suicide attempt were examined. However, in the last 15 years, studies have also addressed stressful and traumatic life events that occurred in childhood and adolescence, and their role in the aetiology of suicidal behaviour. In the following overview of studies on the relationship between stressful and traumatic life events and suicidal behaviour, only research findings that reached statistical significance will be reported.

The Relationship Between Recent Stressful and Traumatic Life Events and Non-Fatal Suicidal Behaviour

Studies focusing on recent life events (i.e., 12 months prior to index suicide attempt) comparing suicide attempters with a general population control group, found that a number of life events, such as recent loss of a family member or friend, relationship problems, psychological and physical problems, problems related to education and work, and financial problems, were more often reported by those having attempted suicide (Paykel et al., 1975; Welz, 1988). In addition, suicide attempters reported more negative life events in the year prior to the index suicide attempt compared to the general population (Cochrane & Robertson, 1975). Studies comparing suicide attempters with non-suicidal depressed patients, reported more often relationship problems, such as divorce and serious physical illness among those attempting suicide (Paykel et al., 1975). On the basis of the data from the first ten centres participating in the WHO/Euro Multicentre Study on Suicidal Behaviour, physical illness in combination with depression was found to be clearly associated with attempted suicide, with physical illness becoming more strongly related to suicidal behaviour with advancing age (De Leo et al., 1999).

Studies comparing depressed suicidal patients to non-depressed suicidal patients found that those being depressed reported more chronic problems prior to the attempt (Farmer & Creed, 1989). In a study among patients with major depression and borderline personality disorder, it appeared that recent life events might elevate the risk of suicidal behaviour, in particular among those with a low degree of social adjustment (Kelly et al., 2000). In a study by Weyrauch et al. (2001), recent stressful life events, in combination with impulsiveness, were associated with an increased risk of attempted suicide, in particular in medically serious attempts.

The Relationship Between Stressful and Traumatic Life Events in Childhood and Adolescence and Non-Fatal Suicidal Behaviour Later in Life

On the basis of a review of studies on the relationship between stressful and traumatic events during childhood and adolescence (< 18 years) and non-fatal suicidal behaviour later in life by Yang & Clum (1996), it appeared that a number of events such as physical maltreatment, sexual abuse and emotional neglect were associated with attempted suicide later in life, in particular among women. These findings were confirmed by other studies, not included in the review, such as a study among female attempted suicide patients by Van Egmond et al. (1993), and a study among women with a history of alcohol problems by Kingree et al. (1999).

Stressful and Traumatic Life Events Related to Non-Fatal Suicidal Behaviour Among Adolescents

In a number of studies, adolescents have been identified as a subgroup among suicide attempters, both with regard to their suicidal behaviour and risk factors for repetition (De Wilde et al., 1992; Burgess et al., 1998; Hawton et al., 1999). With regard to life events, Yang & Clum (1996) found that among adolescents, sexual abuse, emotional neglect, long-term separation from parent(s), divorce or separation of parents, long-term psychopathology of parent(s) and suicidal behaviour by parent(s), were associated with an increased risk of suicidal behaviour. Although in a number of studies, problems with peers were found to be associated with suicidal behaviour among adolescents as well, this was not a consistent finding in all studies (Yang & Clum, 1996). In a study by De Wilde et al. (1992), young attempted suicide patients (14–21 years) were compared to non-suicidal depressed youngsters and a control group from the general population The results indicated that suicidal youngsters were more often separated from their parent(s) in childhood, more often physically maltreated in childhood, and that they reported a higher number of stressful and traumatic events than the non-suicidal depressed youngsters.

As to life events that occurred between age 12 until 1 year prior to index-suicide attempt, those attempting suicide more often reported changes in living situation and caretaking, problems associated with divorce or separation of parents, sexual abuse and a higher total number of stressful and traumatic events. In addition, youngsters attempting suicide more often reported experiences with sexual abuse in the year prior to the index-suicide attempt, changes in living situation and caretaking, problems with school, and they also reported a higher number of events.

Stressful and Traumatic Life Events Related to Non-Fatal Suicidal Behaviour Among the Elderly

Relatively few studies have been carried out on the role of live events in elderly people with non-fatal suicidal behaviour, which may be due to the relatively low prevalence of non-fatal suicidal behaviour in this age group.

The main focus of most studies has been on the influence of physical problems on suicidal behaviour, and less attention has been paid to the influence of psychological and social factors associated with suicidal behaviour among the elderly. Although a number of studies have found a relationship between physical problems and illness and attempted suicide (Nowers, 1993; Draper, 1994), this was not a consistent finding in all studies. With regard to recent life events, in most studies a relationship was found between social isolation, loneliness, relationship problems and an increased risk for non-fatal suicidal behaviour (Draper, 1996).

From the overview of research findings, it appears that there is some consistency among studies with regard to the types of stressful and traumatic life events associated with suicidal behaviour.

On the basis of studies that have focused on the influence of recent life events, it seems that recent events, such as relationship problems, loss of a family member or friend, and physical illness might facilitate suicidal behaviour instead of causing it. Findings from most studies demonstrating that, prior to the attempt, suicide attempters report a higher number of events than controls, also supports this. This fact might represent an indication of an accumulation of events, which itself might be primarily a facilitating factor in the development of suicidal behaviour.

Although studies have not primarily investigated differences between young and old suicide attempters, in terms of types and frequency of stressful and traumatic life events, the findings of individual studies among either younger or older suicide attempters seem to differ. Life events that seem to be specific for suicide attempters in younger age groups are the presence of psychopathology of a parent, suicidal behaviour by a parent, and a high number of events prior to the attempt. Life events that might be more specific for elderly suicide attempters are loss of partner or friend, relationship problems and social isolation.

From research on the development of psychopathology in general, we know that both vulnerability and resilience are influenced by different factors (Dohrenwend, 1998), aspects that in most studies on suicide attempters have not been systematically examined in combination with stressful and traumatic life events. In the Repetition Prediction Project of the WHO/Euro Multicentre Study on Suicidal Behaviour, the psychosocial and psychiatric aspects and prospective design provided a good opportunity to look at relationships between life events and other personal characteristics of suicide attempters. In addition, the predictive value of specific types of stressful and traumatic events for repetition was examined as well.

Findings from the WHO/EURO Multicentre Study on Suicidal Behaviour

Assessment of Life Events

To assess stressful and traumatic life events, various scales and questionnaires have been developed. From a review by Miller (1996), it appeared that most of the existing instruments focus on specific life events or experiences, such as the Harvard Trauma Questionnaire (Mollica et al., 1992), the Hassles Scale (Kanner et al., 1981), and the Social Readjustment Rating Scale (Holmes & Rahe, 1967). So far, no instrument had been developed including both severe traumatic life events and less severe stressful life events, which could be used for a wider patient population. Furthermore, most of the existing instruments do not include information on the type of relationship between victim and perpetrator and neither do they specify different periods in life. Therefore, a new instrument was developed to assess stressful and traumatic life events.

As already mentioned at the beginning of this chapter, a number of methodological problems were identified in previous studies in this field. Most of these issues were taken into account in the new questionnaire: Stressful and Traumatic Events Questionnaire (STEQ, Kerkhof et al., 1989), that was used to assess stressful and traumatic life events. The psychometric properties of the STEQ were examined in a study carried out on a sample of attempted suicide patients. In order to find out whether the subscales can be used to differentiate between subgroups of attempted suicide patients, differences were examined between women versus men, and first evers versus repeaters.

Method

Sample

The Repetition Prediction part of the WHO/EURO Multicentre Study included data from 15 European research centres on suicidal behaviour. The total sample consisted of 1,703 persons aged 15 years and over, who had been referred to a general hospital following a suicide attempt. In ten centres, which were initially included in the study, the data collection was carried out from 1990 until 1992. In five centres, which were included in the study at a later stage, the data collection was carried out from 1996 until 1998 (Table 1).

In each centre, the study was carried out according to a standard protocol. A structured interview, European Parasuicide Interview Schedule (EPSIS I and II, Kerkhof et al., 1993a, 1993b), was conducted shortly after a patient was treated in a general hospital following a suicide attempt. The interview comprised a wide

Table 1 Number of patients (N) in the different centres, mean age (mean) and standard deviation (SD) and ratio females:males in each centre.

Centre	N	Age/Mean (SD)	Ratio women : men
1. Helsinki[1]	224	35.7 (12.0)[a]	1.26
2. Stockholm[1]	202	41.0 (17.0)	1.71
3. Oxford[2]	150	31.6 (13.7)	1.58
4. Leiden[1]	141	34.8 (13.1)	2.06
5. Odense[1]	139	41.6 (14.6)	1.89
6. Würzburg[1]	124	37.0 (13.9)	1.43
7. Umeå[1]	122	35.7 (14.1)	1.97
8. Gent[2]	112	32.4 (12.8)	0.86
9. Padova[1]	106	30.3 (12.6)	2.42
10. Sør-Trøndelag[1]	89	36.6 (11.7)	1.16
11. Pecs[2]	71	35.2 (13.7)	1.84
12. Bern[1]	66	38.2 (16.6)	1.27
13. Lubljana[2]	62	37.2 (14.7)	1.69
14. Emilia-Romagna[1]	56	44.7 (19.2)	2.11
15. Hall[2]	39	33.4 (11.7)	1.29
Total	1703	36.3 (14.5)	1.57

[1]Data collection in the period 1990–1992; [2]Data collection in the period 1996–1998.
[a]Because of the high numbers of DSH in Helsinki, patients were recruited on a sample basis.

range of variables including demographic variables, characteristics of index suicide attempt, previous attempts, depression, hopelessness, substance abuse, and stressful and traumatic life events in different periods of life.

Measurement of Stressful and Traumatic Life Events

The Stressful and Traumatic Events Questionnaire (STEQ), developed by Kerkhof, Bernasco, Bille-Brahe, Platt, and Schmidtke (1989) was designed as part of the European Parasuicide Interview Schedule (EPSIS) for the WHO/EURO Multicentre Study on Parasuicide. The item pool construction for this questionnaire was based on the findings of two studies on attempted suicide in Leiden, The Netherlands (Kerkhof, 1985; Van Egmond et al., 1993).

The STEQ consists of 96 items concerning stressful and traumatic life events in three different periods: (1) childhood and early adolescence (0–15 year), (2) late adolescence and adulthood (> 15 year), and (3) 12 months prior to the index-suicide attempt. In addition, different categories of persons in relationship to whom events had occurred, such as parents, brothers and sisters, partners, children, and other significant persons were distinguished. A number of items, including the complete categories of items regarding partner and own children are not relevant in childhood and early adolescence and therefore, are not applicable for this period. The answers to the questions with regard to whether an event has occurred are structured (yes: score = 1/no: score = 0). The total number of items included in the questionnaire is 96 and, at the end, respondents are asked to point the three most important events in the list. The questionnaire includes items concerning severe traumatic events, e.g., physical maltreatment or sexual abuse, as well as generally regarded less severe stressful events or negative experiences, e.g., problems with education or difficulties in making contact with others.

Measurement of Other Variables

Information on standard demographic information and suicide attempts was obtained as part of the structured interview. For the assessment of psychological characteristics, the following self-report measures were used. Severity of depression at the time of the interview was assessed by the Beck Depression Inventory (BDI, Beck et al., 1961). The Hopelessness Scale (HS, Beck et al., 1974) assessed pessimistic beliefs and attitudes towards the future. Self-esteem was assessed by the Self-Esteem scale (SE, Rosenberg (1965).

Data Analyses

In order to identify subscales among the items of the STEQ, factor analyses were performed for the items in each separate period (childhood and early adolescence, late adolescence and adulthood, 12 months prior to the index-suicide attempt). Reliability analysis was used to examine the internal consistency of the subscales obtained by factor analysis. Intersubscale correlations were calculated to determine whether subscales were interrelated. Differences between first evers and repeaters on the various subscales were investigated with t tests (see also Arensman et al., submitted). The predictive value of risk factors of repeated suicide attempts was analysed using multiple regression analysis.

Results

Sociodemographic Characteristics

The majority (62.6%) of the total sample ($n = 1,703$) comprised women. The ratio women/men was 1.57, with a relatively high proportion of men in Gent, Sør-Trøndelag, Helsinki, Bern and Emilia-Romagna. A relatively high proportion of women was found in Padova, Leiden and Umeå (Table 1).

The mean age of the total sample was 36.3 years, with a range from 15–87 years. The mean age of the samples in the different centres varied, with a significantly younger sample in Padova (mean: 30.3, $p < .01$) and Oxford (mean: 31.6, $p < .05$), and a significantly older sample in Emilia-Romagna (mean: 44.7, $p < .01$) and Stockholm (mean: 41.0, $p < .05$) (Table 1). On the basis of the total sample, no significant difference was found between the mean age for men and women. Most of the patients (91.5%) were native, which means that they were born in the same country where the centre was located.

Response Prediction Project

The prediction part concerns only the sample of the centre in Leiden, which consisted of 89 attempted suicide patients, who were part of a sample ($n = 141$) treated at the Leiden University Medical Centre (LUMC), following a suicide attempt in the period October 1990 until December 1991. The first interview was conducted within one month after treatment at the LUMC. After an average follow-up period of 13 months, those patients who had consented to being seen again were interviewed a second time ($n = 106$; 75%). Of those who participated in the second interview (1st follow-up), 89 patients (84%) consented to be contacted again for a third interview (2nd follow-up), which were conducted from September 1998 until May 1999. The mean follow-up period between 1st follow-up interview and 2nd follow-up interview was 6.6 years, the mean follow-up period between 1st interview and 2nd follow-up interview was 7.7. years. A total of 41 patients agreed to complete a 2nd follow-up interview. This is 30% of the initial sample ($n = 141$). Considering the number of people approached for the 2nd follow-up interview ($n = 89$), the percentage of completed interviews is 47%. A number of 33 persons were traced, but did not participate for various reasons (see also Arensman, et al., submitted). At the final follow-up, the sample consisted of 26 women (mean age: 36.4) and 15 men (mean age: 38.9).

Factor Structure of the STEQ

Table 2 presents an overview of the subscales derived from the original items through factor analyses (see also Arensman et al., submitted). For the period child-

Table 2 Subscales of the STEQ obtained through factor analysis for the three different periods.

STEQ subscales		
Childhood and early adolescence (< 15 years of age)	**Late adolescence and adulthood (> 15 years of age)**	**Last year prior to suicide attempt**
1. Maltreatment (mental/physical) by parent(s), and relationship problems parents	1. Maltreatment (mental/physical), incl. sexual abuse by partner, and addiction of partner	1. Sexual abuse by partner
2. Separation from parent(s) for long periods	2. Sexual abuse by parent(s), brother/sister	2. Maltreatment (mental/physical) by partner, incl. relationship problems with partner
3. Sexual abuse by parent(s)	3. Maltreatment (mental/physical) by parent(s)	3. Mental and physical maltreatment by parent(s)
4. Absence of social network	4. Maltreatment (mental) by other persons, and psychosocial problems	4. Psychological/psychiatric problems of brother/sister
5. Maltreatment (mental/physical) by other important persons, and interpersonal problems with significant others	5. Psychological/psychiatric problems children	5. Mental maltreatment by other persons, and interpersonal problems with significant others
6. Physical illness of patient	6. Psychological/psychiatric problems brother/sister	6. Psychological/psychiatric problems of partner
7. Psychiatric disorders parent(s)	7. Physical illness parent(s)/brother/sister, death of parent(s)	7. Psychosocial problems
8. Victim of crime, physical maltreatment, incl. sexual abuse by brother/sister	8. Victim of crime, and sudden stressful/traumatic event	8. Psychological/psychiatric problems of children
9. Psychiatric problems brother/sister		9. Physical illness of patient
10. Death of parent(s)		10. Psychological/psychiatric problems parent(s)
11. Parent(s) died		

hood and early adolescence, ten subscales were obtained, with most subscales representing life events in relation to parents, such as separation from parent(s) for long periods or sexual abuse by parent(s).

For the period late adolescence and adulthood, eight subscales were obtained, representing life events in relation to various persons, such as parents, partners, brothers and sisters, children, and other people. For the period of 12 months prior to the index-suicide attempt, eleven subscales were obtained, also representing events related to various persons. With regard to internal consistency, moderate to high Cronbach's a coefficients were found for most of the subscales. A number of subscales had low internal consistency, such as the subscale "parent(s) died" (in childhood and early adolescence and in the year prior to suicide attempt), physical illness and psychological or psychiatric problems of parent(s). These life events did not have high loadings on any other subscale, which might be an indication that these events should be considered as separate events.

Overall, the inter-subscale correlations were low, reflecting low common variance among the different subscales, indicating that the different subscales do indeed represent specific stressful and traumatic life events. However, positive correlations were found between similar subscales across the three different periods.

Differences Between Men and Women

Looking at the three periods together, on 14 out of 29 subscales women scored significantly higher than men. Only on the subscale: "Victim of crime, and sudden stressful/traumatic event," did male suicide attempters have a significantly higher score. Examples of subscales on which women had a higher score were "maltreatment (mental or physical) by parent(s), and relationship problems of parents," "sexual abuse by parent(s)," and "psychological/psychiatric problems of children." These findings show that female suicide attempters report more sexual abuse and physical maltreatment throughout life, with parents and brothers/sisters being the main perpetrators early in life and partners being the main perpetrators later in life.

Differences Between First Evers and Repeaters

Suicide attempters who had not made any previous attempts prior to the index suicide attempt (first evers), and those who had made one or more attempts prior to the index attempt (repeaters), were compared as to types and number of life events. The results showed that on 20 out of the 29 subscales repeaters scored significantly higher than first evers.

Except for the subscales "physical illness" and "parent(s) died," during childhood and early adolescence, repeaters had significantly higher scores on eight out of ten subscales. As to the period late adolescence and adulthood, repeaters scored significantly higher than first evers on five out of eight subscales, which were similar to the subscales in the first period. In this period repeaters also reported more often sexual abuse, physical and mental maltreatment by partners. In the last period, i.e., during the 12 months prior to the index suicide attempt, repeaters had significantly higher scores than first evers on seven out of 11 subscales. Although less significant differences were found between the two groups here, sexual abuse and physical maltreatment by partner, and physical and mental maltreatment by parents and other persons were reported more often by repeaters. In addition, repeaters scored significantly higher on subscales representing psychological or psychiatric problems with partners and children, and psychosocial problems experienced by the patient self.

Correlation Between the Number of Events and Psychological Characteristics of Suicide Attempters

In order to investigate whether there is a relationship between the mean total number of events in the different periods and the psychological characteristics of the persons involved, correlations were calculated between the number of events and symptoms of depression, feelings of hopelessness and self-esteem. Significant correlations were found between the number of stressful and traumatic life events in each period and symptoms of depression, actual feelings of hopelessness, and negative self-esteem. However, the strongest correlations were found between the number of events in the year prior to the index suicide attempt, and the psychological characteristics at the time of the index attempt, with relatively high correlations for depression and negative self-esteem.

Predictive Value of Stressful and Traumatic Life Events

Prospective Repetition

During the short-term follow-up period of 13 months, 42% of the attempted suicide patients in the Leiden centre ($N = 106$), had made at least one repeated attempt. Of those who completed the last follow-up interview ($n = 41$), 6.6 years after the first follow-up interview, nearly half (48.8%) had made one or more than one repeated attempt. A significantly higher percentage (69%) of those who had attempted suicide prior to the index suicide attempt than of the first evers (13%), repeated the attempt during the follow-up period (13%) ($p < .001$). Twelve percent of the sample ($n = 41$) engaged in one repeated attempt, 13% repeated twice, 9% repeated 3 to 5 times, and 15% repeated 5 or more times. Comparing first evers and repeaters on the number of repeated attempts, the number among the repeaters was significantly higher (mean: 4.92, *SD*: 8.87) than among first evers (mean: 0.20, *SD*: 0.56; $p < .02$).

A fairly accurate prediction could be made of the number of repeated suicide attempts in both the short-term and long-term. Of the thirteen variables included in the multiple regression analysis, six predictors were found to be associated with the number of repeated attempts within one year following the index suicide attempt, including two subscales of stressful and traumatic life events. Most of the variance was explained by the number of previous suicide attempts, followed by the STEQ subscale "physical, mental maltreatment, incl. sexual abuse by partner, and addiction of partner (> 15 years)" and the STEQ subscale "Long-term separation from parent(s) (< 15 years)." The last three predictors were subsequently hopelessness, method of suicide attempt/self-injury, and the motive "wishing to die."

With regard to prediction of long-term repetition, i.e., 7.7. years after the index suicide attempt, four out of nine variables were selected. Among the predictors one

STEQ subscale was included: "parent(s) died during childhood or early adolescence (< 15 year)." Two other predictors: the number of previous attempts and attempted suicide method (which emerged as long-term predictors of repetition), were also identified as short-term predictors. In addition, the total score of depressive symptoms (measured by the BDI) was also selected as predictor of repeated attempts.

Discussion and Conclusions

Although there appears to be some consistency with regard to the types of stressful and traumatic life events related to both non-fatal and fatal suicidal behaviour, due to methodological differences, such as study design, measurement instrument, and inclusion of other variables that might be related to either life stress and/or psychological and psychiatric characteristics of suicide attempters, it is often not possible to make a strict comparison between the available studies.

The Stressful and Traumatic Events Questionnaire (STEQ) was developed for the purpose of investigating stressful and traumatic events among attempted suicide patients, as part of the WHO/Euro Multicentre Study on Suicidal Behaviour. The factor structure of the STEQ identified in this study supports the idea that certain events are inter-related or that the occurrence of one event increases the risk of experiencing other events, such as sexual abuse, physical maltreatment and mental maltreatment. On the other hand, stressful and traumatic events, represented in specific subscales, can be considered independently, which was confirmed by the low inter-subscale correlations (see also Arensman et al., submitted).

One important disadvantage of the STEQ is that it is a relatively time-consuming instrument. Depending upon the number of categories (e.g., life events in relation to brothers/sisters, partner(s), and children) that are applicable, the average time involved in conducting the STEQ is thirty minutes. However, the advantages might undo the disadvantages, considering the fact that both the content validity and predictive validity of the subscales seem to be sufficient. A high score on most of the subscales is indicative of a pattern of repeated attempts, with two subscales having predictive value for repeated attempts in the short-term and one subscale having predictive value for long-term repetition.

To a great extent, the subscales of the STEQ represent the stressful and traumatic events reported in most previous studies. However, a number of subscales of the STEQ represent events that were not previously reported in relation to suicidal behaviour, such as being a victim of a crime, and psychological or psychiatric problems of brother or sister, partner, or children.

With regard to the identified STEQ subscales representing specific traumatic events, such as sexual abuse and physical maltreatment, the findings are in agreement with the subscales identified in two studies by Bernstein et al. (1994) and Bernstein et al. (1997) using the Childhood Trauma Questionnaire, a retrospective measure for child abuse and neglect. With regard to less severe stressful events, no similarities were found between the STEQ subscales and other instruments. This might be explained by the fact that apparently these events are often labelled as daily hassles, which vary considerably among other instruments developed so far.

Our findings clearly show that most of the STEQ subscales can be used to differentiate between relevant (sub)groups of patients, such as female versus male suicide attempters, and first evers versus repeaters. Although the findings are based on a representative sample of attempted suicide patients, a comparison with a control group was not included, which is important in order to obtain normative data. However, in Leiden, where 141 suicide attempters were included, a comparison was made with the general population, and those who had attempted suicide reported significantly more stressful and traumatic events throughout life (Arensman, 1997).

Since the study was carried out among attempted suicide patients, which can be considered a specific group of patients, an important question is whether the questionnaire can be used for other groups of patients. Taking into account that the population of suicide attempters is heterogeneous in terms of psychopathology, comorbidity and problem history, and the clear association between the number of stressful and traumatic events in the three different periods and depressive symptoms, the STEQ might be useful for both research- and assessment purposes among other patient groups as well.

On the basis of previous studies and the Multicentre Study, it appears that among suicide attempters those who are repeaters report a higher number of events in all periods than those who are first evers. This might be an indication that among repeaters, recurrence of (similar) stressful and traumatic events might be associated with increased vulnerability and less resilience, which itself might elevate the risk of repeated suicidal behaviour, and a pattern of chronic repetition in the long-term. However, information on the types and frequency of stressful and traumatic life events only is not sufficient to answer the question why two persons experiencing the same event may react differently, and which processes mediate between being confronted with a stressful or traumatic event and the occurrence of suicidal behaviour.

According to Dohrenwend (1998) cognitive and emotional processes including appraisal, coping and emotional and behavioural responses are considered important mediating factors between the occurrence of a recent stressful or traumatic life event, and the subsequent changes in functioning and health. In addition, he also assumes a relationship between the occurrence of recent negative life events itself and personal predispositions, biological background and the wider environment.

With regard to the role of psychobiological factors in the aetiology of suicidal behaviour, Van Heeringen (2001) proposed a diathesis-stress model in which genetically determined biological factors interact with early traumatic events, causing a disturbance of the serotonergic system. In addition, sustained stress, leading to a sustained overproduction of cortisol can provoke or aggravate the serotonergic disturbances. A dysregulation of the serotonergic system appears to be associated with dysregulation of anxiety and aggression, which might increase the risk of suicidal behaviour. Since the Multicentre Study was developed at the end of the eighties and started in the beginning of the nineties, with the main objective being to identify psychosocial risk factors for repeated suicidal behaviour, no specific hypotheses were included in order to be able to test these models.

Therefore, future research into the role of life events in the development of suicidal behaviour, should focus more on psychobiological factors, appraisal processes and coping, and subsequent behavioural and emotional responses among attempted suicide patients, in order to identify irrational or inadequate appraisal and coping strategies that maintain the negative circle of the experience of stress and repeated suicide attempts and associated psychopathology. Especially, at the current stage of scientific research in this field, this would be a welcome challenge, since in many different disciplines high quality studies have been conducted, often exclusively focusing on one of the aspects that contribute to the development of suicidal behaviour.

Acknowledgments

We would like to thank Alfred Aardema for his valuable support in the process of data analysis.

References

Appleby, L., Cooper, J., Amos, T., & Faragher, B. (1999). Psychological autopsy study of suicides by people aged under 35. *British Journal of Psychiatry, 175,* 168–174.

Arensman, E., & Kerkhof, A. J. F. M. (1996). Classification of attempted suicide; A review of empirical studies, 1963–1993. *Suicide and Life-Threatening Behavior, 26,* 46–67.

Arensman, E. (1997) *Attempted suicide: Epidemiology and classification.* Dissertation. Leiden: Leiden University.

Arensman, E., Kerkhof, A. J. F. M., Hjelmeland, H., Aardema, A., Bille-Brahe, U., Crepet, P., De Leo, D., Fekete, S., Grad, O., Haring, C., Hawton, K., Van Heeringen, C., Lönnqvist, J. L., Michel, K., Salander-Renberg, E., Schmidtke, A., & Wasserman, D. (submitted). *Psychometric properties of a questionnaire for the assessment of stressful and traumatic life events in a sample of attempted suicide patients.*

Arensman, E., Kerkhof, A. J. F. M., Aardema, A., Verkes, R. J., & Hengeveld, M. W. (submitted). *Short-term and long-term risk factors for repeated deliberate self-harm: A seven year follow-up study.*

Beck, A. T., Ward, C. H., Mendelson, M., Mock. J, & Erbauch J. (1961). An inventory for measuring depression. *Archives of General Psychiatry, 4,* 561–571.

Beck, A. T., Weissman, A., Lester, D., & Trexler, L. (1974). The measurement of pessimism: The Hopelessness Scale. *Journal of Consulting and Clinical Psychology, 6,* 861–865.

Bernstein, D. P., Fink, L., Handelsman, L., & Foote, J. (1994). Initial reliability and validity of a new retrospective measure of child abuse and neglect. *American Journal of Psychiatry, 151,* 1132–1136.

Bernstein, D. P., Ahluvelia, T., Pogge, D., & Handelsman, L. (1997). Validity of the Childhood

Trauma Questionnaire in an adolescent psychiatric population. *Journal of the American Academy of Child and Adolescent Psychiatry, 36,* 340–348.

Bille-Brahe, U., Kerkhof, A. J. F. M., De Leo, D., Schmidtke, A., Crepet, P., Lönnqvist, J., Michel, K., Salander-Renberg, E., Stiles, T. C., Wasserman, D., Aagaard, B., Egebo, H., & Jensen, B. (1997). A repetition-prediction study of European parasuicide populations: A summary of the first report from Part II of the WHO/EURO Multicentre Study on Parasuicide in co-operation with the EC Concerted Action on attempted suicide. *Acta Psychiatrica Scandinavica, 95,* 81–86.

Burgess, S., Hawton, K., & Loveday, G. (1998). Adolescents who take overdoses: Outcome in terms of changes in psychopathology and the adolescents' attitudes to care and to their overdose. *Journal of Adolescence, 21,* 209–218.

Cochrane, R., & Robertson, A. (1975). Stress in the lives of parasuicides. *Social Psychiatry, 10,* 161–171.

De Leo, D., Scocco, P., Marietta, P., Schmidtke, A., Bille-Brahe, U., Kerkhof, A. J. F. M., Lönnqvist, J., Crepet, P., Salander-renberg, E., Wasserman, D., Michel, K., & Bjerke, T. (1999). Physical illness and parasuicide: Evidence from the European Parasuicide Study Interview Schedule (EPSIS/WHO-EURO). *International Journal of Psychiatry in Medicine, 29,* 149–163.

De Wilde, E. J., Kienhorst, C. W. M., Diekstra, R. F. W., & Wolters, W. H. G. (1992). The relationship of life events in childhood and adolescence with adolescent suicidal behavior. *American Journal of Psychiatry, 1,* 45–51.

Dohrenwend, B. P. (1998). *Adversity, stress, and psychopathology.* Oxford: Oxford University Press.

Draijer, N., & Boon, S. (1993). Trauma, dissociation and dissociative disorders. In S. Boon & N. Draijer, *Multiple personality disorder in the Netherlands: A study on reliability and validity of the diagnosis.* Amsterdam: Swets & Zeitlinger.

Draper, B. (1994). Suicidal behaviour in the elderly. *International Journal of Geriatric Psychiatry, 9,* 655–661.

Draper, B. (1996). Attempted suicide in old age. *International Journal of Geriatric Psychiatry, 11,* 577–587.

Farmer, R., & Creed, F. (1989). Life events and hostility in self-poisoning. *British Journal of Psychiatry, 154,* 390–395.

Hawton, K., Kingsbury, S., Steinhardt, K., James, A., & Fagg, J. (1999). Repetition of deliberate self-harm by adolescents: the role of psychological factors. *Journal of Adolescence, 22,* 369–378.

Heikkinen, M., Aro, H. M., & Lönnqvist, J. K. (1993). Life events and social support in suicide. *Suicide and Life-Threatening Behavior, 23,* 343–358.

Heikkinen, M., & Lönnqvist, J. K. (1996). Recent life events in elderly: A nationwide study in Finland. In J. L. Pearson & Y. Conwell (Eds.), *Suicide and aging: International perspectives.* New York: Springer Publishing.

Herman, J. (1992). *Trauma and recovery.* New York: Basic Books.

Holmes, T. H., & Rahe, R. H. (1967). The Social Readjustment Scale. *Journal of Psychosomatic Research, 11,* 213–218.

Houston, K., Hawton, K., & Shepperd, R. (2001). Suicide in young people aged 15–24: A psychological autopsy study. *Journal of Affective Disorders, 63,* 159–170.

Kelly, T. M., Soloff, P. H., Lynch, K. G., Haas, G. L., & Mann, J. J. (2000). Recent life events, social adjustment, and suicide attempts in patients with major depression and borderline personality disorder. *Journal of Personality Disorders, 14,* 316–326.

Kerkhof, A. J. F. M. (1985). *Suicide en de geestelijke gezondheidszorg* [Suicide and mental health care]. Dissertation. Lisse: Swets & Zeitlinger.

Kerkhof, A. J. F. M., Bernasco, W., Bille-Brahe, U., Platt, S., & Schmidtke, A. (1993a). WHO/EURO Multicentre on Parasuicide European Interview Schedule (EPSIS I), version 5.1. In U. Bille-Brahe et al. (Eds.), *Facts and figures*. Copenhagen, WHO/EUR/ICP/PSF.018.

Kerkhof, A. J. F. M., Egmond, M. van, Bille-Brahe, U., Platt, S., & Schmidtke, A. (1993b). European Parasuicide Interview Schedule (EPSIS II) version 3.2. In U. Bille-Brahe et al. (Eds.), *Facts and figures*. Copenhagen, WHO/EUR/ICP/PSF.018.

Kessler, R. C. (1997). The effects of stressful life events on depression. *Annual Review in Psychology, 48,* 191–214.

Kingree, J. B., Thompson, M. P., & Kaslow, N. J. (1999). Risk factors for suicide attempts among low-income women with a history of alcohol problems. *Addictive Behaviors, 24,* 583–587.

Miller, Th. (1997). *Clinical disorders and stressful life events.* Madison, CT: International Universities Press.

Mollica, R. F., Caspi-Yavin, Y., Bollini, P., Truong, T. et al. (1992). The Harvard Trauma Questionnaire: Validating a cross-cultural instrument for measuring torture, trauma, and posttraumatic stress disorder in Indochinese refugees. *Journal of Nervous and Mental Disease, 180,* 111–116.

Nowers, M. (1993). Deliberate self-harm in the elderly: A survey of one London borough. *International Journal of Geriatric Psychiatry, 8,* 609–614.

Paykel, E. S., Prusoff, B. A., & Myers, J. K. (1975). Suicide attempts and recent life events: A controlled comparison. *Archives of General Psychiatry, 32,* 327–333.

Rosenberg, M. (1965). *Society and the adolescent self-image.* Princeton: Princeton University Press.

Sandin, B., Chorot, P., Santed, M. A., Vliente, R. M., & Joiner, T. E. (1998). Negative life events and adolescent suicidal behavior; a critical analysis from the stress process perspective. *Journal of Adolescence, 21,* 415–426.

Saxe, G. N., Van der Kolk, B. A., Berkowitz, M. D., Chinman, G., Hall., K., Lieberg, G., & Schwatrz, J. (1993). Dissociative disorders in psychiatric inpatients. *American Journal of Psychiatry, 150,* 1037–1042.

Terr, L. (1994). *Unchained memories.* New York: Basic Books.

Van Egmond, M., Garnefski, N., Jonker, D., & Kerkhof, A. J. F. M. (1993). The relationship between sexual abuse and female suicidal behavior. *Crisis, 14,* 19–29.

Van der Kolk, B. A., & Fisler, R. E. (1994). Childhood abuse and neglect and loss of self-regulation. *Bulletin of the Menninger Clinic, 58,* 145–168.

Van der Kolk, B. A., Pelcovitz, D., Roth, S., Mandel, F. S., McFarlane, A., & Herman, J. L. (1996). Dissociation, somatization and affect dysregulation: The complexity of adaptation to trauma. *American Journal of Psychiatry, 153,* 83–93.

Van Heeringen, C. (2001). *Understanding suicidal behaviour. The suicidal process: approach to research, treatment and prevention.* Chichester, UK: Wiley.

Welz, R. (1988). Life events, current social stressors, and risk of attempted suicide. In H. J. Moller, A. Schmidtke, & R. Welz (Eds.), *Current issues of suicidology.* Berlin-Heidelberg: Springer-Verlag.

Weyrauch, K. F., Roy, P., Katon, W., & Wilson, L. (2001). Stressful life events and impulsiveness in failed suicide. *Suicide and Life-Threatening Behavior, 31,* 311–319.

Yang, B., & Clum, G. A. (1996). Effects of early negative life experiences on cognitive functioning and risk for suicide: A review. *Clinical Psychology Review, 16,* 177–195.

Chapter 9
Repetition of Attempted Suicide: Frequent, but Hard to Predict

Ad Kerkhof[1] and Ella Arensman[2]

[1]*Department of Clinical Psychology, Vrije Universiteit, Amsterdam, The Netherlands,*
[2]*National Suicide Research Foundation, Cork, Ireland*

Introduction

Repetition is one of the core characteristics of suicidal behaviour. Among those who commit suicide, up to 44% attempted previously, this being revealed by methods that include psychological autopsy studies (Ovenstone & Kreitman, 1974; Clark & Horton-Deutsch, 1992; Maris, 1992; Isometsä & Lönnqvist, 1998). Women more frequently (39%) attempted suicide than men (19%) in the last year before committing suicide (Isometsä & Lönnqvist, 1998). On the basis of several studies, it appears that among suicide attempters "repeaters" are probably commoner than "first-evers." Between 30% and 60% of suicide attempters had made suicide attempts previous to the index attempt, and between 15% and 25% had done so within the last year (Bagley & Greer, 1971; Buglass & Horton, 1974a,b; Morgan et al., 1975, 1976; Bancroft & Marsack, 1977; Kreitman, 1977; Bille-Brahe & Jessen, 1994; Kreitman & Casey, 1988; Hawton et al. 1995; Platt et al., 1988, 1992; Sakinofski, 2000).

Prospectively, suicide attempters have a high risk of committing suicide as between 10% and 15% may eventually die because of suicide (Maris, 1992). Mortality by suicide is even higher among suicide attempters who have made previous attempts (Hawton & Catalan, 1981; Farmer, 1986; Cullberg et al., 1988; Hawton & Fagg, 1988; Rygnestad, 1988; Sellar et al., 1990; Sakinowski, 2000). The risk of repeated suicidal behaviour is highest during the first year after a suicide attempt, and especially within the first three to six months (Bancroft & Marsack, 1977; Goldacre & Hawton, 1985; Wang et al., 1985; Hawton & Fagg, 1988, 1995). In the WHO/EURO Multi-Centre Study on Suicidal Behaviour it was found that at least

56% of the registered attempters had previously attempted, 32% at least twice, and that 29% made another attempt in a one-year follow-up (Arensman et al., 2003).

All this points to the obvious need to know more in order to prevent repetition. Knowledge of antecedents or risk factors may help early identification of persons at risk and also better treatment. Socio-demographic risk factors associated with repetition are the age group of 25–49 years, being divorced, unemployed, and from a lower social class (Arensman & Kerkhof, 1996). Psychiatric and psychosocial characteristics of repeaters are substance abuse, depression, hopelessness, powerlessness, personality disorders, unstable living conditions or living alone, criminal records, previous psychiatric treatment, and a history of stressful traumatic life events, including broken homes, and family violence. Prospectively, a history of previous attempts predicts future non-fatal suicide attempts (Buglass & Horton, 1974; Van Egmond, 1989; Sakinofsky & Roberts, 1990; Kreitman & Foster, 1991; Owens et al, 1994; Arensman & Kerkhof, 1996; Hjelmeland, 1996; Sakinofski, 2000).

However, the predictability of repetition is far from satisfactory. In clinical practice as well as in research projects, the specificity and sensitivity of clinical judgment as well as the actuarial prediction of sets of predictor variables is not optimal. The most important explanation for this lack of predictive power is the heterogeneity of the attempted suicide population; the population consisting of persons with very different characteristics, backgrounds, life problems, motives, and expectations regarding the suicide attempt. The meaning of suicidal behaviour may vary from attention-seeking behaviour or stress management to a nearly successful attempt to die. Repetition of suicidal behaviour may serve quite a different function in borderline patients than in those recently bereft of a partner.

Retrospective studies of repetition are needed in search for risk factors, and so are prospective investigations. Retrospectively it is possible to divide the population in first-evers and repeaters, and to subdivide repeaters in major (grand) and minor repeaters, the cut off sometimes being put at five previous attempts, accounting for 16% of men and 12% of women (Kreitman & Casey, 1988, Stocks & Scott, 1991). Major repeaters are thought to be more often male, of low social class, unmarried, sociopathic personality disordered, and alcoholic.

There are quite a few methodological shortcomings in previous studies. Many studies on attempted suicide populations cannot easily be compared because of differences in definitions (attempted suicide, parasuicide, deliberate self-harm, self-injury, self-poisoning, self-destructive behaviour, etc.), differences in variables being studied, differences in methodologies, catchment areas or settings, differences in representativeness of the samples, the time periods covered, etc. Only few studies have employed personal interviews with a longitudinal design. Attempted suicide populations may differ between countries, or even within countries between areas or cities. A problem often confronted when studying attempted suicide populations is the mobility of the group. It is known that tracing suicide attempters after being treated in hospital is extremely time consuming. Attrition is likely to occur, and selective attrition is probable. The number of repeaters in follow-up studies therefore is often quite small. As a consequence many small studies resulted with limited comparability. For the multi-variate analysis of repetition, a much larger sample would be required. This chapter sets out to contribute to the study of repetition by presenting summarised findings from the WHO/EURO Multi-Centre Study on Suicidal Behaviour, a research project intended to overcome the above-mentioned methodological problems. This chapter concentrates on repetition, using both prospective and retrospective material, from both the Monitoring Study (1989–1992), including 15 centres, and the Repetition-Prediction Project (1991–1997), including 16 participating centres.

The interviews followed structured interview schedules (EPSIS I and EPSIS II) based on research findings and hypotheses about predictors of suicidal behaviour and repetition, containing observer-rated as well as self-rated instruments For the analysis in this chapter, the following variables were selected from the EPSIS I interview: method employed (hard versus soft), socio-demographic information (age, gender, marital status, education, employment status), depression, hopelessness, trait and state anger, suicidal intent, self-esteem, life events, self-reported reasons and motives for the attempted suicide, and treatment history. From the EPSIS II interview information regarding repetition in the follow-up period was collected.

During the study period 1989–1992 a total number of 16,193 persons were treated for 20,850 episodes in the areas under study because of attempted suicide. During the study period 1991–1997, in total 1866 patients were interviewed in the first wave in the repetition-prediction part (with EPSIS I), and 731 were interviewed in the second wave one year later (with EPSIS II). The representativeness of the sample of interviewed persons has been evaluated compared with data from the Monitoring Study. Details of this comparison can be found in Bille-Brahe (1996b). The conclusions are that, compared to the Monitoring Study, somewhat more women took part in the Repetition Study, the age distribution was similar, except at two centres, and there was a tendency towards a somewhat higher proportion of self-poisoners in the EPSIS sample than in the Monitoring Study, while there were fewer that had used one method only. There were no differences between the EPSIS sample and Monitoring groups regarding the proportion having previously attempted suicide. The overrepresentation of women might indicate that female suicide attempters are more inclined to present at a general hospital after the attempted suicide.

The findings will be presented in five sections: the prevalence of repetition; differences between first-evers and repeaters regarding the selected variables; differences between repeaters and non-repeaters in the follow up; prediction of repeated suicidal behaviour, and a tentative analysis of types of repetition.

Findings on Repetition

Based on the data from the Monitoring Study, 44% of all suicide attempters had previously attempted suicide, ranging from 29% in Szeged, Hungary, to 55% in

Bern, Switzerland. The majority of those who made previous attempts had made their last attempt within the 12 months prior to the index attempt (see Arensman et al., 2003).

Based on data from the Repetition-Prediction Study (EPSIS I) 56% of the respondents had made suicide attempts previously at least once (range from 38% in Padova, Italy, to 66% in Leiden, The Netherlands and in Oxford, UK), while 32% had attempted suicide twice or more before the index attempt (range from 17% in Würzburg, Germany, to 45% in Oxford, UK).

As expected, the number of persons reporting previous suicide attempts in personal interviews is equal to, or higher than, the number of persons who report previous attempts while being medically treated in hospital. This holds for all centres except Bern and Helsinki.

In the ongoing Monitoring Study, repeaters were prospectively identified at re-admission. Not all repeated episodes could be monitored in this way because they may not have been treated in hospital or may have been treated outside the catchment area. Therefore, the findings should be considered as a conservative estimation. Based on the pooled data it was found that within 6 months at least 10% of all suicide attempters had repeated (once or more), within 12 months at least 14% had repeated, within 24 months at least 19% had re-attempted, and within 36 months this was 23% (Arensman et al., 2003).

In the Repetition-Prediction Study it appeared from the follow up interviews (EPSIS II) that 29% had repeated at least once, and 17% at least twice, within the 12 month period after the index attempt. This is about twice as much as was observed in the Monitoring Study. The difference is partly due to the fact that the Monitoring System did not reach full coverage of all single attempted suicide episodes, and thus the chances of monitoring pairs of index attempt and repeated attempt are lowered, and partly to the fact that respondents in the follow-up interviews reported repeated attempts that did not lead to hospital admission, or to a hospital admission outside the catchment area. The monitoring through hospital records therefore reveals less repetition than a repetition prediction study using personal interviews at several points in time. As expected, centres with high rates of retrospective repetition (Odense, Leiden, Oxford, Helsinki, Umeå) also had high rates of prospective repetition.

Differences Between First-Evers and Repeaters at the Index Attempt

Based on 1,866 interviews (EPSIS I) from 16 centres, the following significant differences were observed between first-evers (828) and repeaters (1,038) at the time of the index attempt: on socio-demographic variables repeaters were somewhat older than first-evers, were more often divorced or separated, and less economically active. No differences were found for gender (59% women among first-evers versus 61% among repeaters), and level of education. Regarding psychological and psychiatric variables, it appeared that repeaters had been treated more frequently in psychiatric hospitals (64%) than first-evers (28%), were more depressed (BDI = 26.1 versus 20.5), and somewhat more hostile (STAS = 36.8 versus 34.0). No differences were observed on total scores on the scales for Hopelessness, Suicide Intent, Self-Esteem, Motives, or regarding the method chosen for the suicide attempt.

The repeaters reported significantly more often than the non-repeaters problematic events and experiences during childhood. These problems related to their parents (mental and physical maltreatment, no affection, hatred feelings, sexual abuse by parents, parents were absent, divorced or separated, parents' relationship problems, admission to a psychiatric hospital, or attempted suicide), to brothers and sisters (admission to psychiatric hospital, attempted suicide, physical and sexual abuse by brothers), to significant others (physical and mental maltreatment, long lasting bad relationships), and they had more often suffered emotional problems (loneliness, anxiety, problems making friends), and witnessed or had been victim of a serious crime. No differences were observed regarding the death of parents or physical illnesses of the respondent him or herself during childhood.

Regarding later periods in life, repeaters significantly more often than first-evers reported events and experiences related to their partners (physical and sexual abuse, sexual and relationship problems, partner addicted or sentenced to jail), to parents (mental and physical maltreatment and abuse, no affection and hatred feelings), to brothers and sisters (addiction, attempted suicide, admission to psychiatric hospital), and they had more often suffered emotional problems (anxiety, sexual problems, loneliness, failures to achieve important life goals), and witnessed or had been victim of a serious crime or an emergency situation. No differences were observed regarding the death of parents or events related to children.

Regarding events in the year preceding the index attempt, repeaters significantly more often than first-evers reported negative life events and experiences related to their partner (physical and mental maltreatment, sexual and relationship problems), to their children (children in contact with the police, addicted or admitted to a psychiatric hospital), to brothers and sisters (attempted suicide, admitted to psychiatric hospital), to their parents (physical and mental maltreatment), and they more often had suffered from emotional problems (anxiety, eating problems, loneliness, sexual problems). No differences were observed regarding death of parents in the last year preceding the attempt, or physical illnesses. (More details on the relationship between life events and suicidal behaviour can be found in the chapter by Arensman and Kerkhof elsewhere in this volume.)

Retrospective Analysis of Repetition

All selected variables were entered as predictor variables in a stepwise multiple linear regression analysis with retrospective repetition as dependent variable (information on previous attempted suicides from EPSIS I). This was done in order to find the best possible subset of predictors to discriminate repeaters from first-evers, for men and for women, respectively. The cumulative R squares or variances explained are summarized (missing values deleted listwise). It appeared that for women the major predictor of retrospective repetition is the number of times they were treated in a psychiatric hospital (R^2 = .201), followed by psychosocial problems during the previous year (life events subscale, R^2 cum. = .247), low Self-Esteem (.259), important negative life events later in life (.271), parent admitted to psychiatric hospital or attempted suicide in childhood respondent (.281), other problems of parents in childhood respondent (.290), problems at school, in making friends during childhood (.297), sexual abuse by parents during childhood (.301).

For men, too, the most powerful (retrospective) predictor of previous suicide attempts is the frequency of treatments in psychiatric hospitals (.199), followed by addiction, having been victim, witness or convicted for crime (.236), low Self-Esteem (.252), hard method in previous attempted suicide (.264), and being 30–39 years old (.285).

The greater the number of previous inpatient psychiatric treatments, the higher the chance that a person is a repeater at the time of the index attempt. This variable clearly captures best many other differences between repeaters and first-evers. For clinicians, this will not come as a surprise. Additional improvements in explaining variance are observed when entering several other predictors in the model, such as the score on Self Esteem (with low self esteem predictive of retrospective repetition), and negative life events. Many variables that are associated with repetition do not appear in the model because of their co-linearity with the frequency of treatment in psychiatric hospitals (e.g., due to alcohol abuse, problems with medication, etc.). The predictive power of this best possible subset of variables in determining (in retrospect, using EPSIS I information gathered after the index attempt) whether a person is a first-evers or a repeater at the time of the index attempt is limited. About 30% of variance is explained. This indicates that the opportunities for the prediction of future repetition will be even more modest.

Differences at Initial Interview Between Those Who Repeated and Non-Repeaters at the Follow-Up

In total, 731 follow-up interviews were administered (EPSIS II). It appeared that 517 persons did not report repeated attempts in the follow-up period, while 214 reported at least one repeat-attempt (29%). There were 89 respondents who reported one repeat-attempt (12%), and 125 who reported two or more repeat attempts in the follow-up period (17%). Significant differences in characteristics measured at initial interview (EPSIS I) were (summarised): repeaters were somewhat more often women (69%) than non-repeaters (62%), female repeaters tended to be somewhat younger, and less economically active. No differences were found for marital status and level of education. As to psychiatric and psychosocial variables, it appeared that those who repeated an attempt in the follow up significantly more often had been treated in a psychiatric hospital (64%) versus those who did not repeat (39%), had attempted before the index attempt more frequently (75% versus 50% among non-repeaters), had *lower* suicide intent (SIS = 12.2 versus 13.6 among non-repeaters), and were more depressed (BDI = 28.3 versus 22.5 among non-repeaters). No differences were found regarding total scores on the scales for Self-Esteem, Motives for the attempt, Hopelessness, Anger, or the method used in the index attempt. Regarding life events it appeared that repeaters report more maltreatment by parents, partners and others, more psychiatric problems in siblings, and more involvement in criminal events, as a witness or a victim.

Prediction of Repetition in Follow-Up

All variables were entered as predictor variables in a series of stepwise multiple linear regression analyses with non-fatal repetition in follow up as dependent variable (0 = no repetition; 1 = one repeated attempt; 2 = two or more re-attempts). Successive analyses were performed for the group as a whole, for men and women separately, for first-evers and repeaters separately, and finally for male first-evers, male repeaters, female first-evers, and female repeaters. Only cumulative R square or explained variances are presented here for the successive variables entered in the various models (missing values deleted listwise).

- *Group as a whole:* Previous attempted suicide is the most powerful predictor entering the model ($R^2 = .113$), followed by the frequency of treatments in psychiatric hospitals (cumulative $R^2 = .147$), low Self-Esteem ($R^2 = .172$), young Age (.186), and low Suicide Intent (factor 1, seriousness), amounting to $R^2 = .199$ or 20% variance explained. Those with low self-esteem, younger age, and low suicide intent tend to repeat more often.
- *Women:* The same variables enter the model in similar sequence: previous attempted suicide ($R^2 = .133$), followed by frequency of treatment in psychiatric hospitals (cumulative $R^2 = .153$), young Age (.174), low Self-Esteem (.185), and low Suicide Intent (seriousness), amounting to $R^2 = .194$, or 19% variance explained. Women with low self-esteem, younger age and low suicide intent tend to repeat more often.
- *Men:* Frequency of treatments in psychiatric hospitals emerges as the first variable to enter the model (.125), followed by low Self-Esteem (.190), Loss of Control (Motive item 3, R^2 cum = .232), and few precautions against discovery taken at the index attempt (.262). Men with low self-esteem, more impulsivity, and low suicide intent tend to be repeater more often .
- *First-evers:* For those who were first-ever at the time of the index attempt, only low

Self-Esteem enters the model as a significant predictor for becoming a repeater in the follow-up period, albeit amounting only to $R^2 = .033$, or 3% variance explained.

- *Repeaters:* For those who were repeaters at the index attempt, the following predictors entered the model: frequency of treatments in psychiatric hospitals (.080), low Self-Esteem (.120), young Age (.152), low Suicide Intent (.180), and previous attempted suicides (.194), amounting to 19% explained variance.
- *Men, first-evers:* Two factors enter the model: inverse Self-Esteem (.138), followed by Lost Control over myself (.210), indicating impulsivity.
- *Men, repeaters:* Three variables comprise the model: Frequency of treatments in psychiatric hospitals (.124), followed by inverse Precautions taken (Suicide Intent) (.200), and Depression (.260).
- *Women, first-evers:* No predicting risk variables were found for repetition in the follow-up.
- *Women, repeaters:* Frequency of treatments in psychiatric hospitals is the first variable to enter the model (.066), followed by inverse Age (.098), inverse Suicide Intent, Seriousness (.126), and low Self-Esteem (.151).

This series of multiple regression analyses reveals that previous non-fatal suicidal behaviour is the best predictor of future non-fatal suicidal behaviour. Prediction is better among repeaters than among first-evers, and somewhat different variables are relevant for men and women. Prediction of repetition among female first-evers seems to be impossible, among male first-evers it is possible, focussing on low self-esteem and high impulsivity (Lost Control). For those who have a history of non-fatal suicidal behaviour, the frequency of treatments in psychiatric hospitals is the best predictor. In women, young age, low self esteem and low suicide intent are predictive of future suicide attempts, while for men few precautions at the index attempt (hinting at impulsivity), and depression add to the prediction of repetition. It appeared that the inclusion of life events in the regression models did not improve the prediction of repetition.

Two Types of Repetition?

In investigating prediction of repetition the collinearity of many variables result in one or two predictor variables entering the model, while related variables may not come forward although they do have strong relationships with the criterion variable, like depression. Some variables may have curvilinear relationships with the dependent variable that cannot be accounted for in linear regression analyses. Some variables may be of interest for particular groups, like hopelessness in depression, while being of less relevance for other groups, e.g., the non-depressed. In order to tentatively investigate such relationships, a non-linear principle components analysis (PRINCALS) has been carried out with all the major variables of interest, included together with retrospective (attempted suicides previous to the index attempt) and prospective repetition (attempted suicides in the follow-up period). This analysis allows for non-linear relationships, inclusion of categorical variables (like gender), and discrimination of subgroups of respondents on major dimensions. A two-dimensional solution had the best fit (total fit .23). The first dimension reflected the relationships between prospective and retrospective repetition (component loadings .802 and .695 respectively) and frequency of treatments in psychiatric hospitals (.580), Depression (.474), Self-Esteem (.495), and negative life events such as Maltreatment by parents in childhood (.478), and Maltreatment by partner later in life (.457). This dimension is further related to: Motive to Die (.326), or to Interrupt (.321), longstanding mental health problems (.316), and low Suicide Intent (−.311). This first dimension may be conceived as a life-long vulnerability dimension. The second dimension has high loadings on: Hopelessness (.462), Depression (.435), State (.423) and Trait Anger (.397), and female sex (.326).

This solution suggests that there are two different ways in which repetition of attempted suicide can be understood: There seems to be a hopeless and depressed type of repetition, and there seems to be a low-depression, low-hopelessness, instant-relief type of repetition.

The first type of non-fatal repetition is a depressed and hopeless type of recurrent suicidal behaviour. This is characterized by a life-long problem history, e.g., of maltreatment by parents in childhood and by partners later in life, by the experience of having longstanding problems, a history of mental health care treatment, including admissions to psychiatric hospitals, by motives to die, and to a lesser degree to interrupt. We might conceive here of persons with a life-long history of adversity, that at the time of the attempt result in depression and hopelessness and sometimes feelings of anger. Depression, hopelessness and attempted suicide all reflect unsuccessful ways of coping with adversity. It appears that their expectations towards the near or distant future are negative. Repetition here reflects a persisting vulnerability factor.

The other type of non-fatal repetition can be conceived of as a low-depression and low-hopelessness type of recurrent behaviour. This behaviour too is associated with a number of previous treatments in psychiatric hospitals, with motives of appeal and temporary interruption of consciousness, with recent problems with partners (e.g., partner being admitted to a psychiatric hospital, or partner attempted suicide), and with alcohol abuse. The SIS score is low, and there is loss of control. It is tempting to conclude that in this type of recurrent non-fatal suicidal behaviour impulsivity and attention seeking behaviour have to be located. These individuals seem wanting to interrupt consciousness, to appeal to others and they only mildly suffer from depression and hopelessness. The motivation for recurrent non-fatal suicidal behaviour has nothing to do with dying. This type of repetition, too, reflects a way of coping, or self-regulation, but here we may think that it is oriented towards the immediate future: instant relief from negative feelings. The more distant future is not involved.

We might think of splitting recurrent non-fatal suicidal behaviour into two types: a depressed/hopeless type, oriented towards dying, and an impulsive, low-depression, low-hopelessness type, oriented towards instant relief and help. But no matter how well we will be able to define such a distinction, both groups will continue to repeat. In any case, a high score on the Suicide Intent Scale is not predictive for future non-fatal suicidal behaviour. A low score on the SIS is indicative for non-fatal repetition, but the predictive power is limited. The SIS therefore is not a suitable instrument for non-fatal repetition. Whether it is suitable for fatal repetition will be investigated elsewhere.

Discussion

The greater the number of previous suicide attempts before the index attempt, and the greater the number of treatments in psychiatric hospitals, the greater are the chances for repetition of attempted suicide. For clinicians, this will not come as a surprise. Because of the interrelationships with other variables, these two encompass many other variables reflecting vulnerability for future non-fatal suicidal behaviour. For many patients, this vulnerability is related to long-term psychiatric disorders. However, the predictability of future non-fatal suicidal behaviour is limited since much of the variance is unexplained for. Prediction of repetition may be enhanced by focussing on specific high-risk groups, such as borderline patients with a history of repeated self-destructive behaviour, or specific low-risk populations (male adolescent first-evers with no psychiatric treatment history and with stable living conditions), but in general the prediction of repetition suffers from large numbers of false positives and false negatives. Interestingly, *low* suicide intent is associated with repeated non-fatal suicidal behaviour, illustrating clinical experiences that those with low suicide intent, and those who made few precautions for discovery, are those with the highest risk for non-fatal repetition. Together with the predictive power of self-reported loss of control, this again points at the impulsivity of non-fatal suicidal behaviour.

The prediction of recurrent non-fatal suicidal behaviour continues to produce headache. It appears that it will not be possible to devise an instrument that predicts non-fatal repetition without low sensitivity and specificity for the whole group. We might better aim at developing predictive scales for well defined subgroups, but even then the predictive power will be unsatisfactory. This conclusion has been reached before (e.g., Sakinofski, 2000). The prediction of repetition probably is best served by inclusion of cognitive styles and psychological in depth understanding of the meaning of several types of non-fatal suicidal behaviour. Unless we develop a thorough psychological typology of self-destructive behaviour, we will fall short in predicting and therewith preventing repetition.

Acknowledgements

A. Aardema, B. Steunenberg and W. Blees provided invaluable support in the process of data-analysis.

References

American Psychiatric Association. (1987). *DSM-III-R: Diagnostic and statistical manual of mental disorders* (3rd ed. revised). Washington DC: Author.

Appleby, L., & Warner, R. (1993). Parasuicide – Features of repetition and the implications for intervention. *Psychological Medicine, 23*, 13–16.

Arensman, E., & Kerkhof, A. J. F. M. (1996). Classification of attempted suicide: A review of empirical studies, 1963–1993. *Suicide and Life-Threatening Behavior, 26*, 46–67.

Arensman, E., Kerkhof, A. J. F. M., Dirkzwager, A., Verduin, C., Bille-Brahe, U., Crepet, P., De Leo, D., Hawton, K., Hjelmeland, H., Lönnqvist, J., Michel, K., Querejeta, I., Salander-Renberg, E., Schmidtke, A., Temesvary, B., & Wasserman, D. (2003). *Prevalence and risk factors for repeated suicidal behaviour: Results from the WHO/EURO Multicentre Study on Parasuicide, 1989–1992.*

Bagley, C., & Greer, S. (1971). Clinical and social predictors of repeated attempted suicide: A multivariate analysis. *British Journal of Psychiatry, 119*, 515–521.

Bancroft, J.H. J., Skrimshire, A. M., & Simkin, S. (1976). The reasons people give for taking overdoses. *British Journal of Psychiatry, 128*, 538–548.

Bancroft, J.H. J., & Marsack, P. (1977). The repetitiveness of self-poisoning and self-injury. *British Journal of Psychiatry, 131*, 394–399.

Bancroft, J.H. J., Hawton, K., Simkin, S., Kingston, B., Cumming, C., & Whitwell, D. (1979). The reasons people give for taking overdoses: a further inquiry. *British Journal of Modern Psychology, 52*, 353–365.

Beck, A. T., Ward, C. H., Mendelson, M., Mock, J., & Erbaugh, J. (1961). An inventory for Measuring depression. *Archives of General Psychiatry, 4*, 561–571.

Beck, A. T., Schuyler, D., & Herman, J. (1974). Development of Suicidal Intent Scales. In A. T. Beck, H. L. P. Resnik, & D. J. Lettieri (Eds.), *The prediction of suicide* (pp. 45–56). Bowie, MD: Charles Press.

Beck, A. T., Weissman, A., Lester, D., & Trexler, L. (1974). The measurement of pessimism: The hopelessness scale. *Journal of Consulting and Clinical Psychology, 42*, 861–865.

Beck, A. T., Kovacs, M., & Weisman, A. (1979). Assessment of suicidal intention: The Scale for Suicide Ideation. *Journal of Consulting and Clinical Psychology, 47*, 343–352.

Beck, A. T., Steer, R. A., & Ranieri, W. F. (1988). Scale for Suicide Ideation: Psychometric Properties of a Self-Report Version. *Journal of Clinical Psychology, 44*, 499–505.

Bille-Brahe, U., & Jessen, G. (1994). Repeated suicidal behaviour: A two year follow-up. *Crisis, 15*, 77–82.

Bille-Brahe, U., Schmidtke, A., Kerkhof, A. J. F. M., De Leo, D., Lönnqvist, Platt, S., & Sampaio Faria, J. (1995). Background and introduction to the WHO-EURO Multicentre Study on Parasuicide. *Crisis, 16*, 72–84.

Bille Brahe, U., Kerkhof, A. J. F. M., De Leo, D., Schmidtke, A., Crepet, P., Lönnqvist, J., Michel,

K., Salander-Renberg, E., Stiles, T. C., Wasserman, D., & Egebo, H. (1996). A repetition-prediction study on European parasuicide populations. *Crisis, 17,* 22–31.

Bille Brahe, U., Andersen, K., Wasserman, D., Schmidtke, A., Bjerke, T., Crepet, P., De Leo, D., Haring, C., Hawton, K., Kerkhof, A. J. F. M., Lönnqvistr, J., Michel, K., Phillipe, A., Querejeta, I., Salander-Renberg, E., & Temesvary (1996). The WHO-EURO Multicentre Study: Risk of Parasuicide and the comparability of the areas under study. *Crisis, 17,* 32–42.

Bille Brahe, U., Kerkhof, A. J. F. M., De Leo, D., Schmidtke, A., Crepet, P., Lönnqvist, J., Michel, K., Salander-Renberg, E., Stiles, T. C., Wasserman, D., Aagaard, B., Egebo, H., & Jensen, B. (1997). A repetition-prediction study of European parasuicide populations: A summary of the first report from Part II of the WHO/EURO Multicentre Study on Parasuicide in co-operation with the EC Concerted Action on Attempted Suicide. *Acta Psychiatrica Scandinavica, 95,* 81–86.

Buglass, D., & McCullogh, J. W. (1970). Further suicidal behaviour: the development and validation of predictive scales. *British Journal of Psychiatry, 116,* 483–491.

Buglass, D., & Horton, J. (1974a). A scale for predicting subsequent suicidal behaviour. *British Journal of Psychiatry, 124,* 573–578.

Buglass, D., & Horton, J. (1974b). The repetition of parasuicide: A comparison of three cohorts. *British Journal of Psychiatry, 125,* 168–174.

Clark, D. C., & Horton-Deutsch, S. L. (1992). Assessment in absentia: The value of the psychological autopsy method for studying antecedents of suicide and predicting future suicides. In R. W. Maris, A. L. Berman, J. T. Maltsberger, & R. I. Yufit (Eds.), *Assessment and prediction of suicide* (pp. 144–182). New York: Guilford.

Cullberg, J., Wasserman, D., & Stefansson, C. G. (1988). Who commits suicide after a suicide attempt? *Acta Psychiatrica Scandinavica, 77,* 598–603.

Egmond, M. van, & Diekstra, R.F. W. (1989). The predictability of suicidal behaviour: The results of a meta-analysis of published studies. In R.F. W. Diekstra, R. Maris, S. Platt, A. Schmidtke, & G. Sonneck (Eds.), *Suicide and its prevention* (pp. 37–61). Leiden: Brill.

Farmer, R. (1986). Deliberate self-poisoning. *British Journal of Hospital Medicine, 36,* 437–442.

Goldacre, M., & Hawton, K. (1985). Repetition of self-poisoning and subsequent death in adolescents who take overdoses. *British Journal of Psychiatry, 146,* 395–398.

Hawton, K. (1987). Assessment of suicide risk. *British Journal of Psychiatry, 150,* 145–153.

Hawton, K., & Catalan, J. (1981). Psychiatric management of attempted suicide patients. *British Journal of Hospital Medicine, 26,* 365–368.

Hawton, K., & Catalan, J. (1982, 1987). *Attempted suicide.* Oxford: Oxford University Press.

Hawton, K., & Fagg, J. (1988). Suicide and other causes of death, following attempted suicide. *British Journal of Psychiatry, 152,* 359–366.

Hawton, K., & Fagg, J. (1992). Trends in deliberate self-poisoning and self-injury in Oxford, 1976–1990. *British Medical Journal, 304,* 1409–1411.

Hawton, K., & Fagg, J. (1995). Repetition of attempted suicide: The performance of the Edinburgh predictive scales in patients in Oxford. *Archives of Suicide Research, 1,* 261–272.

Hjelmeland, H. (1996). Repetition of parasuicide: A predictive study. *Suicide and Life-Threatening Behavior, 26,* 395–404.

Isometsä, E. T., & Lönnqvist, J. K. (1998). Suicide attempts preceding completed suicide. *British Journal of Psychiatry, 173,* 531–535.

Kerkhof, A. J. F. M., Wal, J. van der, & Hengeveld, M. W. (1988). Typology of persons who attempted suicide with predictive value for repetition: a prospective cohort study. In H. J. Möller, A. Schmidtke, & R. Welz (Eds.), *Current issues of suicidology* (pp. 193–203). Berlin: Springer-Verlag.

Kerkhof, A. J. F. M., Bernasco, W., Bille Brahe, U., Platt, S., & Schmidtke, A. (1993a). European Parasuicide Study Interview Schedule (EPSIS I), version 5.1. In U. Bille-Brahe et al. (Eds.), *Facts and figures.* Copenhagen, WHO/EUR/ICP/PSF.018

Kerkhof, A. J. F. M., Egmond, M. van, Bille-Brahe, U., Platt, S., & Schmidtke, A. (1993b). European Parasuicide Study Interview Schedule (EPSIS II), version 3.2. In U. Bille-Brahe et al. (Eds.), *Facts and figures.* Copenhagen, WHO/EUR/ICP/PSF.018

Kerkhof, A. J. F. M., Schmidtke, A., De Leo, D., Bille-Brahe, U., & Lönnqvist, J. (Eds.), (1994). *Attempted suicide in Europe. Findings from the WHO/EURO Multicentre Study on Parasuicide.* Leiden/Copenhagen: DSWO Press, Leiden University and World Health Organization.

Kreitman, N. (1977). *Parasuicide.* London: Wiley.

Kreitman, N., & Casey, P. (1988). Repetition of parasuicide: an epidemiological and clinical study. *British Journal of Psychiatry, 153,* 792–800.

Kreitman, N., & Foster, J. (1991). Construction and selection of predictive scales, with special reference to parasuicide. *British Journal of Psychiatry, 159,* 185–192.

Maris, R. W. (1992). The relationship of nonfatal suicide attempts to completed suicide. In R. W. Maris, A. L. Berman, J. T. Maltsberger, & R. I. Yufit (Eds.), *Assessment and prediction of suicide* (pp. 362–380). New York: Guilford.

Morgan, H. G., Burns-Cox, C. J., Pocock, H., & Pottle, S. (1975). Deliberate self-harm: Clinical and socio-economic characteristics of 368 patients. *British Journal of Psychiatry, 127,* 564–574.

Morgan, H. G., Barton, J., Pottle, S., Pocock, H., & Burns-Cox, C. J. (1976). Deliberate self-harm: A follow up study of 279 patients. *British Journal of Psychiatry, 128,* 361–368.

Ovenstone, I. M. K., & Kreitman, N. (1974). Two syndromes of suicide. *British Journal of Psychiatry, 123,* 35–39.

Owens, D., Dennis, M., Read, S., & Dacis, N. (1994). Outcome of deliberate self-poisoning. An examination of risk factors for repetition. *British Journal of Psychiatry, 165,* 797–801.

Pallis, D. J., Barraclough, B. M., Levey, A. B., Jenkins, J. S., & Sainsbury, P. (1982). Estimating suicide risk among attempted suicides, I: The development of new clinical scales. *British Journal of Psychiatry, 141,* 37–44.

Pallis, D. J., Gibbons, J. S., & Pierce, D. W. (1984). Estimating suicide risk among attempted suicides, II: Efficiency of predictive scales after the attempt. *British Journal of Psychiatry, 144,* 139–148.

Pierce, D. W. (1981). The predictive validation of a suicide intent scale: A five-year follow up. *British Journal of Psychiatry, 139,* 391–396.

Platt, S., Bille-Brahe, U., Kerkhof, A. J. F. M., Schmidtke, A., Bjerke, T., Crepet, P., De Leo, D., Haring, C., Lönnqvist, J., Michel, K., Phillippe, A., Pommereau, X., Querejeta, I., Salander-Renberg, E., Temesvary, B., Wasserman, D., & Sampaio Faria, J. G. (1992). Parasuicide in Europe: The WHO/EURO Multicenter Study on Parasuicide, I: Introduction and preliminary analysis for 1989. *Acta Psychiatrica Scandinavica, 85,* 97–104.

Platt, S., Hawton, K., Kreitman, N., Fagg, J., & Foster, J. (1988). Recent clinical and epidemiological trends in parasuicide in Edinburgh and Oxford: A tale of two cities. *Psychological Medicine, 18,* 405–418.

Rosenberg, M. (1965). *Society and the adolescent self-image.* Princeton: Princeton University Press.

Rygnestad, T. (1988). A prospective 5-year follow-up study of self-poisoned patients. *Acta Psychiatrica Scandinavica, 72,* 389–394.

Sakinofsky, I., & Roberts, R. S. (1990). What determines repetition of parasuicide? In G. Ferrari, M. Bellini, & P. Crepet (Eds.), *Suicidal behaviour and risk factors* (pp. 951–954). Bologna: Monduzzi Edditore.

Sakinofski, I. (2000). Repetition of Suicidal Behaviour. In K. Hawton & K. van Heeringen (Eds.), *The international handbook of suicide and attempted suicide* (pp. 385–404). Chichester: Wiley.

Schmidtke, A., Bille-Brahe, U., Kerkhof, A. J. F. M., De Leo, D., Platt, S., Sampaio Faria, J., Henderson, J., & Potozky, W. (1993). The WHO/EURO Multicentre Project on Parasuicide: State of the art. *Italian Journal of Suicidology, 3,* 83–95.

Schmidtke, A., Bille-Brahe, U., De Leo, D., Kerkhof, A. J. F. M., Bjerke, T., Crepet, P., Haring, C., Hawton, K., Lönnqvist, J., Michel, K., Pommereau, X., Querejeta, I., Phillipe, A., Salander-Renberg, E., Temesvary, B., Wasserman, D., Fricke, S., Weinacker, B., & Sampaio Faria, J. G. (1996). Attempted suicide in Europe: Rates, trends and sociodemographic characteristics of suicide attempters during the period 1989–1992. Results of the WHO/EURO Multicentre Study on Parasuicide. *Acta Psychiatrica Scandinavica, 93,* 327–338.

Sellar, C., Goldacre, M. J., & Hawton, K. (1990). Reliability of routine hospital data on poisoning as measure of deliberate self-harm in adolescents. *Journal of Epidemiology and Community Health, 44,* 313–315.

Spielberger, C. D. (1980). *Preliminary manual for the State-Trait Anger Scale (STAS).* Unpublished manuscript. University of South Florida, Tampa, FL.

Spielberger, C. D. (1988). *State-Trait Anger Expression Inventory – Research edition.* Odessa, FL: Psychological Assessment Resources, Inc.

Stocks, R., & Scott, A. I. F. (1991). What happens to patients who frequently harm themselves? A retrospective one-year outcome study. *British Journal of Psychiatry, 158,* 375–378.

Tuckman, J., & Youngman, W. F. (1968). A scale for assessing suicide risk of attempted suicides. *Journal of Clinical Psychology, 24,* 17–19.

Wang, A. G., Nielsen, B., Bille-Brahe, U., Hansen, W., & Kolmos, L. (1985). Attempted suicide in Denmark: Assessment of repeated suicidal behaviour. *Acta Psychiatrica Scandinavica, 72,* 389–394.

World Health Organization (1977). *Manual of the International statistical classification of diseases, injuries, and causes of death* (9th revision, Vol. 1). Geneva: World Health Organization.

World Health Organization (1978). *Mental disorders: Glossary and guide to their classification in accordance with the ninth revision of the international classification of diseases.* Geneva: World Health Organization.

World Health Organization (1986). *Summary report, Working Group on Preventive Practices in Suicide and Attempted Suicide.* York, England, 22–26 Sept. 1986. Copenhagen, WHO Regional Office for Europe (ICP/PSF 017).

Chapter 10
Marital Relationships of Suicide Attempters

Cordula Löhr and Armin Schmidtke

Department of Clinical Psychology, University of Würzburg, Germany

Introduction

According to various authors, suicidality is higher among separated and divorced suicide attempters than among single and married people. The original starting-point of this approach was the work of Durkheim (1897/1951), who stated that the subordination of the individual to the needs of other family members lowers the destructive potential of the drive towards individualism. According to this hypothesis divorce reduces family responsibilities and therefore the suicide rates are higher for divorced people. The results of Stack (1992) support this theory: suicide rates for divorced people were 34.9/100,000, whereas for married people it was only 11.9/100,000.

These findings were contradicted by the "status integration view" (Gibbs & Martin, 1964), which contends that infrequent marital statuses go ahead with high role conflict and therefore with a high risk of suicide. Following this view, in a society with a high rate of divorces, divorced people should commit fewer suicides because of lower role conflict; whereas in a society with a low divorce rate, divorced people should commit more suicide because of higher role conflict. Stack (1990) found some support for the status integration view in combination with Durkheim's theory: In accordance with the increase of the divorce rate between 1960 and 1980 (+174%), there was a decline in the ratio of the suicide rate of divorced people to married people for most age groups. However, the suicide rates of divorced people were still three times as high as those of married people. Stack (1990) concluded that "divorced people are not quite as suicidal today as a generation ago" (Stack, 1992, p. 543).

Another approach of looking at this problem is to take a closer look at the kind of interpersonal relations instead of looking at marital statuses – which can be experienced by single, married and divorced people. Despite the fact that many studies emphasised that interpersonal problems have an important impact on the motivation of suicidal behaviour, we know little about the kind of interpersonal problems – as it was already pointed out by Stephens (1988). He found that four major themes dominated the relationships of female suicide attempters: "smothering love," infidelity, battering, and denial of affection. All of them were unhappy in their relationships to males. Canetto, Feldman and Lupei (1989) described the communication of the majority of couples with a suicidal partner (suicide attempt or severe suicidal ideation) as significantly more dysfunctional than in normal couples. According to Schotte, Cools and Payvar (1990) deficits in interpersonal problem-solving skills may predispose individuals to the development of suicidal behaviour. A high degree of psychological and physical violence has been described by Arcel, Mantonakis, Petersson, Jemos and Kaliteraki (1992). Many authors point out that, especially for females, interpersonal problems are an important reason for attempting suicide (e.g., Canetto, 1992–1993; Kushner, 1995; Canetto & Lester, 1998). Lester (1995) and Michel, Valach and Waeber (1994) reported that, especially for young people, interpersonal problems were the main cause of the suicide attempt.

Other than poor social problem-solving skills, problems related to psychiatric illness or alcohol abuse by the suicide attempter her/himself or the partner may be mediating reasons for the relationship between interpersonal problems and suicide attempts (Sadowski & Kelley, 1993). However, Stack and Wasserman (1995) pointed out that the relationship between marital status and attempting suicide holds true even after controlling for alcohol abuse.

The aim of this chapter is to give an overview of the marital relations of suicide attempters, looking at marital status and the quality of the marriage, and to compare between different cultures. Descriptions are based on information from the WHO publication Facts and Figures (Bille-Brahe et al., 1993; Bille-Brahe, 1999) and results from the WHO/EURO Multi-Centre Study on Suicidal Behaviour. The WHO/EURO Multi-Centre Study on Suicidal Behaviour consists of two parts: the Monitoring Study (Schmidtke et al., 1996) and the Repetition-Prediction Study (Bille-Brahe et al., 1996). Analyses from both parts of the study will be presented in the following.

Results from the Monitoring Study

The Monitoring Study provides us with information on socio-demographic variables. Table 1 gives information on 46,605 episodes by 33,386 persons registered in 21 Centres (Ankara, Turkey; Bern, Switzerland; Bordeaux, France; Emilia, Italy; Gent, Belgium; Guipuzcoa, Spain; Innsbruck, Austria; Leiden, The Netherlands; Helsinki, Finland; Ljubljana, Slovenia; Odense, Denmark; Oxford, Great Britain;

Table 1 Number of male and female suicide attempters per centre for the period 1989 to 2000 and percentage of each centre in the total amount.

	Male	Female	Timeframe	Total
	N	*N*		%
Ankara	83	219	1998–2000	0.9
Bern	568	864	1989–1990; 1993–1998	4.3
Bordeaux	348	775	1989	3.4
Emilia	240	551	1989–1994	2.4
Gent	642	772	1996–1999	4.2
Guipuzcoa	71	118	1989–1991	0.6
Helsinki	1545	1555	1989–1996	9.3
Innsbruck	987	1118	1989–1998	6.3
Leiden	230	396	1989–1992	1.9
Ljubljana	357	409	1995–1999	2.3
Odense	2174	2866	1989–1999	15.1
Oxford	1434	1889	1989–1999	10.0
Padua	321	590	1989–1996	2.7
Pecs	219	348	1997–1999	1.7
Rennes	732	1243	1995–1996	5.9
Sør-Trøndelag	1039	1398	1989–1999	7.3
Stockholm	1050	1732	1989–1998	8.3
Szeged	439	543	1989–1991	2.9
Tallinn	480	461	1995–1996	2.8
Umeå	482	712	1989–1995	3.6
Würzburg	529	855	1989–1999	4.1
Total	**13970**	**19414**	**1989–2000**	**100**

Padua, Italy; Pecs, Hungary; Rennes, France; Sør-Trøndelag, Norway; Stockholm, Sweden; Szeged, Hungary; Tallinn, Estonia; Umeå, Sweden; Würzburg, Germany) during the period 1989 to 2000.

Marital Status

Data for marital status were only available from 20 Centres (excluding Rennes, Table 2). In total, 48% of the males and 40% of the females had never been married. Thirteen percent of the males and 14% of the females were separated, 6% of the males and

Table 2 Percentage of marital status for male and female suicide attempters per centre for the period 1989 to 1999 and in total.

	Never Married		Separated		Divorced		Married	
	Male	**Female**	**Male**	**Female**	**Male**	**Female**	**Male**	**Female**
Ankara	52	50	3	2	5	2	40	43
Bern	52	44	10	15	6	5	30	29
Bordeaux	41	36	10	11	8	5	40	44
Emilia	50	36	4	3	9	7	28	40
Gent	52	40	14	18	3	3	28	34
Guipuzcoa	48	42	9	4	14	7	24	42
Innsbruck	57	43	1	1	26	38	3	9
Helsinki	54	44	21	23	2	3	21	26
Leiden	51	44	16	16	1	2	31	32
Ljubljana	54	41	4	5	4	5	32	41
Odense	36	24	15	14	4	3	41	51
Oxford	53	49	9	9	5	4	25	29
Padua	52	47	2	3	7	5	35	35
Pecs	38	30	11	14	5	5	43	43
Sør-Trøndelag	45	34	16	20	6	5	30	34
Stockholm	51	44	21	22	0	0	26	27
Szeged	26	30	16	16	13	12	30	29
Tallinn	38	37	13	11	4	4	43	43
Umeå	44	39	18	15	3	2	32	38
Würzburg	51	47	8	9	6	7	29	29
Total	**46**	**40**	**13**	**14**	**6**	**6**	**28**	**33**

females were divorced and 28% of the males and 33% of the females were married. This means that for males there is a higher percentage of single suicide attempters (48%) than for females (40%), whereas for females there is a higher percentage of married suicide attempters (33%) than for males (28%). For separated and divorced suicide attempters, the percentages are almost the same for both sexes. Because the probability of being married and consequently being separated or divorced is lower among the younger age groups, data were analysed separately for persons aged 25 and above. This analysis showed that the results are age-dependent: the percentages of single people decreased for the age group 25 and above (males: 36%, females: 22%), whereas the percentages for being married (males: 34%, females: 41%), separated (males: 17%, females: 19%) and divorced (males: 7%, females 8%) increased.

For males, $\chi^2(76) = 1718.40$, $p < .001$, and females, $\chi^2(76) = 3053.30$, $p < .001$, there were highly significant differences between the centres. For males in Helsinki, Innsbruck and Oxford, there were more single males who attempted suicide than in general, whereas in Odense and the two Hungarian centres (Szeged and Pecs) there were less single males who attempted suicide than in general. In Helsinki, Umeå, Stockholm and Sør-Trøndelag, there were more separated male suicide attempters than in general, while in Emilia, Padua, Würzburg, Innsbruck, Oxford and Ankara, there were fewer separated male suicide attempters. Whereas more divorced male suicide attempters were found in Innsbruck, Szeged and Guipuzcoa, fewer were found in Odense, Helsinki, Umeå, Leiden, Stockholm, Oxford and Gent. More married male suicide attempters than in general were found in Odense, Bordeaux, Tallinn, Pecs and Ankara and fewer were found in Helsinki and Innsbruck. For females, there were more single suicide attempters in Padua, Helsinki, Würzburg, Stockholm, Oxford and Ankara, whereas fewer single female suicide attempters were found in Odense, Sør-Trøndelag and the two Hungarian Centres (Szeged and Pecs). While more separated female suicide attempters than in general were found in Helsinki, Stockholm, Sør-Trøndelag and Gent, fewer separated female suicide attempters were found in the two Italian centres (Emilia and Padua), Würzburg, Innsbruck, Guipuzcoa, Oxford, Ljubljana and Ankara. More divorced female suicide attempters were found in Innsbruck and Szeged, whereas fewer were found in Odense, Helsinki, Umeå, Leiden, Stockholm, Oxford, Gent and Ankara. More married females suicide attempters were found in Odense, Emilia, Umeå, Bordeaux, Tallinn, Pecs, Ljubljana and Ankara, whereas fewer were found in Helsinki, Würzburg, Stockholm, Innsbruck and Oxford.

These results raise the question: Are the different percentages between the various centres due to different distributions in the total populations in the different countries (e.g., higher divorce rates in the northern European countries like Denmark, Sweden and Great Britain, low divorce rate in Italy – Europarat, 1991) or are these differences peculiar to the suicide attempters? What can be easily seen – when the above data are compared to the data from Facts and Figures (Bille-Brahe, 1999, p. 37) is that, in general, single people are clearly overrepresented among suicide attempters (normal population: 24%), whereas the percentage of divorced people is pretty much the same as in the normal population (6%). Also, we can see from Facts and Figures that the percentage of divorced people does not differ between the centres as much as the percentage of single people.

More specifically, for single people, one can see that, for example, in Odense and Pecs there are rather low percentages of single persons in the total population (Odense: 16%; Pecs: 9%; Szeged: 19%), so unsurprisingly the percentage of single persons among suicide attempters is rather low (Odense: males: 36%, females: 24%; Pecs: males: 38%, females: 30%; Szeged: males: 26%, females: 30%), too, but still higher than in the total population. In contrast, in the two Swedish centres (Stockholm and Umeå) the percentage of single people in the total population is also low, but the percentage of single suicide attempters is rather normal, compared to other centres. The same is true for Bern, Gent, Tallinn and Padua. On the other hand, Leiden (46%), Ljubljana (46%) and Bordeaux (43%) have high percentages of single people in the total population, but have rather normal percentages of single suicide attempters (Leiden: males: 51%, females: 44%; Ljubljana: males: 54%, females: 41%; Bordeaux: males: 41%, females: 36%). In contrast, Oxford (42%) and Helsinki (32%) have high percentages of single persons in the total population (42%) and also high percentages of single suicide attempters (Oxford: males: 53%, females 49%; Helsinki: males: 54%, females: 44%). Innsbruck has a high percentage of single persons in the total population (47%) and a high percentage of male single suicide attempters (57%), but the percentage of female suicide attempters is rather normal (43%).

For divorced people we can see that, for example, Helsinki (13%) and Stockholm (10%) have rather high divorce rates in the normal population, but in both centres the number of divorced people is very low among the suicide attempters (Helsinki: males: 2%, females: 3%; Stockholm: males and females 0%). In contrast, Padua has a rather low rate of divorced people in the normal population (2%), but has a normal percentage of divorced people among suicide attempters (males: 7%, females: 5%). For Ankara, this is only true for males, whereas for females the percentage of divorced suicide attempters is also low. Pecs has a rather high rate of divorced people in the normal population and normal rates of divorced people among suicide attempters. On the other hand, in Innsbruck one finds very high percentages of divorced male (26%) and female suicide attempters (38%), but the divorce rate in the normal population is rather normal (5%). Also for Szeged one finds rather high percentages of divorced male (13%) and female (12%) suicide attempters, whereas the percentage of divorced people in the normal population is rather normal (4%). The same is true for males from Guipuzcoa (suicides attempters: 14%; normal population: 1%), Umeå (males: 3%, females: 2%) and Gent (males: 3%, females: 3%), who have rather low percentages of divorced male and female suicide attempters, whereas the divorce rates in the normal population seem to be rather normal. The same seems to be true for Odense, Oxford and Helsinki. In Bordeaux, the percentage of male and female suicide attempters is very similar to the European average, as too is the percentage of divorced people in the normal population.

Household Composition

Table 3 shows the results with regard to the usual household composition. Thirty-five percent of the male and 40% of the female suicide attempters are living with their partners – either alone with partner or with partner and children. Another third of the males (33%) and females (31%) is living without a partner (either alone or alone with children). The rest is either living with parents, other relatives or in an institution (males: 26%, females: 25%). For males and females, the centres differ

Table 3 Percentage of usual household situation for male and female suicide attempters per centre for the period 1989 to 1999 and in total.

	Alone (with children)		Partner (and children)		Parents/other relatives/institution	
	Male	**Female**	**Male**	**Female**	**Male**	**Female**
Ankara	4	4	35	39	58	51
Bern	29	32	42	41	24	24
Bordeaux	0	0	30	27	66	69
Emilia	24	21	24	45	52	34
Gent	32	27	41	48	23	23
Guipuzcoa	11	10	27	46	55	43
Innsbruck	24	26	30	48	42	25
Helsinki	66	60	30	37	3	2
Leiden	29	32	48	46	23	21
Ljubljana	17	21	32	43	39	36
Odense	42	33	44	51	13	14
Oxford	14	19	27	30	31	31
Padua	16	18	35	36	49	45
Pecs	17	21	41	45	39	26
Sør-Trøndelag	37	40	34	42	27	15
Stockholm	42	43	38	39	18	18
Szeged	41	47	32	29	24	22
Tallinn	21	19	42	43	34	35
Umeå	52	43	36	42	11	14
Würzburg	30	29	42	41	26	28
Total	**33**	**31**	**35**	**40**	**26**	**25**

significantly from each other, males: $\chi^2(57) = 2934.51$, $p < .001$; females: $\chi^2(57) = 3578.55$, $p < .001$.

Compared to the total figures, more male suicide attempters living alone were found in Odense, Helsinki, Umeå, Stockholm and Szeged, whereas fewer were found in Padova, Bordeaux, Innsbruck, Guipuzcoa, Oxford, Tallinn, Pecs, Ljubljana and Ankara. More males living alone with a partner or with a partner and children were found in Odense, Würzburg and Leiden, but fewer were found in Emilia, Helsinki, Innsbruck and Oxford. More males living with their parents, other relatives or in an institution were found in Emilia, Padua, Bordeaux, Innsbruck, Guipuzcoa, Oxford, Pecs, Ljubljana and Ankara, and fewer were found in Odense, Helsinki, Umeå and Stockholm. More female suicide attempters living alone or alone with children were found in Helsinki, Umeå, Stockholm, Sør-Trøndelag and Szeged, whereas fewer were found in Emilia, Padua, Bordeaux, Guipuzcoa, Oxford, Tallinn, Pecs, Ljubljana and Ankara. More female suicide attempters living alone with a partner or with a partner and children were found in Odense, Innsbruck and Gent, whereas fewer were found in Bordeaux, Szeged and Oxford. More females living with parents, other relatives or in an institution were found in Padua, Bordeaux, Guipuzcoa, Oxford, Ljubljana and Ankara, but fewer were found in Odense, Helsinki, Umeå, Stockholm and Sør-Trøndelag.

Results from the Repetition-Prediction Study

Results from the Repetition-Prediction Study provide more detailed information on the intimate relationships of suicide attempters. Of the centres participating in the Monitoring Study, 15 Centres, namely Bern (Switzerland), Emilia (Italy), Gent (Belgium), Helsinki (Finland), Innsbruck (Austria), Leiden (The Netherlands), Ljubljana (Slovenia), Odense (Denmark), Oxford (Great Britain), Padua (Italy), Pecs (Hungary), Sør-Trøndelag (Norway), Stockholm (Sweden), Umeå (Sweden) and Würzburg (Germany) carried out the first wave of the European Parasuicide Study Interview Schedule (EPSIS I; Bille-Brahe et al., 1996).

In total, 1,756 patients who attempted suicide and entered the medical care system between the years 1990 to 1999 were investigated (all of them also took part in the Monitoring Study). Females constituted 61% of the sample. The mean age was 40 years (range: 15–87 years). Socio-demographic characteristics were in line with international findings (e.g., Schmidtke, 1997).

Forty eight percent of the males and 44% of the females were single, 26% of the males and 28% of the females were married, and 24% of the males and 22% of the females were divorced or separated. Almost half of the patients (45%) were living in a stable relationship (married or cohabiting for at least 12 months, $N = 788$). Mean duration of marriage or cohabiting was 13 years.

Marital quality of Suicide Attempters Living in a Stable Relationship

Looking at the reasons that caused the suicide attempt, among suicide attempters living in a stable relationship, "problems with partner" were among the three most frequently reported reasons. About two thirds of all suicide attempters reported "problems with partner," "problems with loneliness" and "mental illness and psychiatric symptoms."

For all three reasons, significantly higher percentages were found for females than for males.

Furthermore, the kind of problems with the partner reported during the interview for the last year before the suicide attempt was assessed: The five by far most reported relationship problems were "serious relationship problems," "sexual problems," "rows with partner," "mentally mistreated by partner" and "financial problems with partner." For the first four kinds of relationship problems, no significant differences between males and females were found. In contrast, males significantly more often described "financial problems with partner."

A high degree of physical and psychological violence – especially against female suicide attempters was described: about one third of the female suicide attempters described that they have been mentally mistreated by their partner and about one fifth reported that achievements had been prevented by the partner. Also almost one fifth of the females answered that their partner had beaten them.

Differences between Suicide Attempters with and Without Relationship Problems

Forty six percent of the total sample reported that they had experienced serious relationship problems during the last year before the suicide attempt. Thirty seven percent of those were male suicide attempters and 63% were female suicide attempters. However, there was no significant gender difference between those experiencing relationship problems and those not experiencing any relationship problems.

Furthermore, there was no significant difference between those with and without relationship problems with regard to methods (poisoning and hard methods) of the suicide attempt.

There was a significant difference between the two groups with regard to the number of suicide attempts: There were relatively few suicide attempters with relationship problems who only made one suicide attempt (43%, versus 48% of the suicide attempters without relationship problems), mostly they made two to four attempts (46%, versus 38% of the suicide attempters without relationship problems), and 11% made five or more attempts (versus 14% of the suicide attempters without relationship problems; see Table 4).

Furthermore there was a highly significant difference with regard to diagnoses: there were significantly fewer suicide attempters with relationship problems that were diagnosed with affective disorders (Table 5). In contrast, there was no significant difference with regard to the depression score in suicide attempters with ($M = 24.0$, $SD = 11.6$) or without relationship problems ($M = 23.0$, $SD = 11.7$).

For most people who experienced relationship issues, these problems were the reason for attempting suicide (90%).

Table 4 Number of suicide attempts of suicide attempters with and without relationship problems (%).

Number of suicide attempts:	Suicide attempters with relationship problems	Suicide attempters without relationship problems	Total
1	43	48	45
2–4	46	38	42
≥5	11	14	13

Table 5. Diagnoses of suicide attempters with and without relationship problems (%).

	Suicide attempters with relationship problems	Suicide attempters without relationship problems	Total
Schizophrenia	1	2	1
Affective disorders	5	10	8
Acute stress disorder	1	1	1
Adjustment disorder	10	6	8
Substance abuse	11	8	9
Personality disorders	18	19	18
Others	2	2	2
No psychiatric diagnoses	53	53	53

Table 6. Problems with partner as a reason for attempting suicide of suicide attempters with and without relationship problems (%).

		Suicide attempters with relationship problems	Suicide attempters without relationship problems	Total
No		10	58	36
Yes	Minor	19	20	20
	Major	70	23	44

Conclusions

To summarise the results from the Monitoring Study with regard to the marital status, we can conclude that single persons are clearly over-represented among suicide attempters, whereas the percentage of divorced people is nearly the same among suicide attempters and in the total population. These results somewhat support the findings of Stack (1990). Whereas earlier results of this study showed that single and divorced people were over-represented among suicide attempters (e.g.,

Schmidtke, 1997), now divorced people are no longer over-represented. In accordance with the increasing divorce rates all over Europe these results give evidence for the status integration view of Gibbs and Martin (1964), whereas the theory of Durkheim (1951) can no longer be supported by these data, since the percentage of divorced among suicide attempters is not higher than in the normal population.

There were highly significant differences between the centres. Overall, in centres where a high divorce rate is present in the normal population (Helsinki, Stockholm and Pecs), divorce does not seem to be a special risk factor for attempting suicide. But also in centres with a low percentage of divorced people in the normal population (Padua, Ankara), we find rather normal percentages of divorced people among suicide attempters, which do not support the status integration theory. In Innsbruck, one finds an extremely high percentage of divorced suicide attempters, even though the divorce rate in the normal population seems to be rather normal. However, it remains speculative if it is divorce that causes people in Austria to attempt suicide, or if there are other reasons that cause the divorce as well as the suicide attempts. On the other hand, marriage seems to be a very protective factor in Innsbruck: only 3% of the male suicide attempters and 9% of the female suicide attempters are married. Unfortunately, one does do not know the percentage of married people in the normal population, but it is highly probable that the percentage is higher.

The picture is different for being single. In Leiden and Ljubljana one finds high percentages of single people in the normal population, but being single does not seem to be a special problem for suicide attempters, because, when compared to other centres, the percentages of single suicide attempters are rather normal. In contrast, in Oxford there is a high percentage of single persons in the general population, but the percentage of single suicide attempters is even higher. The same seems to be true for males from Innsbruck. Centres with low rates of single people in the general population have either also lower percentage of single suicide attempters (Odense and Pecs) or rather normal percentages of single suicide attempters (Stockholm, Umeå, Bern, Gent, Tallinn and Padua).

The results from the Repetition-Prediction Study show that relationship problems have an important impact on the decision to attempt suicide: for more than two thirds of all suicide attempters who live in a stable relationship, problems with their partner influenced the decision to attempt suicide. These results are in line with findings from other authors (e.g., Stephens, 1988; Canetto, et al., 1989; Schotte, et al., 1990).

The results also show that having a relationship problem has a stronger impact on attempting suicide in females than in males. This finding is in line with the findings of other authors (Canetto, 1992–1993; Kushner, 1995; Canetto & Lester, 1998). However, it is important to point out that also almost two thirds of the male suicide attempters were motivated by problems with their partners.

The kinds of problems with partners were mostly described as "serious relationship problems," "sexual problems," "rows with partner," "mentally mistreated by partner" and "financial problems with partner." Physical abuse was reported by about one fifth of the females and it can be assumed that – like in other reports (e.g., Bergman & Brismar, 1991) – far more were abused but did not report on it.

Interestingly, there are significant differences between suicide attempters with and without relationship problems: suicide attempters with relationship problems mostly made two to four suicide attempts. Fewer suicide attempters with affective disorders experienced relationship problems. Depression (measured by the BDI; Beck & Steer, 1987) was investigated as a possible mediating variable, but it was the same in suicide attempters with and without relationship problems. Suicide attempters with relationship problems did not use different methods than suicide attempters without relationship problems. For 90% of the suicide attempters with relationship problems, those problems were the reason for attempting suicide.

From the results of the current study it becomes clear that single people are clearly over-represented among suicide attempters. Furthermore it was shown that in general divorced people are no longer over-represented among suicide attempters, even though there are differences between the individual centres. About 45% of all suicide attempters are living in a stable relationship. About two thirds of them experience major impairments of marital quality, and interpersonal problems have an important impact on the decision to attempt suicide. Therefore, relationship problems have important treatment implications in the therapy of suicide attempters. During clinical diagnostic processes – before the beginning of therapy – it should be clarified if there are impairments of marital quality. Behaviour analysis then might indicate that the training of interpersonal skills like problem solving is one of the main therapeutic goals.

Since the method of the current study gives a rather rough picture of marital quality, future research is needed to evaluate marital quality in a more detailed way.

References

Arcel, L.T., Mantonakis, J., Petersson, B., Jemos, J., & Kaliteraki, E. (1992). Suicide attempts among Greek and Danish women and the quality of their relationships with husbands or boyfriends. *Acta Psychiatrica Scandinavica, 85,* 189–195.

Beck, A.T., & Steer, R.A. (1987). *Beck Depression Inventory. Manual.* San Antonio: The Psychological Corporation.

Bergman, B., & Brismar, B. (1991). Suicide attempts by battered wives. *Acta Psychiatrica Scandinavica, 83,* 380–384.

Bille-Brahe, U. (1999). *WHO/EURO Multicentre Study on Parasuicide. Facts and figures.* Copenhagen: WHO Regional Office for Europe.

Bille-Brahe, U., Kerkhof, A. J. F. M., DeLeo, D., & Schmidtke, A. (1996). A repetition-prediction study on European parasuicide populations. *Crisis, 17,* 22–31.

Bille-Brahe, U., Bjerke, T., Crepet, P., DeLeo, D., Haring, C., Hawton, K., Kerkhof, A. J. F. M., Lönnqvist, J., Michel, K., Philippe, A., Pommereau, X., Querejeta, I., Salander Renberg, E., Schmidtke, A., Temesvary, B., Wasserman, D., Sampaio-Faria, J.G. (1993). *WHO/EURO*

Multicentre Study on Parasuicide. Facts and figures. Copenhagen: WHO Regional Office for Europe.

Canetto, S.S. (1992–1993). She died for love and he for glory: Gender myths of suicidal behavior. *Omega: Journal of Death and Dying, 26,* 1–17.

Canetto, S.S., Feldman L.B., & Lupei, R.L. (1989). Suicidal persons and their partners: Individual and interpersonal dynamics. *Suicide and Life-Threatening Behavior, 19,* 237–248.

Canetto, S.S., & Lester, D. (1998). Gender, Culture, and Suicidal Behavior. *Transcultural Psychiatry, 35,* 163–190.

Durkheim, E. (1951). *Suicide: A study in sociology.* Glencoe, IL: Free Press. (Original work published 1897).

Europarat (1991). *Recent demographic developments in the member states of the council of Europa.* Strasbourg: Council of Europe Publishing.

Gibbs, J., & Martin, W.T. (1964). *Status integration and suicide.* Eugene: University of Oregon Press.

Kushner, H.I. (1995). Women and suicidal behavior: Epidemiology, gender and lethality in historical perspective. In S.S. Canetto & D. Lester (Eds.), Women and suicidal behavior (pp. 11–34). New York: Springer.

Lester, D. (1995). An examination of Leenaars' theory of suicide. *Perceptual and Motor Skills, 80,* 578.

Michel, K., Valach, L., & Waeber, V. (1994). Understanding deliberate self-harm: The patients' views. *Crisis, 15,* 172–186.

Rotheram-Borus, M.J., Trautman, P.D., Dopkins S.C., & Shrout, P.E. (1990). Cognitive style and pleasant activities among female adolescent suicide attempters. *Journal of Consulting and Clinical Psychology, 58,* 554–561.

Sadowski, C., & Kelley, M.L. (1993). Social problem solving in suicidal adolescents. *Journal of Consulting and Clinical Psychology, 61,* 121–127.

Schmidtke, A. (1997). Perspective: Suicide in Europe. *Suicide and Life-Threatening Behavior, 27,* 127–136.

Schmidtke, A., Bille-Brahe, U., DeLeo, D., Kerkhof, A.J.F.M., Bjerke, T., Crepet, P., Haring, C., Hawton, K., Lönnqvist, J., Michel, K., Pommereau, X., Querejeta, I., Philippe, A., Salander-Renberg, E., Temesvary, B., Wasserman, D., Fricke, S., Weinacker, B., Sampaio-Faria, J.G. (1996). Attempted suicide in Europe: Rates, trends and sociodemographic characteristics of suicide attempters during the period 1989–1992. Results of the WHO/EURO Multicentre Study on Parasuicide. *Acta Psychiatrica Scandinavica, 93,* 327–338.

Schotte, D., Cools, J., & Payvar, S. (1990). Problem-solving deficits in suicidal patients: Trait vulnerability or state phenomenon? *Journal of Consulting and Clinical Psychology, 58,* 562–564.

Stack, S. (1990). New micro level data on the impact of divorce on suicide, 1959–1980: A test of two theories. *Journal of Marriage and the Family, 52,* 119–127.

Stack, S. (1992). Marriage, Family, Religion, and Suicide. In R.W. Maris, A.L. Berman, J.T. Maltsberger, & R.I. Yufit (Eds.), *Assessment and prediction of suicide* (pp. 540–552). New York: Guilford.

Stack, S., & Wasserman, I.M. (1995). Marital status, alcohol abuse and attempted suicide: A logit model. *Journal of Addictive Diseases, 14,* 43–51.

Stephens, B.J. (1988). The social relationships of suicidal women. In D. Lester (Ed.), *Why women kill themselves* (pp. 73–85). Springfield, IL: CC Thomas.

Chapter 11
Physical Illness and Suicidal Behaviour

Jacinta Hawgood, Kym Spathonis and Diego De Leo

Australian Institute for Suicide Research and Prevention, Griffith University, Brisbane, Australia

The role of physical illness in suicidal behaviour has gained interest by researchers since the mid-19th century. Only recently, has the complexity of the relationship between physical illness and suicide been acknowledged, and researchers have taken initial steps toward recognising the need for carefully constructed and standardised approaches to methodological investigation. The quality of many studies in this area has, in the past, rendered research findings inconclusive. The lack of uniform definitions and the inconsistent use of terminology in reference to "physical illness" and "suicidal behaviour" have contributed to ambiguous research findings. Nonetheless, scientific inquiry is increasingly attending to several complex issues, including differences in the association between physical illness and suicidal behaviour across the lifespan, improvements in clinical/health screening and suicide assessment, cultural factors, and research design.

This chapter will comprehensively review and critically evaluate research that has investigated physical illness and suicide. Throughout the review, particular attention will be afforded to methodological issues including study design, and the conceptualisation and operationalization of the constructs investigated. A unique appraisal of the role that physical illness may play in non-fatal suicidal behaviour will be presented, with reference to recent findings from the WHO/EURO MultiCentre Study on Suicidal Behaviour. The specific psychological and clinical characteristics associated with particular forms of physical illnesses will also be discussed with regard to the outcome of both fatal and non-fatal suicidal behaviour. A final discussion of the implications for clinical and health practice and suicide prevention policy will concord with suggestions for future research endeavours.

Background

The quantity of research conducted in relation to physical illness and suicidal behaviour is minimal compared to studies investigating suicidal behaviour in association with psychiatric conditions such as depression and substance abuse, and psychosocial factors including marital and employment status, anomie, and social isolation. Notwithstanding, some researchers have studied this phenomenon since 1928 (Sainsbury, 1955; Dorpat et al., 1968; Barraclough, 1980; Mackenzie & Popkin, 1987). These studies have focused either specifically on illnesses such as cancer and neurological conditions (Louhivouri & Hakama, 1979; Bolund, 1985; Crocetti, et al., 1998; Levi et al., 1991; Stenager et al., 1992), or on physical illnesses that occur more often in the general population such as diabetes mellitus (Goldston et al., 1994; Kyvik et al., 1994), pulmonary diseases such as asthma and bronchitis, gastrointestinal disorders, rheumatological disorders, cardiovascular disorders, and physical conditions associated with pain (Chenoweth et al., 1980; Ross et al., 1982; Wells et al., 1989; North et al., 1990; Grabbe et al., 1997; Quan et al., 2002). Studies conducted on the more frequently experienced physical conditions are often methodologically flawed compared to studies on cancer and most neurological conditions, which tend to be more acceptable and have lead to more conclusive findings. One reason for this is a lack of uniform definitions of, and criteria for physical illnesses. Consequently, investigations are difficult to compare and this has resulted in an unclear understanding of the relationship between physical conditions and suicidal behaviour.

Unfortunately, many studies that investigated the relationship between physical illness and suicide in the general population did not pay heed to age stratification, and the results of these studies cannot be specifically generalized to either younger or older populations. A paucity of literature exists on the association between physical illness and suicidal behaviour in younger people (Beautrais et al., 1996; Druss & Pincus, 2000) compared to older people. This is particularly the case even in relation to more extensively and closely examined studies on illnesses such as cancer and suicide. The reasons for this are varied and may relate to the fact that global rates of suicide among the elderly are often the highest. It has been further speculated that physical complications and conditions of a terminal nature appear more often in older age groups compared to younger age groups (Mackenzie & Popkin, 1990). Furthermore, the association between psychosocial factors and physical illness, particularly loss of mobility, autonomy and social isolation, may exacerbate existing feelings of seclusion and increased dependency is common in older age, leading to an increased risk of suicidal behaviour.

Finally, the majority of studies in this area have focused on the relationship between fatal suicidal behaviour and physical illness, while less attention has been given to suicide ideation, and non-fatal suicidal behaviour. This is true for the general population, and even more so for younger people. As well as this, only recently has the epidemiology of non-fatal suicidal behaviour and physical illness been investigated in a large-scale international comparison (De Leo et al., 1999a).

Compared to studies on fatal suicidal behaviour, those that have investigated non-fatal suicidal behaviour are even more methodologically complicated. Studies that have been undertaken in this domain are methodologically diverse, not easily comparable, and primarily lack a uniform and standardised definition of non-fatal suicidal behaviour.

Methodological Considerations

Physical Illness

A primary complication in determining the association between physical illness and suicide is the way in which physical illness is defined and interpreted. While most research has used the term *physical illness* axiomatically, this condition has also been conceptualised as *medical illness* or *somatic illness*, usually with little delineation between terms. Hence, ambiguities surround the diagnostic criteria used to define and distinguish such conditions as cancer, pain, and gastrointestinal disorders. Furthermore, recent studies have proposed separate identifiable phases of physical illness, such as chronic, acute, chronic in relapse, or terminal (De Leo et al., 1999a). In addition, specific diagnostic categories may be subdivided into a range of conditions differentiated by particular characteristics, for example various types of cancer and epilepsy. Finally, a common limitation of most studies is the failure to acknowledge the concomitant effect of different types of physical illness on suicidal behaviour. As a consequence, physical illness has often been rendered as a generic "summatory" entity, with a lack of acknowledgement of the specific contributions of different illnesses. This methodological problem has been particularly evident for a number of age-related conditions, such as hypertension, poly-arthrosis, and diabetes mellitus, whose contributory role has been largely overlooked.

The quality of study design used for the investigation of level of risk and suicide in different physical conditions is questionable. Variations across studies in the selection of the population has resulted in biased research findings, particularly where samples of convenience are drawn, for example, from hospital inpatients only. Between samples, the severity of physical illness may differ, as for example in the case of spinal cord injured patients (Hartkopp et al., 1998). The defining characteristics of the control group and difficulty in the selection process may also vary. In light of this, few studies have utilised case-control design methods where individuals, who exhibit either non-fatal suicidal behaviours or suicidal ideation, are compared with a control group.

According to Stenager and Stenager (2000), the most acceptable method for investigating the relationship between physical illness and fatal suicidal behaviour is through the use of national and state registers which contain all persons with a particular condition derived through specific diagnostic criteria. Such studies allow for comparisons to be made between the register population (i.e., those with a particular physical illness) and deaths in a larger population death register, marked by a particular geographic area (e.g., nation, state and local community). Thus, the relative risk of suicide can be calculated with the availability of comparable ratios of population groups, during a particular period of time. Register studies also allow for investigation and comparison of persons with a specific physical illness, and those at different stages of illness. It must be remembered, however, that although this method is ideal, funding registers is very expensive and it takes many years of monitoring persons with particular physical conditions to establish a basis for sound analyses.

Increasingly, epidemiological studies have made use of standardised mortality ratios (SMRs), which constitute the observed number of suicides in a population completed by individuals with a particular physical illness, divided by the expected number of deaths of the general population. This statistic is adjusted for gender, age, and year of observation, allowing for the comparison between SMRs. Because much larger populations are engaged, suicide mortality figures are therefore more reliable.

Epidemiology

Fatal Suicidal Behaviour

To the authors' knowledge, Ruth Cavan first recognised an association between suicide and physical illness in 1928 (Mackenzie & Popkin, 1987). Based on 391 cases of suicide in Chicago in 1923, 23% of deceased subjects were found to have been suffering from a physical illness, in 16% of which the physical illness was considered to have had a direct relationship with the suicide. Sainsbury (1955) identified physical illness as a risk factor for suicide using autopsy methodology in his renowned North London study during the period of 1936–1938. He found that 29% ($n = 111$) of 390 suicides investigated were associated with physical illness. In 18% of these cases, physical illness was the major contributing factor, and the only contributing factor in 6% of cases. Moreover, a review of earlier studies in this area has found physical illness to be prevalent in approximately 25% to 70% of suicides (Whitlock, 1986; Mackenzie & Popkin, 1990).

Internationally, epidemiological studies have identified an increased suicidal risk associated with many physical illnesses (Harris & Barraclough, 1994; Stenager & Stenager, 2000). Robust evidence supports the association between increased suicide risk for patients with cancer, ischemic heart disease, chronic pulmonary disease, (Quan et al., 2002), some neurological diseases including multiple sclerosis, stroke, epilepsy, and Huntington's chorea, and immune disorders such as HIV/AIDS (Stenager & Stenager, 1992; Harris & Barraclough, 1994). However, the level of suicide risk is less clear for gastrointestinal problems (e.g., peptic ulcers) and spinal cord injuries (Harris & Barraclough, 1994), where some studies have shown positive associations with such illnesses and suicidal behaviour, and others have found a negative or no relationship. To a lesser extent, illnesses including diabetes mellitus (also juvenile diabetes), rheumatoid arthritis and neoplasms of the cervix and prostate are thought to increase the risk of suicide (Stenager & Stenager, 1992; Harris & Barraclough, 1994).

Fatal suicidal behaviour among individuals with physical illness may vary across the life cycle, where a concurrent increase in age corresponds with an increase in the number of suicides by individuals with existing physical illnesses (Dorpat et al., 1968; Klerman, 1987). Klerman (1987) reported that physical illness posed a considerable risk for individuals aged 30 years and over, compared to individuals under the age of 30. Dorpat and colleagues (1968) also found that the prevalence of physical illness in subjects who died by suicide predominated in older age, where 69.7% of the sample was aged 60 years and older, compared to 13.3% under the age of 39 years. This trend was also observed in the WHO/EURO Multi-Centre Study on Suicidal Behaviour by De Leo and colleagues (1999a) where the lowest level of physical illness was observed among individuals aged 15–34 year (40%) compared to 53% in those aged 35 to 64 years, and 72% in those over 65 years. Moreover, individuals aged 65 years and older were more likely to suffer from physical illnesses that were chronic in relapse.

More recent studies have paid a close attention to the examination of specific physical illnesses, as opposed to measuring physical illness as one generic entity. Table 1 presents a chronological list of various studies published over the last 15 years. As mentioned before, studies on cancer and neurological conditions dominate this area, although other illnesses that are more common in the general population have received increasing attention.

Overall, register studies have demonstrated a prevalence of fatal suicidal behaviour in deceased cancer patients that ranges from 0.2% (Levi et al., 1991; Crocetti et al., 1998) to 34.7% (Storm et al., 1991). Levi and colleagues suggested that the risk of suicide in the first year after diagnosis is significantly higher (SMR = 3.9) compared to the risk attenuated in subsequent years (SMR = 2.2 between 1 and 5 years, and SMR = 1.5 over 5 years). These findings are consistent with those reported in a Swedish Cancer Register where substantial excess risk was found during the first year after diagnosis (SMR = 16.0 in males, and 15.4 in females) (Allebeck et al., 1989). Crocetti et al. (1998) found that the period of highest suicide risk occurred during the first 6 months after diagnosis (SMR = 27.7), a risk that dropped to 18.8 during the first year thereafter. These findings contrast significantly with the risk of suicide in the general population, and exceed the risk reported in other studies. The findings from these two studies also differ from those reported in an earlier Finnish Register study (Louhivuori & Hakama, 1979), where the risk was found to be greatest after 5 years post-diagnosis (SMR = 1.3 for males, and 1.9 for females).

Table 1 Fatal suicidal behaviour in patients with physical illnesses.

Source	Location	Study Design	No. participants	Physical illness (PI) subtype		Participants with PI who completed suicide (CS)	
				N	%	N	%
Stensman & Sundqvist-Stensman (1988)	Uppsala, Switzerland	Register study (1977–1984)	416	All somatic illnesses 416	100.0	70	17.0*
				Subgroups with suicide rate > general population			
				Multiple sclerosis		2	0.5
				Parkinson's disease		4	1.0
				Malignant neoplasms		13	3.1
Allebeck & Bolund (1991)	Stockholm, Switzerland	Register study (1975–1985)	59845	Cancer 3744	6.3	144	3.8
Levi et al. (1991)	Canton of Vaud, Switzerland	Register study (1976–1987)	24166	Cancer 24166	100.0	55	0.2
Storm et al. (1991)	Denmark	Register study (1971–1986)	296330	Cancer 296330	100.0	All participants 568 / All deaths (N = 1637) 568	0.2 / 34.7
Stenanger et al. (1992)	Denmark	Register study (1953–1985)	6088	Multiple sclerosis (MS) 5525	90.8	All MS patients 53 / All deaths (N = 1444) 53	0.96 / 3.7
Henderson & Ord (1997)	Maryland, USA	Register study (1991–1996)	241	Head & neck cancer 241	100.0	3	1.2
Grabbe et al.(1997)	USA	Register study (1985–1986)	9181	Death by suicide (N = 41)			
				Cancer		6	15.1
				Stroke		2	5.7
				Myocardial infarction		8	21.9
				Asthma		6	16.6
				Lung condition		14	34.3
				Angina		8	19.6
				High blood pressure		15	37.2
				Diabetes		2	5.5
				Alzheimer's disease		4	11.1

Table 1 continued.

Source	Location	Study Design	No. participants	Physical illness (PI) subtype		Participants with PI who completed suicide (CS)
Stenager et al. (1998)	Funen, Denmark	Follow-up study (1973–1989)	37869	Stroke 37869	100.0	
Crocetti et al. (1998)	Florence and Prato, Italy	Register study (1985–1989)	27123	Cancer 27123	100.0	
Hartkopp et al. (1998)	Denmark	Follow-up study (1953–1990)	888	Spinal chord injury 888	100.0	
Teasdale & Engberg (2001a)	Denmark	Register study (1979–1993)	114098	Stroke 114098	100.0	
Teasdale & Engberg (2001b)	Denmark	Register study (1979–1993)	145440	Concussion 126114	86.7	
				Cranial fracture 7560	5.2	
				Cerebral contusion or traumatic intracranial haemorrhage 11766	8.1	
Quan et al. (2002)	Alberta, Canada	Case-control study (1984–1995)	Cases/suicides (N = 822) Controls/Motor vehicle accident deaths (N = 944)	Cancer		95 11.6
				Ischemic heart disease		155 18.9
				Cerebrovascular disease		60 7.3
				Chronic pulmonary disease		133 16.2
				Peptic ulcer		55 6.7
				Diabetes mellitus		73 8.9
				Prostate disorder		118 18.3
				Death by suicide		
Nilsson et al. (2002)	Stockholm, Switzerland	Case-control study (1980–1989)	Cases/deceased N = 148 Controls/alive N = 171	Epilepsy 148	100.0	Death by suicide 26 17.6
				171	100.0	Possible/Undetermined suicide 49 28.7

*Where physical illness was of major importance in the suicide.

Table 2 Non-fatal suicidal behaviour in patients with physical illnesses.

Source	Location	Study Design	No. of participants	Physical illness (PI) subtype		Participants with PI who completed suicide (CS)	
				N	%	N	%
Allebech & Bolund (1991)	Stockholm, Switzerland	Register study/Follow-up	59845	Cancer 3744	6.3	196	5.24
Goldston et al. (1994)	Pittsburgh, USA	Follow-up study	95	Insulin-Dependent Diabetes Mellitus (IDDM) 95	100.0	ATS shortly after diagnosis 0.0	0.0
						ATS after onset 6	7.3
Skoog et al. (1996)	Gothenburg, Switzerland	Cross-sectional	345	Myocardial infarction		–	32.1
				Peptic ulcer		–	31.7
				3 defined physical illnesses		–	21,4
Forsell et al. (1997)	Stockholm, Switzerland	Cross-sectional	969	Major health problem 279	28.8	Fleeting SI (N = 105) 36	34.5
						Common SI (N = 24) 9	37.5
De Leo et al. (1999a)	15 centres from 13 European countries	Cross-sectional multi-centre study	1269	Any physical illness 517	48.0	283	55.0*
Akechi et al.(1999)	Kashiwa, Japan	Register study	362	Cancer 14	3.9	3	37.5
Druss & Pincus (2000)	USA	Cross-sectional	7589	Any physical illness 1901	25	169	8.9
				2 physical illnesses 406	5.3	65	16.2
				Asthma 504	6.6	94	18.7
				Chronic bronchitis 271	3.6	49	18.4
				Cancer 66	0.9	14	22.6

Table 2 continued.

Source	Location	Study Design	No. of partici-pants	Physical Illness (PI) subtype		Participants with PI who completed suicide (CS)	
Gili-Planas et al. (2001)	Formentera Island, Spain	Cross-sectional (two-stage design)	3815	Any medical illness	48	1.3	6	14.3
Kishi et al. (2001)	Maryland, USA	Follow-up study	496	Stroke	301	60.7	Acute-onset SI (all participants)	
							36	7.3
				Traumatic brain injury	65	13.1	Delayed-onset SI (all participants)	
							56	11.3
				Myocardial infarction	70	14.1		
				Spinal chord injury	60	12.0		
Ikeda et al. (2001)	Houston, Texas	Case-control study	Cases: 153 Controls: 513	Serious medical problem or disability				
				Cases	47	30.7	153	100.0
				Controls	62	12.1	–	

*Where physical illness was of major importance in the suicide.

However, some studies have found suicide risk to be higher shortly after diagnosis for specific cancer sites such as gastrointestinal, upper airways and lungs, central nervous system, breast, male genital, blood and lymphatic system, pancreas and kidney (Allebeck & Bolund, 1991; Levi et al., 1991; Storm et al., 1992). Most studies of cancer sufferers report a higher suicide risk for males, as opposed to female sufferers of cancer (Fox et al., 1982; Grabbe et al., 1997; Henderson et al., 1997). However, some studies have found no gender differences (Crocetti, et al., 1998) and, others still, have found that women present with a higher suicide risk compared to men (Allebeck et al., 1989).

A recent case-control study (Nilsson et al., 2002) investigated suicide risk in persons with epilepsy finding a nine-fold increased suicide risk for individuals with a co-morbid psychiatric illness, and a 10-fold increased risk where antipsychotic medications were used. Among individuals with epilepsy onset prior to the age of 18 years (early-onset), compared to those with onset at the age of 29 years or older, the risk of suicide increased significantly (Nilsson et al., 2002).

Non-Fatal Suicidal Behaviour

Across all studies investigating non-fatal suicidal behaviour, the prevalence of physical illness (generic and specific combined) ranges from 5.24% (Allebeck & Bolund, 1991) and 48% (De Leo et al., 1999a), with a mean prevalence of 33%. The prevalence of physical illness among repeaters may be even more pronounced (55%). Across all types of studies the highest prevalence of non-fatal suicidal behaviour amongst individuals with specific illnesses was found in cancer patients (22.6%) (Druss & Pincus, 2000). Interestingly, the prevalence of non-fatal suicidal behaviour did not differ between younger or older age groups. Though, this is probably due to the lack of comparability between studies, in terms of age and illness grouping, as well as both generic and specific illnesses.

The effects of asthma, particularly at a younger age, and suicidal behaviour are unclear. However due to the potentially chronic, acute, disabling and life-threatening nature of asthma, the risk of suicidal behaviour may increase. Some recent evidence has identified a four-times higher risk of non-fatal suicidal behaviour among asthma patients (Druss & Pincus, 2000).

The prevalence of suicidal ideation also differs between physical illnesses. Compared to the general population, increased levels of suicidal ideation have been observed among insulin dependent diabetes mellitus patients (58.5%) (Goldston et al., 1994) and cancer patients (37.5%) (Akechi et al., 1999), with lowest levels observed among stroke patients (7.3%) (Kishi et al., 2001). The results of previous studies, however, have yielded a remarkably lower prevalence of suicidal ideation. For example, the prevalence of suicidal ideation among primary care patients (Lish et al., 1996), and urban medical outpatients (Zimmerman et al., 1995) ranged from

2% to 7%. Further fluctuations of suicidal ideation exist among the general population, with life prevalence ranging from 4.8% (Paykel et al., 1974) to 15% (Schwab et al., 1972). However, it is probable that the high prevalence of suicidal ideation reported in these studies is not entirely associated with physical illness. For example, Forsell and colleagues (1997) found that 50% of elderly subjects who had frequent suicidal ideation also suffered from major depression. Thus, it appears that populations suffering from physical illness, as opposed to the general population, may experience increased levels of suicidal ideation as a result of a concurrent psychiatric disorder.

With overall regard to methodological design and the studies presented in Table 2, those that have measured physical illness as a generic entity, as opposed to those measuring specific illnesses, have demonstrated seemingly higher frequencies of non-fatal suicidal behaviour. This pattern can be seen also with regard to the prevalence of suicidal ideation. The reasons for such variation in findings may be attributed to the fact that the individual effects of specific illnesses may not be accounted for when combined as a 'generic' illness. Different illnesses may result in unique outcomes, particularly in relation to well being, participation in activities and quality of life (De Leo et al., 1999a). Thus, the differential psychological and physical impact of a specific illness on an individual may result in an overall additive effect, particularly in regard to psychiatric conditions and suicidal behaviour. Consequently, great caution must be taken when interpreting these findings.

The Role of Predisposing and Precipitating Factors

Whether or not physical illness contributes independently, and/or has a direct influence on fatal and non-fatal suicidal behaviour has been widely disputed. Syme (1977) proposed a framework for explaining suicidal behaviour that includes two conceptually distinct phases, namely "predisposition" and "precipitation." In this model, physical illness is considered to precipitate suicidal behaviour in distressed individuals who may experience several predisposing conditions, which may occur in conjunction with other precipitants (such as trauma, job loss, marital/relationship break up etc). However, the downfall of this seemingly simplistic framework is the disregard of the interactive/reciprocal role of mediating factors, which may have a stronger influence upon suicidal behaviour. For example, Gangat and colleagues (1987) found that of people who died by suicide and also had a physical illness prior to death, 65% were taking a prescribed medication that is renown for its potential to induce depression. Therefore, it was suggested that, at least in part, the influence of physical illness as a risk factor for suicide might in fact be overestimated. As well as this, the impact of a previous history of non-fatal suicidal behaviour is also important, as it has been shown to be more common among individuals with a physical illness (55%) compared to individuals not suffering from a physical illness (49%) (De Leo et al., 1999a). Thus, the impact of physical illness upon suicide, when examined closely is far more complex. Furthermore, a design based on this framework does not permit for a distinction between precipitating and predisposing events to be made, nor does it distinguish the changing role of factors based on individual attributes. This makes it considerably more difficult to generalise findings across individuals with specific illnesses and of different age groups. Nonetheless, the analysis of predisposing and precipitating factors requires high scrutiny and an acknowledgement of the possibility that the same factors may interact or mediate themselves differently between individuals, and at different stages of life.

The Stress-Diathesis Model

A more sophisticated approach for understanding suicidal behaviour is the stress-diathesis model (Mann et al., 1999). In this model, genetic influences and other factors that render an individual vulnerable to suicidal behaviour may predispose an individual to suicidal behaviour. Conditions of a chronic nature, including drug and alcohol use and other psychiatric illnesses, as well as sexual, physical and emotional trauma during early childhood, may contribute to an individual's overall suicidal predisposition (Lönnqvist, 2001). The composite of these factors, together with the individual's ability to cope and respond to stresses including acute physical or psychiatric illness, socio-economic crises, family and/or relationship break-up, and losses are believed to influence the extent to which a person may become suicidal. This model also considers the impact of hormones, neurological factors including neurotransmission, as well and protective factors such as problem solving ability, social and emotional support, and efficient coping skills in altering the individual's ability to respond effectively to stress (Wasserman, 2001). Thus, in this context, physical illness may be considered as a precipitating factor for suicide through limiting the ability of a person to cope.

Physical Illness as a Risk Factor for Fatal and Non-Fatal Suicidal Behaviour

Nature of the Physical Illness

In general, illnesses that are chronic in nature (lasting over time), debilitating (interfering with activities of daily living), painful (unresponsive to conventional treatments), stigmatising, cognitively impairing, potentially life-threatening (Goldblatt,

2000) and incurable (Harris & Barraclough, 1994) present the greatest risk for suicide. Research has also demonstrated that a chronic progressive course of illness (chronic, and chronic in relapse states), such as that associated with serious neurological conditions, is associated with an increased suicide risk, particularly during the first 5 years after diagnosis (Stenager & Stenager, 1992; Harris & Barraclough, 1994; De Leo et al., 1999a). Chronic conditions and those that are chronic in relapse have been directly related to depression. For example, individuals with a diagnosed acute physical illness and a history of non-fatal suicidal behaviour have been found to experience lower levels of depression compared to both chronically ill individuals, and individuals whose condition may be chronic in relapse (De Leo et al., 1999a). Harris & Barraclough (1997) have proposed that some terminal illnesses in the late stages (e.g., some neurological conditions that can result in dementia) may actually act as a "buffer" against suicidal behaviour due to decreased mental ability and organic deterioration.

Goldblatt (2000) suggested that the way in which these characteristics are experienced by the patient might determine the impact of the illness in terms of mood, coping, recovery, and cooperation in their own treatment and rehabilitation. Individual differences in the progression of physical illness, the age of illness onset, gender differences, the degree of disability, and the perceived threat to life imposed by an illness are also important considerations for study designs. These factors combined may contribute to a better understanding of the total stress experience.

Co-Morbid Psychiatric Conditions

Research investigating the link between concurrent physical illness, psychiatric disorder and non-fatal suicidal behaviour has progressed only modestly over time. Some findings have indicated that psychiatric illnesses may form a link between physical illness and suicide. Co-morbid non-organic mental disorders, particularly depressive disorders and substance abuse, may increase the risk of suicide (Stenager et al., 1996). In suicide attempters, present psychiatric illness has been observed in 76% of those physically ill, and depressive symptomatology has been found to differ significantly in conditions that are acute, chronic and chronic in relapse (De Leo et al., 1999a).

A number of cross-sectional and longitudinal studies have found a close relationship between physical symptoms and psychiatric illnesses (Hotopf et al., 1998; Simon & Von Korff, 1991). However, what is not known is whether this relationship is indicative of a reciprocal causal process. Hotopf and colleagues (1998) investigated this relationship and found that the presence of a psychiatric disorder at the time of initial assessment was shown to be predictive of multiple physical symptoms at follow-up. In turn, physical symptoms reported at follow-up predicted a new onset of psychiatric symptoms. In the case of the role of multiple sclerosis (MS) in suicidal behaviour, a probable link between depressive symptoms and suicidal behaviour has been observed (Berman & Samuel, 1990). However, the difficulty in determining whether depressive symptoms preceded the onset of MS, or whether MS may trigger depression, or whether depressive symptoms are an intrinsic part of the illness (i.e., a clinical manifestation of demyelination), remains undetermined. Thus acknowledgement of neurological processes (e.g., neurotransmitter modification and alteration) appears to be a critical component of understanding their role (particularly in regards to psychiatric factors) in suicidal behaviour.

Druss and Pincus (2000) conducted a cross sectional study investigating generic and specific physical illnesses, non-fatal suicidal behaviour and suicidal ideation, and clinical characteristics in a total of 7589 eligible individuals from a stratified random sample. Consistent with other studies conducted in the past two decades, depression and alcohol use were strongly associated with having a physical illness. A lifetime history of depression was more prevalent among people with one (11.3%) or more (20.3%) physical illnesses, compared to people who did not report a physical illness (7.1%). A greater level of alcohol consumption was common among people with one (12.5%) or more (22.6%) physical illnesses. Non-fatal suicidal behaviour and suicidal ideation was reported amongst people with physical illness in 8.9% and 25.2% cases respectively. Controlling for alcohol use, depressive disorder and/or symptomatology resulted in a 1.3 increased risk of suicidal ideation and a 1.6 increased risk of non-fatal suicidal behaviour in individuals suffering from a physical illness. The contribution of depression, alcohol use, and physical illness contributed to increased suicide risk independently of one another, and together provided an additive risk for ideation and attempts. Consequently, the increase in odds of suicidal ideation in those suffering from more than one physical illness was 1.8 times, and 2.4 times for non-fatal suicidal behaviour.

Findings from the WHO/EURO Multi-Centre Study on Suicidal Behaviour indicated that physical illness or disability, and suffering from psychiatric illness were significant triggering factors for non-fatal suicidal behaviour (De Leo et al., 1999a). Of the forty-two percent of respondents in the study who reported physical illness as a precipitating factor, 20% believed it to be a minor, and 22% as a major precipitating factor for non-fatal suicidal behaviour. Psychiatric illness or symptoms were also considered to be a major precipitating factor in 60% of participants who considered physical illness to have a major role in triggering their behaviour. Compared to those without a physical illness, psychiatric illness was reported as a precipitating factor more often by younger (15 to 34 years) and middle-aged individuals (35 to 64 years) suffering from a physical illness than the older age group (65 years and older). Furthermore, these differences were reported regardless of the apparent absence of significant differences in depressive symptomatology (Beck Depression Inventory – BDI scores) for these age groups. A significantly higher BDI score was observed in individuals aged 35 to 64 years, compared to 15–34 years, and significant differences in BDI scores were found for each status of physical illness within this group. This finding is in line with the premise that middle age is apparently a stage of the life span where the incidence of depression is markedly higher. The prevalence of paranoid schizophrenia/psychosis was found to differ in groups according to their illness status, where these disorders frequented more so in those with relapsing physical illnesses (De Leo et al., 1999a).

In a case-control study, Kontaxakis and colleagues (1988) compared the incidence of non-fatal suicidal behaviour among patients with concurrent physical and psychiatric conditions, and patients with a psychiatric disorder only. In the case group, the most frequently reported physical illnesses included cancer and cardiovascular conditions. Findings revealed that patients with a coexisting illnesses (physical and psychiatric), were more likely to have been diagnosed as suffering from organic psychotic disorder or affective disorder, more likely to be older, and more likely to have employed a violent suicide method. Furthermore, the precise effect of psychiatric factors (e.g., depression), particularly in the association between neurological illnesses and non-fatal suicidal behaviour remained unclear.

Patient Reactions to Physical Illness

The subjective experience of the individual suffering from a physical illness is an important consideration in understanding suicidal behaviour. The impact of what is often unexpected news, regarding a diagnosis of acute or even terminal physical illness, may relate to alterations in the patient's psychological, emotional and behavioural state of being. Such a transition may result in a reduction of autonomy, isolation, changes in the individual's perception of him/herself, diminished relationships with family and friends, and negative consequences for daily activities and life style (De Leo et al., 1999b; Breitbart et al., 2000; Filiberti et al., 2001). A lowered self-esteem level (De Leo et al., 1999b) may result either as a direct consequence of reduced mobility, increased dependency and fear, or an apparent deficiency prior to diagnosis. Further studies, however, are required to determine the exact contribution of patient subjective reactions to physical illnesses, and specifically, the association with different types of physical illnesses.

The extent to which a physical illness may lead to suicidal behaviour may, in part, be related to an altering of psychological reaction to treatment course and an individual's subjective perception of quality of life (De Leo et al., 1999a). An understanding of exactly which factors relate to these psychological reactions is important for subsequent treatment and intervention responses. The WHO/EURO Multi-Centre Study on Suicidal Behaviour demonstrated that significant patient perceptions of physical illness might precipitate non-fatal suicidal behaviour in individuals suffering acute, chronic and chronic in relapse (physical) conditions (De Leo et al., 1999a). The study found that those perceiving their physical illness to be either a major or minor precipitating factor for subsequent non-fatal suicidal behaviour had a higher mean age, and higher scores on both the Suicide Intent Scale (SIS) and the Self-Esteem Scale (SES). Age and scores on the SES were shown to have independent discriminatory effects (De Leo et al., 1999a).

The adverse effects of conditions, particularly those that are chronic and potentially life threatening such as cancer and HIV/AIDS, may induce psychological distress, depression, hopelessness, frustration, and irritability, especially in regard to the experience of treatment and adverse physical consequences. It has been suggested that the diagnosis of a severe physical illness, and the associated experience of hospitalisation and/or medical treatment, may lead to a greater increased negative perception of the illness (Hamman et al., 1985). It is also permissible that the severity of depression and anxiety symptoms experienced in response to the diagnosis may be proportionately associated with suicidal thoughts or behaviours (Brent et al., 1986). However, the extent to which other psychosocial factors such as previous experience of illness, family and cultural influences, and premorbid personality variables may impact upon the subjective reactions of physically ill patients is less clear.

Patient Fear

The uncertainties surrounding death may also play an important role in the patient's psychological, behavioural and emotional state, which may, in turn, impact upon prognosis (Goldblatt, 2000). The impact of fear spurn by a physical illness may result in various outcomes of both social and personal detriment. Such outcomes may include dependency on others, stigma and altered perception of others, as well as a loss of dignity, a fear of pain and/or death, and the experience of negative side effects from medical treatment. It is possible that such outcomes may provoke a situational crisis or be implicated in the onset of depressive symptoms. Further, fear of the physical illness itself, and general loss of control over one's life, may increase the risk of suicidal behaviour (MacKenzie & Popkin, 1990; De Leo et al., 1999b, 2000).

Patient Perception of Self-Suffering

The subjective view of self-suffering from physical illness may play an important role in the association between physical illness and suicidal behaviour. The patient's beliefs and perceptions of their illness may act as a link to suicide and constitute a higher risk for suicidal outcomes than merely the illness itself.

In a controlled prospective study of suicide in subjects over the age of 50 years, Conwell and colleagues (1990) investigated the suicidal impulses of cancer patients in relation to patients' beliefs about cancer and death. They found that in eight cases (all males), it was the patient's belief that the cancer played a major role in the decision to end one's own life. Other factors were correlated with the decision to end one's life including an active relationship with a primary care physician, numerous losses, prior experience with cancer or a debilitating disease, and a rigid, self-sufficient personality (Conwell et al., 1990).

The impact of socio-cultural factors on the outcome of attitudes toward assisted suicide and euthanasia was investigated in a survey of 100 patients with terminal cancer (Suarez-Almazor et al., 2002). Albeit the fact that 69% of the sample supported euthanasia and physician assisted suicide, no association between attitude and symptomatologic constructs including pain, nausea, well-being, loss of appetite, depression, or subsequent survival was found. Rather, the authors found that socio-cultural characteristics including male gender, a lack of religious beliefs, and a perception that cancer patients are a heavy burden on their families correlated most significantly with the acceptability of assisted suicide.

Ability to Cope

The role of protective factors in the development, maintenance and outcome of physical illnesses has received minimal attention in the literature. Particularly, the ability of individuals to cope with a physical illness has not been comprehensively studied in relation to fatal and non-fatal suicidal behaviour. In addition, individual strengths and resiliency are not often considered in the progression of suicidal behaviour among the physically ill. It has been suggested that certain physiological, psychological, and behavioural learning elements of coping responses may distinguish between adaptive and maladaptive outcomes in individuals diagnosed with a physical condition (Peterson, 1974). More recently, findings from the WHO/EURO Multi-Centre Study on Suicidal Behaviour have provided invaluable insights on the possible protective role of psychosocial factors including social supports, coping, life events and other protective factors that may operate to lower the risk of non-fatal suicidal behaviour among individuals with physical illnesses (De Leo et al., 1999a). However, a better understanding of individual patterns of coping, and the characterisation of adaptive versus maladaptive coping styles in terms of their impact upon suicidal behaviour is required.

Implications for Intervention, Treatment and Prevention

Risk Assessment

The cumulative results from the literature on physical illness and suicidal behaviour suggest that several risk factors for suicidal behaviour that may manifest in the physically ill ought to be assessed by clinicians. These risk factors include being of an older age, being of male gender (for some illnesses), experiencing a chronic or chronic in relapse physical illness, suffering from a pre-existing depression and/or depressive symptoms that may arise subsequent to the illness, having a history of heavy alcohol use, suffering from an organic disorder, and suffering from cancer, multiple sclerosis, Huntington's Chorea, epilepsy or HIV/AIDS. Furthermore, current research findings indicate that for both young and older aged persons, the period of most increased risk occurs immediately following the diagnosis of a physical illness. It also appears that the specific physical illnesses associated with increased suicide risk are also associated with some psychiatric illnesses, particularly depression.

The literature over the last decade has pointed to the importance of the subjective experience of the patient and his/her perception of the physical illness, and his/her motivations for suicidal behaviour. The patient's subjective accounts of the illness may assist in determining the level of patient fear, rationality, and willingness to participate in treatment, thus providing important information regarding the association between the experience of illness and suicidal behaviour. Furthermore, the impact of the illness on quality of life should be assessed based on the subjective response of the patient. The extent to which the patient recognises the presence and severity of the physical illness, and its association with participation in future life events should be established (Mackenzie & Popkin, 1990). An appropriate time to elicit such information is during assessment of level of hopelessness and future orientation. Also pertinent to this area of investigation is the assessment of patient coping and problem solving ability, including past experiences of coping with stressful life changes or events.

Although it is not clear what role protective factors play in the relationship between physical illness and suicidal behaviour, several protective factors deserve consideration in general suicide risk assessment. It is particularly important to gauge the level of perceived ability to cope, and perceptions of dependency on those who might provide needed support. A thorough understanding of the social, emotional and cultural experience of the illness from the subjective view of the patient is paramount to ensuring a comprehensive and thorough investigation and subsequent management plan.

Further Research

It has been demonstrated that there is a considerable link between physical illness and fatal suicidal behaviour, however, further studies are needed to determine whether it is the illness itself that is responsible for an increased suicide risk. Also, more studies are needed to investigate illnesses that both reduce quality of life and occur more frequently within the population, for example, heart disease, asthma and bronchitis.

The role of psychosocial and cultural factors in predicting suicidal behaviour in physically ill people is not clearly understood. In addition, the role of both psychiatric and psychosocial factors at different phases of physical illness requires further attention in the study of non-fatal suicidal behaviour. It is probable, given recent cross-cultural evidence derived from the WHO/EURO Multi-Centre Study on Suicidal Behaviour, that the subjective experience of a physical illness may have significant impact on the suicidal behaviour of sufferers. Further research into areas such as this, combined with the investigation of coping ability, protective factors and specific illnesses across different ages of the life span, as well as cultural differences, is needed. In addition, recognition of the variation of physical illness prevalence in suicidal behaviour across the life span emphasises a need for more carefully designed and focused studies.

In addition to complications with the conceptualisation of physical illness and suicidal behaviour, there is a lack of sophistication in measurement of mediating constructs believed to perpetuate or 'add' to the risk of suicidal behaviour. Often, the research questions that have been asked in order to estimate risk of suicidal behaviour in this population are based on the implicit assumption that the individual's response to the physical condition is "abnormal." Consequently, operationalisation of the constructs being studied has occurred within a paradigm that suggests a level of abnormality as the outcome of experience of physical illness.

Psychiatric illness has consistently been found to share a co-morbid relationship with physical illness in contributing to suicidal behaviour, particularly, depressive symptoms and/or depressive disorder. Generally, the assumption has been that depressive symptoms experienced by individuals who are physically ill represent a depressive disorder. Thus the symptoms of depression, which provide the basis for the diagnosis of depressive disorder, may be associated with suicidal behaviour in those who are physically ill. However, this framework fails to take into consideration what constitutes *normal* and *abnormal* responses to physical illness and thresholds for the subjective experience thereof.

Hence, a determination of the point at which a "normal" level of depression (i.e., a normal response to diagnosis of illness) in the physically ill person becomes "abnormal" (i.e., an indicator of psychiatric illness, such as depression) is required. In doing so, however, it should be acknowledged that regardless of whether an individual's reaction to the physical illness is perceived as normal or abnormal, the presence of depressive symptomatology nonetheless, requires subsequent intervention and treatment. It is not suitable for the evaluating physician or health care worker to interpret depressive symptomatology as *appropriate* to the individual's physical condition.

Conclusion

A primary focus of this review has been on the chronological changes in the literature and research findings concerning the role of physical illness and fatal and non-fatal suicidal behaviour. Critical methodological design issues that require attention by researchers in this area of investigation have been highlighted. Currently, knowledge of differences between fatal and non-fatal suicidal outcomes in sufferers of physical illness is not clearly understood. While the association between certain illnesses and fatal suicidal behaviour has been demonstrated, these same relationships based on similar methodological designs have not been demonstrated for non-fatal suicidal behaviour. Following the process of inductive research, questions investigating such differences will be dependent upon clarification and validation, firstly, of the differences regarding fatal versus non-fatal suicidal behaviour in the general population. Only then, can the understanding of differences in suicidal behaviours of physically ill populations be clarified.

Finally, it is important to understand and manage suicidal behaviour in this population within a framework that assumes variation between normal and abnormal indicators of psychic distress or disorder. Assessment of suicide risk in this population must consider general risk factors for suicidal behaviour, and more specifically, those that characterise physical illness.

References

Akano, T., Okuyama, T., Mikami, I., Shima, Y., Yamawaki, S., & Uchitomi, Y. (1999). Suicidal thoughts in cancer patients: Clinical experience in psycho-oncology. *Psychiatry and Clinical Neurosciences, 53,* 569–573.

Akechi, T., Kugaya, A., Okamura, H., Nakano, T., Okuyama, T., Mikami, I., Shima, Y., Yamawaki, S., & Uchitomi, Y. (1999). Suicidal thoughts in cancer patients: Clinical experience in psycho-oncology. *Psychiatry and Clinical Neurosciences, 53,* 569–573.

Allebeck, P., & Bolund, C. (1991). Suicide and suicide attempts in cancer patients. *Psychological Medicine, 21,* 979–984.

Allebeck, P., Bolund, C., & Ringback, G. (1989). Increased suicide rates in cancer patients. A cohort study based on the Swedish Cancer-Environment Register. *Journal of Clinical Epidemiology, 42,* 611–616.

Beautrais, A. L., Joyce, P. R., & Mulder, R. T. (1996). Risk factors for serious suicide attempts among youths aged 13 through 24 years. *Journal of the American Academy of Child and Adolescent Psychiatry, 35,* 1174–82.

Beck, A. T., Steer, R. A. Kovacs, M., & Garrison, B. (1985). Hopelessness and eventual suicide: A 10-year prospective study of patients hospitalised with suicidal ideation. *American Journal of Psychiatry, 142,* 559–563.

Benson, V., & Marano, M. A. (1998). Current estimates from the National Health Interview Survey, 1995. National Center for Health Statistics. *Vital Health Statistics, 10,* 199.

Berman, A. L., & Samuel, L. (1990). Suicide among multiple sclerosis patients. *Proceedings of the 23rd Annual Meeting of the American Association of Suicidology*, New Orleans, LA, USA (pp. 267–268). Washington DC: American Association of Suicidology.

Bille-Brahe, U., & Jessen, G. (1994). Repeated suicidal behavior: A two-year follow-up. *Crisis, 15*, 77–82.

Bille-Brahe, U. (1993). *Background documents of the WHO/EURO Multi-Centre Study on Parasuicide.* Document EUR/ICO/PSF 018)

Bille-Brahe, U. (1982). Persons attempting suicide as clients in the Danish welfare system. *Social Psychiatry, 17*, 181–187.

Bille-Brahe, U., Kerkhof, A. J. F. M., De Leo, D. Schmidtke, A., Crepet, P., Lönnqvist, J., Michel, K., Salander-Renberg, E., Stiles, T. C., Wasserman, D., Aagaard, B., Egebo, H., & Jensen, B. (1997). A repetition-prediction study of European parasuicide populations: a summary of the first report from Part II of the WHO/EURO Multi-Centre Study on Parasuicide in co-operation with the EC Concerted Action on Attempted Suicide. *Acta Psychiatrica Scandinavica, 95*, 81–86.

Blumenthal, S. J., & Kupfer, D. J. (Eds.). (1990). *Suicide Over the life cycle: Risk factors, assessment and treatment of suicidal patients.* Washington, DC: American Psychiatric Association.

Bohannon, P. (1960). *African homicide and suicide.* Princeton: Princeton University Press.

Bolund, C. (1985). Suicide and cancer, I: Demographic and social characteristics of cancer patients who committed suicide in Sweden, 1973–1976. *Journal of Psychosocial Oncology, 3*, 17–30.

Breitbart, W., Rosenfeld, B., Pessin, H., Kaim, M., Funesti-Esch, J., Galietta, M., Nelson, C. J., & Brescia, R. (2000). Depression, hopelessness, and desire for hastened death in terminally ill patients with cancer. *Journal of American Medical Association, 284*, 2907–2911.

Brent, D. A., Kalas, R., Edelbrock, C., Costello, A. J., Dulcan, M. K., & Conover, N. (1986). Psychopathology and its relationship to suicidal ideation in childhood and adolescence. *Journal of American Child Psychiatry, 25*, 666–673.

Breslau, N., Davis, G. C., & Adreski, P. (1991). Migraine, psychiatric disorders, and suicide attempts: An epidemiological study of young adults. *Psychiatry Research, 37*, 11–23.

Chenoweth, R., Tonge, J., & Armstrong, J. (1980). Suicide in Brisbane: A retrospective psychosocial study. *Australia and New Zealand Journal of Psychiatry, 14*, 37–46.

Conwell, Y., Caine, E. D., & Olsen, K. (1990). Suicide and cancer in late life. *Hospital and Community Psychiatry, 41*, 1334–1339.

Crocetti, E. Arniani, S., Acciai, S., Barchielli, A., & Buiatti, E. (1998). High suicide mortality soon after diagnosis among cancer patients in central Italy. *British Journal of Cancer, 77*, 1194–1196.

De Leo, D., Scocco, P., Schmidtke, A., Bille-Brahe, U., Kerkhof, A. J. F. M., Lönnqvist J., Crepet, P., Salander-Renberg, E., Wasserman, D., Michel, K., & Bjerke, T. (1999a). Physical illness and parasuicide: Evidence from the European Parasuicide Study Interview Schedule (EPSIS/WHO-EURO). *International Journal of Psychiatry Medicine, 29*, 149–63.

De Leo, D., Hickey, P., Meneghel, G., Cantor, C. H. (1999b). Blindness, fear of sight loss, and suicide. *Psychosomatics, 40*, 339–344.

De Leo, D., Hickey, P., Meneghel, G., Cantor, C. H. (2000). Blindness and high suicide risk? In reply (letter). *Psychosomatics, 41*, 371.

Diekstra, R. F. W. (1982). Epidemiology of attempted suicide in the EEC. In J. Wilmott, C. Mandlewicz, & J. Mendlewicz (Eds.), *New trends in suicide prevention* (pp. 1–16). New York: Karger.

Dorpat, T. L., Anderson, W. F., & Ripley, H. S. (1968). The relationship of physical illness to suicide. In H. L. P. Resnik (Ed.), *Suicidal behaviours: Diagnosis and management*. Boston: Little, Brown.

Druss, B., & Pincus, H. (2000). Suicidal ideation and suicide attempts in general medical illnesses. *Archives of Internal Medicine, 160,* 1522–1526.

Durant, T. M., & Swahn, M. H. (2001). Medical conditions and nearly lethal suicide attempts. *Suicide and Life Threatening Behavior, 32 (Suppl. 1),* 60–67.

Emanuel, E. J., Fairclough, D. L., Daniels, E. R., & Clarridge, B. R. (1996). Euthanasia and physician-assisted suicide: Attitudes and experiences of oncology patients, oncologists, and the public. *Lancet, 347,* 1805–1810.

Fife, B. L., Kennedy, V. N., & Robinson, L. (1994). Gender and adjustment to cancer: Clinical implications. *Journal of Psychosocial Oncology, 12,* 1–21.

Filiberti, A., Ripamonti, C., Totis, A., Ventafridda, V., De Conno, F., Contiero, P., & Tamburini, M. (2001). Characteristics of terminal cancer patients who committed suicide during a home palliative care program. *Journal of Pain and Symptom Management, 22,* 544–553.

Fisher, B. J., Haythornthwaite, J. A., Heinberg, L. J., Clark, M., & Reed, J. (2001). Suicidal intent in patients with chronic pain. *Pain, 89,* 199–206.

Forsell, Y., Jorm, A. F., & Winblad, B. (1997). Suicidal thoughts and associated factors in an elderly population. *Acta Psychiatrica Scandinavica, 95,* 108–111.

Fox, B. H., Stanek, E. J., Boyd, S. C., & Flannery, J. T. (1982). Suicide rates among cancer patients in Connecticut, *Journal of Chronic Disorders, 35,* 89–100.

Gangat, A. E., Naidoo, L. R., & Simpson, M. A. (1987). Iatrogenesis and suicide in South African Indians. *South African Medicine Journal, 71,* 171–173.

Ganzini, L., Johnston, W. S., & Hoffman, W. F. (1999). Correlates of suffering in amyotrophic lateral sclerosis. *Neurology, 52,* 1434–1440.

Gili-Planas, M., Roca-Bennasar, M., Ferrer-Perez, V., & Bernardo-Arroyo, M. (2001). Suicidal ideation, psychiatric disorder, and medical illness in a community epidemiological study. *Suicide and Life Threatening Behavior, 31,* 207–213.

Goldblatt, M. (2000). Physical illness and suicide. In R. W. Maris, A. L. Berman, & M. M. Silverman (Eds.), *Comprehensive textbook of suicidology*. New York: Guilford.

Goldston, D. B., Kovacs, M., Ho, V. Y., Parrone, P. L., & Stiffler, L. (1994). Suicidal ideation and suicide attempts among youth with insulin-dependent diabetes mellitus. *Journal of the American Academy of Child and Adolescent Psychiatry, 33,* 240–246.

Grabbe, L., Demi, A., Camann, M. A., & Potter, L. (1997). The health status of elderly persons in the last year of life: A comparison of deaths by suicide, injury, and natural causes. *American Journal of Public Health, 87,* 434–437.

Green, G. (1995). Aids and euthanasia. *Aids Care, Suppl. 2(7),* 169–173.

Hamman, R. F., Cook, M., & Keefer, S., Young, W. F., Finch, J. L., Lezotte, D., McLaren, B., Orleans, M., Klingensmith, G., & Chase, H. P. (1985). Medical care patterns at the onset of insulin-dependent diabetes mellitus: Association with severity and subsequent complications. *Diabetes Care, 8,* 94–100.

Harris, E. C., & Barraclough, B. M. (1994). Suicide as an outcome for medical disorders. *Medicine, 73,* 281–296.

Harris, E. C., & Barraclough, B. M. (1997). Suicide as an outcome for mental disorders. A meta-analysis. *British Journal of Psychiatry, 170,* 205–28.

Hartkopp, A., Bronnum-Hansen, H., Seidenschnur, A. M., & Biering-Sorensen, F. (1998). Suicide in spinal cord injured population: It's relation to functional status. *Archives of Physical Medicine and Rehabilitation, 79,* 1356–1361.

Henderson, J. M., & Ord, R. A. (1997). Suicide in head and neck cancer patients. *Journal of Oral Maxillofacial Surgeons, 55,* 1217–1221.

Hendin, H. (1999). Suicide, assisted suicide, and medical illness. *Journal of Clinical Psychiatry, 60* (Suppl. 2), 46–50.

Hotopf, M., Mayou, R., Wadsworth, M., & Wessely, S. (1998). Temporal relationships between physical symptoms and psychiatric disorders. *British Journal of Psychiatry, 173,* 255–261.

Hyllested, K., Jensen, K., & Bille-Brahe, U. (1992). Multiple sclerosis and suicide: An epidemiological study. *Journal of Neurology, Neurosurgery and Psychiatry, 55,* 542–545.

Ikeda, R. M., Kresnow, M., Mercy, J. A., Powell, K. E., Simon, T. R., Potter, L. B., Ikeda, R. M., Kresnow, M., Mercy, J. A., Powell, K. E., Simon, T. R., Potter, L. B., Durant, T. M., & Swahn, M. H. (2001). Medical conditions and nearly lethal suicide attempts. *Suicide and Life Threatening Behavior, 32* (Suppl.), 60–67.

Jones, L. J. (1994). *The social context of health and health work.* Basingstoke: Macmillan Press.

Jorm, A. F., Henderson, A. S., Scott, R., Korten, A. E., Christensen, H., & Mackinnon, A. J. (1995). Factors associated with the wish to die in elderly people. *Age and Ageing, 24,* 389–392.

Kerkhof, A. J. F. M., Schmidtke, A., De Leo, D., Bille-Brahe, U., & Lönnqvist, J. (Eds.). (1994). *Attempted suicide in Europe. Findings from the WHO/EURO Multi-centre Study on Parasuicide.* Leiden and Copenhagen: DSWO Press, Leiden University and World Health Organisation, Europe Region.

Kishi, Y. Robinson, R. G., & Kosier, J. T. (in press). Suicidal ideation among patients with acute life-threatening physical illness: Patients with stroke, traumatic brain injury, myocardial infarction, and spinal cord injury. *Psychosomatics.*

Kishi, Y., Robinson, R.G, & Kosier, J. T. (2001). Suicidal ideation among patients with acute life-threatening physical illness. *Psychosomatics, 42,* 382–390.

Kishi, Y., Robinson, R. G., & Kosier, J. T. (2001). Suicidal ideation among patients during the rehabilitation period after life-threatening physical illness. *Journal of Nervous and Mental Disease, 189,* 623–628.

Kleespies, P. M., Hughes, D. H., & Gallacher, F. P. (2000). Suicide in the medically and terminally ill: Psychological and ethical considerations. *Journal of Clinical Psychology, 56,* 1153–1171.

Klerman, GL. (1987). Clinical epidemiology of suicide. *Journal of Clinical Psychiatry, 48,* 33–38.

Kontaxakis, V. P., Christodoulou, G. N., Mavreas, V. G., & Havaki-Kontaki, B. J. (1988). Attempted suicide in psychiatric outpatients with concurrent physical illness. *Psychotherapy and Psychosomatics, 50,* 201–206.

Kyvik, K., Stenager, E., Green, A., & Svendsen, A. (1994). Suicides in men with IDDM. *Diabetes Care, 17,* 210–212.

Levi, F., Builliard, J. L., & la Vecchia, C. (1991). Suicide risk among incident cases of cancer in the Swiss canton Vaud. *Oncology, 48,* 44–47.

Lish, J. D., Zimmerman, M., Farber, N. J., Lush, D. T., Kuzma, M. A., & Plescia, G. (1996). Suicide screening in primary care setting at a veterans affairs medical centre. *Psychosomatics, 37,* 413–424.

Lönnqvist, J. (2001). Physical illness and suicide. In D. Wasserman (Ed.), *Suicide: An unnecessary death* (pp. 93–98). Martin Dunitz: London.

Louhivouri, K. A., & Hakama, M. (1979). Risk of suicide among cancer patients. *American Journal of Epidemiology, 109,* 59–64.

Louhivuori, K. A., & Hakama, M. (1979). Risk of suicide among cancer patients. *American Journal of Epidemiology, 109,* 59–65.

Mackenzie, T. B., & Popkin, M. K. (1987). Suicide in the medical patient. *International Journal of Psychiatry in Medicine, 17,* 3–22.

Mackenzie, T. B., & Popkin, M. K. (1990). Medical illness and suicide. In S. J. Blumentahl & D. J. Kupfer (Eds.), *Suicide over the life cycle: Risk factors, assessment, and treatment of suicidal patients* (pp. 205–232). Washington, DC: American Psychiatric Press.

Mann, J. J., Waternaux, C., Haas, G., & Malone, K. (1999). Toward a clinical model of suicidal behaviour in psychiatric patients. *American Journal of Psychiatry, 156,* 181–189.

Nilsson, L., Ahlbom, A., Farahmand, B. Y., Asberg, M., Tomson, T. (2002). Risk factors for suicide in epilepsy: A case control study. *Epilepsia, 43,* 644–651.

North, C. S., Ray, E.C, Spitznael, E. L., & Alpers, D. H. (1990). The relation of ulcerative colitis to psychiatric factors: A review of findings and methods. *American Journal of Psychiatry, 147,* 974–981.

Padoani, W., Marini, M., & De Leo, D. (2001). Cognitive impairment, insight, depression, and suicidal ideation. *Archives of Gerontology and Geriatrics, suppl. 7,* 295–298.

Paykel, E. S., Myers, J. K., Lindenthal, J. J., & Tanner, J. (1974). Suicidal feelings in the general population: A prevalence study. *British Journal of Psychiatry, 124,* 460–469.

Quan, H., Arboleda-Florez, J., Fick, G. H., Stuart, H. L., Love, E. J. (2002). Association between physical illness and suicide among the elderly. *Social Psychiatry and Psychiatric Epidemiology, 37,* 190–197.

Rihmer, Z., Rutz, W., & Pihlgren, H. (1995). Depression and suicide on Gotland: An intensive study of all suicides before and after a depression-training programme for general practitioners. *Journal of Affective Disorders, 35,* 147–152.

Ross, A. H., Smith, M. A., Anderson, J. R., & Small, W. P. (1982). Late mortality after surgery for peptic ulcer. *NEHJM 307,* 519–522.

Sainsbury, P. (1955). *Suicide in London: An ecological study.* London: Chapman & Hall Ltd.

Schwab, J. J., Warheit, G. J., & Holzer, C. E. (1972). Suicidal ideation and behaviour in a general population. *Diseases of the Nervous System, 33,* 745–748.

Simon, G. E., & von Korff, M. (1991). Somatization and psychiatric disorder in the NIMH epidemiologic catchment area study. *American Journal of Psychiatry, 148,* 1494–1500.

Skoog, I., Aevarsson, O., Beskow, J., Larsson, L., Palsson, S., Waern, M., Landahl, S., & Ostling, S. (1996). Suicidal feelings in a population sample of nondemented 85 year olds. *American Journal of Psychiatry, 153,* 1015–1020.

Stenager, E. N., Koch-Henriksen, N., & Stenager, E. (1996). Risk factors for suicide in multiple sclerosis. *Psychotherapy Psychosomatics, 65,* 86–90.

Stenanger, E. N., Madsen, C., Stenanger, E., & Boldsen, J. (1998). Suicide in patients with stroke: Epidemiological study. *British Medical Journal, 316,* 1206.

Stenager, E. N., & Stenager, E. (2000). Physical illness and suicidal behaviour. In K. Hawton, K. van Heeringen (Eds.), *Suicide and attempted suicide* (pp. 405–420). Chichester: Wiley.

Stenager, E. N., & Stenager, E. (1998). *Disease, pain and suicidal behavior.* New York: Hawthorn Medical Press.

Stenager, E. N., & Stenager, E. (1992). Suicide in patients with neurological diseases: Methodological problems. Literature Review. *Archives of Neurology, 49,* 1296–1303.

Stenager, E. N., Stenager, E., Koch-Henriksen, N., Bronnum-Hansen, H., Stenager, E. N., & Stanager, E. (1992). Suicide and patients with neurologic diseases. *Archives on Neurology, 49,* 1296–1303.

Stenanger, E. N., Stanager, E., Koch-Henriksen, N., Brønnum-Hansen, H., Hyllested, K., Jensen, K., & Bille-Brahe, U. (1991). Suicide and multiple sclerosis: An epidemiological investigation. *Journal of Neurology, Neurosurgery, and Psychiatry, 55*, 542–545.

Storm, H. H., Christensen, N., & Jensen, O. M. (1991). Suicides among Danish patients with cancer: 1971 to 1986. *Cancer, 69*, 1507–1512.

Suarez-Almazor, M. E., Newman, C., Hanson, J., & Bruera, E. (2002). Attitudes of terminally ill cancer patients about euthanasia and assisted suicide: Predominance of psychosocial determinants and beliefs over symptom distress and subsequent survival. *Journal of Clinical Oncology, 20*, 2134–2141.

Sullivan, M., Rapp, S., Fitzgibbon, D., Chapman, E. R. (1997). Pain and the choice to hasten death in patients with painful metastatic cancer. *Journal of Palliative Care, 13*, 18–28.

Syme, S. L. (1977). Behavioural factors associated with the etiology of physical disease: A social epidemiological approach. *American Journal of Public Health, 64*, 1043–1045.

Thakur, U. (1963). *The history of suicide in India.* Delhi: Munshiram Manoharlal.

Verbrugge, L. M. (1989). The twain meet: Empirical explanations of sex differences in health and mortality. *Journal of Health and Social Behaviour, 26*, 156–182.

Vilhjalmsson, R., Kristjansdottir, G., & Sveinbjarnardottir, E. (1998). Factors associated with suicide ideation in adults. *Social Psychiatry and Psychiatric Epidemiology, 33*, 97–103.

Viney, L. L., & Westbrook, M. T. (1981). Psychological reactions to chronic illness-related disability as a function of its severity and type. *Journal of Psychosomatic Research, 25*, 513–523.

Wasserman, D. (2001). A stress-vulnerability model and the development of the suicidal process. In D. Wasserman (Ed.), *Suicide: An unnecessary death* (pp. 13–27). Martin Dunitz: London.

Wells, K. B., Golding, J. M., & Burnam, M. A. (1989). Affective, substance use, and anxiety disorders in persons with arthritis, diabetes, heart disease, high blood pressure, or chronic lung condition. *General Hospital of Psychiatry, 11*, 320–327.

Whitlock, F. A. (1986). Suicide and physical illness. In A. Roy (Ed.), *Suicide* (pp. 151–170). Baltimore: Williams & Wilkins.

WHO (1986). *Summary report: Working group on preventive practices in suicide and attempted suicide.* York, PA: Author.

World Health Organisation (1999). *Figures and facts about suicide.* Geneva: WHO/MNH/MBD.

Zimmerman, M., Lish, J. D., Lush, D. T., Farber, N. J., Plescia, G., & Kuzma, M. A. (1995). Suicidal ideation among urban medical outpatients. *Journal of General International Medicine, 10*, 573–576.

Chapter 12
Addiction and Suicidal Behaviour: Questions and Answers in the EPSIS

Helen S. Keeley[1], Paul Corcoran[1] and Unni Bille-Brahe[2]

[1]National Suicide Research Foundation, Cork, Ireland, [2]Centre for Suicidological Research, WHO Collaborating Centre for Prevention of Suicide, Denmark

Introduction: What Do We Need to Know?

In modern Europe, there are few more emotive topics than those of suicidal behaviour and abuse of alcohol and other substances. The WHO/EURO Multi-Centre European Parasuicide Study Interview Schedule (EPSIS) included questions regarding family and personal history of substance misuse. This chapter will attempt to use the information collected to help us to get a better understanding of the connection(s) between these behaviours.

The literature is suggestive of a strong association between suicidal behaviour and alcohol consumption. The Canadian Task Force on Suicide Prevention reported "the rate of alcoholism among suicide completers may be as high as 21% and as many as 15–18% of alcoholics may ultimately complete suicide" (National Task Force on Suicide, 1994). Alcohol and substance misuse are frequently cited as major risk factors especially in reviews of youth suicide (McQuillan & Rodriguez, 2000). It has been estimated that between 25 and 50% of all suicides are committed by alcoholics and drug addicts (Berglund & Ojehagen, 1998), and that 40% of suicides have presented with alcohol and/or drug misuse (Lejoyeux et al., 2000). Recently there has been increased reporting of a link between suicide and other addictions, e.g., cigarette smoking (Miller et al., 2000) and gambling (Oakley-Browne et al., 2000).

However, the exact nature of the link or links remains poorly understood and results are sometimes contradictory and may vary with age and gender. Depression and alcoholism and their comorbidity are common in Finnish suicide attempters (Suominen et al., 1996). In a cohort of 46 490 Swedish male conscripts, a significantly higher proportion of alcohol abusers were found among the suicide attempters (33%) than among the suicides (10%) and suicide attempters who abused alcohol were less likely to die by suicide (Rossow et al., 1999). The authors concluded that intoxication may have caused an increase in impulsiveness resulting in a higher number of less serious attempts. This may be associated with the fact that the population was entirely composed of young and middle-aged men. Current substance use, even without abuse or dependence, has been suggested as a significant risk factor for unplanned (impulsive) suicide attempts among those with suicidal ideation (Borges et al., 2000). It has been found that completed suicide in alcoholics most often occurs in late middle age precipitated by interpersonal loss and problems with employment (Barraclough et al., 1974).

The association between suicidal behaviour and drug misuse is less well studied than the association with alcohol. It has been stated that there is "a strong relationship between the severity of substance misuse and risk of non-fatal suicidal behaviour" (Neeleman & Farrell, 1997), while a US population study concluded that in predicting suicidal behaviour, the number of substances used is more important than the type (Borges et al., 2000).

Suicidal behaviour associated with misuse of substances is reported far more often among men than among women. An American study found a positive and significant association between per capita alcohol consumption and male suicide rates (Gruenewald et al., 1995). In a study of the role of drugs in suicide, alcohol was found twice as often in male suicides as in female suicides (Ohberg et al., 1996). Cultural influences may provide a more likely explanation of these gender differences than personal history, since it is not likely that, e.g., life events associated with a family history of addiction, would affect men more than women. A study of alcohol abusing youth suicides that reported a gender ratio of 1:5 (F:M) found no gender differences as to the type and degree of stressors (Marttunen et al., 1994).

A question to be addressed is whether the association between substance misuse and suicidal behaviour is a direct one, or whether it is mediated by other factors. A number of explanations for the association have been proposed which may be divided into three main categories (Rossow, 1996).

– The long-term effect(s) of substance misuse is a causal factor in suicidal behaviour (mediated through the effects of neurotransmitters, especially in the serotonergic system; social disintegration; personal losses; depression).
– There is an underlying common vulnerability to both kinds of behaviours, i.e., some people are predisposed to develop both addictive and suicidal behaviour due to life events and traits of personality such as avoidance and/or genetic origin.
– Acute intoxication triggers self-harming behaviour by enforcing depressive cognitions, increasing feelings of hopelessness and reducing internal controls on impulsive behaviour.

A family history of alcohol and/or substance misuse might also predispose towards suicidal behaviour in a number of ways. If a parent or an significant other has addictive problems, there is an increased likelihood that the person has been exposed to adverse psychological stresses during their lifetime, including early childhood. Experiences of social problems, similar to those associated with addictive lifestyles, which might include witnessing violence and suicidal behaviour, have been found to be more common among adolescent suicide attempters with alcohol abuse than among those who are diagnosed with depression (Marttunen et al., 1994). This allows us to understand one way in which those who have had a disturbed family history with an absence of or reduction in parental support are more likely, in their turn, to abuse substances and attempt suicide. The conclusion has been made that experiences of childhood trauma contribute to the initiation of self-destructive behaviour and lack of secure attachments helps maintain it (as would be expected if there was a history of disrupted parental care due to addictive behaviour) (van der Kolk et al., 1991). Another potential explanation is, as mentioned above, that there is a common inherited genetic or personality trait, such as impulsivity, that predisposes the person to either or both addiction and suicidal behaviour.

Another confounding factor is the attitudes towards suicidal behaviour and alcohol and substance misuse in force in the society. In some areas, there may be "cultural prescriptions" for using suicidal behaviour as a reaction to problems or trauma, whereas in others, drinking alcohol may be the more accepted solution (Rossow, 1996). In "wetter" societies, this might lead to fewer completed suicides and more impulsive attempts in the younger men, while there would be a tendency towards completed suicide among older men. Similar gender specific societal influences may also operate to keep the rate of alcohol and substance misuse lower among women, which again might help to explain their historically higher rate of non-fatal attempts.

In summary, it is generally accepted that there is a strong link between the misuse of alcohol and other substances, and the risk of suicidal behaviour. The link has been confirmed in many studies, but the details of how the interaction works in different situations remains unclear. It seems likely, however, that more than one mechanism is involved; for instance, that impulsiveness associated with drunkenness increases the risk of a suicide attempt among younger males, while the long-term biological and social effects of addictive behaviour is a more important risk factor when it comes to completed suicide by older men. The reason why women with a family background of addiction are less likely to develop substance misuse associated with suicidal behaviour than their male counterparts, remains an important question to be answered.

In this chapter, we examine the way in which the EPSIS study may provide some answers to the above questions.

Materials and Methods: What Questions Did We Ask?

Data collected by the in-depth interviews of 1,910 suicide attempters in 16 centres were analysed. All questions relating directly to alcohol and drug use, either personal or within the persons' social network were noted. Some of the scales (see below) were summarised and basic demographic data was also included.

Personal Characteristics

- Age and gender

Characteristics of the Index Suicide Attempt and Prevalence of Previous Attempt(s)

- Method of attempt, i.e., whether self poisoning or self injury or both
- Whether alcohol was one of the methods used in the attempt
- Suicide intent as measured by Beck's Suicide Intent Scale (SIS)
- Addiction given as a reason for the index attempt
- Whether a previous suicide attempt was made

Psychiatric Diagnosis

- Whether substance misuse or other

Psychological Characteristics

- Mean Beck Depression Inventory (BDI) score
- Mean Beck Hopelessness Scale (BHS) score
- Mean Rosenberg Self-Esteem Scale (SES) score (note: the higher the score, the lower the self-esteem)
- Proportion who indicated that they have suffered from anxiety in such a way that it hindered their life

Prevalence of Reported Problems with Addiction

- Proportion who indicated that alcohol was currently a problem
- Proportion indicated by the CAGE screen to be problem drinkers
- Proportion who indicated that drugs/medicines were a current problem
- Proportion who indicated that they were ever addicted to alcohol, drugs or medicines for a year or more

Life Events Questionnaire

Questions regarding personal and family history of addiction, attempted and completed suicide and admission to psychiatric hospital were included. Individual questions which related to "Early childhood," "Later in life" and "In the last year" were re-analysed to produce a summed variable "Ever" that indicated that the event had occurred any time in the person's life. The following questions were included in the analysis:

- Parent ever in psychiatric hospital
- Parent ever died by suicide
- Parent ever addicted
- Parent ever attempted suicide
- Brother/sister ever died by suicide
- Brother/sister ever in psychiatric hospital
- Brother/sister ever attempted suicide
- Brother/sister ever addicted
- Partner ever addicted
- Children ever addicted
- Children ever attempted suicide

Results: What Did We Find?

Personal Characteristics, Gender and Age

Of the 1,910 interviewed suicide attempters, 1,152 were women (60%), 757 men (40%), and one was transsexual. The gender ratio varied significantly between centres ($p < .05$). There were twice as many female as male attempters interviewed in Odense, Emilia-Romagna, Padova, Umeå, and Leiden, whereas in the Helsinki, Sør-Trøndelag, Hall and Cork samples there was only a small majority of women, and in the Gent area there was an excess of male attempters.

The age of the suicide attempters ranged from 13 to 87 years with a median age of 34 years (interquartile range: 25–44 years). In general, the age distribution was skewed with about one in seven aged over 50 years, but the distribution varied significantly between the areas under study (p fs24 .001). The median age ranged from 27, 28, 29 and 31 years in Padova, Oxford, Cork and Gent, respectively, to 39, 39 and 45.5 years in Odense, Stockholm and Emilia-Romagna. Overall, the men and women had the same age distribution.

Characteristics of the Index Suicide Attempt and Prevalence of Previous Attempt(s)

Self-poisoning alone was the method used in four out of every five suicide attempts and self-injury the sole method in 14% of cases, while the remaining 7% involved a combination of methods. The choice of method varied significantly by gender $(p < .001)$. The vast majority of the women (945, 84%) used self-poisoning only, compared to less than three quarters of the men (541, 72%), while men were more likely to self-injure, either alone (men: 133, 18%; women; 125, 11%) or in combination with self-poisoning (men: 77, 10%; women: 60, 5%). Alcohol (ICD-10 X65) was used in combination with other methods in 318 cases (17%), and as a single method in only 17 (1%) of the cases. Alcohol was used more often by men than by women (men; 169, 23%; women: 149, 13%; $p < .001$).

As detailed in Table 1, the methods used for the suicide attempt varied significantly across the 16 centres for both men $(p < .001)$ and for women $(p < .001)$. In all areas under study, self-poisoning was the most common single method used, but, while over 90% of male and female suicide attempters in Sør-Trøndelag and Oxford used this method, it was less frequent in Hall and Würzburg. The frequency with which alcohol was used as one of the methods also varied significantly between the centres for both men $(p$ fs24 .001) and women $(p < .001)$. In the two Italian centres (Emilia-Romagna and Padova) and in three of the Scandinavian centres (Odense, Helsinki and Umeå), the method was uncommon among both male and female attempters, and in Ljubljana among the male attempters. Contrary, in Sør-Trøndelag the majority of both male and female attempts involved alcohol, and the percentage was also high in Gent and among men in Leiden.

From a closed checklist, 535 (29%) of the suicide attempters interviewed gave addiction as a reason for their attempt. More than half of them (289, 54%) said that addiction was the major reason, while to the rest, 246 (46%), it had been a minor reason. Significantly more men than women gave addiction as a reason for their attempt (men: 279, 37%; women: 256, 23%, $p < .001$).

The proportion of male and female attempters who said that addiction was a reason for their attempt varied highly significantly across centres (men: $p < .001$; women: $p < .001$). It was relatively rarely cited by women in the two Italian centres and in Würzburg, Ljubljana and Bern, while it was cited by at least half of the male

Table 1 Characteristics of the index suicide attempt and prevalence of previous attempt(s).

Centre	Men										Women									
	Self-poisoning only		Alcohol as a method		Addiction a reason		Mean SIS score	Previous attempt(s) made			Self-poisoning only		Alcohol as a method		Addiction a reason		Mean SIS score	Previous attempt(s) made		
Bern	18	(62%)	11	(38%)	14	(48%)	15.4	12	(41%)		25	(69%)	7	(19%)	3	(8%)	16.2	16	(43%)	
Cork	41	(62%)	16	(24%)	35	(51%)	16.0	41	(61%)		60	(81%)	8	(11%)	14	(19%)	15.0	43	(63%)	
Emilia-Romagna	15	(83%)	1	(6%)	2	(12%)	18.3	7	(39%)		32	(84%)	2	(5%)	3	(8%)	14.5	17	(45%)	
Gent	39	(65%)	28	(47%)	13	(22%)	15.8	27	(47%)		44	(85%)	16	(31%)	12	(24%)	12.3	27	(56%)	
Hall	13	(41%)	11	(35%)	16	(50%)	16.2	20	(63%)		23	(61%)	8	(21%)	14	(37%)	16.3	21	(57%)	
Helsinki	79	(80%)	3	(3%)	51	(53%)	12.3	49	(53%)		114	(91%)	1	(1%)	44	(38%)	12.9	65	(54%)	
Leiden	40	(87%)	19	(41%)	17	(37%)	12.8	28	(61%)		75	(79%)	17	(18%)	17	(18%)	11.4	64	(69%)	
Ljubljana	13	(57%)	1	(4%)	4	(17%)	16.7	10	(43%)		29	(74%)	6	(15%)	0	(0%)	18.2	17	(44%)	
Odense	38	(79%)	1	(2%)	16	(33%)	15.1	31	(65%)		76	(84%)	3	(3%)	32	(36%)	14.4	59	(65%)	
Oxford	53	(91%)	9	(16%)	26	(45%)	13.4	37	(65%)		86	(95%)	14	(15%)	27	(29%)	1.8	61	(67%)	
Padova	25	(81%)	0	(0%)	5	(16%)	15.0	12	(40%)		69	(93%)	3	(4%)	12	(16%)	12.5	27	(37%)	
Pecs	29	(76%)	8	(21%)	13	(35%)	14.2	23	(61%)		57	(90%)	6	(10%)	14	(22%)	14.2	40	(63%)	
Sør-Trøndelag	39	(98%)	26	(65%)	12	(31%)	12.3	25	(61%)		43	(98%)	24	(55%)	8	(18%)	11.1	27	(57%)	
Stockholm	51	(69%)	20	(27%)	28	(38%)	15.1	32	(44%)		111	(88%)	21	(17%)	31	(24%)	13.4	71	(57%)	
Umeå	26	(63%)	4	(10%)	17	(43%)	14.0	28	(68%)		58	(73%)	2	(3%)	22	(28%)	13.1	49	(61%)	
Würzburg	22	(46%)	11	(23%)	10	(20%)	13.5	20	(39%)		43	(67%)	11	(17%)	3	(4%)	12.8	31	(44%)	
All centres	541	(72%)	169	(23%)	279	(37%)	14.5	402	(54%)		945	(84%)	149	(13%)	256	(23%)	13.3	635	(57%)	

attempters in Helsinki, Hall and Cork, and by more than one third of the female attempters in Helsinki, Hall and Odense. In most centres, if addiction was cited, it was most often as a major reason.

Suicide intent was higher among the male than among the female attempters ($p < .001$). Across the centres, the level of suicide intent associated with the attempt varied significantly for both men ($p < .05$) and for women ($p < .001$). Among the men, suicide intent was low in Sør-Trøndelag, Helsinki and Leiden, and high in Emilia-Romagna, Ljubljana and Hall. Female attempters in Oxford, Sør-Trøndelag and Leiden had, in general, low suicide intent, which contrasted with Ljubljana, Hall and Bern.

The majority of both male and female attempters had a history of previous suicide attempts (men: 402, 54%, women: 635, 57%). The prevalence of previous attempts varied significantly between the centres for both men and women (men: $p < .05$; women: $p < .001$). Two thirds of the male attempters in Umeå, of the female attempters in Leiden, and of both genders in Odense and Oxford had made at least one previous suicide attempt. Among both men and women in Padova, and among men in Emilia-Romagna and Würzburg, less than 40% had previously attempted suicide. One third of the male attempters in Odense, Hall and Oxford and of the female attempters in Umeå, Leiden and Oxford had a history of three or more previous suicide attempts.

Psychiatric Diagnosis

Psychiatric diagnosis varied significantly between the centres for both men ($p < .001$) and women ($p < .001$). An equal number of male and female attempters were not diagnosed as suffering from any psychiatric illness.

Men were twice as likely as women to be diagnosed as substance abusers (men: 24%; women: 12%). The proportion varied, however, from zero in Sør-Trøndelag, Helsinki and Emilia-Romagna for both genders, to just over 30% of female attempters in Odense and Hall and to 47, 42, and 59%, respectively, of the male attempters in Oxford, Odense and Hall.

Problems with Alcohol, Drugs and Medicines

Problems with alcohol were twice as common among men as among women ($p < .001$). Furthermore, one in four men felt that alcohol was a major problem, compared to only 10% of the women. Men and women were equally likely to admit that they had a current problem with drugs and/or medicines, but men were more than twice as likely as women to have had contact with a consultation service for alcohol and/or drug problems (men: 132, 18%; women: 86, 8%; $p < .001$).

Table 2 Psychiatric diagnosis of suicide attempters.

Centre	Men						Women					
	No psychiatric diagnosis		Non-substance abuse diagnosis		Substance abuse diagnosis		No psychiatric diagnosis		Non-substance abuse diagnosis		Substance abuse diagnosis	
Bern	0	(0%)	18	(64%)	10	(36%)	0	(0%)	28	(88%)	4	(13%)
Cork	7	(10%)	52	(78%)	8	(12%)	10	(14%)	55	(75%)	8	(11%)
Emilia-Romagna	0	(0%)	17	(100%)	0	(0%)	1	(3%)	37	(97%)	0	(0%)
Gent	9	(15%)	38	(63%)	13	(22%)	3	(6%)	38	(73%)	11	(21%)
Hall	0	(0%)	13	(41%)	19	(59%)	0	(0%)	26	(68%)	12	(32%)
Helsinki	0	(0%)	55	(100%)	0	(0%)	4	(6%)	60	(94%)	0	(0%)
Leiden	19	(41%)	14	(30%)	13	(28%)	52	(55%)	37	(39%)	6	(6%)
Ljubljana	0	(0%)	17	(74%)	6	(26%)	0	(0%)	38	(97%)	1	(3%)
Odense	8	(17%)	20	(42%)	20	(42%)	36	(40%)	27	(30%)	28	(31%)
Oxford	0	(0%)	31	(53%)	27	(47%)	0	(0%)	70	(76%)	22	(24%)
Padova	1	(3%)	25	(86%)	3	(10%)	4	(6%)	63	(91%)	2	(3%)
Pecs	0	(0%)	28	(74%)	10	(26%)	0	(0%)	57	(91%)	6	(10%)
Sør-Trøndelag	40	(100%)	0	(0%)	0	(0%)	47	(98%)	1	(2%)	0	(0%)
Stockholm	7	(10%)	51	(70%)	15	(20%)	3	(2%)	112	(90%)	10	(8%)
Umeå	0	(0%)	28	(68%)	13	(32%)	0	(0%)	65	(82%)	14	(18%)
Würzburg	0	(0%)	29	(71%)	12	(29%)	0	(0%)	55	(93%)	4	(7%)
All centres	91	(13%)	436	(63%)	169	(24%)	160	(15%)	769	(73%)	128	(12%)

Table 3 Prevalence of current problems with alcohol, drugs and medicines and addiction.

Centre	Men				Women			
	Alcohol a problem now	Problem drinker (CAGE = 2)	Drugs/meds a problem now	Ever addicted (> one year)	Alcohol a problem now	Problem drinker (CAGE = 2)	Drugs/meds a problem now	Ever addicted (> one year)
Bern	6 (21%)	9 (31%)	8 (28%)	13 (45%)	2 (5%)	5 (14%)	9 (24%)	5 (14%)
Cork	34 (52%)	34 (57%)	10 (16%)	34 (53%)	14 (20%)	17 (27%)	13 (19%)	18 (27%)
Emilia-Romagna	2 (13%)	2 (13%)	1 (6%)	1 (6%)	1 (3%)	0 (0%)	13 (35%)	7 (19%)
Gent	11 (20%)	20 (36%)	13 (23%)	18 (32%)	7 (15%)	10 (22%)	15 (32%)	18 (36%)
Hall	16 (52%)	17 (55%)	10 (32%)	19 (59%)	9 (24%)	12 (33%)	6 (16%)	12 (33%)
Helsinki	61 (64%)	59 (72%)	20 (22%)	72 (84%)	42 (35%)	46 (41%)	28 (24%)	48 (52%)
Leiden	14 (30%)	16 (35%)	12 (27%)	25 (56%)	13 (14%)	15 (16%)	20 (21%)	22 (26%)
Ljubljana	6 (26%)	8 (36%)	4 (17%)	10 (44%)	1 (3%)	5 (13%)	2 (5%)	1 (3%)
Odense	20 (43%)	24 (52%)	na	32 (68%)	26 (29%)	30 (34%)	na	37 (41%)
Oxford	22 (39%)	27 (50%)	12 (21%)	29 (50%)	20 (22%)	27 (30%)	11 (12%)	28 (31%)
Padova	3 (10%)	4 (14%)	9 (31%)	7 (23%)	6 (8%)	4 (6%)	12 (16%)	15 (21%)
Pecs	14 (37%)	17 (45%)	2 (5%)	10 (26%)	13 (21%)	21 (34%)	11 (18%)	12 (19%)
Sør-Trøndelag	19 (48%)	21 (54%)	3 (8%)	15 (37%)	14 (30%)	12 (27%)	6 (13%)	17 (36%)
Stockholm	22 (31%)	16 (23%)	3 (4%)	28 (39%)	23 (19%)	27 (22%)	10 (8%)	30 (25%)
Umeå	14 (37%)	15 (46%)	6 (17%)	17 (42%)	18 (23%)	20 (39%)	13 (17%)	23 (28%)
Würzburg	9 (18%)	11 (24%)	6 (12%)	17 (33%)	4 (7%)	5 (9%)	13 (19%)	8 (11%)
All centres	273 (38%)	300 (43%)	119 (18%)	347 (48%)	213 (19%)	256 (24%)	182 (18%)	301 (28%)

For both men and women, the prevalence of current problems with alcohol and with drugs/medicines varied significantly between the centres (alcohol: men: $p < .001$; women: $p < .001$; drugs/meds: men: $p < .05$; women: $< .05$).

The proportion of male and female suicide attempters having problems with alcohol was highest in Helsinki (men: 64%; women: 35%). About half of the men interviewed in Sør-Trøndelag, Cork and Hall reported an alcohol problem compared to only 10 and 13% in the Italian centres of Padova and Emilia-Romagna, and 18% in Würzburg. Although the prevalence was consistently lower in women, the pattern across the centres was similar to that for the men.

According to their CAGE score, almost one third of the suicide attempters (556, 32%) were problem drinkers. Problem drinking was significantly more common among men than among women (men: 300, 43%; women 256, 24%; $p < .001$).

The CAGE score indicated that the prevalence of problem drinking varied significantly between the centres for both men $(p < .001)$ and women $(p < .001)$. Helsinki had the highest rates for both genders (71%, 41%). At least half of the men in Sør-Trøndelag, Oxford, Odense, Cork and Hall and at least one third of the women in Umeå, Pecs, Odense and Hall were problem drinkers.

About 30% of the male attempters in Leiden, Padova, Bern and Hall and of the female attempters in Gent and Emilia-Romagna had a current problem with drugs and/or medicines. At the other end of the scale, the proportion was less than 10% among the male attempters in Sør-Trøndelag, Stockholm, Pecs and Emilia-Romagna and among the female attempters in Stockholm and Ljubljana.

For both genders and in virtually all centres, the proportion identified as problem drinkers by the CAGE exceeded the proportion who reported that alcohol was currently a problem for them. However, the sensitivity and specificity of the CAGE were high with 84% and 88% of those with and without a current alcohol problem being correctly identified.

In general, the male attempters were significantly more likely than the female attempters to have had a period of one year or more in their life when they had been addicted to alcohol, drugs or medicine $(p < .001)$, but there were significant differences between the centres (men: $p < .001$; women: $p < .001$). A previous history of addiction was highly prevalent among both male and female attempters in Helsinki in particular, and also in Odense.

Psychological Characteristics

In general, female suicide attempters were significantly more depressed, feeling more hopeless and having a lower self-esteem than the male attempters (depression: $p < .001$; hopelessness: $p < .05$; self-esteem: $p < .001$). The levels of depression and self-esteem among men varied significantly between the centres, ($p < .001$ and $p < .001$, respectively) but hopelessness did not. Especially high depression scores were

Table 4 Psychological characteristics.

Centre	Men				Women			
	Depression (mean BDI score)	Hopelessness (mean BHS score)	Self-esteem (mean SES score)	Ever suffered from anxiety	Depression (mean BDI score)	Hopelessness (mean BHS score)	Self-esteem (mean SES score)	Ever suffered from anxiety
Bern	2.1	9.2	22.4	14 (48%)	17.3	1.7	23.5	13 (35%)
Cork	25.5	1.5	25.7	35 (55%)	27.7	1.9	27.4	42 (63%)
Emilia-Romagna	12.3	9.3	23.3	3 (17%)	23.1	12.2	25.5	13 (35%)
Gent	23.8	1.7	25.4	21 (37%)	27.0	1.8	27.4	27 (54%)
Hall	21.9	9.8	23.3	12 (38%)	24.9	11.2	24.7	8 (22%)
Helsinki	19.5	na	25.9	29 (53%)	23.2	na	27.6	48 (61%)
Leiden	22.8	1.5	25.2	15 (33%)	25.6	1.6	27.4	51 (60%)
Ljubljana	23.4	9.0	25.5	8 (35%)	21.8	9.7	25.4	8 (20%)
Odense	28.1	8.5	25.5	9 (20%)	29.5	8.4	25.6	34 (38%)
Oxford	24.5	12.5	27.4	31 (54%)	28.6	12.6	28.9	49 (56%)
Padova	23.9	1.1	25.2	14 (47%)	24.0	12.5	26.0	41 (60%)
Pecs	23.8	1.2	26.5	10 (26%)	27.0	11.2	27.1	25 (40%)
Sør-Trøndelag	18.3	1.3	25.2	20 (50%)	21.8	1.8	26.1	26 (54%)
Stockholm	2.3	9.3	23.0	15 (21%)	23.1	11.3	26.5	44 (37%)
Umeå	19.1	1.2	24.6	11 (27%)	24.8	11.5	28.3	34 (44%)
Würzburg	19.1	9.9	24.4	23 (45%)	18.0	9.9	23.8	33 (47%)
All centres	22.1	1.2	25.1	270 (39%)	24.7	1.9	26.6	496 (47%)

recorded among men in Odense, which contrasted sharply with the very low scores among men in Emilia-Romagna. The male attempters in the Oxford area had the lowest self-esteem, though only differing significantly from men in the Bern and Stockholm areas.

Among the female suicide attempters, all three psychological characteristics varied significantly across the centres (depression: $p < .001$; hopelessness: $p < .001$; self-esteem: $p < .001$). High depression levels were recorded for the women in Odense, Oxford, Cork, Gent, and Pecs, although only significantly higher than in Bern and Würzburg. A similar pattern was shown across the centres regarding the women's self-esteem; low self-esteem was reported from Oxford, Umeå, Helsinki, Cork, Leiden and Gent, particularly in contrast to the levels in Bern and Würzburg. The level of hopelessness among women varied less but was significantly higher in Oxford and Padova than in Odense.

In general, female suicide attempters were significantly more likely than the male attempters to have suffered from anxiety in such a way that it had affected their life $(p < .001)$. The prevalence of such anxiety varied significantly between the centres for both genders too (men: $p < .001$; women: $p < .001$). About half of the male suicide attempters in Sør-Trøndelag, Oxford, Helsinki and Cork suffered from such anxiety as did about 60% of the female attempters in Leiden, Helsinki, Padova and Cork. This contrasted with a frequency of approximately 20% among men in Stockholm, Odense and Emilia Romagna, and among women in Hall and Ljubljana.

Life Events Questionnaire

Table 5 shows the frequencies of a range of addiction-relevant life events experienced by the interviewed suicide attempters. The variation between the areas under study was statistically significant $(p < .05)$ for the majority of variables, but Bonferroni's adjustment indicated that the only statistically significant difference related to the lifetime likelihood of having an addicted parent, an addicted sibling or an addicted partner. Suicide attempters from the two Italian centres were among the least likely to have been related to an addicted person. Almost half of the attempters from the Helsinki area had an addicted parent, whereas this was the case for about 40% from Umeå, Hall, Cork, Pecs, and Ljubljana. About one in three attempters from Helsinki, Umeå, Cork and Odense had an addicted sibling, while an addicted partner was common in Hall and Ljubljana, and in particular in Helsinki and in Odense.

Table 5 Prevalence of life events relevant to addiction.

Centre	Parent in psych hospital P7	Parent died by suicide P13	Parent ever addicted P14*	Parent ever attempted P21	Sibling died by suicide BS25	Sibling in psych hospital BS30	Sibling ever attempted BS31	Sibling ever addicted BS32*	Partner ever addicted Pr36*	Children ever addicted Ch58	Children ever attempted Ch61
Bern	5 (8%)	2 (3%)	14 (21%)	9 (14%)	0 (0%)	9 (15%)	7 (12%)	12 (20%)	11 (22%)	3 (9%)	3 (9%)
Cork	29 (22%)	2 (2%)	50 (37%)	14 (10%)	3 (2%)	21 (16%)	18 (13%)	41 (31%)	21 (25%)	10 (12%)	6 (7%)
Emilia-Romagna	3 (5%)	0 (0%)	7 (13%)	1 (2%)	0 (0%)	1 (2%)	1 (2%)	1 (2%)	5 (12%)	1 (3%)	1 (3%)
Gent	27 (25%)	5 (5%)	29 (27%)	18 (17%)	6 (6%)	19 (20%)	13 (14%)	16 (17%)	20 (26%)	9 (19%)	1 (2%)
Hall	12 (18%)	2 (3%)	29 (43%)	7 (10%)	2 (3%)	6 (10%)	9 (14%)	14 (22%)	16 (32%)	2 (6%)	0 (0%)
Helsinki	25 (18%)	10 (6%)	77 (48%)	12 (9%)	7 (4%)	11 (8%)	18 (13%)	39 (30%)	52 (41%)	na	2 (3%)
Leiden	14 (11%)	3 (2%)	41 (31%)	11 (8%)	3 (2%)	15 (12%)	14 (11%)	25 (20%)	22 (22%)	4 (7%)	3 (5%)
Ljubljana	7 (11%)	5 (8%)	25 (40%)	7 (11%)	0 (0%)	5 (9%)	3 (5%)	10 (17%)	14 (31%)	1 (2%)	1 (2%)
Odense	33 (44%)	10 (7%)	41 (30%)	17 (12%)	7 (6%)	22 (18%)	19 (16%)	39 (32%)	45 (37%)	13 (13%)	2 (2%)
Oxford	21 (15%)	2 (1%)	47 (32%)	24 (17%)	2 (1%)	18 (13%)	24 (18%)	24 (18%)	18 (24%)	4 (6%)	3 (8%)
Padova	11 (11%)	1 (1%)	24 (23%)	8 (8%)	1 (1%)	8 (8%)	6 (7%)	13 (14%)	7 (15%)	1 (3%)	0 (0%)
Pecs	19 (19%)	4 (4%)	39 (39%)	19 (19%)	1 (1%)	14 (15%)	14 (15%)	25 (27%)	22 (27%)	0 (0%)	5 (7%)
Sør-Trøndelag	14 (16%)	0 (0%)	23 (26%)	7 (8%)	2 (2%)	14 (16%)	11 (13%)	18 (21%)	21 (28%)	1 (2%)	3 (5%)
Stockholm	35 (18%)	7 (4%)	58 (30%)	22 (12%)	7 (4%)	26 (15%)	18 (10%)	30 (17%)	41 (27%)	9 (8%)	2 (2%)
Umeå	19 (16%)	2 (2%)	44 (37%)	11 (9%)	1 (1%)	25 (22%)	14 (12%)	39 (34%)	27 (28%)	3 (4%)	3 (4%)
Würzburg	17 (14%)	2 (2%)	30 (25%)	7 (6%)	2 (2%)	17 (16%)	16 (15%)	14 (13%)	17 (19%)	3 (5%)	2 (4%)
All centres	291 (17%)	57 (3%)	578 (32%)	194 (11%)	44 (3%)	231 (14%)	205 (12%)	360 (22%)	359 (27%)	64 (7%)	39 (4%)

na = data not available/question not asked
Significant after Bonferroni adjustment, i.e., $p < .00454545$ (.05/11)

Table 6 Male and female suicide attempters who were problem drinkers compared to those who were not.

Characteristic	Men				Women			
	Problem drinker (CAGE = 2)		Not a problem drinker (CAGE < 2)		Problem drinker (CAGE = 2)		Not a problem drinker (CAGE < 2)	
Self-poisoning as only method	215	(72%)	285	(73%)	211	(83%)	658	(85%)
Alcohol as a method	99	(33%)	63	(16%)	64	(25%)	78	(10%)
Addiction as a reason for attempt	205	(70%)	55	(14%)	149	(59%)	93	(12%)
Mean SIS score	14.4		14.6		12.2		13.7	
Previous suicide attempt(s)	184	(62%)	191	(48%)	184	(72%)	410	(52%)
Mean age	35.6		35.9		36.0		36.1	
Psychiatric diagnosis								
– none	39	(14%)	47	(13%)	30	(13%)	124	(17%)
– non-substance abuse diagnosis	123	(45%)	273	(74%)	121	(52%)	575	(78%)
– substance abuse diagnosis	112	(41%)	51	(14%)	82	(35%)	37	(5%)
Alcohol a problem now	229	(76%)	33	(8%)	170	(66%)	42	(5%)
Drugs/meds a problem now	60	(22%)	53	(14%)	54	(24%)	116	(16%)
Ever addicted (> one year)	220	(75%)	107	(27%)	159	(65%)	127	(17%)
Depression (mean BDI score)	23.3		2.6		26.6		24.2	
Hopelessness (mean BHS score)	1.7		9.5		1.9		11.0	
Self-esteem (mean SES score)	25.9		24.3		27.6		26.1	
Ever suffered from anxiety	121	(45%)	130	(34%)	130	(56%)	333	(45%)
Parent in psych hospital (P7)	45	(17%)	62	(16%)	44	(19%)	119	(16%)
Parent died by suicide (P13)	10	(4%)	13	(3%)	9	(4%)	22	(3%)
Parent ever addicted (P14)	109	(39%)	103	(27%)	113	(47%)	210	(28%)
Parent ever attempted (P21)	34	(13%)	32	(9%)	34	(14%)	83	(11%)
Sibling died by suicide (BS25)	7	(3%)	9	(3%)	10	(4%)	15	(2%)
Sibling in psych hospital (BS30)	42	(17%)	44	(12%)	39	(17%)	89	(13%)
Sibling ever attempted (BS31)	33	(13%)	36	(10%)	38	(17%)	89	(13%)
Sibling ever addicted (BS32)	79	(31%)	61	(17%)	72	(32%)	125	(18%)
Partner ever addicted (Pr36)	50	(23%)	25	(10%)	103	(50%)	161	(29%)
Children ever addicted (Ch58)	3	(2%)	10	(6%)	15	(12%)	33	(9%)
Children ever attempted (Ch61)	4	(3%)	4	(2%)	9	(6%)	20	(5%)

Bonferroni adjustment (significance level = .05/25 = .002)

Comparison of Suicide Attempters, Who Are Problem Drinkers to Those, Who Are Not

As reported above, 40% of the suicide attempters were men, and men made up the majority of the problem drinkers (54%) compared to only one in three of the male attempters (33%) who were not problem drinkers (*p* fs24 .001). Table 6 summarises the aggregate comparison of the male and female suicide attempters with and without drinking problems across a range of characteristics relevant to their attempt as well as their personal profiles and life event history (the differences reported are based on Bonferroni's adjustment of the assessment of statistical significance). The validity of the aggregate comparison depends on the extent to which the differences between those with and without problem drinking are similar across centres.

Both the male and the female suicide attempters, who were problem drinkers, were at least twice as likely to use alcohol as one of their methods to attempt suicide than the not problem drinkers (men: $p < .001$; women: $p < .001$), and they were far more likely to give addiction as the reason for their suicide attempt (men: $p < .001$; women: $p < .001$). Among the female attempters, problem drinkers had a lower level of suicide intent, though not quite significantly so according to Bonferroni's adjustment. Irrespective of gender, the problem drinkers were more likely to have a history of at least one previous suicide attempt (men: $p < .001$; women: $p < .001$) and far more likely to have made at least three previous attempts (men: 26% vs. 11%, $p < .001$; women: 32% vs. 19%, $p < .001$).

Unsurprisingly, problem drinkers were far more likely to have been diagnosed as substance abusers than the attempters with no drinking problems (men: $p < .001$; women: $p < .001$), they were also far more likely to have said that alcohol was a current problem to them (men: $p < .001$; women: $p < .001$) and that they had been addicted to alcohol, drugs and/or medicines for a period of one year or more during their life (men: $p < .001$; women: $p < .001$).

At their index attempt, both male and female problem drinkers had significantly lower self-esteem than those with no drinking problems (men: $p < .001$; women: $p < .001$). For both genders, suicide attempters with drinking problems were somewhat more likely to have suffered from anxiety in such a way that it been a hindrance in their life (men: $p < .01$; women: $p < .01$). Furthermore, they were more likely to have had a parent (men: $p < .01$; women: $p < .001$), a sibling (men: $p < .001$; women: $p < .001$) or a partner (men: $p < .001$; women: $p < .001$) who was addicted.

Discussion

This preliminary overview of some of the data from the EPSIS study will concentrate on the extent to which the results presented have helped to clarify some of the questions posed in the introduction, where we outlined Rossow's three hypotheses regarding the association between substance misuse and suicidal behaviour. While there is little in terms of conclusive evidence, the data, nevertheless, give information relevant to each of the proposed explanations that will be discussed below.

1. Long Term Effects of Substance Misuse as a Causal Factor in Suicidal Behaviour

Close to 30% of the attempters cited addiction as a reason for their attempt, thus implying that substance misuse does contribute substantially to the risk of attempted suicide. As only 17% of the episodes included alcohol intake as part of the method, this would indicate that for the majority of attempters the act was not directly related to acute intoxication. International literature would argue that these effects are more likely to be evident in cases of completed attempts in older people, who have had to cope with the longer term outcome of substance misuse, including substantial losses in the personal, familial, financial and wider social arenas.

2. An Underlying Common Vulnerability to Both Difficulties

The data provided rather impressive evidence in favour of this hypothesis. While a substantial minority (29%) cited addiction as the reason for their attempt, Table 3 shows clearly an intergenerational pattern of substance misuse and suicidal behaviour. An average of 32% of interviewees (varying from a staggering 43% in Hall to 13% in Emilia-Romagna) said that at least one of their parents had been addicted. The wider implications can be glimpsed when one considers that an average of 22% of siblings were also reported as addicts, and 12% had also harmed themselves. The consequences on a person's life of such a family background can be clearly seen in the fact that it was reported that 27% of the partners were also addicted. Given the young age of the population under study, it is also noteworthy that even at such an early stage, 7% of the interviewees' children were already addicted and 4% had made attempts at harming themselves. The degree to which these results are due to *nature* (i.e., genetic and other biological factors) or *nurture* (attachment difficulties and modelling due to early life events), or a combination of both, cannot be decided here. However, it seems that for some families, substance misuse and suicidal behaviour, either separately or in combination, form a large part of their family life-story, and our data therefore strongly underline the importance of further investigations into both current and previous family backgrounds of suicide attempters.

3. Acute Intoxication May Trigger Self-Harm

The hypothesis seems to be validated to some extent by our data. It was not possible to determine the level of intoxication involved in episodes, but we could estimate how frequent alcohol was used as a method. As mentioned above, an average of 17% of the cases involved alcohol, but it was rarely used as the only method. Among men, suicide intent was the same for problem drinkers and non-problem drinkers, but among women, the intent was lower among problem drinkers, a fact that perhaps is related to the greater propensity for alcohol to trigger impulsive attempts among females.

The EPSIS data proved useful as instruments for gaining a further perspective on the question of gender and substance misuse. In all the areas under study, men and women were equally likely to be diagnosed as suffering from a mental disease (87% and 85%, respectively) but men were twice as often as women diagnosed as substance misusers (24% versus 12%). There are, however, questions to be asked about the accuracy of these data from some of the centres. In particular, two of the Nordic centres, namely Sør-Trøndelag and Helsinki, did not diagnose either men or women as substance misusers, which seems highly unlikely as 45% of the respondents from Helsinki and 24% from Sør-Trøndelag identified addiction as a reason for their attempt, and that Sør-Trøndelag was the centre with the highest number of cases involving alcohol as a method (60%.). A similar situation pertained in Emilia-Romagna, in that no one was diagnosed as a substance misuser, although 9% of the interviewed attempters identified addiction as a reason for their attempt.

Another question that requires further clarification is why more of the men than of the women with a family history of alcohol abuse became abusers themselves. A recent report by Lieb et al. (2002) suggests that it is more likely that women will become problem drinkers if it is their mother, rather than their father, who is abusing alcohol. This question cannot be answered by the EPSIS data, because no distinction was made as to which of the parents was an addict. They showed, however, that there was a higher rate of addiction in children of the female attempters, who were problem drinkers, especially when compared with the same group of male attempters (12% vs 2%). While acknowledging that the numbers involved are small, these data could be seen as supportive of Lieb's hypothesis. Given the reduction in the social constraints on female drinking, this is clearly an important area for future investigation.

Implications for Clinical Tests and Treatment

The information provided from this study underline the need for further research in several specific areas such as:

- Family patterns of abuse, especially gender-specific issues
- The relative contributions of biological and social influences to the development of both addiction and suicidal behaviours in subsequent generations
- The degree to which addictive and self-harm behaviours promote or substitute each other is a complex but potentially rewarding area for future investigation

There are also a number of important treatment implications arising from this study:

– The presence of addiction to alcohol and/or other substances should be taken as poor prognostic factors when assessing people regarding risk of suicidal behaviours. Consequently, enquiries into the presence of abuse should form part of routine assessments.

– There may be a case to be made for more integration of the treatment of addiction and other co-morbid factors in those vulnerable to suicidal behaviours. Increased integration would allow recurrent suicidal ideation and/or depressive features to be identified and treated within the context of an established confiding relationship that is allowing the person to deal with addictive behaviours. For historical reasons, among others, these services tend to be separated, but when the conditions interact to the extent shown in this and other studies, this may not be the best treatment model.

– Successful treatment of those who are suicidal must address co-morbid problems and of these, addiction is one of the most common and relevant. One can only echo the Finnish Suicide Strategy who concluded that effective tackling of abuse issues is the most effective way to reduce the levels of suicidal behaviour in a society (National Research and Development Centre for Welfare and Health, 1993).

References

Barraclough, B., Bunch, J., Nelson, B., & Sainsbury, P. (1974). A hundred cases of suicide: Clinical aspects. *British Journal of Psychiatry, 125,* 355–373.

Berglund, M., & Ojehagen, A. (1998). The influence of alcohol drinking and alcohol use disorders on psychiatric disorders and suicidal behavior. *Alcohol, Clinical and Experimental Research, 22,* 333S–345S.

Borges, G., Walters, E. E., & Kessler, R. C. (2000). Associations of substance use, abuse, and dependence with subsequent suicidal behavior. *American Journal of Epidemiology, 151,* 781–789.

Gruenewald, P. J., Ponicki, W. R., & Mitchell, P. R. (1995). Suicide rates and alcohol consumption in the United States, 1970–1989. *Addiction, 90,* 1063–1075.

Lejoyeux, M., Boulenguiez, S., Fichelle, A., McLoughlin, M., Claudon, M., & Ades, J. (2000). Alcohol dependence among patients admitted to psychiatric emergency services. *General Hospital Psychiatry, 22,* 206–212.

Lieb, R., Merikangas, K. R., Hofler, M., Pfister, H., Isensee, B., & Wittchen, H. U. (2002). Parental alcohol use disorders and alcohol use and disorders in offspring: A community study. *Psychological Medicine, 32,* 63–78.

Marttunen, M. J., Aro, H. M., Henriksson, M. M., & Lönnqvist, J. K. (1994). Psychosocial stressors more common in adolescent suicides with alcohol abuse compared with depressive adolescent suicides. *Journal of American Academy of Child and Adolescent Psychiatry, 33,* 490–497.

McQuillan, C. T., & Rodriguez, J. (2000). Adolescent suicide: A review of the literature. *Bolivian Asoc Med P R, 92,* 30–38.

Miller, M., Hemenway, D., & Rimm, E. (2000). Cigarettes and suicide: A prospective study of 50,000 men. *American Journal of Public Health, 90,* 768–773.

National Research and Development Centre for Welfare and Health, Helsinki (1993). *National Research and Development Centre for Welfare and Health. National Task Force on Suicide.* Ottawa: Minister of National Health and Welfare.

Neeleman, J., & Farrell, M. (1997). Suicide and substance misuse. *British Journal of Psychiatry, 171,* 303–4.

Oakley-Browne, M. A., Adams, P., & Mobberley, P. M. (2000). Interventions for pathological gambling. *Cochrane Database Systematic Review* CD001521.

Ohberg, A., Vuori, E., Ojanpera, I., & Lönngvist, J. (1996). Alcohol and drugs in suicides. *British Journal of Psychiatry, 169,* 75–78.

Rossow, I. (1996). Alcohol and suicide – Beyond the link at the individual level. *Addiction, 91,* 1413–1416.

Rossow, I., Romelsjo, A., & Leifman, H. (1999). Alcohol abuse and suicidal behaviour in young and middle aged men: Differentiating between attempted and completed suicide. *Addiction, 94,* 1199–1207.

Suominen, K., Henriksson, M., Suokas, J., Isometsa, E., Ostamo, A., & Lönnqvist, J. (1996). Mental disorders and comorbidity in attempted suicide. *Acta Psychiatrica Scandinavica, 94,* 234–234.

van der Kolk, B. A., Perry, J. C., & Herman, J. L. (1991). Childhood origins of self-destructive behavior. *American Journal of Psychiatry, 148,* 1665–1671.

Chapter 13
Sexual Abuse and Suicidal Behaviour

Ellenor Salander Renberg, Sibylla Lindgren and Inger Österberg

Umeå University, Sweden

Introduction

Most of current models and theories on suicide and suicidal behaviour cover multidimensional aspects, involving both internal and external factors. Earlier life events constitute such factors, and this chapter will deal with the importance of especially one type of life event that has attracted growing attention in research, namely sexual abuse.

Definitions and Prevalence of Sexual Abuse

It is only until the last 20 years that knowledge about prevalence and consequences of sexual abuse has been more generally acknowledged and spread. The prevalence presented varies considerably between studies, probably reflecting contrasting definitions and operational criteria. The definitions can mainly be characterized as being either broad and inclusive or narrow. As an example, the Swedish National Board of Health and Welfare (2000) present a wide and inclusive definition of sexual abuse of children: *"Acts or situations of a sexual nature in which an adult or young person uses a minor for the gratification of his or her own sexual or other needs."* This definition includes both physical and non-physical contact, as well as sexual exploitation of children and young persons in commercial and suchlike contexts. Narrow and strict definitions mainly focus on different sub-groups, with a continuous increase in the severity of the abuse, ranging from speech and gestures to penetration (Coll et al., 1998; Haugaard, 2000). Consequently, there is no definite consensus in how to define and measure childhood sexual abuse, ultimately reflected in a situation where the meaning of all three terms involved, *childhood, sexual* and *abuse*, are actually operationalized differently (Haugaard, 2000) in literature and research. Childhood is, in some studies, defined as below 18, in others below 16 or below 15. Sexual behaviour can, as already mentioned, be defined as acts or gestures, speech or as being exposed to sexual acts. Finally, the definition of abuse diverges, and mainly concerns whether a situation actually causes direct harm or not. This is especially in focus when describing short-term and long-term consequences of childhood sexual abuse. Also, depending on the population under study, prevalence of sexual abuse varies. In general population surveys, about 8–13% of women and about 3% of men report experiences of sexual abuse during childhood (Ernst et al., 1993; Molnar et al., 2001; Romans et al., 1995). In psychiatric populations the prevalence is higher. Palmer and colleagues (1993) and Wurr and Patridge (1996) report that about 33–50% of female psychiatric patients have experienced sexual abuse during childhood.

Associations Between Suicidal Behaviour and Sexual Abuse

There are basically two approaches addressing the relationship between suicidal behaviour and sexual abuse: how common suicidal behaviour is among those abused, and how common sexual abuse is among persons involved in suicidal acts. With the first alternative, different studies have shown that there is an overrepresentation of suicidal behaviours among those abused. In a study from Switzerland (Ernst et al., 1993), suicide attempts were about five times more common among those sexually abused during childhood as compared to the non-abused, and in a study from New Zealand (Romans et al., 1995), about 9% of sexually abused women reported a history of deliberate self-harm, as compared to 3% in the non-abused group. In a review of studies conducted between 1988 and 1998 (Santa Mina & Gallop, 1998), the odds ratio for suicide attempts among adults reporting childhood sexual abuse was estimated to be 1.3 to 25.6 times higher than among the non-abused. Concerning the latter approach, sexual abuse among suicide attempters, prevalence presented in different studies also varies considerably. Coll and colleagues (1998) reported for a group of female overdose patients in England a prevalence of sexual abuse in childhood of about 73% when using a broad definition, and about 51% when using a more narrow definition. In a recent study (Coll et al., 2001), the same authors showed that female overdose patients were 15 times more likely to have experienced sexual abuse than matched controls. Two Dutch studies report on prevalences of sexual abuse among female suicide attempters of 39% (Draijer, 1985) and 50% (Van Egmond et al., 1993). In a Norwegian study, 24% of women and 9% of men admitted to hospital after a suicide attempt had experienced childhood sexual abuse (Hjelmeland & Bjerke, 1996). Again, differences in prevalence are probably due to differences in data collection procedures, definitions and the populations under study, as well as the time frame studied.

Consequences of Sexual Abuse

It is evident that the prevalence and associations presented reveal a considerable overlap between sexual abuse and suicide attempts, clearly demonstrating increased risk for self-destructive behaviour in the group of sexually abused persons. Therefore, it is important to look more clearly at the specific consequences of sexual abuse with regard to suicidal behaviour. There are authors who argue that sexual abuse during childhood should be considered as an extremely serious life event, to be compared with those experienced by soldiers at war or survivors from concentration camps or hostages (Finkelhor & Browne, 1985; Herman, 1992; Silverman et al., 1996). Finkelhor and Browne's model (1985) of the development of the trauma associated with sexual abuse describes the potential impact of the child as including sexual traumatisation, betrayal by the adult, stigmatization and powerlessness, with an increased risk for self-destructive behaviour and suicide. The long-term psychological consequences of childhood sexual abuse described in the literature are depressive symptoms, low self-esteem, anxiety syndromes, guilt, sleep disturbances, substance abuse, somatisation, sexual problems and self-injuries (e.g., Briere & Runtz, 1988; Malinosky-Rummel & Hansen, 1993), as well as dissociative experiences (Anderson et al., 1993). The high prevalence of sexual abuse among psychiatric patients confirm these severe psychological consequences, as well as studies showing that childhood sexual abuse is linked to most major psychiatric disorders (e.g., Molnar et al., 2001; Fergusson et al., 1996), and to post-traumatic stress disorder (PTSD) (Herman, 1992; Winfield et al., 1990). In this context, Herman (1992) argues that many traumatized persons are inaccurately diagnosed as having borderline personality disorder (BPD) or multiple personality disorder (MPD), instead of PTSD, and consequently, do not receive adequate treatment, i.e., not sufficient support to work through the trauma. However, researchers have also discussed the sequel link and the role of psychopathology, as well as adverse family, social and interpersonal experiences, as being mediating factors (Molnar et al., 2001), suggesting some caution in interpreting any simplistic etiological relationships.

Findings from the WHO/EURO Study on Suicidal Behaviour

Within the WHO/EURO Multi-Centre Study on Suicidal Behaviour (Bille-Brahe, 1999; Bille-Brahe et al., 1997), involving several European regions, consecutive cases of attempted suicide attending health facilities were approached. The study has been described in detail elsewhere, as well as participating regions (Bille-Brahe et al., 1996; Bille-Brahe et al., 1999). This non-selected material of suicide attempters of both genders, based on common definitions and data collection procedures, offers unique possibilities for cross-cultural comparisons. In one part of the study, a comprehensive interview instrument, the EPSIS (European Parasuicide Study Interview Schedule) (Kerkhof et al., 1989), was applied, including a questionnaire on life-events as one of several instruments. This questionnaire, which was filled in by the respondent in the presence of an interviewer, included, among other aspects, a number of questions on sexual abuse, referring to different periods in life: during childhood (–15 years of age), later in life and in the last year. The specific questions on sexual abuse included in the instrument are presented in Table 1.

The questions cover different types of forced sexual activities (including intercourse, other sexual activities, prostitution and rape) related to different persons (parents, siblings, partner, others) and to three different periods in life. In the following presentation, childhood sexual abuse (CSA), refers to reporting on any type of sexual abuse before the age of 16, while adult sexual abuse (ASA) refers to any type of sexual abuse after the age of 15.

The findings are based on ten of the centres participating in the first wave of the EPSIS Study conducted during 1990–1991 (Salander Renberg et al., 1998). Interviews were conducted in the different regions with a total of 1,116 persons, 410 males and 706 females, attending health facilities after a parasuicide. According to drop-out analyses, the group interviewed constituted about 54% of the parasuicide population attending health facilities. With regard to most background factors, the interviewed group did not differ from the total parasuicide population in most centres regarding basic demographic variables such as age and gender (Bille-Brahe et al., 1996).

Table 1 Questions included in the EPSIS covering different types of sexual abuse.

Question area	Period
Forced sexual intercourse by parent	Childhood, later in life, last year
Forced to endure other sexual activities by parent	Childhood, later in life, last year
Forced sexual intercourse by brother/sister	Childhood, later in life, last year
Forced to endure other sexual activities by brother/sister	Childhood, later in life, last year
Forced sexual intercourse by partner	Later in life, last year
Forced to endure other sexual activities by partner	Later in life, last year
Forced by partner to prostitute oneself	Later in life, last year
Raped by other person/stranger	Childhood, later in life, last year
Had to prostitute oneself	Childhood, later in life, last year

Prevalence in Different Regions

The total prevalence of CSA and LSA was 11% and 19%, respectively. A proportion of 44% of CSA also reported on ASA, and, reversed, 24% of persons reporting ASA also reported CSA. A total of 29% of CSA cases had experienced more than one type of CSA, and 33% of the CSA group were abused by their parents.

Table 2 shows substantial differences between centres concerning reporting CSA. The total rates vary from 2% in Emilia Romagna, Italy to 17% in Umeå, Sweden. The lowest rates were found in Italy, Germany and Finland, while the highest rates were found in Sweden, Norway, Denmark, the Netherlands and in Switzerland.

The prevalence later in life, ASA, was nearly twice as high as CSA, but the rank order remained stable, except for Helsinki which had a more Nordic pattern, i.e., higher prevalence.

Table 2 Self-reported prevalence of childhood sexual abuse (CSA) among suicide attempters in different regions in Europe.

Centre	Females		Male		Total	
	N	%	*N*	%	*N*	%
Odense, Denmark	16	18%	2	4%	18	13%
Emilia Romagna, Italy	1	3%	–	–	1	2%
Padova, Italy	8	11%	1	3%	9	8%
Helsinki, Finland	3	7%	1	3%	4	6%
Würzburg, Germany	7	10%	–	–	7	6%
Umeå, Sweden	19	23%	2	5%	21	17%
Leiden, The Netherlands	16	17%	3	7%	19	13%
Stockholm, Sweden	20	16%	2	3%	22	11%
Sør-Trøndelag, Norway	9	19%	–	–	9	10%
Bern, Switzerland	5	14%	2	7%	7	11%
Total	104	15%	13	3%	117	11%

Gender Differences

Self-reported CSA was generally about five times more common among females than among males, but with different gender specific patterns in different countries. In Norway (Sør-Trøndelag), as well as in Italy (Emilia Romagna) and Germany (Würzburg), there were no males at all reporting CSA, while in Switzerland (Bern) the female rates were only about twice as high as male rates.

Concerning ASA, the total prevalence was about three to four times higher among females. Exceptions were found in Padua and Bern, where female and male

Table 3 Self-reported prevalence of adult sexual abuse (ASA) among suicide attempters in different regions in Europe.

Centre	Females		Male		Total	
	N	%	N	%	N	%
Odense, Denmark	25	28%	2	4%	27	19%
Emilia Romagna, Italy	7	18%	–	–	7	13%
Padova, Italy	9	12%	4	13%	13	12%
Helsinki, Finland	16	39%	1	3%	17	24%
Würzburg, Germany	12	16%	2	4%	14	11%
Umeå, Sweden	23	28%	5	12%	28	23%
Leiden, The Netherlands	34	36%	4	9%	38	27%
Stockholm, Sweden	30	36%	6	8%	36	18%
Sør-Trøndelag, Norway	19	24%	1	2%	20	23%
Bern, Switzerland	6	16%	3	10%	9	14%
Total	181	26%	28	7%	209	19%
TOTAL	34%	237	9%	38	25%	275

Table 4 Gender-specific comparisons between the group of sexually abused and the non-abused, in childhood (CSA), and later in life (LSA).

Factor	Females		Males		Females		Males	
	CSA N=104	No CSA N=602	CSA N=13	No CSA N=397	LSA N=180	No LSA N=524	LSA N=28	No LSA N=382
Mean age	35 y	37 y	38 y	39 y	36 y	37 y	34 y	39 y
Divorced	37%	26%*	46%	28%	41%	23%***	28%	28%
Motive: wanted to die	76%	74%	54%	76%	77%	74%	75%	75%
Method: sharp object	13%	11%	7%	11%	8%	12%	7%	11%
Previous parasuicide	75%	52%***	85%	51%*	74%	49%***	57%	52%
Psych. inpatient care	63%	49%**	69%	44%	64%	46%***	68%	43%*

χ^2 test: *$p < .05$, **$p < .01$, ***$p < .001$

prevalence's were quite similar, and in Norway where there was a huge gap between the gender-specific rates.

Non-abused Group Versus Sexually Abused Group, Gender Specific

Comparisons shown in Table 4, based on some selected basic characteristics, reveal differences between the abused and non-abused concerning previous parasuicide, psychiatric inpatient care and divorce rates. No significant differences were found concerning age, seriousness of intent, wish to die or use of sharp objects as the method for suicide attempt.

Discussion

For the very first time we have data available for cross-cultural comparisons on sexual abuse among suicide attempters, representing eight European countries. The findings show that sexual abuse is common among attempters, especially among females, which is in line with earlier findings. However, the prevalence is generally rather low as compared to most other studies. Data also reveal substantial differences in the prevalence of sexual abuse in different parts of Europe. Sexual abuse was reported to a higher extent among suicide attempters in northern and some central European regions, while prevalence was significantly lower in southern parts of Europe. Whether these results reflect a true difference in prevalence of sexual abuse or mainly cultural differences in reporting on sexual abuse can be questioned. It is reasonable to assume that the self-reported prevalence, to a certain degree, is influenced by cultural-specific values and norms regarding sexual abuse in the regions, e.g., internalised societal and religious attitudes and taboos, as well as legal aspects. In this respect, cultural specific taboos and values might influence both the occurrence per se and the willingness to report. We can have a situation where sexual abuse is not reported, despite occurrence, or the opposite, where it is not regarded as serious and consequently not reported. We can even expect a situation where there is a total denial that such things ever take place.

Despite good representativeness, according to drop out analyses, there is still a risk for response bias, since nearly half of the group was not interviewed. This is a well-known problem when approaching suicide attempters (Coll et al., 2001), and especially in a cross-cultural setting controlling for response bias is essential, however difficult it may be to handle. It is undoubtedly a methodological strength that common definitions and procedures for data collection have been used, but still additional methodological considerations are to be mentioned. Studies have demonstrated a general inconstancy in reporting on CSA, i.e., a substantial degree of unreliability in reporting mainly consisting of false negative reports, leading to a serious underestimation of the true prevalence of the abuse, which is especially evident for males (Fergusson et al. 2000; Widom & Morris, 1997). In the current study, this phenomena is probably valid for all regions.

Another more specific methodological aspect is the assessment of the impact of using self-reporting scales. In this study, the person filled in the questionnaire him/herself, but in the presence of an interviewer. The participants may have found it easier to give reliable answers in a questionnaire as they had more distance than in a personal interview (Coll et al., 1998). Some interviewers actually reported on situations were the interviewee could report about sexual abuse for the very first time, speaking in favour of the method applied. Of course an opposite situation with over-reporting could also exist. However, the definition applied in current study mainly suggests an under-reporting since the term *forced to* is used in most of the items. It is not certain that the person would agree on that formulation as they could regard themselves as being in part responsible, i.e., implicated in the act and therefore do not consider the act as something they have been forced to do, even using the same defence mechanisms as the perpetrator; normalizing, minimizing, denial, dissociation and depersonalization. One way of getting around this is to ask very concrete questions, describe what actually happened, e.g., touched, pinched or fondled in a sexual manner, and that it was something that the person did not want to happen (Coll et al., 1998).

To summarize the findings, we have found quite high prevalence of sexual abuse among suicide attempters, however, they are probably under-reported, especially in some regions. We have also found substantial gender differences in reporting on CSA, probably overestimated due to higher underreporting among males. With regard the limited comparisons made between those sexually abuse and those not abused, differences were found concerning previous parasuicides and psychiatric contacts, indicating a more manifest self destructive behaviour in the abused group, as well as more psychiatric symptoms. Earlier findings of more unstable personal relationships (e.g., Bagley & Ramsey, 1985) were supported by the higher divorce rate in the abused group. Earlier studies have demonstrated no difference between the abused and non-abused with concern to the severity of the attempt (Brodsky et al., 2001). Severity was not directly assessed in the current study, but our finding of no difference in wish to die between the two groups indirectly confirms earlier findings.

Clinical Implications

The presented results partly confirm findings from other studies of a high prevalence of sexual abuse among suicide attempters, at least in the majority of the centres. Findings reinforce the importance of enquiring about this trauma among suicide attempters. The following recommendations are based on both findings in this study and the clinical experiences of two of the authors (SL and IÖ) and will hopefully serve as a basis for further development and evaluation of interventions directed towards the group of suicide attempters, with special focus on those with experience of sexual abuse.

Recommendations

In the acute phase it of crucial importance to provide immediate management of the acute crisis, i.e., appropriate support during this period. As soon as possible, it is essential to conduct a risk assessment for repeated suicidal behaviours, preferably including a self-assessment by the patient, where protective as well as provoking factors are considered. The assessment should include a thorough analysis and evaluation of the suicide attempt with special focus on earlier suicidal behaviour as well as questions about adverse life events such as sexual abuse. In this context, it is important to take cultural aspects, such as taboos, into consideration when evaluating the responses, including risk of general reporting failure and gender specific reporting patterns. If sexual abuse is reported, it is important to make further enquiries about any possible ongoing abuse, and, if so, immediate steps must be taken to protect the person from further abuse.

The *treatment phase* should besides providing optimal treatment offer continuous risk assessment and provide possibilities for persons with experience of sexual abuse to work through the trauma. It is important to *develop knowledge* and specific competence for management of persons with severe consequences of sexual abuse. It is also important to develop knowledge on the consequences of sexual abuse, involving protective as well as risk factors. Finally, in a clinical setting, increased knowledge of reliable diagnostic procedures for traumatized patients should be targeted, especially with reference to PTSD and sexual abuse.

Conclusions

To conclude, we have for the first time data available for cross-cultural comparisons on sexual abuse among suicide attempters. The main results disclose substantial differences in the reporting of sexual abuse among parasuicide patients in different parts of Europe, and between genders. With prevalence being relatively low, this indicates a general under-reporting. Failure to report sexual abuse should therefore be taken into consideration in a clinical setting when evaluating responses to enquires about sexual abuse among parasuicide patients. Cultural taboos as well as other kind of response biases can probably influence the reporting to a high extent.

References

Anderson, G., Yasenik, L., & Ross, C. (1993). Dissociative experiences and disorders among women who identify themselves as sexual abuse survivors. *Child Abuse and Neglect, 17*, 677–686.

Bagley, C., & Ramsey, R. (1985). Sexual abuse in childhood, psychosexual outcomes. *Journal of Social Work and Human Sexuality, 4*, 33–84.

Bille-Brahe, U., Andersen, K., Wasserman, D., Schmidtke, A., Bjerke, T., Crepet, P., DeLeo, D., Haring, C., Hawton, K., Kerkhof, A., Lönnqvist, J., Michel, K., Phillipe, I., Querejeta, I., Salander Renberg, E., & Temesváry, B. (1996). The WHO-EURO Multicentre Study: Risk of parasuicide and the comparability of the areas under study. *Crisis, 17*, 32–42.

Bille-Brahe, U. (Ed). (1999). *WHO/EURO Multicentre Study on Parasuicide. Facts and figures* (2nd ed.). Copenhagen: World Health Organization, Regional Office for Europe.

Bille-Brahe, U., Kerkhof, A., De Leo, D., Schmidtke, A., Crepet, P., Lönnqvist, J., Michel, K., Salander Renberg, E., Stiles, T. C., Wasserman, D., Aagaard, B., Egebo, H., & Jensen, B. (1997). A repetition-prediction study on European parasuicide populations: A summary of the first report from part II of the WHO/Euro Multicentre Study on Parasuicide in co-operation with the EC Concerted Action on Attempted Suicide. *Acta Psychiatrica Scandinavica, 95*, 81–86.

Brier, J., & Runtz, M. (1988). Symptomatology associated with childhood sexual victimization in a nonclinical sample. *Child Abuse and Neglect, 12*, 51–59.

Brodsky, B., Oquendo, M., Ellis, S., Haas., G, Malone, K., & Mann, J. (2001). The relationship of childhood abuse to impulsivity and suicidal behaviour in adults with major depression. *American Journal of Psychiatry, 158*, 1871–1877.

Coll, X., Law, F., Tobias, A., & Hawton, K. (1998). Child sexual abuse among women who take overdoses, I: A study of prevalence and severity. *Archives of Suicide Research, 4*, 291–306.

Coll, X., Law, F., Tobias, A., Hawton, K., & Tomas, J. (2001). Abuse and deliberate self-poisoning in women: A matched case-control study. *Child Abuse and Neglect, 25*, 1291–1302.

Draijer, N. (1985). De omvang van seksueel misbruik van kinderen in het gezin [The extent of child sexual abuse in the family]. *Maanblad Geestelijke Volksgezondheid, 40*, 587–608.

Ernst, C., Angst, J., & Földenyi, M. (1993). The Zurich Study. XVII. Sexual abuse in childhood. Frequency and relevance for adult morbidity data of a longitudinal epidemiological study. *European Archives of Psychiatry and Clinical Neuroscience, 242*, 293–300.

Fergusson, D., Horwood, L., & Lynskey, M. (1996). Childhood sexual abuse and psychiatric disorders in young adulthood, Part II: Psychiatric outcomes of sexual abuse . *Journal of the American Academy of Child and Adolescent Psychiatry, 35*, 1365–1374.

Fergusson, D., Horwood, L., & Woodward, L. (2000). The stability of child abuse reports: A longitudinal study of the reporting behaviour of young adults. *Psychological Medicine, 30*, 529–544.

Finkelhor, D., & Browne, A. (1985). The traumatic impact of child sexual abuse: A conceptualization. *American Journal of Orthopsychiatry, 55*, 530–541.

Haugaard, J. (2000). The challenge of defining child sexual abuse. *American Psychologist, 55*, 1036–1039.

Herman, J. (1992). *Trauma and recovery*. New York: Basic Books.

Hjelmeland, H., & Bjerke, T. (1996). Parasuicide in the county of Sør-Trøndelag, Norway. General epidemiology and psychological factors. *Social Psychiatry and Psychiatric Epidemiology, 31*, 272–283.

Kerkhof, A., Bernasco, W., Bille-Brahe, U., Platt, S., & Schmidtke, A. (1989). *European Parasuicide Study Interview Schedule (EPSIS) for the WHO (Euro) Multicentre Study on Parasuicide.* Leiden, The Netherlands: Department of Clinical and Health Psychology, University of Leiden.

Malinosky-Rummel, R., & Hansen, D. (1993). Long-term consequences of childhood psychical abuse. *Psychological Bulletin, 114,* 68–79.

Molnar, B., Buka, S., & Kessler, R. (2001). Child sexual abuse and subsequent psychopathology: Results from the National Comorbidity Survey. *American Journal of Public Health, 91,* 753–760.

Palmer, R., Coleman, L., Chaloner, D., Oppenheimer, R., & Smith, J. (1993). Childhood sexual experience with adults. A comparison of reports by women psychiatric patients and general-practice attenders. *British Journal of Psychiatry, 163,* 499–504.

Romans, S., Martin, J., Anderson, J., Herbison, P., & Mullen P. (1995). Sexual abuse in childhood and deliberate self-harm. *American Journal of Psychiatry, 152,* 1336–1342.

Salander Renberg, E., Lindgren, S., Österberg, I., Bille-Brahe, U., Crepet, P., De Leo, D., Hjelmeland, H., Kerkhof, A., Lönnqvist, J., Michel, K., Schmidtke, A., & Wasserman, D. (1998, September). *Parasuicide and sexual abuse – Findings from the WHO/EURO Multicentre Study on Parasuicide – Repetition-Prediction Study (EPSIS).* Paper presented at the Seventh European Symposium on Suicidal Behaviour, Gent.

Santa Mina, E., & Gallop, R. (1998). Childhood sexual and physical abuse and adult self-harm and suicidal behaviour: A literature review. *Canadian Journal of Psychiatry, 43,* 793–800.

Silverman, A., Reinherz, H., & Gianconia, R. (1996). The long-term sequelae of child and adolescent abuse: A longitudinal community study. *Child Abuse and Neglect, 20,* 709–723.

Swedish National Board of Health and Welfare. (2001). *Sexual abuse of children. A survey of current knowledge.* Stockholm: Author.

Van Egmond, M., Garnefski, N., Jonker, D., & Kerkhof, A. (1993). The relationship between sexual abuse and female suicidal behavior. *Crisis, 14,* 129–139.

Widom, C., & Morris, S. (1997). Accuracy of adult recollections of childhood victimization, Part 2: Childhood sexual abuse. *Psychological Assessment, 9,* 34–46.

Wurr J., & Patridge I. (1996). The prevalence of history of childhood sexual abuse in a acute inpatient population. *Child Abuse and Neglect, 20,* 867–872.

Chapter 14
The Importance of Social Support

Unni Bille-Brahe and Borge Jensen

Suicide Research Centre, Odense, Denmark

Introduction

Since the publication in the seventies of reviews reported by, e.g., Caplan (1974) and Cassel (1976), the concept of social support has been frequently discussed in international literature, and "The term 'social support' has been widely accepted within both medicine and psychiatry to denote those aspects of relationships thought to confer a beneficial effect on physical and psychological health" (Brugha, 1988). Furthermore, several studies have shown that social disintegration and lack of social support are major risk factors for suicidal behaviour as well (Bille-Brahe, 1985; Brugha, 1988; D'Attilio et al., 1992; Bjarnason, 1994; Eskin, 1995). The problem is, however, that even though a general agreement seems to exist that there is a "... theoretical basis and strong empirical evidence for the causal impact of social relationships on health" (House et al., 1988), there is very little agreement as to definitions and indicators, how or what to measure, and regarding mechanisms at work (Kaplan et al., 1977; House, 1981; Veiel, 1985; Brugha, 1991). A greater part of the studies reported focus on the access to support, and social support is often measured, as in, e.g., IMSR (Brugha et al., 1987), by how many and what kind of people the individual is surrounded by, how often they meet, what kind of support they have been offered, etc.

In a previous paper (Bille-Brahe et al., 1999), a model for measuring social support was introduced in which social support was seen as an aspect of social integration and as a function of interactions between people. It was therefore taken into consideration that the feeling of being needed by others is as important to the well-being of the individual as having his or her own need fulfilled, and that the way people see things may not always reflect what actually takes place. Consequently, the crucial question is to what degree the individual himself feels that his needs regarding social support are met. In the following, results from the previous study will be briefly reported, and the results from more detailed analyses of the material will be presented.

The Theoretical Background

The theoretical considerations behind the construct of the model were discussed in detail in a previous paper (Bille-Brahe et al., 1999), but as they are important for reading the results, they will be briefly discussed here too. Basically, the construction of the model has taken its point of departure partly in the theory on social integration as developed by Émile Durkheim (1897), and partly by the work of Unni Poulsson Kramer (1981) on what she terms "social anchorage."

The relationship between suicidal behaviour and social integration/disintegration has been discussed elsewhere, where social integration refers to the relationship between the individual and his/her community (Bille-Brahe, 1985, 1987, 2000). Here, the concept also refers to the interaction between the individuals, where the main element is the giving and the receiving of support.

Interaction between people is a complex phenomenon, and one way of trying to understand it is by describing it according to the degree of dependency or interdependency between the interacting persons. Using the terms proposed by Poulsson Kramer, we will discern between *shared*, *balanced*, and *negative* interdependency or reciprocity.

– *Shared reciprocity* refers to the situation where support is given unconditionally – e.g., a person may support another without demanding anything in return. Usually, however, the person expects that if and when he himself is in need of support he will get it. No account is kept, but there is a general feeling of confidence and trust in the existence of those mutual obligations that ensures that one will be supported when needing it. The establishment and the maintenance of this type of interaction imply the adherence to those common norms and values that usually exist within families or groups of friend, among neighbours, and the like.

– *Balanced reciprocity,* on the other hand, is to be looked upon as a kind of trade – people are exchanging services that are more or less of the same value to those involved. Balanced reciprocity is to some degree also based on confidence and common interest, but there is a time element to it; the "pay back" is supposed to take place within a definite period of time. This kind of interaction may take place on a highly personal level, but more often it is referring to interactions in a more neutral and non-personal sense.

– A *negative reciprocity* is in actual fact not an interaction, but rather a kind of one-sided relationship where the function or the task in itself is the only object of the interaction: a person (or a group) is looking for the best bargain, i.e., to get as much as possible for as little as possible. Often this kind of interaction reflects differences in or conflict between interests, and at times a skewed distribution of power, too. Usually, however, it is a question of non-personal or neutral relationships of exchange, such as selling or buying goods or manpower, receiving public benefits, etc. – or for that matter, watching television.

All three types of interactions are normal parts of everyone's daily life, but when we talk about social support as something that may "reduce stress, improve heath, and, especially, buffer the impact of stress on health" (House, 1981), we are obviously concentrating on situations where the type of interaction can be described as *shared reciprocity*, i.e., by mutual, personal interdependency.

Another dimension of interactions lies in the fact that the interaction between people can be both instrumental and expressive, i.e., the tasks or functions carried out can be seen as practical (instrumental) support or emotional (expressive) support (cf. also House, 1981). Furthermore, the interaction may also concern one or several tasks or functions; versatile functions typically taking place within the family or among close friends, where emotional needs are taken care of and practical support is given as well.

Material and Method

Our model for measuring social support comprises four components or dimensions, and all four include information on emotional and practical support, as well as on whether family and/or friends are involved.

The functions and mechanisms of social support have to be seen in their cultural context, and so do people's expectations and perceptions. Therefore, the balance between what the individual needs and his perception of what he gets is used as a kind of "neutral" measure of social support.

The instrument for measuring social support was especially constructed for the Repetition-Prediction Study, and it is included in the European Parasuicide Study Interview Schedule (EPSIS I and II) (Kerkhof et al., 1993a, 1993b.). The Repetition-Prediction Study is a follow-up interview study; the initial interview carried out on suicide attempters within one week after the index attempt, and the second one year after (Bille-Brahe et al., 1996). The material under study comprises information on 937 suicide attempters who completed the initial interview (EPSIS I), and on 535 attempters who completed both the initial and the follow-up interview (EPSIS I and EPSIS II).

Analyses carried out during the previous study on the representativeness of the interview population showed that, in general, there was a disproportionate number of women, both in relation to the total population of suicide attempters treated at the hospitals and in relation to the drop-outs between the initial and the follow-up interview. The mean age of those interviewed was a little lower, but not significantly so; the number of previous attempts was more or less the same, but the interviewed attempters had a longer stay in hospital.

The results presented showed – perhaps somewhat to our surprise – that apparently most of the European suicide attempters under study felt that their need for support was met, and that they also felt that they themselves were needed and able to give the support asked for (Bille-Brahe et al., 1999). Looking at the four dimensions separately, there were significant differences between the areas as to the level of support on some of the dimensions, but when looking at the balance between the dimensions, the differences were surprisingly few. The general conclusion was therefore that, judging by the level of the need for support, there were differences between the areas, but, judging by the individual perception of the degree a person's needs were met, the majority of suicide attempters in the various European areas under study agreed that their needs were met to a great extent.

The results raised, however, several questions. One in particular was about whether gender could be a confounding variable; another was whether the level of social support in some way correlates with the repetition of the suicide attempt.

Results

Table 1 gives an overview of the suicide attempters under study (inapplicable and missing values were excluded.

As in the previous study, the robustness of the material, now divided by gender, was examined using an explorative principal component analyses carried out for each of the 16 variables in the model. The 1st principal component described the general level of the social support (high scores indicating a high level of support), the 2nd component described the importance of who is giving the support, and the 3rd principal component the interdependent impact of the 16 variables. The analyses showed that the material under study had a high degree of consistency. At all centres, the general level of emotional support was of most importance. In most areas, it was also important whether the support was given by family or by friends. Finally, the two dimensions "needing/receiving" and "being needed/giving" seemed to be of some significance.

Carried out on the two genders independently, the analyses showed the same robustness of the material. The 1st principal component indicated that the level of emotional support was relatively more important to men than to women in Odense, Padova and Umeå, and more important to women than to men in Leiden, Stockholm, Sør-Trøndelag and Bern. The 2nd principal component indicated that women in Padova and Umeå, in particular, first and foremost received support from their families. Analyses on the 3rd component showed no differences between men and women as to the interdependent impact of the 16 variables.

Table 1 Overview of the model used and the suicide attempters under study.

	Family			Friends		
	Not at all	**To some extent**	**Very much**	**Not at all**	**To some extent**	**Very much**
EMOTIONAL						
Needing support	142	225	492	146	288	392
Receiving support	218	291	327	164	346	286
Needed for support	211	271	378	209	333	279
Giving support	189	353	292	160	355	273
PRACTICAL						
Needing support	242	288	327	310	333	181
Receiving support	180	260	377	197	305	269
Needed for support	238	268	357	285	326	204
Giving support	182	333	311	192	355	225

Support Within the Family

When looking at the balance between support needed and support received within the family, it turned out that while, on the average, about half of the attempters (52%) were receiving the amount of support they were asking for, more women (39%) than men (26%) did not feel that their need was met – on the other hand, more men (17%) than women (12%) felt that they got more than they asked for ($p = .000$). This was more or less the case in all areas with the exception of Denmark, where, on the contrary, more men than women were dissatisfied with the amount of emotional support they received (44% and 39%, respectively), and more women than men received more support than they asked for (11%, 6%). The differences between the genders were, however, significant only in Padova ($p = .002$), in Helsinki ($p = .004$), and in Stockholm ($p = .003$).

When it came to practical support within the family, the overall pattern showed, to some extent, the same traits: more women than men (22%, 15%) did not feel they received the practical support they needed, and only slightly more men than women (26%, 25%) got more than needed. Here too, there were variations between the centres – it is, for instance interesting to note that in Bern none of the male suicide attempters felt that they did not get the practical support they needed, while in Odense, 25% thought so. The differences between the genders were, however, significant in Bern only ($p = .045$).

As to the dimensions "being needed for/giving" emotional support, there was generally a better balance between the two: on average, 65% felt that there was a balance between how much they were needed and how much they were giving. There were, however, still some differences between the genders: 23% of the female attempters felt that they were not able to give the emotional support asked for, as against only 17% of the men (ns), and there were some interesting variations between the areas. In the two Italian areas under study, Emilia Romagna and Padova, and in the two Scandinavian areas, Stockholm and Sør-Trøndelag, more men than women felt there was a negative balance between what was needed from them and how much they were able to give, while in Helsinki, in particular, significantly more women felt that way.

As to the practical element of these dimensions, there was generally a good balance. On average, 60% felt there were a balance between being needed and giving, and there were no significant differences between the genders. The pattern was a little different though in Leiden, Padova, Sør-Trøndelag and Bern, where there was a disproportionate number of men feeling the imbalance between being needed and being able to give support.

Social Support Among Friends

The overall pattern of social support within the group of friends was to some extent the same as within the family: about 60% felt that their needs both for emotional and for practical support were met. On average, a few more women (29%) than men (27%) felt that they received less emotional support than they needed (ns), while an equal proportion of both men and women (13%) said that they got more than they needed. In none of the areas under study was the difference between the genders significant – except for in Emilia Romagna, where there was a marked difference between the genders.

As to practical support, again somewhat more female than male attempters did not get what they needed (16%–13%), but at the same time, 25% of the women and 22% of the men said that they got more than they needed (ns). There were, however, some differences between the areas. In Bern, a few more men than women received from their friends the practical support they needed; in Emilia Romagna, a few men missed this support, while close to one third got more than they needed. Also in Odense and in Sør-Trøndelag, more men than women did not get quite the support they needed, while more women got more than they asked for.

In general, there was a rather good balance between the two dimensions of "being needed for" and "giving" social support; on average, 70% seemed to be satisfied with the situation, and neither regarding emotional nor practical support was there in general any significant difference between the genders. In most areas, there were some differences between the genders regarding emotional support, but none were significant. As to practical support, in all areas except for in Padova and Umeå, there was a preponderance of men feeling they were not able to give the support expected from them. In Stockholm, the preponderance of men was significant, while in contrast, in Padova, there was a significant excess of women holding this view.

In a previous paper, correlation coefficients were calculated to see whether there would be some kind of trade-off between the two areas of support, namely within the family and among the friends. The results indicated that, in general, no trade-off was taking place – on the contrary, much need for support from family was usually accompanied by much need from friends, and this seemed to be the case in most areas under study. Based on pooled data, all the correlations were significant ($p = .000$), indicating that, in general, trade-off do not take place on any of the dimensions, neither among men nor among women. However, when the calculation is carried out for each area separately, it turned out that a slight trade-off could be seen on some of the dimensions.

Regarding emotional support, no trade-off took place at all in Odense, Stockholm and Umeå, and in Emilia Romagna and Padova, trade-off only took place regarding giving support, and then only among men. On the contrary, trade-off was more common in Helsinki, Sør-Trøndelag and Würzburg, where emotional support from the family was more often substituted by support from friends.

As to practical support, the picture was a bit different. No trade-off took place, not only in Odense, Stockholm and Umeå, but also in Leiden, while in Bern and Würzburg, in particular, trade-off took place on several dimensions. It is interesting to note that in, e.g., Bern, there was no trade-off among men when needing emotional support was concerned, but a significant trade-off regarding practical support.

Level of Social Support and Repetition of Suicide Attempts

Finally, correlations between the level of social support and repetition of suicide attempts were studied. Unfortunately, combining the many variables resulted in

Table 2 Receiving/needing social support by repeated suicide attempts.

	Only index attempt		Attempt(s) only before index att.		Attempt(s) only after index att.		Attempts both before and after index att.		Total
	Obs	Exp	Obs	Exp	Obs	Exp	Obs	Exp	
High under-balance	21	28	23	23	2	4	28	17	72
Some under-balance	41	45	42	38	5	7	29	28	117
Balance	52	46	35	38	8	7	24	28	119
Some over-balance	37	37	26	31	8	6	25	28	96
High over-balance	23	19	19	15	3	3	3	11	48

Pearson χ^2 $p = .051$; Obs = observed values, Exp = expected values

Table 3 Being needed for/giving social support by repeated suicide attempts.

	Only index attempt		Attempt(s) only before index att.		Attempt(s) only after index att.		Attempts both before and after index att.		Total
	Obs	Exp	Obs	Exp	Obs	Exp	Obs	Exp	
High under-balance	13	14	11	12	2	2	11	91	37
Some under-balance	31	39	36	32	6	6	28	24	101
Balance	83	77	69	64	10	11	37	47	199
Some over-balance	33	29	16	24	7	4	20	18	76
High over-balance	14	15	13	13	1	2	11	9	39

many missing values, and the number of persons under study was therefore reduced to 452. Of these, 278 (62%) had attempted suicide more than once (the index attempt).

A social support balance scale based on a probability distribution was developed. The values for each dimension ranged from −2 to +2, and the sum from −8 to +8 (high under-balance −8 to −3; low under-balance −2 to −1; balance = 0; low over-balance +1 to +2; high over-balance +3 to +8). A preliminary cross-tabulation indicated a correlation between the balance on the needing/receiving dimension, and the repetition of the attempt.

The result was supported by a chi square test carried out on the expected values for the two populations (EPSIS I and EPSIS II), the conclusion of which was that the balance between needing and receiving support during the follow-up period has an influence on the pattern of repetition.

A similar cross tabulation, carried out regarding the other dimension of support, namely being needed for and giving support, did, however, not yield any significant correlation. It has to be kept in mind, though, that in both tables, there are problems with very small values in some of the cells. In the following, the suicide attempters are therefore divided in two groups only, namely repeaters and non-repeaters.

From Table 4 it can be seen that there is a significant difference between the repeaters and the non-repeaters on the need/receiving dimension.

Finally, Table 5 sums up the relationship between social support and the risk of repeating the suicide attempt.

The table confirms what has been shown above, namely, that with the lack of social support the risk of repeating the suicide attempt appears to increase. It was, however, somewhat unexpected that the feeling of not receiving sufficient support seems to be harder on men than on women (odds ratios 2.07:1.31).

Among men, the lack of support seems to inflict the overall risk rather than the risk during the follow-up period. On the other hand, receiving too much support

Table 4 Needing/receiving and being needed for/giving social support by repeaters and non-repeaters.

	Repeaters		Non-repeaters	
	Obs.	**Exp.**	**Obs.**	**Exp.**
Receiving less than needed	127	116	62	73
Receiving enough or more than needed	151	162	112	101
Giving less than needed	94	85	44	53
Giving enough or more than being needed for	184	193	130	121

Not enough support, Fischer's exact test 1-tailed = .022; too many demands, Fischer's exact test 1-tailed = .034

Table 5 Social support and the overall risk of repeating a suicide attempt, and the risk during the follow-up period.

	Men		Women		All	
	Overall	**During follow-up**	**Overall**	**During follow-up**	**Overall**	**During follow-up**
Receiving less than needed	p = .028 odds ratio 2.07	p = .340 odds ratio 1.24	p = .159 odds ratio 1.31	p = .142 odds ratio 1.36	p = .0022 odds ratio 1.52	p = .109 odds ratio 1.32
Needing less than receiving	p = .290 odds ratio 0.79	p = .287 odds ratio 1.30	p = .307 odds ratio 0.85	p = .086 odds ratio 0.64	p = .199 odds ratio 0.82	p = .263 odds ratio 0.85
Giving less than being needed for	p = .144 odds ratio 1.59	p = .409 odds ratio 1,17	p = .090 odds ratio 1.48	p = .095 odds ratio 1.48	p = .034 odds ratio 1.51	p = .094 odds ratio 1.37
Being needed for less than giving	p = .488 odds ratio 1.08	p = .080 odds ratio 1.80	p = .211 odds ratio 0.77	p = .431 odds ratio 1.10	p = .309 odds ratio 0.87	p = .135 odds ratio 1.33

seems to decrease the overall risk for men, while too much increases the risk during the follow-up period.

As far as the female suicide attempters were concerned, the overall risk and the risk during the follow-up period were affected more or less to the same extent, with the exception that, as with men, women were more vulnerable during the follow-up period when they were needed for less than giving.

Discussion and Conclusion

According to our previous study, in general, most of the European suicide attempters felt that their need for social support was met to a great extent, and also that they felt they themselves were needed for giving support, and also able to give the support asked for. The first aim of this study was to see if there would be any differences between the genders regarding the four dimensions used in our model for measuring social support, namely needing/receiving and being needed for/giving emotional and practical support within the family and among friends. The results indicate that there are differences between male and female attempters both when it comes to support within the family and support among friends, but – except for emotional support within the family – it is difficult to find any unambiguous pattern in these differences. Looking at the balance (which was chosen as a "neutral" measurement for support) between, for instance, needing and receiving, the distribution on genders varies at times markedly between the areas under study, and this is also the case when it comes to types of support (i.e., emotional or practical), or whether we are talking about support within the family or among friends. It is noteworthy, however, that in all the areas, except for Denmark, significantly more women than men did not feel that they got the emotional support they needed.

As to the trade-off between family and friends, the results show that in some areas no trade-off takes place at all, but that in others, support within family, in some cases, can be obviously substituted by support among friends or vice versa. There are differences between the genders, but again there are no systematic differences between the centres in this respect.

The second aim of our study was to try and see if a lack of social support correlates with the risk of repeated suicide attempts. The results showed that in spite of the apparent general satisfaction among the suicide attempters with the level of social support, the risk of repeating the attempts are affected by the level of social support: the risk increases if the attempter receives less social support than he/she needs, or if he/she is not able to give what is asked or expected from him/her. The fact that these "deficits" have a general influence on the overall risk of repetition underlines the importance of taking the question of social support into consideration when assessing and treating a suicidal patient – in particular male patients, who seem to be especially vulnerable when it comes to the level of social support.

References

Bille-Brahe, U., & Wang, A. G. (1985). Attempted suicide in Denmark II. Social integration. *Social Psychiatry, 20,* 163–170.

Bille-Brahe, U. (1987. Suicide and social integration. In N. Juel Nielsen, N. Retterstøl, & U.

Bille-Brahe (Eds.), *Suicide in Scandinavia. Acta Psychiatrica Scandinavica* (suppl. 336;76), pp. 45–62.

Bille-Brahe, U. (1988). En sociologisk angrebsvinkel [A sociological approach]. In U. Bille-Brahe, N. Juel Nielsen & A. G. Wang (Eds.), Komparativ forskning vedrørende destruktiv og selvdestruktiv adfærd i Norden [Comparative research on destructive and self-destructive behaviour in the Nordic countries] (pp. 102–118). Odense: Odense University Press.

Bille-Brahe, U. (Ed.). (1999). *Facts and figures.* Copenhagen: WHO Regional Office for Europe.

Bille-Brahe, U. (1994). En sociologisk indfaldsvinkel på suicidal adfærd [A sociological approach to suicidal behaviour]. In E. Fleischer (Ed.), *Elementer til et tværvidenkabelig suicidalforskningsparadigme* [Elements of an interdisciplinary research paradigm]. Odense: Odense University Press.

Bille-Brahe, U. et al. (1999). Social support among European suicide attempts. *Archives of Suicide Research, 5,* 215–231.

Bille-Brahe, U., Andersen, K., Wasserman, D. et al. (1996a). The WHO/Euro Multicentre Study; Risk of parasuicide and the comparability of the areas under study. *Crisis, 171,* 32–42.

Bille-Brahe, U., Kerkhof, A., De Leo, D., Schmidtke, A. et al. (1996b). A repetition-prediction study on European parasuicide populations. *Crisis, 171,* 22–31.

Bjarnason, T. (1994). The influence of social support, suggestion and depression on suicidal behaviour among Icelandic youth. *Acta Sociologica, 37,* 195–206.

Brugha, T. S., Stuart, E., MacCarthy, B., Potter, J. et al. (1987). The interview measure of social relationships: The description and evaluation of a survey instrument for assessing personal resources. *Social Psychiatry, 22,* 123–128.

Brugha, T. (1988). The interview measure of social relationship. In C. Thompson (Ed.), *The instrument of psychiatric research.* Chichester: Wiley.

Caplan, G. (1974). Support systems. In G. Caplan, *Support systems and community health.* New York: Basic Books.

Cassel, J. (1979). The contribution of social environment to host resistance. *American Journal of Epidemiology, 104,* 107–123.

Champion, L. (1995). A developmental perspective on social support networks. In T. S. Brugha (Ed.), *Social support and psychiatric disorder. Research findings and guidelines for clinical practice* (pp. 61–95). Cambridge: University Press.

Dáttilio, J. P., Campbell, B. M., Lubold, P. et al. (1992). Social support and suicide potential: Preliminary findings for adolescent populations. *Psychological Reports, 70,* 76–76.

Durkheim, É. (1951). *Suicide: A study in sociology.* London: The Free Press (original work published 1897).

Eskin, M. (1995). Suicidal behaviour as related to social support and assertiveness among Swedish and Turkish high school students: A cross-cultural investigation. *Journal of Clinical Psychology, 51,* 158–172.

House, J. S. (1981). *Work stress and social support.* Massachusetts: Addison-Wesley.

House, J. S., Landis, K. R., & Umberson, S. (1988). Social relationships and health. *Science, 241,* 540–545.

Kaplan, B. H., Cassel, J. C., & Gore, S. (1977). Social support and health. *Medical Care, 15* (suppl.), 47–58.

Kerkhof, A., Bernasco, W., Bille-Brahe, U., Platt, S., & Schmidtke, A. (1993a). European Parasuicide Interview Schedule (EPSIS I). In U. Bille-Brahe (Ed.), *Facts and figures.* Copenhagen: WHO Regional Office for Europe.

Kerkhof, A., van Egmond, M., Bille-Brahe, U., Platt, S., & Schmidtke, A. (1993b). European

Parasuicide Interview Schedule (EPSIS II). In U. Bille-Brahe (Ed.), *Facts and figures.* Copenhagen: WHO Regional Office for Europe.

Lakey, B., & Cassady, P. B. (1990). Cognitive processes in received social support. *Journal of Personality and Social Psychology, 59,* 337–343.

Poulsson Kramer, U. (1981). En tilnærmingsmade for studier av sosial forankring [Approaches to studies on social anchoring]. In *Planleggningssekretariatets rapport: Deltaking og sosial foranking* [Report from the Planning Committee: Participation and social anchorage]. Oslo: Oslo University Press.

Veiel, H. O. F. (1985). Dimensions of social support: A conceptual framework for research. *Social Psychiatry, 20,* 156–162.

Chapter 15
Imitation of Suicidal Behaviour

Armin Schmidtke[1], Cordula Löhr[1] and Diego De Leo[2]

[1]Department of Clinical Psychology, University of Würzburg, Germany, [2]Australian Institute for Suicide Research and Prevention, Griffith University, Brisbane, Australia

Introduction

It has frequently been suggested that suicidal behaviour might be learnt by a process of imitation, especially among children, adolescents, young adults and psychiatric patients (Kreitman et al., 1969, 1970; Schmidtke & Schaller, 2000). Explanations for the temporal clustering of use of particular methods for suicide, or the use of special locations like bridges must also include the social transmission of suicidal behaviour.

Often imitation and identification processes were used to explain clusters of suicides or suicide attempts among special subgroups like schoolchildren, psychiatric inpatients, prison inmates, army units, or people in reservations. The social transmission of suicidal behaviour may also influence a nation's attitude towards suicidal behaviour and thus influence the magnitude of the suicide rate in a country (Fekete & Schmidtke, 1966). Therefore, knowledge of suicidal behaviour in a social environment was frequently regarded as a risk factor in the assessment of suicide risk. Kreitman et al. (1969, 1970) viewed suicide attempts as a form of communication ("a sub-cultural language").

With regard to imitation of inpatient behaviour, in light of earlier accounts, it is evident that the idea of committing suicide can spread among inpatients. There are four main factors contributing to suicide contagion among psychiatric inpatients: (1) suggestion, or the "Werther effect"; (2) breakdown in the professional self-confidence of the staff – after several consecutive suicides, the personnel may lose their professional self-confidence and become insecure. During imitation episodes, the number of employees with lowered self-confidence is exceptionally high. Birtchnell (1983) has noted that the more anxious the therapist appears to be, the more likely the patient is to believe himself capable of self-destruction. When patients sense the insecurity of the staff, they may lose their faith in the possibility of recovery and give up hope (Beck et al., 1985). (3) Propagation of a hopeless atmosphere; and (4) psychotic identification.

Therefore, when an inpatient commits or attempts suicide, this may facilitate others to think of suicide as a possible way of escaping a hopeless situation.

Most inpatient suicides are committed outside the hospital grounds (Taiminen et al., 1992), and this may alleviate the effect of direct exposure on other inpatients. However, the Werther effect can be mediated indirectly via the staff, and even via the press from outside the hospital to the inpatients.

The majority of studies show that imitation has an effect on aggression and suicide (Cantor & Sheehan, 1996; Schmidtke & Schaller, 2000; Schmidtke et al., 2001). However, there are some exceptions, for example, the study of Kirch and Lester (1990), and some investigation results are not too consistent.

In studying imitative and preventive effects, it is necessary to clearly understand the conceptual framework of learning by modelling or imitation. Imitative effects should be distinguished from contagious effects on suicidal behaviour, which are also commonly mentioned in the literature (see, e.g., Phillips & Resnik, 1969, 1985; Steede & Range, 1989). From a psychological point of view, the theory of imitation should be preferred, as its theoretical framework makes it easier to explain some of the findings with regard to imitative behaviours in the field of suicidology, including some that appear contradictory. In contrast to imitation, contagion implies a kind of infectious disease concept, not allowing the "infected" person to act independently and make individual choices. Learning by modelling refers to the acquisition of new patterns of behaviour through the observation of the behaviour of one or more models. Therefore, imitation is not limited to learning from real-life models.

Thus, learning by modelling can be regarded as a function of certain characteristics of both the model and the observer. Personality characteristics of the observer may also moderate the probability of exhibiting the learned behaviour. Stimulating events or motivating processes determine whether responses acquired by observation are actually performed at a specific point in time. In fact, a behavioural strategy learned by observation may be used a considerable amount of time after the observation has taken place, and, in the meantime, even contrary behaviour may occur. As a consequence, films aimed at preventing suicide may cause imitative behaviour (see, for example, Gould & Shaffer, 1986). On the other hand, it is not surprising that extremely publicised mass suicides, such as those in Jonestown, Waco, or in San Diego, and the mass suicides of the Order of the Solar Temple in Canada, France and Switzerland were apparently not followed by imitation effects. At least, in part, this can be explained by the involuntary nature of the suicides (e.g., Kroth, 1984) and the "unattractiveness" of some of the group leaders.

Currently available knowledge indicates that the imitation effects of reported or portrayed suicidal behaviour depend on a number of factors (Schmidtke & Schaller, 2000).

Kind of Behaviour

The most important variable is whether the behaviour shown is real or fictional, and whether acts or thoughts of an individual person or general theories about aggressive and suicidal behaviour are presented. In general, with regard to suicidal behaviour, it is assumed that it is the real rather than the fictional behaviour that more easily generates imitation (Pirkis & Blood, 2001; Stack 2003).

Kind of Model and Observer Variables

Similarities between specific characteristics of the model and those of the observer play an important role, even in learning from symbolic models. The effect of imitation clearly depends on similarities between the model and the potential imitators. This effect was already shown for aggression phenomena in studies by Phillips and co-workers: after boxing contests, the level of aggression depended on whether a white person or an Afro-American won the fight (Phillips et al., 1992). For suicide, this evidence was supported by studies from Phillips (1974, 1977) and Schmidtke and Häfner (1988): white actors were more often imitated by whites, and young male suicides more by young males. Suicidal methods appeared to have been imitated in a study by Gould and Shaffer (1986), as well as in one case and in studies by Schmidtke and Häfner (1988) on railway suicide, and in an investigation by Etzersdorfer et al. (2001) on shooting.

The variables that determine the probability of imitation firstly include age, as younger people are more suggestible and thus more prone to imitate their peers than older persons. However, also the elderly may be exposed to copycat effects, whereas middle-aged people may be relatively protected since they are more highly integrated in society (Stack, 2000). Consequently, newspaper or television reports and films have been shown to disproportionately influence young people, especially when the models are young (Phillips, 1974; Bollen & Phillips, 1982; Phillips & Cartensens, 1988; Schmidtke & Häfner, 1988ab). If a story is about an elderly suicide victim, the increase in copycat suicides is also very high (Stack, 2000). Secondly, gender is thought to play a role, as females in general are, for example, more field dependent.

Other important characteristics include self-esteem and self-efficacy, which, according to Bandura (1977), are among of the most important variables in social learning as well as extroversion, impulsiveness, and mood congruence (i.e., when model and observer are in the same mood condition).

Ethnic model preferences apparently also exist, as suicides of foreigners do not trigger copycat suicides among native individuals (Stack, 1996, 2000). The influence of race was clearly demonstrated by Molock (1994) and Stack (1996). As suicidal behaviour in the USA is commonly viewed by African Americans as a problem afflicting white Americans, the former may be less likely to engage in imitative behaviour when exposed to white models. In the study of Stack (1996) in Japan, the imitation effect was restricted to Japanese victims.

When the models are particular celebrities who are unknown to large audiences or to vulnerable sub-groups such as youngsters or the elderly, as in the study of Jonas (1992), an imitation effect is unlikely to occur because the model characteristics are not relevant for those potentially most inclined to imitation.

According to Meichenbaum (1971), it is also important that model characteristics include a coping model (e.g., not to use suicidal behaviour as a problem solving strategy) or a master model (in which the model is shown as an expert).

Consequences of the Act

The imitation effect also depends on the degree to which the behaviour of the model is reinforced (i.e., appears to be positive or approved).

Kind of "Transporting" of the Model Behaviour

The effects clearly depend on how the model behaviour is "transported" to the potential imitator. It is a different matter whether the suicidal model behaviour is shown or portrayed as real (most adolescents report that their parents and peers are the best models for behaviour) in printed media (books, journals, magazines), music, theatre (plays or operas), or in films or television, or in the new electronic media (e.g., Internet). Therefore, various combinations of behaviour shown and type of media are possible. Up to now, there exists no systematic study examining the differences of the various media with regard to imitation effects of suicidal behaviour. However, in the last years some authors have claimed that the Internet, due to its interactive possibilities, may be more dangerous than other media (Baume et al., 1998). This could be especially true for youngsters. With the Internet they can be reached easily, can quickly be in contact with other persons, while their postings and exchanged suicidal thoughts and plans remain anonymous. With the help of the Internet, they could very quickly arrange suicide pacts.

With regard to the possible imitation effect through the Internet, it has to be kept in mind that the amount of online material is immense, the access is not controllable, and the model behaviour can be accessed or read repeatedly. Press reports about Internet suicide Forums can in themselves be an advertisement of such forums and attract more people, thus creating a multiplicative effect.

Dosage Effect

The imitation depends also on the "dosage" of reporting. As early as in the studies of Phillips (1974, 1977), it was already shown that imitation effects clearly depend on the quantity of reporting and the size of the audience, e.g., the number of possible imitators. Simply put: the bigger the reporting, the higher the probability of imitation effects. Even newer studies show a clear association between the number of presentations (Schmidtke & Häfner, 1988), the size of distribution (Etzersdorfer et al., 2001) and the size of the imitation effect.

Size of Audience or Number of Possible Imitators

Some studies have also clearly shown the importance of the size of the audience. The increase of suicides is proportionate to the size of audience (Schmidtke & Häfner, 1988; Etzersdorfer et al., 2001).

Short- and Long-Term Influences

A further hypothesis in exploring the reasons for different findings is based on the fact that the reporting or portrayal of suicidal behaviour or the presentation of fictional suicide models might influence a population's suicidal behaviour either in the short or in the long term. Impulsive imitators can already be in a state of mood predisposing them to such behaviour, and may be consequently triggered to quick reactions. Another group may instead be influenced by the media in the long run, with the view that this form of behaviour is "a common and understandable way" of problem solving (Schmidtke & Schaller, 2000).

The WHO/EURO Multi-Centre Study on Suicidal Behaviour (Schmidtke et al., 1998) allowed, for the first time, the opportunity to study the frequency of suicidal models among suicide attempters, and to investigate these imitation hypotheses and effects on a cross-cultural basis.

Findings

Data were available for 15 European centres participating in the Repetition-Prediction part of the WHO/EURO Multi-Centre Study. Within one week after the index suicide attempt, an interview (EPSIS I), taking 2–2.5 hours to complete, was performed. Questions referring to the imitation of suicidal acts dealt with the relationship of the model to the subject, the type of model behaviour, the method of the model event, and the time elapsed between the model event and the present parasuicide.

Of all suicide attempters, 54% reported at least one suicidal model (suicide or suicide attempt). Females reported models at a slightly higher percentage than males (55% vs 52%). Four percent of the males and females reported four or five suicidal models. The various catchment areas differed significantly with regard to the frequency of models. There seemed to be a slight north-south gradient. The lowest percentages were found for the Italian centres, the highest percentage in Sweden. The age distribution for all suicidal models was significantly different between the various age groups.

For males, the type of suicidal behaviour of the latest model was to a greater proportion (51%) a suicide. In contrast, females in most centres reported more parasuicidal model behaviour (on average: 61%). The frequency of parasuicidal models was significantly different, with the highest percentage for the female age groups below 35 years; however, this was not true for the youngest age group. The oldest age groups had the lowest frequency of suicide models.

The majority of the model events took place more than twelve months before the index suicide attempt. Only 14% reported that the latest model event was made during the 12 months before the present parasuicide. Model events in the week before the index parasuicide were found for only 1% of the males and females.

In most cases, the latest model for male and female suicide attempters was a friend or a colleague. Thirty-six percent of the males and 29% of the females had a friend with a history of suicidal behaviour. There was no co-variation of the relationship between suicidal model and age.

Model frequencies for certain persons increase if one counts all models: the latest model and all previous models. Forty-three percent of the male suicide attempters and 37% of the female suicide attempters reported a friend with a history of suicidal behaviour. The next largest model group was constituted by "other relatives" (members of the extended family).

More than one in every fourth suicide attempter had his or her contact with the model behaviour in a treatment facility (30% of the male suicide attempters and 29% of the female suicide attempters).

Twenty-three percent of the males and 27% of the females were either physically present during the model act, in telephone contact with the model or contacted immediately before or after the model act.

There was no clear relation between the method of the last model and the method of the index suicide attempt, neither for males nor for females.

To test the hypothesis of a relationship between a greater availability of suicide models and the frequency of model behaviour among suicide attempters, the co-variations between the density of the population in the catchment area or in the country with the frequency of suicidal models were computed. There was no significant correlation between suicide attempt data and population density of a given catchment area, $r = -.10$, ns. However, significant co-variation between suicide attempt data of each catchment area and population density of the country was found, $r = -.66$, $p < .04$, where there was only one centre per country, and $r = -.62$, $p < .097$, where there were two centres in the same country (the averaged data were used).

Discussion

Knowledge of and experience with suicidal models is a frequent phenomenon among suicide attempters (Kreitman et al., 1969, 1970). The results of the WHO/EURO Multi-Centre Study on Suicidal Behaviour clearly reflect an interesting socio-cultural difference. Both Italian centres showed the lowest frequency of suicidal models, whereas the Nordic centres had higher frequencies. There is no significant relation between the possible availability of suicidal models, measured by the density of population, and the frequency of suicidal models.

In all countries suicide attempters have significantly more contact with suicidal models than psychiatric patients and, with great probability, also when compared to normal controls (based on data from a conservative control group of Hungarian people, see Fekete & Schmidtke, 1966). However, previously reported findings that women and young people follow models more frequently were not supported by these results, although older age groups did have lower model frequencies. In addition, the specific method of the model suicidal behaviour resulted only infrequently in imitation. Therefore, the hypothesis that there may also be different types of responders should be re-examined. "Early responders" may be more impulsive and may already have contemplated suicidal behaviour. In particular, among young people undergoing a crisis resembling that of the model, the model behaviour may precipitate the suicidal action, perhaps more probably with the same method. In contrast, "late responders" may exhibit a less impulsive, more considered response to a model. In such cases, the model behaviour may only help to "sow the seeds of suicide in the distant future" (Barraclough et al. 1977, p. 531) and lead to or support the view that this form of behaviour is a "common and understandable way" of problem solving, as Littmann already stated in 1985. This would eventually increase the likelihood that a person chooses suicidal behaviour as a problem-solving strategy when in a stress situation, although not necessarily with the same method.

With regard to preventive measures, since many suicide attempters can directly observe suicide models in a psychiatric hospital, it is of crucial importance to identify strategies that can interrupt copycat suicides or attempted suicides. One possibility could be providing better information to patients in the aftermath of such acts, not hiding such acts, and – like in school programs – developing special strategies for persons at risk in the hospital.

Apart from the possibility of imitation within hospitals, it might be dangerous to report about suicide events in a sensational way. The reporting may trigger the same attitude and behaviour in persons who find themselves in a similar state of mood.

That it would be possible to use the media also for preventing suicidal acts, has clearly been shown by some investigations. A study by Sonneck and co-workers (1993), for example, illustrates very well the opportunities for prevention offered by the mass media. Since the opening of the Vienna subway in 1978, the system has been used as a way of attempting or committing suicide. The number of these events was very low in the early years, but from 1984 on, suicides and suicide attempts increased. This trend was neither due to an extension of the Viennese subway system nor to an increase in the number of passengers. However, major Austrian newspapers reported these suicides in a very sensational and dramatic way. As a response to this dangerous habit, the Austrian Association for Suicide Prevention created media guidelines and requested the press to follow them, beginning in June 1987. After these guidelines were published, the general quality of reporting changed markedly. Instead of printing sensational articles, papers printed either short reports (rarely on front page) or did not report suicides at all. At the same time, the number of suicides in the subway significantly decreased from the first to the second half of 1987, and the rates remained low. A similar effort was made in Switzerland. In the context of the Swiss National Suicide Prevention Program, the Swiss Association for Suicide Prevention tried to persuade the press not to report about suicides in a sensational way. The results also showed a decrease in suicide rates (Michel et al., 1998).

It was hypothesized that the media coverage portraying the suicide of the singer Kurt Cobain, the leader of the rock band *Nirvana,* as an unreasonable act and a useless way of problem solving (especially as derived from the interview with his widow) actually prevented copycat suicides (Kienhorst, 1994; Jobes et al., 1996; Berman, et al., 1998).

Therefore, the striking relation between the change in style of reporting by print media and the number of suicides supports the hypothesis that reports and portrayals of suicidal, and perhaps also amok behaviour (Schmidtke & Schaller, 2000), may trigger additional suicides and amok events; *vice versa* toning down press reports may have a preventive effect.

References

Bandura, A. (1977). *Social learning theory.* Englewood Cliffs, NJ: Prentice Hall.

Barraclough, B., Shepherd, D., & Jennings, C. (1977). Do newspaper reports of coroner's inquests incite people to commit suicide? *British Journal of Psychiatry, 131,* 528–532.

Baume, P., Cantor, C. H., & Rolfe, A. (1988). Cyber suicide: Interactive suicide on the Internet. *Crisis, 18,* 73–79.

Beck, A. T., Steer, R. A., Kovacs, M., & Garrison, B. (1985). Hopelessness and eventual suicide: A 10-year prospective study of patients hospitalised with suicidal ideation. *American Journal of Psychiatry, 145,* 559–563.

Berman, A. L., Jobes, D. A., & O'Carroll, P. (1998). The aftermath of Kurt Cobain's suicide. In D. DeLeo, A. Schmidtke, R. F. W. Diekstra (Eds.), *Suicide prevention: A holistic approach* (pp. 139–143). Dordrecht: Kluwer.

Birtchnell, J. (1983). Psychotherapeutic considerations in the management of the suicidal patient. *American Journal of Psychotherapy, 37*, 24–36.

Bollen, K. A., & Phillips, D. P. (1982). Imitation suicides: a national study of effects of television news stories. *American Sociological Review, 47*, 802–809.

Cantor, C. H., & Sheehan, P. W. (1996). Violence and media reports. A connection with Hungerford? *Archives of Suicide Research, 2*, 255–266.

Etzersdorfer, E., Voracek, M., Sonneck, G. (2001). A dose-response relationship of imitational suicides with newspaper distribution. *Australian and New Zealand Journal of Psychiatry, 35*, 251.

Fekete, S., & Schmidtke A (1996). The impact of mass media reports on suicide and attitudes towards self-destruction: Previous studies and some new data from Hungary and Germany. In B. Mishara (Ed.), *The impact of suicide* (pp. 142–155). New York: Springer.

Gould, M. S., & Shaffer, D. (1986). The impact of suicide in television movies. *New England Journal of Medicine, 315*, 690–694.

Jobes, D. A., Berman, A. L., O'Carroll, P. W., Eastgard, S., & Knickmeyer, S. (1996). The Kurt Cobain suicide crisis: Perspectives from research, public health, and the news media. *Suicide and Life-Threatening Behavior, 26*, 260–271.

Jonas, K. (1992). Modelling and suicide. A test of the Werther effect. *British Journal of Social Psychology, 31*, 295–306.

Kienhorst, I. (1994). Kurt Cobain. *Crisis, 15*, 62–63.

Kirch, M. R., Lester, D. (1990). Is a spate of suicides a cluster? *Perceptual and Motor Skills, 70*, 46.

Kreitman, N., Smith, P., & Tan, E. S. (1969), Attempted suicide in social networks. *British Journal of Preventive and Social Medicine, 23*, 116–123.

Kreitman, N., Smith, P., & Tan, E. S. (1970). Attempted suicide as language: An empirical study. *British Journal of Psychiatry, 116*, 465–473.

Kroth, J. (1984). Recapitulating Jonestown. *Journal of Psychohistory, 11*, 383–393.

Littmann, S. K. (1985). Suicide epidemics and newspaper reporting. *Suicide and Life-Threatening Behavior, 15*, 43–50.

Meichenbaum, D. (1971). Examination of model characteristics in reducing avoidance behaviour. *Journal of Personality and Social Psychology, 17*, 298–307.

Michel, K., Frey, C., & Valach, L. (1998, September). *Suicide reporting in print media: An evaluation of the effect of guidelines issued to editors and journalists.* Paper presented at the 7th European Symposium on Suicide and Suicidal Behaviour, Gent, Belgium.

Molock, S. D., Williams, S., Lacy, M., & Kimborough, R. (1994, April). *Werther effects in a black college sample.* Paper presented at the 27th Annual Congress of the American Association of Suicidology, New York.

Phillips, D. P. (1974). The influence of suggestion on suicide. Substantive and theoretical implications of the Werther effect. *American Sociological Review, 39*, 340–354.

Phillips, D. P. (1977). Motor vehicle fatalities increase just after publicized suicide stories. *Sciences, 196*, 1464–1465.

Phillips, D. P. (1985). The Werther effect. Suicide, and other forms of violence are contagious. *Sciences, 25*, 32–39.

Phillips, D. P., & Carstensen, L. L. (1988). The effect of suicide stories on various demographic groups, 1968–1985. *Suicide and Life-Threatening Behavior, 18*, 100–114.

Phillips, D. P., Lesyna, K., Paight, D. J. (1992). Suicide and the media. In R. W. Maris, A. L. Berman, J. T. Maltsberger et al. (Eds.), *Assessment and prediction of suicide.* New York: Guilford.

Pirkis, J., & Blood, R. W. (2001). Suicide and the media, 2: Portrayal in fictional media. *Crisis, 22,* 155–162.

Schmidtke, A., Fricke, S., Weinacker, B., Bille-Brahe, U., De Leo, D., Kerkhof, A., Bjerke, T., Crepet, P., Haring, C., Hawton, K., Lönnqvist, J., Michel, K., Phillipe, A., Pommereau, I., Querejeta, I., Salander-Renberg, E., Temesvary, B., Wasserman, D., & Sampaio-Faria, J. (1998). Suicide and suicide attempt rates in Europe, 1989–1993: Rates, changes and epidemiological results of the WHO/EURO Multicentre Study on Parasuicide. In De Leo, D., Schmidtke, A., & R. F. W. Diekstra (Eds.), *Suicide prevention – A holistic approach* (pp. 67–80). Dordrecht: Kluwer.

Schmidtke, A., Hafner, H. (1988). The Werther effect after television films: New evidence for an old hypothesis. *Psychological Medicine, 18,* 665–676.

Schmidtke, A., & Schaller, S. (2000). The role of mass media in suicide prevention. In K. Hawton & K. van Heeringen (Eds.), *International handbook of suicide and attempted suicide* (pp. 675–697). New York: Wiley.

Schmidtke, A. Schaller, S., & Wasserman, D. (2001). Suicide clusters and media coverage of suicide. In D. Wasserman (Ed.), *Suicide – An unnecessary death* (pp. 265–268). London: Dunitz.

Sonneck, G., Hetzersdorfer, E., & Nagel-Kuess, S. (1993). Imitation effect in suicidal behavior. Subway suicide in Vienna. In K. Bohme (Ed.), *Suicidal behaviour: The state of the art* (pp. 65–66). Regensburg: Roderer Verlag.

Stack, S. (1996). The effect of the media on suicide: Evidence from Japan, 1955–1985. *Suicide and Life-Threatening Behavior, 26,* 132–142.

Stack, S. (2000). Media impacts on suicide: A quantitative review of 293 findings. *Social Science Quarterly, 81,* 957–971.

Stack, S. (2003). Suicide influences and factors: Media effects. In R. Kastenbaum (Ed.), *Encyclopedia of death and dying* (pp. 821–824). New York: MacMillan.

Steede, K. K., & Range, L. M. (1989). Does television induce suicidal contagion with adolescents? *Journal of Community Psychology, 17,* 166–172.

Taiminen, T., Salmenpera, T., & Lehtinen, K. (1992). A suicide epidemic in a psychiatric hospital. *Suicide and Life-Threatening Behavior, 22,* 350–363.

Chapter 16
Seasonality and Other Temporal Fluctuations in Suicidal Behaviour: Myths, Realities and Results

Gert Jessen

Suicide Research Centre, Odense, Denmark

Introduction

Seasonal variations and other temporal fluctuations in the frequency of suicidal behaviour has been the object of a wide range of studies, with the vast majority being published during the last two or three decades. Throughout history special attention has been paid to a particular so-called "Spring-fever"; as early as in the 19th century, Morselli (1881) noted specific seasonal variations in the frequency of suicide with a peak in late spring and early summer, and Durkheim (1897/1951) presented European data that showed a marked peak in the frequency of suicide in the first summer month of June. Other older and minor studies have pointed at the same tendency; for example, two Danish studies carried out in the middle of the 19th century by Kayser (1846) and the beginning of the 20th century by Pontoppidan (1908) gave similar observations.

Time of the Year

The seasonality of suicide has become a ubiquitous phenomenon, and Kevan (1980), Massing and Angermeier (1985), Jessen et al. (1998), Jessen (2003) and others have discussed the majority of studies in the field published during the 20th century, but due to the rareness of studies from the Southern hemisphere they mainly deal with the Northern hemisphere. Generally, these studies showed that the frequency of suicide peaks during springtime (March to May), but also to some extent in the autumn, especially in October. In 49 of 80 studies, Kevan (1980) documented a spring-maximum.

During later years, seasonal variations in the frequency of suicide have been observed in various studies with peaks in late spring and to a somewhat lesser extent in late autumn (Dreyer, 1959; Eastwood & Peacocke, 1976; Eastwood & Stiasny, 1978; Pflug, 1978; Kreitman, 1980; Näyhä, 1982, 1983; Lester, 1983, 1988; Warren et al., 1983; Souêtre et al., 1987; Micciolo et al., 1989;Chew & McCleary, 1995; Hakko et al., 1998; Jessen et al., 1998; Preti & Miotto, 1998; Jessen & Jensen, 1999; Rocchi & Perlini 2002). The spring peak was also confirmed by Stack (1995), but only for whites and not for non-whites. Preti et al. (2000) mentioned that violent suicide methods follow clearer seasonal patterns than suicides by less violent methods. Hakko et al. (1998) found that suicides among senior citizens as well as non-violent suicides occur more often during autumn than would be expected, and Rasanen et al. (2002) found that suicides by hanging peaked in spring and suicides by drowning, jumping and gassing peaked in summer for both genders, and that suicides by poisoning and drowning peaked in autumn only for females. This finding was supported by a study of all suicides in Italy from 1984 to 1995 (Preti & Miotto, 1998). Ajdacic-Gross et al. (2003) found in a large Swiss study that the seasonality largely depended on specific violent suicide methods and different cyclical dynamics. Among others, the mentioned studies indicated that the seasonality in suicide throughout the year could be related to violent suicide methods in particular.

Gender differences in the seasonal variation have been discussed in some of the studies mentioned above, and a tendency has been shown for the frequency of female suicides in particular to peak during the autumn, too. However, among others, neither Lester (1971) nor Sanborn and Sanborn (1978), nor Ho et al. (1997) found any significant differences between the genders.

A tendency towards the seasonal variations being dependent on age has been demonstrated in some studies. Kok and Tsoi (1993) found a higher correlation for the younger groups than for the somewhat older, and Danneel (1975) found that young people commit suicide more often during autumn and winter than old people. In a Japanese study, Takahasi (1964) found that the younger the group, the earlier in the spring the peak appears, a finding that was supported by Wallenstein et al. (1989), who found that the frequency among adolescents in USA peaked during the first three months of the year, a pattern that was significantly different from that of adults.

The Cycle Tendency Theory

At the end of the 19th century, Durkheim maintained that the frequency of suicide is cyclical and that the number of suicides tends to be higher at the beginning of each cycle, but that no "cosmic factors" could explain the cycles. He argued that the rhythm of this cyclical tendency could be seen as a parallel to the rhythm of social life, where the level of activity tends to be higher at the beginning of every new cycle, e.g., at the beginning of a new year, a month or a week. Durkheim wanted to relate the temporal fluctuations in the frequency of suicides to temporal or cyclical aspects of social interaction and he stated that the rhythm of social life seems to follow the calendar. Based on a large study on suicides in England from 1958 to 1974, Meares et al. (1981) supported Durkheim's cyclical hypothesis, finding one single cycle for men and two cycles for women within each year.

Large-scale studies on suicide carried out by among others Schramm (1968), Zung and Green (1974), Rogot et al. (1976), Dixon and Shulman (1983), Mac-Mahon (1983), Massing and Angermeier (1985), Maldonado and Kraus (1991), Hassan (1994) and Jessen et al. (1998) have demonstrated the existence of weekly cycles as a specific aspect of the cyclical phenomenon. According to these studies, the frequency of suicide peaks on Mondays, in popular terms called "blue Mondays." The Monday peak was confirmed by Stack (1995), but again for whites only and not for non-whites. Other studies, for example, by Heigel (1974), indicate a peak on Tuesdays.

Massing and Angermeier (1995) and Jessen and Jensen (1999) suggested that this tendency towards more suicides at the beginning of the week is more prominent now than it used to be, and that the difference between the frequency of suicides during weekends and other weekdays are becoming more distinct than was the case a hundred years ago.

Birthdays and major public holidays are other cyclic events, which have been the object of many studies on the temporal fluctuation of suicides. Both are, on one hand, normally periods that we all look forward to and which most people associate with pleasant things, such as getting together, joy, gifts, and the like. On the other hand, there may be people to whom, e.g., Christmas brings at least some kind of disappointment, anxiety, or even sadness (Sattin, 1975). Also major holidays may often bring stressors, such as too much drinking, changes in day and night and sleep rhythms, increased financial burdens and various family conflicts.

Christmas, the most mythical and emotional major public holiday, is often seen as symptomatic with the time for changes between good and evil, light and darkness. The psychoanalyst Eisenbud (1941) 60 years ago considered the Christmas season to be the most emotional period: "It is the season when the solid citizen becomes liquid and 'the devil is raised,'" and Cattel (1955) noted that during this special holiday period individuals wish for some magical solutions to their problems. Later, Reid (1967) simply stated that basically Christmas is a crisis of love versus aggression. The ambiguity of Christmas described by the term "Christmas blues" or "Christmas syndrome" might be the reason why there is still a widespread belief held by the general public and also by health professionals that the frequency of suicide tends to increase during holidays, especially around Christmas.

A great variety of literature has focused on the negative aspects of holidays (e.g., Eisenbud, 1941; Cattel, 1955; Reid, 1967; Pollock, 1971; Shaffer, 1974; Sattin, 1975;

Barraclough & Shephard, 1976; Kunz, 1978; Albin, 1981; Hillard et al., 1981; Jessen et al., 1999a; Jessen & Jensen, 1999b). The negative aspects of holidays are summed up in the following statement by Sattin (1975): "The holiday season, then, is characterized by the arousal of dependency needs, by regression, by anxiety and depression associated with the fulfilment of interpersonal needs, by awareness of one's mortality, and by the memory of past disappointments and losses." If this rather gloomy view on holidays should, however, be the prevalent one, we should expect a lot more suicides around major public holidays than actually occur. Fortunately, most of the time and to most people holidays are pleasant events.

The Death-Dip Hypothesis

It is still commonly believed that some people may tend to postpone death until after a special positive or important event such as a birth, a birthday, a presidential election, a religious feast or a major public holiday. In his discussion on this topic, Durkheim argued that, generally, the individual is strongly attached to his/her society and its ceremonies and other social rhythms, and he held that the strength of the individual's integration varies between two extremes: some are poorly integrated in their society and therefore not involved or interested in its ceremonies; others are too highly integrated and therefore too much involved or bound by its ceremonies, feasts and rhythms. This latter group may be the ones most likely to try and postpone their death until after a major social ceremony or holiday (Durkheim, 1897/1951; Phillips & Feldman, 1973).

As mentioned, a large number of studies have reported various temporal fluctuations in suicidal behaviour, but few theories have been able to explain the relationship between the temporal variables and an eventual timing of the suicide. Thirty years ago, however, Phillips (1972) put forward his "death-dip hypothesis," suggesting that some consciously postponed their suicide in order to be able to witness their birthday or another special event, and he stated that the month of death might therefore be related to the month of birth. This simple hypothesis is based on the assumptions mentioned above, arguing that in case of a coming special and positive event, some will try to postpone death until after this event has occurred. It is also indicated that famous people and celebrities may be more likely to postpone death than "ordinary people" because less attention is paid to birthdays of the latter. Some studies support this "death-dip hypothesis" by demonstrating that suicides are more likely to occur during the months of the birthday than during the rest of the year (Shaffer, 1974; Barraclough & Shephard, 1976; Kunz, 1978), but other similar studies have failed to support the universality of the "Birthday blues" phenomenon (Danneel, 1975, 1977; Bradshaw, 1981; Lester, 1986; Jessen & Jensen, 1999).

However, with regard to major public holidays, Phillips and Feldman (1973), Lester and Beck (1975), Phillips and Liu (1980), Phillips (1984), Sparhawk (1987),

Jessen et al. (1998), and Jessen and Jensen (1999) supported the death-dip hypothesis by finding evidence that specific holidays, to some extent, have a postponing effect on suicide; especially for Christmas a significant suppressing effect on suicide was found. It is noteworthy that a similar tendency in the frequency of psychiatric hospitalisations was found by Hillard et al. (1981), with a decrease in the number of visits to a psychiatric emergency service before Christmas and an increase after. A Norwegian large-scale study of seasonal variations of violence found that the pattern of violent episodes resembles the seasonal pattern found in suicide and hospitalisation for affective disorders (Morken & Linaker, 2000).

In general, many studies have demonstrated the same pattern around all major public holidays, namely a decrease in suicides before and an increase after the holiday. The greatest impact on the frequency of suicide seems to take place around the major holidays such as Christmas and Easter, especially compared to the pattern of suicides around shorter or minor holidays or holidays that are partially working days.

There is, however, no reason to believe that this postponing or suppressing effect provokes the actual number of suicides, as the effect seems only to transpose some of the suicides from before until after the holiday, i.e., the increase in suicides during the period after a holiday is generally counterbalanced by the decrease in suicides that took place before the holiday (Phillips & Liu, 1980; Phillips, 1984; Jessen & Jensen, 1999). It is also noteworthy that, in general, suicides do not seem to be affected in a way that directly "moves" them from one date to another, but the question of what it is that characterizes the individuals who are affected by this phenomenon still remains to be answered.

The Broken-Promise Effect

Trying to explain the overall seasonal variation in the frequency of suicide, Gabennesch (1988) put forward a comprehensive psychosocial theory of the "broken-promise effect," stating that springtime, weekends, birthdays, and holidays are usually affectively positive events, but that they also at times may promise more than they can fulfil. Gabennesch (1988), Stack (1995), and Jessen & Jensen (1999) point out that the theory is consistent with Durkheim's work on various cyclic phenomena. The psychosocial broken-promise effect contributes to a better understanding of temporal variations in suicidal behaviour as, e.g., the distribution of suicide around major public holidays. According to the hypothesis of Gabennesch, approaching events such as spring, weekends, holidays etc., may influence both psychiatric and non-psychiatric suicidal individuals, because such events tend to promote hope or expectations of getting better or feeling better than before. The forthcoming event is seen as synonymous with a new beginning in the sense of "things will get better then or thereafter." However, if individuals, who for some reason are especially vulnerable and therefore at risk of suicidal behaviour, are building up expectations that are unrealistic and therefore cannot or will not be met, the result-ing frustration and disappointment may trigger reactions such as completed suicide or even homicide, as shown by Stack (1995). An example could be a depression that may deepen during or after the positive event, because it failed to deliver the hoped-for change in the mental condition. Furthermore, the frustration and disappoint-ment that can be felt during a holiday period might be worsened because of the changes mentioned above in daily routines such as more heavy drinking, increased financial burdens, family arguments and conflicts, and therefore the overall positive effect of holidays may tend to lose its power during the day(s). For some individuals, the positive effect may fade away completely and instead turn negative. Also, the absence of various social contacts experienced by many suicidal people could in-crease the negative impact on how they perceive public holidays, when they com-pare themselves with people who have family and friends with whom they can share activities related to these holidays. The effect of positive experienced events can then be described as a kind of suicidal immune system (Jessen et al., 1999b), which un-fortunately breaks down at the end of or after the positive event such as a major public holiday or even springtime. If it is true that social interactions have a higher intensity during spring than in winter, individuals who are feeling isolated, de-pressed or lonely will consequently become even more acutely aware of their own unhappy situation, thereby contributing to the belief in the so-called Spring-fever.

Meteorological Factors

Very few people, indeed, can deny that the weather in one way or another influences them, but the influence seems to be felt in particular if the weather does not follow the well-known and expected pattern. More than a century ago, Morselli (1881) pointed to changes in the weather as a crucial aspect when trying to understand co-variations between seasons and suicides, and he concluded that seasonal varia-tions in the frequency of suicide were presumably mainly due to meteorological factors. According to his hypothesis, it was not the temperature per se, but rather changes in the temperature that caused the increase in suicides in the months of late spring. The hypothesis was supported by Mills (1934), who argued that an in-crease in the number of suicides were to be seen in relation to marked changes in pressure and temperature, such as those occurring in connection with heavy storms. Bouma and Tromp (1972) found a significant positive correlation between suicidal behaviour and periods with strong meteorological turbulence, such as drastic changes in the thermal balance and sudden changes from dry weather to heavy precipitation. Breuer et al. (1986) found suicidal behaviour correlated to meteoro-logical factors such as stable and labile upslide, fog, thunderstorm, warm air and weather drier than on the two proceeding days. In a German study, Heigel (1974) found that more suicides than expected took place during foggy weather or during sudden changes in the weather. Dixon and Shulman (1983) pointed at the correlation between rapidly increasing temperatures and the building up of warm fronts, and an increasing number of suicides, and Barker et al. (1994) found significant co-variations between female suicidal behaviour and ambient temperature, intra-day temperature amplitude and rainfall on the preceding day, and significant co-variations between male suicidal behaviour and rain, cloud, poor visibility, and windy days. Geltzer et al. (2000) showed in a study from Seattle a significant correlation between carbon monoxide poisoning and mean and total precipitation.

Linkowski et al. (1992) found in their study correlations between temperature and the amount of (sun) light, and the frequency of (violent) suicides, and Thorson and Kasworm (1984) and Linkowski et al. (1992) both demonstrated a correlation between suicide and hours of sunlight: the more sunlight, the fewer suicides. Contrary to these findings Salib (1997) and Salib and Gray (1997) reported that suicide and other fatal self-harm appear to be inversely related to fine weather conditions as defined by hours of sunshine, and Petridou et al. (2002) described an association between the frequency of suicide and hours of sunshine and concluded that sunshine may have a triggering effect on suicide. Also Lambert et al. (2003) found that the number of suicides paralleled closely the number of bright sunlight hours. It has also been mentioned that the seasonal pattering might diminish closer to equatorial regions (Parker et al., 2001). However, the co-variation between sunshine and suicide could probably be related to the broken-promise effect, too.

As it is known that some types of depressive illness are sensitive to the intensity of light, this could be another interacting factor behind the correlation, especially when regarding seasonal affective disorders (SAD)(Zung & Green, 1974; Rosenthal et al., 1983, 1984; Wehr, 1988; Kunz & Kunz, 1997; Lam et al., 2001). SAD is classified as a seasonal pattern of recurrent major depressive episodes in winter with full remission of symptoms in summer. However, other groups of seasonal affective disorders have been identified, such as patients with incomplete summer remission (ISR) and patients with winter depressive symptoms that do not meet criteria for major depression (sub-SAD). Differences in both the patterns of clinical symptoms and in the response to light therapy have been demonstrated in these three groups (Lam et al., 2001). In a review, Rosenthal (1983) mentioned that unipolar affective disorders show temporal fluctuations with a peak in spring, and major spring and minor autumn peaks for bipolar affective disorders. As demonstrated by Maes et al. (1993) and Morken et al. (2002), there seems to be a true seasonality in the severity of illness of depressed individuals and a significant positive correlation between the severity of illness and the chronograms of suicide. Following this, Rihmer et al. (1998) suggested that a decreasing tendency of seasonality in suicide might indicate the lowering rate of depressive suicides in a given population.

Results from a large Danish methodological study on possible co-variations between suicide and weather factors (Jessen et al., 1998) confirmed, to some extent, a direct relationship between meteorological factors and the frequency of suicide. The study to some degree also supported the findings of Howarth and Hoffman (1984), stating that of a variety of meteorological variables, humidity, temperature and sunshine had the greatest impact on human mood. Analysis performed on the Danish climatological data showed that one of the most important factors is a combination of various weather variables for "nice weather" with positive factor loadings for the amount of sunlight, visibility and temperature, and negative loadings for relative humidity and precipitation (Jessen et al., 1998). It means that if the levels of sunlight, visibility and temperature are high (sunny, with high visibility and relatively high temperatures) and the levels of relative humidity and precipitation are low (no rain or fog and low humidity), the nice weather factor will be high. The results of the analysis confirm that there are co-variations between the frequency of suicides and various meteorological parameters, such as a negative co-variation between nice weather and the frequency of suicide and a positive correlation between rapidly or unexpected changing weather and suicides. However, in total, the effect of the weather on the frequency of suicidal behaviour seems to be small (Barker et al., 1994; Jessen et al., 1999), especially in the young (Marion et al., 1999).

Lunar Phases and other Cosmic Factors

Throughout the ages, from the old Egyptians and Mayas up till our modern days of science and technology, there has been a persistent myth called the "lunar hypothesis," which says that the moon affects human behaviour in various ways, e.g., emotional distress, antisocial and violent behaviour or other deviant behaviours. It is a fact that this belief still exists (Vance, 1995), but many studies have been conducted with poor or conflicting results. Jones and Jones (1977) found a relationship between the timing of suicide and the lunar phases, but this finding was not supported by many other studies (Garth & Lester, 1978; Maldonado & Krauss, 1991; Rogers et al., 1991; Martin et al., 1992).

Even though many people believe in various forms of spiritual, religious or extraterrestrial factors in suicidal behaviour, studies of various "cosmic factors" (such as numerology, biorhythms, sunspots, comet's orbits and astrological signs) have generally demonstrated no significant correlations with suicidal behaviour (Buckley et al., 1993).

Suicide Versus Suicide Attempts

Literature on seasonality and temporal fluctuations in attempted suicide is far less common than literature on completed suicide, mainly because of the absence of national data on suicide attempts. However, since 1989 the WHO/EURO Multi-Centre Study on Suicidal Behaviour has produced valid and standardised data on attempted suicide from a number of defined catchment areas in several countries in Europe (Platt et al., 1992; Kerkhof et al., 1994; Bille-Brahe et al., 1995; Schmidtke et al., 1996). The large pool of data has provided a solid base for reliable studies on, e.g., temporal fluctuations in the frequency of suicide attempts in Europe.

Results from two studies based on data on 13,533 and 24,388 suicide attempts, respectively, from 13 centres participating in the Multi-Centre Study have provided an overview of the characteristics of major temporal fluctuations and seasonality in suicide attempts (Jessen et al., 1999a, 1999b; Jessen 2003), and for the first time it has been possible to examine whether the patterns of temporal fluctuations and seasonality found for suicides can be replicated for suicide attempts, and also whether the patterns for suicide attempts are consistent throughout Europe.

Month of Year

With regard to monthly fluctuations, there seems to be no major differences between suicide and suicide attempts, although the seasonal pattern for suicide attempts is not as marked as that for suicide. The highest mean number of suicide attempts was found in May, especially for females, and there was consistency in the occurrence of more suicide attempts in the first half of the year than in the second half (Jessen et al., 1999a, 1999b). Masterton (1991) found evidence for a seasonal pattern in female suicide attempts with an increase in summer, a decline over winter and a pronounced December nadir. Barker et al. (1994) supported this by finding a peak in May and June and a trough in December and January. Pflug (1978) and Doganay et al. (2003) demonstrated a peak for suicide attempts in late spring and early summer. There seems to be a general agreement that an overall seasonality in suicide attempts can be observed with a maximum in (early) summer and a minimum in winter. Thus the temporal fluctuations in suicide attempts tend to replicate the pattern for suicides, although the spring peak seems to be somewhat less pronounced for attempts.

Day of Week

When studying the daily fluctuation in the frequency of suicide attempts, Sunday appears to be the peak day, and the lowest frequency of suicide attempts was found on Fridays. This pattern is, however, not consistent throughout Europe and it has to be noted that, as was the case in the monthly distribution, the daily pattern is far less marked among suicide attempts than among suicides.

More than 60 years ago, Piker (1938), too, found that the highest frequency of suicide attempts occurred on Sundays, and that, in general, the last part of the week had fewer suicide attempts than the first. The cyclic weekly distribution in suicides with a marked peak on Mondays and decreasing frequencies throughout the week seems to be somewhat displaced for suicide attempts. This may be related to the fact that interpersonal factors in particular are strongly implicated in suicide attempts, particularly in females, and maximum interaction within families tends to occur during weekends. Completed suicide, on the other hand, tends to be more directly related to personal problems such as psychiatric disorders, especially depression, and these disorders, too, peak on Mondays (Barraclough et al., 1974; Bancroft et al., 1976).

Time of Day

In contrast to the monthly and daily pattern of the frequency for suicide attempts, intra-day fluctuations show a marked pattern that is more consistent throughout Europe. More than half of both male and female suicide attempts occurred during the four hours between 20.00–23.59, and close to one half occurred in the afternoon and evening between 16.00–23.59, while only few suicide attempts took place during the night between 04.00–07.59. That means that in comparison with the time pattern for suicide, suicide attempts take place somewhat later in the day. Already in 1938, Piker noted that only few suicide attempts took place between midnight and early morning (06.00 o'clock), while the majority were carried out during the evenings. In the Multi-Centre Study, an exception from this overall picture was found in the two Italian areas under study, namely Padua and Emilia Romagna, where most attempts occurred after midnight, i.e., between 00.00–03.59 o'clock (Jessen et al., 1999a). Altamura et al. (1999) also found a highly significant variation by time of the day in suicide in Cagliari, Italy. One possible explanation may be the special Mediterranean "chrono-social" life, in which the level of interaction between people is usually higher during late evening than in Northern European countries. This late evening peak may be related to the assumption that attempted suicide and other self-destructive acts often are behaviours symptomatic of disturbed personal relationships, the act frequently tends to express interpersonal communication, rather than a "real" suicidal intent (Bancroft et al., 1976; Shneidman et al., 1994; Fleischer 2000). The high frequency of non-fatal suicidal acts after midnight in the Southern part of Europe may be due to the fact that the time around midnight is the Mediterranean time for intimacy, but also the time during which violent arguments may take place in families.

Major Public Holidays

Results from the Multi-Centre Study on the distribution of suicide attempts around major public holidays showed a similar pattern for suicide and suicide attempts, namely a decrease before and during the holiday, and an increase after. Also, the pattern was the same with regard to the transposition of acts from before a holiday to after. Major holidays such as Christmas and Easter showed the largest fluctuation or transposition, especially compared to the pattern of suicide attempts around minor holidays. A marked fluctuation in suicidal acts during the Christmas and New Year periods was also found for attempted suicide by Cullum et al. (1993), who reported significantly fewer attempts on Christmas Day than on control days.

Summing Up and Conclusion

As seen from Figure 1, the patterns of temporal fluctuations in the frequencies of completed suicides and suicide attempts are similar only to a certain extent.

The peaks in the frequency of suicide attempts appear somewhat later than the peaks in the frequency of suicide, and, while the frequency of suicide peaks on Mondays, the frequency of attempted suicide peaks on Sundays, and furthermore, suicide attempts take place later in the evening or at night than completed suicides. Birthdays seem to have no effect on suicidal behaviour, but major public holidays have. For both suicide and attempted suicide, however, an obvious transposition takes place in the frequencies from before till after the holiday. Metrological factors, too, have a small and rather complex impact on both types of suicidal behaviour.

The review of the literature on the topic of temporal fluctuation in suicidal behaviour shows clearly that psychosocial, sociodemographic and climatic elements in various combinations affect the propensity to commit suicidal acts and thereby the frequency of suicidal behaviour. As yet, however, we are far from having a com-

Figure 1 Temporal fluctuations of suicides and suicide attempts.

Temporal fluctuations of suicides and suicide attempts		
Factor	**Suicides**	**Suicide attempts**
Month of the year	Spring peak (April–May) Autumn peak (female)	Spring/early summer peak (May peak/December nadir)
Day of the week	Monday peak/low weekend Decrease during the week	No clear weekly cycle (Sunday peak/Friday nadir)
Time of the day	During the day During light hours	During evening/early night (20.00–24.00/00.00–04.00)
Birthday	No or small postponing effect	No clear postponing effect
Major public holidays	Marked transposition from before and during until after	Transposition from before and during until after
Weather	Small and complex covariations	Small and complex covariations
Lunar phases, biorhythms, etc.	No or minor effect	No or minor effect

plete picture of the possible combinations and their effect on suicidal behaviour and prevention of it.

It may seem odd that phenomena such as changes in the weather still have this influence on modern man of today, but although the factor may not be a major one, it ought to be taken seriously if we want to reach a better understanding of the co-variation between seasons, metrological and other factors and suicidal behaviour. The fact that seasonality and temporal fluctuations in suicidal behaviour exist, and that there are high risk periods where individuals already at risk may be even more vulnerable, should, to a greater extent, be brought to the attention of all health professionals, volunteers and relatives. Phenomena such as the broken-promise effect could then be more relevant in prevention, especially in terms of help at crisis centres or telephone hot lines for people in temporal crisis. It is also important to be aware of the possible effect of holidays, when the intake of alcohol increases markedly as it does for instance on the 1st of May, on New Year's Eve or on various national holidays, such as the Norwegian Constitution Day, the Hungarian Day of St Stephan or the 4th of July in USA.

The complexity of the multivariable and multifactorial phenomenon will have to be analysed in future research taking into account the large number of underlying and interacting aspects such as psychiatric disorders (especially seasonal affective disorders), psychosocial problems and other cyclical phenomena such as changing economy etc. Much is still to be gained from various multidisciplinary approaches. Also the inconsistencies of the large amount of the various findings will have to be looked deeper into, in particular, with regard to adequate sizes of samples, larger comparative and intercontinental studies, sufficient length of periods of study, the appropriateness of statistical techniques etc. Finally, the impact of seasonality on suicide prevention strategies and treatment of suicidal behaviour will have to be evaluated.

Literature

Ajdacic-Gross, V., Wang, J., Bopp, M., Eich, D., Rossler, W., & Gutzwiller, F. (2003). Are seasonalities in suicide dependent on suicide methods? A reappraisal. *Social Science and Medicine, 57,* 1183–1171.

Albin, R. (1981). The holiday blues: A Christmas fable? *Psychology Today, 15,* 10–11.

Altamura, C., VanGastel, A., Pioli, R., Mannu, P., & Maes, M. (1999). Seasonal and circadian rhythms in suicide in Cagliari, Italy. *Journal of Affective Disorders 9, 53,* 77–85.

Bancroft, J.H.J., Skrimshire, A.M., & Simkin, S. (1976). The reason people give for taking overdoses. *British Journal of Psychiatry, 128,* 538–548.

Barker, A., Hawton, K., Fagg, J., & Jennison, C. (1994). Seasonal and weather factors in parasuicide. *British Journal of Psychiatry, 165,* 375–380.

Barraclough, B., Bunch, J., Nelson, B., & Sainsbury, P. (1974). A hundred cases of suicide: Clinical aspects. *British Journal of Psychiatry, 125,* 255–273.

Barraclough, B., & Shephard, D. (1976). Birthday blues: The association of birthday with self-inflicted death in the elderly. *Acta Psychiatrica Scandinavica, 54,* 146–149.

Bille-Brahe, U., Schmidtke, A., Kerkhof, A. J.F. M., De Leo, D., Lönnqvist, J., Platt, S., & Faria, J. S. (1995). Background and introduction to the WHO/EURO Multicentre Study on Parasuicide. *Crisis, 16,* 72–84.

Bouma, J. J., & Tromp, S. W. (1972). Daily, monthly and yearly fluctuations in the total number of suicides and suicide attempts in the western part of the Netherlands. *Journal of Interdisciplinary Cycle Research, 3,* 269–270.

Bradshaw, C. W. (1981). A re-examination of Phillips' death-dip hypothesis. *Journal of General Psychology, 105,* 265–267.

Breuer, H. W. M., Breuer, J., & Fischbach-Breuer, B. R. (1986). Social, toxicological and meteorological data on suicide attempts. *European Archives of Psychiatry and Neurological Sciences, 235,* 367–370.

Buckley, N.A, Whyte, I. M., & Dawson, A. H.. (1993). There are days and moons. Self-poisoning is not lunacy. *Medical Journal of Australia, 1159,* 786–789.

Cattel, J. (1955). The holiday syndrome. *Psychoanalytic Review, 42,* 39–43.

Chew, K. S. Y., & McCleary, R. (1995). The spring peak in suicides: A cross-national analysis. *Social Science and Medicine, 40,* 223–230.

Cullum, S. J., Catalan, J., Berelowitz, K., O'Brian, S., Millington, H. T., & Preston, D. (1993). Deliberate self-harm and public holidays: Is there a link? *Crisis, 14,* 39–42.

Danneel, R. (1975). Jahreszeitlich bedingte Unterschiede der Selbstmordhäufigkeit bei jungen und alten Menschen [Season conditioned differences in the suicide rates of young and old people]. *Archiv für Psychiatrie und Nervenkrankheiten, 221,* 11–13.

Danneel, R. (1977). Häufigkeitsverteilung der Geburtstage von Selbstmördern [Frequency distribution of birth dates of suicide]. *Archiv für Psychiatrie und Nervenkrankheiten, 224,* 23–25.

Dixon, K. W., & Shulman, M. D. (1983). A statistical investigation into the relationship between meteorological parameters and suicide. *International Journal of Biometeorology, 27,* 93–105.

Doganay, Z., Sunter, A. T., Guz, H., Ozkan, A., Altintop, L., Kati, C., Colak, I., Aygun, D., & Guven, H. (2003). Climatic and diurnal variation in suicide attempts in the ED. *American Journal of Emergency Medicine, 21,* 271–5.

Dreyer, K. (1959). Comparative suicide statistics. *Danish Medical Bulletin, 6,* 75–81.

Durkheim, É. (1897/1951). *Suicide. A study in sociology.* New York: Free Press

Eastwood, M. R., & Peacocke, J. (1976). Seasonal patterns of suicide, depression and electroconvulsive therapy. *British Journal of Psychiatry, 129,* 472–475.

Eastwood, M. R., & Stiasny, S. (1978). Psychiatric disorder, hospital admissions, and suicide. *Archives of General Psychiatry, 35,* 769–771.

Eisenbud, J. (1941). Negative reactions to Christmas. *Psychoanalytic Quarterly, 10,* 639–645.

Fleischer E. (2000). *Den talende tavshed. Selvmord og selvmordsforsøg som talehandling* [The talking silence: Suicide and attempted suicide as acts of speech]. Odense: Odense University Press.

Gabennesch H. (1988). When promises fail: A theory of temporal fluctuations in suicide. *Social Forces, 67,* 129–145.

Garth, J., & Lester, D. (1978). The moon and suicide. *Psychological Reports, 43,* 678.

Geltzer, A. J., Geltzer, A. M., Dunford, R. G., & Hampton, N. B. (2000). Effects of weather on incidence of attempted suicide by carbon monoxide poisoning. *Undersea and Hyperbaric Medicine Journal, 27,* 9–14.

Hakko, H., Rasanen, P., & Tiihonen, J. (1998). Seasonal variation in suicide occurrence in Finland. *Acta Psychiatrica Scandinavica, 98,* 92–97.

Hassan, R. (1994). Temporal variations in suicide occurrence in Australia: A research note. *The Australian and New Zealand Journal of Sociology, 30,* 194–202.

Heigel, K. (1974). Der Einfluß des Wetters auf Suizide und Suizidversuche in einer süddeutschen Großstadt (Augsburg) [The influence of the weather on suicide and suicide attempts in a south German city (Augsburg)]. *Wetter und Leben, 26,* 11–17.

Hillard, J. M., Holland, R. N., & Ramm, D. (1981). Christmas and psychopathology. *Archives of General Psychiatry, 38,* 1377–1381.

Ho, T. P., Chao, A., & Yip, P. (1997). Seasonal variations in suicides re-examined: No sex difference in Hong Kong and Taiwan. *Acta Psychiatrica Scandinavica, 95,* 26–31.

Howarth, E., & Hoffmann, M. S. (1984). A multidimensional approach to the relationship between mood and weather. *British Journal of Psychology, 75,* 15–23.

Jessen, G., Steffensen, P., & Jensen, B. (1998). Seasons and meteorological factors in suicidal behaviour. Findings and methodological considerations from a Danish study. *Archives of Suicide Research, 4,* 263–280.

Jessen, G., & Jensen, B. F. (1999). Postponed suicide death? Suicides around birthdays and major public holidays. *Suicide and Life-Threatening Behaviour, 29,* 272–283.

Jessen, G., Andersen, K., Arensman, E., Bille-Brahe, U., Crepet, P., De Leo, D., Hawton, K., Haring, C., Hjelmeland, H., Michel, K., Ostamo, A., Salander-Renberg, E., Schmidtke, A., Temesvary, B., & Wasserman, D. (1999a). Temporal fluctuations and seasonality in attempted suicide in Europe. WHO/EURO Multicentre Study on Parasuicide. *Archives of Suicide Research, 5,* 57–69.

Jessen, G., Jensen, B. F., Arensman, E., Bille-Brahe, U., Crepet, P., De Leo, D., Hawton, K., Haring, C., Hjelmeland, H., Michel, K., Ostamo, A., Salander-Renberg, E., Schmidtke, A., Temesvary, B., & Wasserman, D. (1999b). Attempted suicide and major public holidays in Europe. Findings from the WHO/EURO Multicentre Study on Parasuicide. *Acta Psychiatrica Scandinavica, 99,* 412–418.

Jessen, G. (2003). Sæson for selvmordsadfærd. Myter og resultater [Seasons for suicidal behaviour: Myths and facts]. *Suicidologi, 1,* 14–15.

Jones P. K. & Jones, S. L. (1977). Lunar association with suicide. *Suicide and Life Threatening Behavior, 7,* 31–39.

Kayser, C. J. (1846). *Om selvmord i Kongeriget Danmark. Et bidrag til dette Lands moralske Statistik* [Suicide in Denmark: A contribution to the land's moral statistics]. Copenhagen: Saertryk af Dansk Folkeblad.

Kerkhof, A. J. F.M, Schmidtke, A., Bille-Brahe, U., De Leo, D., & Lönnqvist, J. (1994). *Attempted suicide in Europe.* Leiden: DSWO Press.

Kevan, S. M. (1980). Perspectives on season of suicide: A review. *Social Science and Medicine, 14,* 369–378.

Kok, L. P., & Tsoi, W. F. (1993). Season, climate and suicide in Singapore. *Medicine, Science and the Law, 33,* 247–252.

Kreitman, N. (1980). Die Epidemiologie von Suizid und Parasuizid [The epidemiology of suicide and parasuicide]. *Nervenarzt, 51,* 131–138.

Kunz, P. R.. (1978). Relationship between suicide and month of birth. *Psychological Reports, 42,* 794.

Kunz, P. R., & Kunz, J. (1997). Depression and suicide in the dark months. *Perceptual and Motor Skills, 84,* 537–538.

Lam, R. W., Tam, E. M., Yatham, L. N., Shiah, I. S., & Zis, A. P. (2001). Seasonal depression: The dual vulnerability hypothesis revisited. *Journal of Affective Disorder, 63,* 123–132.

Lambert, G., Reid, C., Kaye, D., Jennings, G., & Esler, M. (2003). Increased suicide rate in the middle-aged and its association with hours of sunlight. *American Journal of Psychiatry, 160,* 793–5.

Lester, D. (1971). Seasonal variation in suicidal deaths. *British Journal of Psychiatry, 118,* 627–628.

Lester, D. (1983). Monthly variation of suicidal and accidental poisoning deaths. *British Journal of Psychiatry, 143,* 204–205.

Lester, D. (1986). The birthday blues revisited: The timing of suicide, homicide, and natural deaths. *Acta Psychiatrica Scandinavica, 73,* 322–323.

Lester, D. (1988). Geophysical variables and behavior: XLV–III. Climate and personal violence. *Perceptual and Motor Skills, 66,* 602.

Lester, D., & Beck, A. T. (1975). Suicide and national holidays. *Psychological Reports, 36,* 52.

Linkowski, P., Martin, F., & Maertelaer, V. D. (1992). Effect of some climatic factors on violent and non-violent suicides in Belgium. *Journal of Affective Disorders, 25,* 161–166.

MacMahon, K. (1983). Short-term temporal cycles in the frequency of suicide, United States, 1972–1978. *American Journal of Epidemiology, 117,* 744–750.

Maes, M., Meltzer, H. Y., Suy, E., & De Meyer, F. (1993). Seasonality in severity of depression: Relationships to suicide and homicide occurrence. *Acta Psychiatrica Scandinavica, 88,* 156–161.

Maldonado, G., & Kraus, J. F. (1991). Variation in suicide occurrence, by time of day, day of week, month, and lunar phase. *Suicide and Life-Threatening Behavior, 21,* 174–187.

Marion, S. A., Agbayewa, M. O., & Wiggins, S. (1999). The effect of season and weather on suicide rates in the elderly in British Columbia. *Canadian Journal of Public Health, 90,* 418–422.

Martin, S. J., Kelly, I. W., & Saklofske, D. H. (1992). Suicide and lunar cycles: A critical review over 28 years. *Psychological Reports, 71,* 787–795.

Massing, W., & Angermeier, M. C. (1985). The monthly and weekly distribution of suicide. *Social Science and Medicine, 21,* 433–441.

Masterton, G. (1991). Monthly and seasonal variation in parasuicide. A sex difference. *British Journal of Psychiatry, 158,* 155–157.

Meares, R., Mendelson, F.A. O., & Milgrom-Friedman, J. (1981). A sex difference in the seasonal variation of suicide rate: A single cycle for men, two cycles for women. *British Journal of Psychiatry, 138,* 321–325.

Micciolo, R., Zimmermann-Tansella, C., Williams, P., & Tansella, M. (1989). Seasonal variation in suicide: Is there a sex difference? *Psychological Medicine, 19,* 199–203.

Mills, C. A. (1934). Suicides and homicides in their relation to weather changes. *American Journal of Psychiatry, 91,* 669–671.

Morken, G., & Linaker, O. M. (2000). Seasonal variation of violence in Norway. *American Journal of Psychiatry, 157,* 1674–1678.

Morken, G., Lilleeng, S., & Linaker, O. M. (2002). Seasonal variation in suicides and in admission to hospital for mania and depression. *Journal of Affective Disorders, 69,* 39–45.

Morselli, E. (1881). *Suicide. An essay on comparative moral statistics.* London: Kegan Paul.

Näyhä, S. (1982). Autumn incidence of suicides re-examined: Data from Finland by sex, age, and occupation. *British Journal of Psychiatry, 141,* 512–517.

Näyhä, S. (1983). The bi-seasonal incidence of some suicides. Experiences from Finland by marital status, 1961–1976. *Acta Psychiatrica Scandinavica, 67,* 32–42.

Parker, G., Gao, F., & Machin, D. (2001). Seasonality of suicide in Singapore: Data from the equator. *Psychological Medicine, 31,* 549–553.

Petridou, E., Papadopoulos, F. C., Frangakis, C. E., Skalkidou, A., & Trichopoulos, D. (2002). A role of sunshine in the triggering of suicide. *Epidemiology, 13,* 106–109.

Pflug, B. (1978). Untersuchungen über jahreszeitlichen Schwankungen von Suizid und Suizidversuchen [An investigation of seasonal fluctuations in suicide and suicide attempts]. In W. Engelmann (Ed.), *Rhythmusprobleme in der Psychiatrie* [Rhythm problems in psychiatry]. München: Urban & Fischer.

Phillips, D. P. (1972). Deathday and birthday: An unexpected connection. In J. M. Tanur et al. (Eds.), *Statistics: A guide to the unknown* (pp. 52–65). San Francisco: Holden-Day.

Phillips, D. P., & Feldman, K. A. (1973). A dip in deaths before ceremonial occasions: Some new relationships between social integration and mortality. *American Sociological Review, 38,* 678–696.

Phillips, D. P., & Liu, J. (1980). The frequency of suicides around major public holidays: Some surprising findings. *Suicide and Life-Threatening Behavior, 10,* 41–50.

Phillips, D. P. (1984). Teenage and adult temporal fluctuations in suicide and auto fatalities. In H. Sudak et al. (Eds.), *Suicide in the young.* Boston: John Wright/PSG, Inc.

Piker, P. (1938). Eighteen hundred and seventeen cases of suicidal attempt. A preliminary statistical survey. *American Journal of Psychiatry, 95,* 97–115.

Platt, S., Bille-Brahe, U., Kerkhof, A. J.F. M., Schmidtke, A., Bjerke, T., Crepet, P., De Leo, D., Harring, C., Lönnqvist, J., Michel, M., Philippe, A., Pommereau, X., Querejeat, I., Salander-Renberg, E., Temesvary, B., Wasserman, D., & Faria, J. S. (1992). Parasuicide in Europe: the WHO/EURO Multicentre Study on Parasuicide, I: Introduction and preliminary analysis for 1989. *Acta Psychiatrica Scandinavica, 85,* 97–104.

Pollock, G. (1971). On time, death, and immortality. *Psychoanalytic Quarterly, 40,* 435–446.

Pontoppidan, K. (1907). *Retsmedicinske Forelæsninger og Studier. Aarstiden* [Lectures and studies in forensic medicine]. Copenhagen: Nordisk Forlag.

Preti, A., & Miotto, P. (1998). Seasonality of suicides: the influence of suicide method, gender and age on suicide distribution in Italy. *Psychiatry Research, 81,* 219–231.

Preti, A., Miotto, P., & De Coppi, M. (2000). Season and suicide: Recent findings from Italy. *Crisis, 21,* 59–70.

Rasanen, P., Hakko, H., Jokelainen, J., & Tiihonen, J. (2002). Seasonal variation in specific methods of suicide: A national register study of 20,234 Finnish people. *Journal of Affective Disorders, 71,* 51–9.

Reid, R. (1967). *Infantile crisis associated with Christmas: A psychoanalytic interpretation.* Dissertation Abstracts 29(A), 321A (University Microfilms No. 68–9429).

Rihmer, Z., Rutz, W., Pihlgren, H., & Pestality, P. (1998). Decreasing tendency of seasonality in suicide may indicate lowering rate of depressive suicides in the population. *Psychiatry Research, 81,* 233–240.

Rocchi, M. B., & Perlini, C. (2002). Is the time of suicide a random choice? A new statistical perspective. *Crisis, 23,* 161–6.

Rogers, T. D., Masterton, G., & McGuire, R. (1991). Parasuicide and the lunar cycle. *Psychological Medicine, 21,* 393–397.

Rogot, E., Fabsitz, R., & Feinleib, M. (1976). Daily variation in USA mortality. *American Journal of Epidemiology, 103,* 198–211.

Rosenthal, N. E., Sack, D. A., & Wehr, T. A. (1983). Seasonal variation in affective disorders. In T. A. Wehr & F. K. Goodwin (Eds.), *Circadian rhythms in psychiatry.* Pacific Grove, CA: Boxwood Press.

Rosenthal, N. E., Sack, D. A., Gillin, J. C., Lewy, A. J., Goodwin, F. K., Mueller, P. S., Newsome, D. A., & Wehr, T. A. (1984). Seasonal affective disorder. *Archive of General Psychiatry, 41,* 72–80.

Salib, E. (1997). Elderly suicide and weather conditions: is there a link? *International Journal of Geriatric Psychiatry, 12,* 937–941.

Salib, E., & Gray, N. (1997). Weather conditions and fatal self-harm in North Cheshire 1989–1993. *British Journal of Psychiatry, 177,* 473–477.

Sanborn, D. E., & Sanborn, C. J. (1978). Sex, season and suicide. *Psychological Reports, 42,* 1332.

Sattin, S. M. (1975). The psychodynamics of the holiday syndrome. *Perspectives in Psychiatric Care, 4,* 156–162.

Schaffer, D. (1974). Suicide in childhood and early adolescence. *Journal of Child Psychology and Psychiatry, 15,* 275–291.

Schmidtke, A., Bille-Brahe, U., De Leo, D., Kerkhof, A. J.F. M., Platt, S., Bjerke, T., Crepet, P., Harring, C., Hawton, K., Lönnqvist, J., Michel, M., Pommereau, X., Querejeat, I., Philippe, A., Salander-Renberg, E., Temesvary, B., Wasserman, D., Friecke, S., Weinacker, B., & Faria, J. S. (1996). Attempted suicide in Europe: Rates, trends and sociodemographic characteristics of suicide attempters during the period 1989–1992. Results from the WHO/EURO Multicentre Study on Parasuicide. *Acta Psychiatrica Scandinavica, 93,* 327–38.

Schramm, P. (1968). Untersuchungen über statistische Zusammenhänge zwischen Selbstmorden und Wetter in West-Berlin während der Jahre 1956–1965 [An investigation of the statistical relationship between suicide and the weather in West Berlin between 1956 and 1965]. *Meteorologische Abhandlungen, 87*(2). Berlin: Dietrich Reimer Verlag.

Shneidman, E. S., Farberow, N. L., & Litman, R. E. (1994). *Psychology of suicide: A clinician's guide to evaluation and treatment.* Aronson, NJ: Northvale.

Souêtre, E., Salvati, E., Belugou, J. L., Douillet, P., Braccini, T., & Darcourt, G. (1987). Seasonality of suicides: Environ-mental, sociological and biological covariations. *Journal of Affective Disorders, 13,* 215–225.

Sparhawk, T. G. (1987). Traditional holidays and suicide. *Psychological Reports, 60,* 245–246.

Stack, S. (1995). Temporal disappointment, homicide and suicide: An analysis of nonwhites and whites. *Sociological Focus, 28,* 313–328.

Takahasi, E. (1964). Seasonal variation of conception and suicide. *Tohoku Journal of Experimental Medicine, 84,* 215–227.

Thorson, J. A., & Kasworm, C. (1984). Sunshine and suicide: Possible influences of climate on behavior. *Death Education, 8,* 125–136.

Vance, D. E. (1995). Belief in lunar effects on human behavior. *Psychological Reports, 76,* 32–34.

Wallenstein, S., Weinberg, C. R., & Gould, M. (1989). Testing for a pulse in seasonal event data. *Biometrics, 45,* 817–830.

Warren, W. W., Smith, J. C., & Tylor, C. W. (1983). Seasonal variation in suicide and homicide: A question of consistency. *Journal of Biosocial Science, 15,* 349–356.

Wehr, T. A. (1988). Chronobiology of affective illness. *Advances in the Biosciences, 73,* 367–379.

Zung, W. K., & Green, R. L. (1974). Seasonal variation of suicide and depression. *Archives of General Psychiatry, 30,* 89–91.

Part 4

Suicidal Behaviour in Special Interest Groups

Chapter 17
Suicidal Behaviour Among Young People

Ella Arensman[1] and Keith Hawton[2]

[1]*National Suicide Research Foundation, Cork, Ireland,* [2]*Centre for Suicide Research, University of Oxford, UK*

Introduction

Suicidal behaviour among young people has become a growing health problem in many countries. This is true for both suicide and non-fatal suicidal behaviour (Schmidtke et al., 1996; Cantor & Neulinger, 2000).

For many years, information on suicide has been recorded at a national level in most European and non-European countries (WHO, Annual World Health Statistics). However, until recently, internationally comparable data on non-fatal suicidal behaviour were lacking. This was one of the reasons for the initiation of a Multi-Centre Study (WHO/EURO Multi-Centre Study on Suicidal Behaviour), which began in 1989 (Platt et al., 1992; Schmidtke et al., 1996). One of the main objectives of this study was to monitor trends in the epidemiology of attempted suicide* and to identify risk factors for repeated suicidal behaviour using a standardised methodology in all participating centres.

Findings from the first years of the study, 1989 until 1992, indicated that in most countries the highest rates of attempted suicide were found in girls and young women aged 15–24 years (Schmidtke et al., 1996). Although the peak rates for males were found in the age group 25–34 years, the rates for boys and young men aged 15–24 years also appeared to be relatively high. Comparison of these findings with those reported

---

* The term "attempted suicide" is used in this chapter for all non-fatal deliberate acts of self-poisoning or self-injury, irrespective of the intention. While this can be viewed as misleading, since many such acts are not associated with serious suicidal intent, it is a term that is used widely across countries in the context that it is used here.

in earlier studies showed that rates appeared to have increased since the mid 1980s (Hawton & Fagg, 1992; Diekstra, 1996; McLoone & Crombie, 1996). Among boys and young men, marked increases in rates of attempted suicide at the beginning of the nineties resulted in a narrowing of the female to male ratio (Kerkhof et al., 1994; McLoone & Crombie, 1996). This pattern appeared to parallel the rise in young male suicides found in several, but not all, European countries (Cantor & Neulinger, 2000). The relationship between rates of suicide and attempted suicide has, however, received little attention. This was therefore examined across countries participating in the Multi-Centre Study for the period 1989–1992 (Hawton et al., 1998).

Repetition of attempted suicide is a well-recognised problem in both adults and adolescents (Hawton et al., 1982; Arensman & Kerkhof, 1996). However, little was known about how this might vary in young people in terms of gender and between countries in Europe. These issues were examined by Hultén et al. (2001). Variations in repetition according to methods used in adolescents were also investigated.

A number of studies from individual countries have focused on risk factors for repeated non-fatal suicidal behaviour among young people (Brent et al., 1993; Pfeffer et al., 1993; Larsson & Ivarsson, 1998). Indications of a high risk of repeated suicide attempts within the year following the index attempt were found, especially in young males. Compared to young females, males more often used relatively lethal methods (e.g., strangulation, jumping from a high place or jumping in front of a moving object), and they tended to repeat more often (Gasquet & Choquet, 1993; Beautrais et al., 1996). The long-term period over which monitoring of attempted suicide has been carried out in the European collaborative project enabled us to investigate repetition from a prospective viewpoint and also to study the factors associated with repetition among young people. These issues were examined by Hultén, Jiang, Wasserman, Hawton, Hjelmeland, De Leo et al. (2001) using data from 7 centres covering the period 1989–1995.

The size of the problem of suicidal behaviour among the young means that provision of aftercare is of major importance. In general, we know that having a history of one or more suicide attempts is one of the strongest predictors of repetition in the future. Therefore, it is important to provide adequate care, directly following a suicide attempt, in order to try to reduce the risk of repetition in those who have made their first-ever attempt, and also to try to prevent a chronic pattern of repetition among those with a history of one or more previous attempts. We have relatively little information about the extent to which aftercare is recommended following attempted suicide in young people, and about the specific types of care. Available studies indicate that the percentage of young people in the USA receiving psychiatric consultation or other types of aftercare following a suicide attempt varies between 50% (Conn et al., 1984) and 83% (Spirito et al., 1992). The Multi-Centre Study provided a unique opportunity to examine the extent to which aftercare is being recommended for adolescents in Europe after attempted suicide and the factors which may have a bearing on this. This was done using data from nine centres for the period 1989–1992 (Hultén et al., 2000).

This chapter provides an overview of the most important findings from the European collaborative study concerning non-fatal and fatal suicidal behaviour among young people in Europe. In addition, the merits and implications of the study will be discussed, taking into account research findings from other studies focusing on suicidal behaviour among the young. Finally, recommendations for further research in this area are presented.

Prevalence of Attempted Suicide

Compared to older age groups, the prevalence of attempted suicide in the WHO/EURO Multi-Centre Study was highest among females aged 15–24 years in seven out of fifteen centres (Schmidtke et al., 1996). The average person-based rates of attempted suicide per 100,000 population over the period 1989–1992 for females in this age group varied between 99 in Guipuzcoa (Spain) to 766 in Cergy-Pontoise (France). Other centres reporting relatively high rates were Oxford (England) (629 per 100,000), Helsinki (Finland) (347 per 100,000) and Szeged (Hungary) (323 per 100,000). In all other centres except Helsinki, higher attempted suicide rates were found for females than males. Among males aged 15–24, the average attempted suicide rates over the same period varied from 54 per 100,000 population in Emilia Romagna (Italy) to 372 in Helsinki. As for young females, relatively high rates were also found in Cergy Pontoise (337 per 100,000), Oxford (314 per 100,000) and Szeged (253 per 100,000).

Within the age range 15–24 years, in most centres, higher attempted suicide rates were found for females aged 15–19 compared to those aged 20–24. Only in Helsinki and Sør-Trøndelag (Norway) were higher rates found for those aged 20–24, and in Bern (Switzerland) similar rates were found for girls aged 15–19 (266 per 100,000) and women aged 20–24 (267 per 100,000). Among males, the pattern was reversed, with all centres reporting higher rates for those aged 20–24 compared to 15–19 year-olds. Relatively low rates of attempted suicide for both young males and females were found in Guipuzcoa (Spain) and the two Italian centres: Padova and Emilia-Romagna.

In most centres, the attempted suicide rates decreased between 1989 and 1992, which was true for both sexes. However, in most centres there were no indications of a continuous decrease. Moreover, considering the relatively short period, it is difficult to interpret these findings as a downward trend.

Prevalence of Suicide

For fatal suicidal behaviour among males and females aged 15–24, both average regional (i.e., region in which the research centres were based) and national suicide rates per 100,000 population were calculated for the period 1989 to 1992. The highest regional suicide rates for both young males and females were found in Szeged (females: 48 per 100,000; males: 44 per 100,000). For females, however, the regional suicide rates were not representative of the national Hungarian suicide rates, the latter being considerably lower. In the Helsinki region of Finland, there were also high suicide rates, with, as in nearly all other centres, higher rates for males (42 per 100,000) than females (18 per 100,000).

At the national level, the highest suicide rate among females aged 15–19 was found in Norway (7 per 100,000), and among those aged 20–24 the highest rate was in Finland (11 per 100,000). The highest national suicide rate for 15–19 year old males was found in Hungary (50 per 100,000), and for 20–24 year old males in Finland (57 per 100,000). Other countries reporting relatively high national suicide rates in 15–24 year old males were Switzerland (29 per 100,000) and Austria (22 per 100,000). As for the rates of attempted suicide, relatively low suicide rates (nationally) for both young males and females were found in Spain and Italy. Due to the small numbers, no regional suicide rates could be obtained for Guipuzcoa and the two Italian centres.

Relationships Between Rates of Attempted Suicide and Suicide

Since previous studies have reported an increased risk of suicide among those with previous suicide attempts, the question of whether this association is reflected in an association between rates of attempted suicide and suicide across different countries was investigated (Hawton et al., 1998).

Both regional and national suicide rates were positively correlated with attempted suicide rates for 15–24 year-olds. However, only in males were the correlations statistically significant. Among males aged 15–24 years, significant correlations were found between attempted suicide rates and both regional ($r = .65$, $p < .02$) and national suicide rates ($r = .55$, $p < .02$). While a relatively high correlation was found between attempted suicide rates and regional suicide rates in men aged 20–24 years, this did not reach statistical significance ($r = .57$, $p < .09$). The correlations between attempted suicide and suicide rates for females were, while all positive, lower and non-significant.

Repetition of Non-Fatal Suicidal Behaviour

Using data on repeated non-fatal suicidal behaviour obtained from seven centres in the Multi-Centre Study, Hultén et al. (2001) studied prospective repetition rates in 15–19 year-olds over a maximum period of seven years (1989–1995). They also investigated factors associated with repetition. The average follow-up period was 204 weeks (*SD* = 108.9), and the total number of persons attempting suicide in the seven-year period was 1,264, comprising 73% girls and 27% boys. During the follow-up period, 17.2% of the entire group made at least one repeated attempt, the majority repeating within the first year following the index suicide attempt.

Factors Associated with Repetition

Previous Suicide Attempts

Risk of repetition in the Hultén et al. (2001) study was significantly higher among those who had already made one or more suicide attempts prior to the index attempt. This applied to both genders. Among those with a history of previous suicidal behaviour, 30% made at least one further attempt during follow-up, versus 10% of those without such a history (odds ratio 3.27, 95% CI 2.40–4.44).

Other Factors

In the Hultén et al. study (2001), no significant differences between future repeaters and non-repeaters were found for gender and type of aftercare offered. There was also no difference in repetition between those who used "hard" methods (e.g., cutting, hanging or jumping from a high place) and those who used "soft" methods (e.g., overdoses).

Recommended Care after Attempted Suicide

What are the types of care recommended for young people after attempted suicide, and to what extent is this associated with gender and features of the suicidal behaviour? These questions were addressed using the data from nine centres in the European Multi-Centre Study over the period 1989 to 1992 (Hultén et al., 2000).

Recommended aftercare refers to the care recommended after conclusion of emergency somatic treatment following attempted suicide. In the collaborative study, the types of aftercare included inpatient psychiatric care, outpatient psychiatric care with a psychiatrist, psychologist and/or counsellor for psychotherapy, or supportive contact for both the individual and family, and non-psychiatric care, for example, with a school counsellor, social welfare office, or general practitioner. The analyses were based on the data from nine centres, in which there were 1,540 suicide attempts (episodes) involving 1,294 individuals aged 15–19 years, of which 73% were females.

Factors Associated with Aftercare

Previous Suicide Attempts

In most centres, attempted suicide patients who had made one or more prior attempts before the index suicide attempt (repeaters) were more often recommended aftercare compared to those who had never made an attempt prior to the index attempt (first evers). Here, no distinction was made between different types of aftercare. In the two Swedish centres, Stockholm and Umeå, all boys and girls who were repeaters at the time of the index attempt were recommended aftercare. In five other centres, aftercare was recommended more often for male repeaters than female repeaters. However, these differences were not significant.

Looking at the relative risk of care being recommended after a suicide attempt between first evers and repeaters in the individual centres, it appeared that only in Oxford was the chance of being recommended care significantly higher among those who were repeaters at the time of the index attempt compared to those who were first ever (relative risk 1.37, 95% CI 1.20–1.56).

Method of Suicide Attempt

On the basis of the data from all nine centres, it was found that young people who had used a hard method in their index attempts, were significantly more likely to be recommended aftercare than those who used soft methods. In addition, differences were found between specific type of method used and the chance of being recommended aftercare. Males and females who took an overdose of prescribed drugs and those who cut themselves with a sharp object were more likely to be recommended aftercare compared to those who took an overdose of non-prescribed drugs. This is probably related to the fact that those using the first two methods are more likely to be in current care at the time of their attempts.

Comparing first evers and repeaters, it was found that first evers taking an overdose with prescribed drugs or those cutting themselves had the highest chance of being recommended aftercare following their attempts. Among repeaters, those who used cutting as method of index attempt were significantly more likely to be recommended aftercare compared to those using other methods. Logistic regression analysis showed that a history of previous attempts (OR 2.0, 95% CI 1.53–2.61) and using a hard method at the time of the index attempt (OR 1.71, 95% CI 1.49–1.96) were significantly associated with the likelihood of being recommended aftercare.

Discussion and Conclusions

The European collaborative study has provided unique longitudinal data on trends in non-fatal and fatal suicidal behaviour and associated factors among young people in Europe. We will now summarise the key findings and consider their implications.

Relationship Between Attempted Suicide and Suicide

For both males and females aged 15–24 years, there are positive correlations between rates of attempted suicide and suicide rates, but these are more pronounced and only statistically significant in males. These correlations were stronger at the regional level, i.e., where the centres monitoring attempted suicide were based, compared to the national level. The question whether this represents a consistent pattern cannot yet be confirmed, since not all centres were able to provide regional suicide rates.

Looking at the different age groups, the relationship between rates of attempted suicide and suicide was stronger in both sexes in the overall 15–24 year age group compared to within the five-year age bands 15–19 and 20–24 years. However, this conclusion is limited because only 10 out of 15 centres were able to provide suicide statistics in these age bands and hence the findings reflect this fact. Another methodological point concerns the fact that there appear to be differences in the ways in which suicides are registered between the European countries participating in this study. Thus the risk of misclassification of suicides to other categories of death, for example, undetermined or accidental deaths, varies between countries. The extent to which this may have influenced our findings is not clear since this study was based only on official suicide statistics.

The association between rates of attempted suicide and suicide among young males is clearly important because, since a history of attempted suicide is the best predictor of future suicide risk (Sakinofsky, 2000), it implies that changes in the former may be followed by an increase in suicides. The stronger association between rates of attempted suicide and suicide in young males compared to young females is in keeping with the fact that attempts in males tend to be associated with higher suicidal intent (Bancroft et al., 1976; Motto, 1984.). In contrast, young female suicide attempters more often report motives to do with communication of despair and influencing others, which are usually associated with lower suicidal intent. This probably also explains why rates of attempted suicide are generally much higher in young females. From follow-up studies, reviewed by Spirito, Boergers, Donaldson (2000), we know that the risk of suicide following attempted suicide among youngsters is much greater in male than female subjects, with the highest risk of suicide in the first year following the suicide attempt. This is in line with the findings of Hawton, Houston, Shepperd (1999), who conducted a retrospective study of 174 cases of suicide under the age of 25 years, based on data obtained from coroners' and medical records. They found that among those who had made previous attempts, 80% had made their last non-fatal attempt within the year before they committed suicide.

Other factors that appear to be associated with an increased risk of suicide among young males are the use of hard methods at the time of the initial suicide attempt and the presence of substance abuse (Spirito et al., 2000).

Relationship Between Attempted Suicide and Non-Fatal Repetition

Looking at the risk of non-fatal repetition among young males and females aged 15–19 years, the findings indicate that those with a history of suicide attempts are significantly more likely to repeat, the majority repeating within the first year following the last suicide attempt. The percentage of all patients who made at least one repeated attempt was 17.2% during the follow-up period, with 10% repeating within the first year following the index suicide attempt.

Although a standardised methodology was used in all research centres, and validity and reliability checks were carried out on a regular basis, information would have been lacking on repeated suicide attempts that were referred to another hospital outside the catchment area. There would also have been no information on repeat attempts that did not come to medical attention. In a recent study in England of adolescents who had engaged in deliberate self-harm, ranging from minor self-injury to an overdose of medication, only 12.6% had been referred to hospital following these acts (Hawton et al., 2002). Thus the full extent of repetition in young people will have been considerably underestimated in the European Multi-Centre Study, as in other similar studies in the field. In addition, the number of missing values varied between centres, with a relatively large number of missing values for the variable "previous suicide attempts." This may be due to prompt self-discharge from the emergency department before the interviewer could obtain all relevant information from the patient.

The findings with respect to repetition are somewhat higher compared to previous prospective studies using a similar methodology. Thus Goldacre and Hawton (1985) and Sellar, Hawton, Goldacre (1990) reported an annual repetition rate of 6% in 12–18 year-olds in the Oxford region, with the greatest risk of repetition during the first 3 months following the index attempt. Among studies of patients who are re-contacted directly at follow-up, the rates of repetition tend to be somewhat higher, ranging from 10% within 3 months following the index attempt (Hawton et al., 1982; Spirito et al., 1992) to 12% at one year (White, 1974; Kienhorst et al., 1991).

Among those with a history of previous attempts, a significantly higher proportion (30%) made at least one repeated attempt during the entire follow-up, compared to those who were first evers at the time of the index attempt (10.5%). This is in line with findings from a study by Goldston et al. (1999).

In contrast with the risk of eventual for suicide, no gender differences were found with respect to non-fatal repetition of attempts. History of previous attempts appeared to be the only independent predictor for future repetition, emphasising the need for risk assessment directly following a suicide attempt and provision of adequate aftercare. The absence of a difference in repetition between those who used hard and those who used soft methods in their attempts is perhaps surprising given that the majority of episodes involving a hard method would have been self-cutting, a behaviour that is often repeated. Many episodes involving this method, however, do not present to hospital (Hawton et al., 2002) so that repeated cutting often will not be detected by means of hospital registers.

Recommended Aftercare Following Attempted Suicide

A minority of adolescents aged 15–19 years appears to be offered aftercare following emergency medical treatment due to attempted suicide. This is a remarkable finding considering the high risk of repetition directly following the index attempt. It is difficult to explain this finding since few studies have focused on the issue of recommended aftercare. According to Spirito et al. (1992), one quarter of the young people admitted to hospital following suicide attempts denied immediately on arrival that the event had actually been a suicide attempt, and an equally high proportion retracted their admission the following day. Furthermore, in those cases where aftercare has been offered, attendance of treatment sessions tends to be low (Spirito et al., 2000).

The extent to which aftercare is being recommended clearly varies between European countries. It also appears to be related to the type of method used for the attempt as well as the presence or absence of previous attempts. The proportion of adolescents being recommended aftercare following their suicide attempt is somewhat higher in those with a history of previous attempts than in first timers. While this may in part reflect the fact that repeaters are also more likely to be in current care, it also indicates that there is still an important proportion of adolescents, including those with high risk of repeated suicidal behaviour, who are not being recommended aftercare.

Comparing the different European centres, it appears that there is no standard policy with respect to recommended aftercare following attempted suicide. Of all centres included in this study, only in Oxford was aftercare significantly more often recommended to those with a history of previous attempts compared to those had carried out their first ever attempts. Risk of repetition is highest among those with a history of previous attempts and they also appear to have more psychological and psychiatric disorders (Brent et al., 1993; Marttunen et al., 1994). This emphasises the need to offer effective treatment programmes for these individuals following a suicide attempt. However, adequate aftercare directly following the index suicide attempt is also important for those who are first evers, in order to prevent a repeated attempt in the short term and, perhaps, a chronic pattern of repetition in the longer term.

Overall, adolescents who attempted suicide using hard methods in the European collaborative study had a significantly greater chance of being recommended care following their attempt compared to those using soft methods. However, this pattern was not consistent across different countries, indicating a lack of consensus in policies for aftercare. Previous studies have indicated a higher suicide mortality among those who use hard methods (Otto, 1972; Brent et al., 1988). Although the proportions with self-cutting may have been lower in those studies than in the European study, nevertheless recommending aftercare to these individuals should have high priority in treatment policies of general hospitals.

Inconsistency in recommending aftercare may also be explained by the fact that among those using hard methods, a large proportion comprised girls using a sharp object to cut their wrists, an act which is more often associated with tension and other non-suicidal motives rather than relief, suicidal intent, and often associated with borderline personality disorders. Among those who frequently repeat this behaviour, there is a risk of increased lethality of the behaviour over time (Iancu et al., 1997). Although this behaviour is different to much other non-fatal suicidal behaviour, more clearly associated with high suicide risk, assessment of the risk of repetition and adequate treatment for adolescents with this pattern of self harm should also be a priority for healthcare professionals.

Recommendations for Further Research

One of the implications of the European Multi-Centre Study is that an increase in rates of attempted suicide might be associated with an increase in suicide. This association is expected to be higher among young males compared to young females. In order to verify this, trends in attempted suicide and suicide rates need to be examined over a relatively long time, for example, a ten-year period. We also require further information on other factors associated with increased suicide risk in young people, in order to improve procedures for suicide risk assessment. These may include psychological characteristics (e.g., aggression, impulsivity, problem-solving skills) as well as psychiatric and sociodemographic factors.

Among adolescents who are being recommended aftercare following a suicide attempt, the proportion of those who actually receive the recommended care is not known. It is important to verify this, especially in view of the high risk of repeated non-fatal and fatal suicidal behaviour in the first few months following an attempt. From this study, it is apparent that that there are considerable differences between countries in their policies for recommending care to attempted suicide patients following an attempt, which cannot yet be completely explained. Therefore, the reasons underlying these differences should be further investigated, including implications of the different policies in terms of prevention of repeated suicidal behaviour. In addition, information on the efficacy of treatment programmes specifically designed for young suicide attempters is limited. Therefore, further research into the efficacy of treatment interventions, including psychological and psychopharmacological approaches for adolescents and other young people who engage in suicidal behaviour, is clearly needed.

References

Arensman, E., & Kerkhof, A. J.F. M. (1996). Classification of attempted suicide: A review of empirical studies, 1963–1993. *Suicide and Life-Threatening Behavior, 26,* 46–67.

Bancroft, J., Skrimshire, A. M., & Simkin, S. (1976). The reasons people give for taking overdoses. *British Journal of Psychiatry, 128,* 538–548.

Beautrais, A. L., Joyce, P. R., & Mulder, R. T. (1996). Risk factors for serious suicide attempts among youths aged 13 through 24 years. *Journal of the American Academy of Child and Adolescent Psychiatry, 35,* 1174–1182.

Brent, D. A., Perper, J. A., Goldstein, C. E., Kolko, D. J., Allan, M. J., Allman, C. J., & Zelenak, J. P. (1988). Risk factors for adolescent suicide. A comparison of adolescent suicide victims with suicidal inpatients. *Archives of General Psychiatry, 45,* 581–588.

Brent, D. A., Johnson, B., Bartle, S., Bridge, J., Rather, C., Matta, J., Connolly, J., & Constantine, D. (1993). Personality disorder, tendency to impulsive violence, and suicidal behavior in adolescents. *Journal of the American Academy of Child and Adolescent Psychiatry, 32,* 69–75.

Brent, D. A., Kolko, D. J., Wartella, M. E., Boylan, M. B., Moritz, G., Baugher, M., & Zelenak, J. P. (1993). Adolescent psychiatric inpatients' risk of suicide attempt at 6-month follow-up. *Journal of the American Academy of Child and Adolescent Psychiatry, 32,* 95–105.

Cantor, C., & Neulinger, K. (2000). The epidemiology of suicide and attempted suicide among young Australians. *Australian and New Zealand Journal of Psychiatry, 34,* 370–387.

Conn, L., Rudnick, B. F., & Lion, J. R. (1984). Psychiatric care for patients with self-inflicted gunshot wounds. *American Journal of Psychiatry, 141,* 261–263.

Diekstra, R.F. W. (1996). The epidemiology of suicide and parasuicide. *Archives of Suicide Research, 2,* 1–29.

Gasquet, I., & Choquet, M. (1993). Gender role in adolescent suicidal behavior: Observations and therapeutic implications. *Acta Psychiatrica Scandinavica, 87,* 59–65.

Goldacre, M., & Hawton, K. (1985). Repetition of deliberate self-poisoning and subsequent death in adolescents who take overdoses. *British Journal of Psychiatry, 146,* 395–398.

Goldston, D. B., Daniel, S. S., Reboussin, D. M., Reboussin, B. A., Frazier, P. H., & Kelley, A. E. (1999). Suicide attempts among formerly hospitalized adolescents: A prospective naturalistic study of risk during the first 5 years after discharge. *Journal of the American Academy of Child and Adolescent Psychiatry, 38,* 660–671.

Hawton, K., O'Grady, J., Osborn, M., & Cole, D. (1982). Adolescents who take overdoses: Their characteristics, problems and contacts with helping agencies. *British Journal of Psychiatry, 140,* 118–123.

Hawton, K., & Fagg, J. (1992). Deliberate self-poisoning and self-injury in adolescents. A study of characteristics and trends in Oxford, 1976–89. *British Journal of Psychiatry, 161,* 816–823.

Hawton, K., Arensman, E., Wasserman, Hultén, A., Bille-Brahe, U., Bjerke, T., Crepet, P., Deisenhammer, E., Kerkhof, A., De Leo, D., Michel, K., Ostamo, A. Philippe, A., Querejeta, I., Salander-Renberg, E., Schmidtke, A., & Temesvary, B. (1998). Relation between attempted suicide and suicide rates among young people in Europe. *Journal of Epidemiology and Community Health, 52,* 191–194.

Hawton, K., Houston, K., & Shepperd, R. (1999). Suicide in young people. Study of 174 cases, aged under 25 years, based on coroners' and medical records. *British Journal of Psychiatry, 175,* 271–276

Hawton, K., Rodham, K., Evans, E., & Weatherall, R. (2002). Deliberate self harm in adolescents: Self report survey in schools in England. *British Medical Journal, 325,* 1207–1211.

Hultén, A., Wasserman, D., Hawton, K., Jiang, G. X., Salander-Renberg, E. Schmidtke, A., Bille-Brahe, U., Bjerke, T., Kerkhof, A., Michel, K., & Querejeta, I. (2000). Recommended care for young people (15–19 years) after suicide attempts in certain European countries. *European Child and Adolescent Psychiatry, 9,* 100–108.

Hultén, A., Jiang, G. X., Wasserman, D., Hawton, K., Hjelmeland, H., De Leo, D., Ostamo, A., Salander-Renberg, E., & Schmidtke A. (2001). Repetition of attempted suicide among teenagers in Europe: Frequency, timing and risk factors. *European Child and Adolescent Psychiatry, 10,* 161–169.

Iancu, I., Laufer, N., Dannon, P. N., Zohar-Kadouch, R., Apter, A., & Zohar, J. (1997) A general hospital study of attempted suicide in adolescence: Age and method of attempt. *Israel Journal of Psychiatry and Related Sciences, 34,* 228–234.

Kerkhof, A. J.F. M., Schmidtke, A., Bille-Brahe, U., De Leo, D., & Lönnqvist, J. (1994). *Attempted suicide in Europe. Findings from the WHO Regional Office for Europe.* Leiden: DSWO Press.

Kienhorst, C. W. M., De Wilde, E. J., Diekstra, R.F. W., & Wolters, W.H. G. (1991). Differences between adolescent suicide attempters and depressed adolescents. *Acta Psychiatrica Scandinavica, 85,* 222–228.

Larsson, B., & Ivarsson, T. (1998). Clinical characteristics of adolescent psychiatric inpatients who have attempted suicide. *European Child and Adolescent Psychiatry, 7,* 201–208.

Marttunen, M. J., Aro, H. M., Henriksson, M. M., & Lönnqvist, J. K. (1994). Antisocial behaviour in adolescent suicide. *Acta Psychiatrica Scandinavica, 89,* 167–173.

McLoone, P., & Crombie, I. K. (1996). Hospitalisation for deliberate self-poisoning in Scotland from 1981 to 1993: Trends in rates and types of drugs used. *British Journal of Psychiatry, 169,* 81–85.

Motto, J. (1984). Suicide in male adolescents. In H. S. Sudak, A. B. Ford, & N. B. Rushforth (Eds.), *Suicide in the young.* Boston: PSG Inc.

Otto, U. (1972). Suicidal acts by children and adolescents: A follow-up study. *Acta Psychiatrica Scandinavica. Suppl., 233,* 7–123.

Pfeffer, C. R., Klerman, G. L., Hurt, S. W., Kakuma, T., Peskin, J. R., & Siefker, C. A. (1993). Suicidal children grow up: Rates and psychosocial risk factors for suicide attempts during follow-up. *Journal of the American Academy of Child and Adolescent Psychiatry, 32,* 106–113

Platt, S., Bille-Brahe, U., Kerkhof, A., Schmidtke, A., Bjerke, T., Crepet, P., De Leo, D., Haring, C., Lönnqvist, J., Michel, Philippe, A., Pommereau, X., Querejeta, I., Salander-Renberg, E.,

Temesvary, B., Wasserman, D., & Sampaio Faria, J. (1992). Parasuicide in Europe: The WHO/EURO Multicentre Study on Parasuicide. I. Introduction and preliminary analysis for 1989. *Acta Psychiatrica Scandinavica, 85*, 97–104.

Sakinofsky, I. (2000). Repetition of suicidal behaviour. In Hawton, K. & Van Heeringen, K. (Eds.). *The international handbook of suicide and attempted suicide* (pp. 385–404). Chichester: Wiley.

Schmidtke, A., Bille-Brahe, U., De Leo, D., Kerkhof, A., Bjerke, T., Crepet, P., Haring, C., Hawton, K., Lönnqvist, J., Michel, K., Philippe, A., Pommereau, X., Querejeta, I., Salander-Renberg, E., Temesvary, B., Wasserman, D., Fricke, S., Weinacker, B., & Sampaio-Faria, J. G. (1996). Attempted suicide in Europe: Rates, trends and sociodemographic characteristics of suicide attempters during the period 1989–1992. Results of the WHO/EURO Multicentre Study on Parasuicide. *Acta Psychiatrica Scandinavica, 93*, 327–338.

Sellar, C., Hawton, K., & Goldacre, M. (1990). Self-poisoning in adolescents. Hospital admission and deaths in the Oxford region 1980–1985. *British Journal of Psychiatry, 156*, 866–870.

Spirito, A., Plummer, B., Gispert, M., Levy, S., Kurkijan, J., Lewander, W., Hagberg, S., & Devost, L. (1992). Adolescent suicide attempts: Outcomes at follow-up. *American Journal of Orthopsychiatry, 62*, 464–468.

Spirito, A., Boergers, J., & Donaldson, D. (2000). Adolescent suicide attempters: Post-attempt course and implications for treatment. *Clinical Psychology and Psychotherapy, 7*, 161–173.

White, H. C. (1974). Self-poisoning in adolescents. *British Journal of Psychiatry, 124*, 24–35.

World Health Organisation (WHO). *Annual World Health Statistics.* Geneva: Author.

Chapter 18
Suicide and Suicidal Behaviour in Late-Life

Diego De Leo and Kym Spathonis

Australian Institute for Suicide Research and Prevention, Griffith University, Brisbane, Australia

The rationale by which an individual completes suicide at an older age has long been a focus of research efforts in suicidology. Scholars in fields ranging from sociology, philosophy, psychology and psychiatry, to biology and genetics have long investigated suicidal phenomenon in a quest to understand, predict and prevent suicidal behaviour. Decades of suicide research have revealed that social and cultural variables amplify any biological and psychological predisposition to suicidal behaviour. These findings transcend both age and sex. However, diverse rates of suicide among specific population groups indicate that these variables may interact to a varying degree and present a unique risk among individuals of an older age.

In the last few decades, there has been a relevant increase in suicide rates in older age, particularly in a number of Asian and Latin countries. Nations such as Hungary, Lithuania and Latvia, which are marked by distinct cultures and social environments traditionally associated with very high levels of suicidality, have recently experienced an increase in elderly suicide, and markedly lowered rates of youth suicide. Conversely, Anglo-Saxon nations have evidenced the reverse, whereby soaring rates of youth suicides outnumber the rate of suicide completed by elderly individuals (Lester, 2001). The similar trends in elderly suicide found in nations of similar socio-cultural background leads to speculation that the intrinsic nature of suicidal behaviour is embedded in the socio-environmental surrounds in which one exists. Emile Durkheim (1897/1951) speculated this hypothesis over a century ago by indicating that "suicide varies inversely [or negatively] with the degree of social integration of the social group of which the individual forms a part" (p. 209). However, a model formulated purely on a sociological interpretation of suicidal behaviour among the elderly, or any other single interpretation for that matter, will inevitably fail to take into consideration the full spectrum of interrelating factors that contribute to suicidal outcomes. Hence, suicidal behaviour among the elderly must be considered in the realm of empirical evidence that depicts a myriad of risk factors and unique characteristics of suicidal behaviour in late-life.

Identifying the reasons why so many elderly individuals seek to end their own lives is important due to the fact that the number of elderly suicides might be destined to increase. The aged constitute the fastest-growing segment of the population, a phenomenon also associated with a marked increase in longevity. Simultaneously, we are facing the ageing of the "baby boom generation" (Conwell 1992; Harwood & Jacoby 2000). It has been estimated that by the year 2025, the total population will have expanded six-fold since 1950, and people aged 60 years or older will represent about 14 percent of the world's total population (Steinberg et al., 1997).

This chapter begins by presenting an epidemiological depiction of suicidal behaviour in late-life. It is important to note, however, that although elderly rates of suicide may appear to be high, suicidal behaviour (attempted and completed) is often underreported (Tsuang & Simpson, 1985; Robins & Kulbok, 1988; Simpson, 1988) and many actual suicides are recorded by coroners as accidental death (Brooke & Atkinson, 1974) or open verdicts, that is, verdicts indicating possible but not proven suicide (Shaw & Sims, 1984). In addition, variability in defining and reporting cases has called into question the reliability of official rates in some countries (Sainsbury & Jenkins, 1982; Farmer, 1988). Moreover, "passive" suicidal behaviours such as refusal to eat and drink, medication and treatment non-compliance, the use of alcohol and psychotropic drugs, and social withdrawal are often unrecognised in the elderly and are not often considered when examining suicidal behaviour (Hasegawa et al., 1992; Kishi et al., 1996a; Kishi et al., 1996b). Such behaviours have been associated with overtly reported suicidal ideations (Nelson & Farberow, 1980), and the premature ending of life (Osgood et al., 1991). Hence, it is likely that the true prevalence of suicidal behaviour among older-aged populations is misrepresented, and statistics must therefore be interpreted with caution.

When considering the risk of suicide in older age, it is also important to recognise that, as a whole, the elderly population face similar inevitabilities, such as physical decline, increasing limitations on physical and mental functioning, and an increasing need to rely on others for help with activities of everyday living.

This chapter will also pay heed to the nature and capacity of intervention measures to prevent suicide in older age, with particular reference to the potential of primary health care, religious and community sectors. The chapter will conclude with a final reflection on the potential for specifically targeted research and offer a realistic stance upon the likelihood of a future international decrease in suicide rates in late-life.

Epidemiological Trends in Suicidal Behaviour in Late-Life

Fatal Suicidal Behaviour

Internationally, suicide rates increase with age, however, this pattern is not found in every nation. The general global rate of suicide among those aged 75 years and older is approximately three times higher compared to youth under the age of 25 years (see Figure 1). Over the last 30 years, international trends have changed markedly whereby Anglo-Saxon countries, particularly the USA, have experienced up to a 50% decline in rates of elderly suicide, particularly among white males, and a corresponding increase in suicide among younger age groups.

The international progression of suicide rates over time (1960–1990) depicts a significant increase in the rate of elderly/youth suicide in Asian countries (two-fold), and to a lesser extent in Europe (Gulbinat, 1995). Since 1980, Latin countries, Finland and Ireland have experienced the highest increased rates of suicide among individuals aged 75 and older. Contrarily, an increase in suicide among individuals aged 15–24 and a subsequent decline among the elderly has been observed particularly in Anglo-Saxon countries, such as Australia, New Zealand, Canada and the United States (Gulbinat, 1995). A similar trend has been observed in South American countries (Diekstra & Gulbinat, 1993). Table 1 compares the rate of suicide (per 100,000) among individuals aged 75 years and older and youth 15–24 years for a

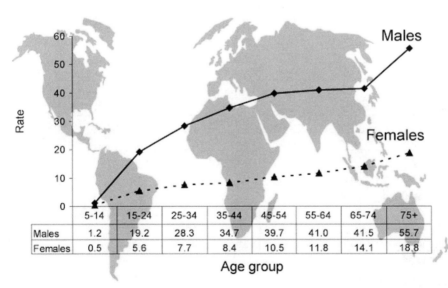

Age group	5-14	15-24	25-34	35-44	45-54	55-64	65-74	75+
Males	1.2	19.2	28.3	34.7	39.7	41.0	41.5	55.7
Females	0.5	5.6	7.7	8.4	10.5	11.8	14.1	18.8

Figure 1 Global suicide rates (per 100,000) by gender and age, selected countries, 1998 (World Health Organisation, 2003).

Table 1 Suicide rates (per 100,000) in world countries by gender and older age and youth (most recent year available). Source: WHO, 2003.

	Year	≥ 75 years			15–24 years		
		Males	**Females**	**Total**	**Males**	**Females**	**Total**
AFRICAN COUNTRIES							
Mauritius	1999	34.5	0.0	12.8	12.3	17.5	14.9
Sao Tome-Principe	1987	0.0	0.0	0.0	0.0	0.0	0.0
Seychelles	1985	0.0	0.0	0.0	39.0	13.3	26.3
Zimbabwe	1990	0.0	0.0	–	13.0	12.1	12.5
AMERICAN COUNTRIES							
Argentina	1996	42.4	7.7	20.5	8.8	3.4	6.1
Belize	1995	50.0	0.0	25.0	16.7	4.3	10.6
Bahamas	1995	0.0	0.0	0.0	0.0	0.0	0.0
Barbados	1995	0.0	0.0	0.0	4.3	9.1	6.7
Brazil	1995	18.3	3.1	9.5	6.9	2.2	4.6
Canada	1997	27.0	4.3	12.8	22.4	4.5	13.7
Chile	1994	26.7	1.4	10.9	10.9	1.5	6.3
Colombia	1994	13.4	0.7	6.3	9.2	3.9	6.6
Costa Rica	1995	8.4	0.0	3.7	11.8	4.0	8.0
Cuba	1996	113.2	27.3	68.0	14.2	13.1	13.7
Ecuador	1995	10.7	1.0	5.2	9.5	8.2	8.9
El Salvador	1993	19.9	8.8	13.2	19.0	13.4	16.2
Guatemala	1984	0.0	0.0	–	0.5	0.0	0.3
Guyana	1994	25.0	0.0	10.0	24.4	10.8	17.8
Jamaica	1985	3.4	2.6	3.0	1.2	0.0	0.6
Mexico	1995	18.0	1.0	8.6	7.6	2.0	4.7
Nicaragua	1994	18.8	4.2	10.0	9.8	5.5	7.6
Panama	1987	19.2	0.0	9.3	6.6	3.4	5.0
Paraguay	1994	9.0	5.7	7.0	4.9	1.6	3.3
Peru	1989	3.0	0.0	1.3	0.7	1.1	0.9
Puerto Rico	1992	24.3	2.4	16.7	9.7	1.6	5.7
Suriname	1992	0.0	0.0	0.0	19.0	12.8	16.0
Trinidad & Tobago	1994	21.2	0.0	10.0	15.8	9.3	12.7
United States of America	1998	45.2	5.2	20.0	18.5	3.3	11.1
Uruguay	1990	71.2	10.0	32.4	13.4	2.9	8.2
Venezuela	1994	28.6	2.0	13.2	11.5	3.9	7.7
SOUTH-EAST ASIA							
Peoples Republic of Korea	2000	81.5	32.4	–	10.2	7.0	–
Sri Lanka	1991	–	–	–	59.0	42.0	–

Table 1 continued.

	Year	≥ 75 years			15–24 years		
		Males	**Females**	**Total**	**Males**	**Females**	**Total**
Thailand	1994	9.5	2.0	5.0	7.8	4.3	6.1
EUROPEAN COUNTRIES							
Albania	1998	11.6	0.0	4.4	10.9	10.8	10.8
Armenia	2000	10.6	7.5	8.6	1.7	0.0	0.9
Austria	2000	95.7	23.0	45.5	21.8	5.7	13.9
Azerbaijan	2000	2.6	2.4	2.5	1.5	0.5	1.0
Belarus	1999	85.5	20.7	37.0	37.3	6.5	22.2
Belgium	1995	80.0	19.9	39.9	21.6	6.2	14.0
Bulgaria	1999	99.1	28.1	56.4	12.0	3.4	7.8
Croatia	2000	104.1	34.6	58.1	18.8	3.1	11.1
Czech. Republic	2000	72.9	16.6	35.2	17.4	3.3	10.5
Denmark	1998	54.2	16.0	29.9	10.4	2.8	6.7
Estonia	1999	119.2	39.4	59.8	44.2	6.8	25.7
Finland	1999	51.7	4.9	19.2	36.3	5.9	21.4
France	1998	84.6	17.9	41.4	13.2	3.6	8.5
Georgia	2000	10.3	4.9	6.8	2.3	0.0	1.2
Germany	1999	62.0	18.5	31.3	12.7	3.0	8.0
Greece	1998	13.7	1.0	6.3	3.1	0.4	1.8
Hungary	2000	144.2	51.4	81.8	17.5	4.0	10.9
Iceland	1997	36.8	0.0	15.2	13.8	9.6	11.8
Ireland	1998	15.9	2.7	7.7	33.6	4.1	19.2
Israel	1997	44.1	15.4	27.5	12.6	1.6	7.2
Italy	1998	42.7	7.0	19.6	7.5	1.9	4.8
Kazakhstan	1999	73.0	24.0	35.5	45.1	9.1	27.1
Kyrgyzstan	1999	21.4	20.1	51.8	18.5	5.0	11.8
Latvia	2000	115.6	31.2	20.5	30.5	4.8	17.9
Lithuania	2000	74.1	28.9	42.6	49.0	9.6	29.5
Luxembourg	2000	87.5	11.2	34.9	12.0	4.1	8.1
Malta	1999	14.1	9.2	11.1	3.4	3.6	3.5
The Netherlands	1999	27.1	9.3	15.5	8.5	4.4	6.5
Norway	1998	19.8	5.1	10.5	23.7	7.7	15.9
Poland	1999	32.9	6.2	15.0	21.5	2.6	12.3
Portugal	2000	44.9	7.8	21.5	3.7	1.0	2.4
Republic of Moldova	2000	49.3	8.2	21.9	11.4	2.5	7.0
Romania	2000	30.4	10.4	17.9	10.2	1.8	6.1
Russian Federation	1998	88.0	32.3	44.6	51.9	8.6	30.5

Table 1 continued.

	Year	≥ 75 years			15–24 years		
		Males	**Females**	**Total**	**Males**	**Females**	**Total**
Slovakia	2000	42.6	9.6	20.9	14.1	2.0	8.2
Slovenia	1999	107.6	19.0	45.2	23.5	7.0	15.4
Spain	1998	46.1	9.2	22.8	8.0	1.5	4.8
Sweden	1998	43.4	12.3	24.2	10.7	5.5	8.1
Switzerland	1996	80.2	23.5	43.5	24.8	5.6	15.3
Tajikistan	1995	23.3	11.0	15.4	5.1	2.6	3.9
The Former Yugo-slav Republic of Macedonia	2000	34.1	11.4	21.1	5.3	2.5	3.9
Turkmenistan	1998	12.9	17.5	16.1	19.9	8.1	14.1
Ukraine	2000	70.3	23.6	35.5	29.3	5.4	17.5
United Kingdom of Great Britain & Northern Ireland	1999	15.5	5.1	8.8	10.6	2.5	6.7
Uzbekistan	1998	11.7	5.9	7.7	11.4	6.6	9.0
Yugoslavia	1990	97.3	32.3	57.3	9.6	3.6	6.7
EASTERN MEDITERRANEAN COUNTRIES							
Bahrain	1988	0.0	0.0	0.0	2.3	0.0	1.2
Egypt	1987	0.0	0.5	0.2	0.0	0.0	0.0
Iran	1991	2.0	0.0	1.0	0.4	0.2	0.3
Kuwait	2000	0.0	0.0	0.0	1.8	1.4	1.6
Syrian Arab Repub-lic	1981	0.0	0.0	0.0	0.5	0.3	0.4
WESTERN PACIFIC COUNTRIES							
Australia	1999	30.0	3.4	13.7	22.1	5.3	13.9
China (mainland, selected areas)	1998	88.0	62.4	72.8	5.8	9.8	7.7
China (mainland, selected rural ar-eas)	1998	170.0	104.4	129.1	8.4	15.2	11.8
China (mainland, selected urban ar-eas)	1998	35.7	29.3	32.1	3.4	4.4	3.9
China (Hong Kong)	1999	53.1	38.4	44.2	9.0	6.8	7.9
Japan	1999	60.7	34.1	43.4	16.5	7.3	12.0
Korea	2000	81.5	32.4	48.1	16.5	7.3	8.7
New Zealand	1998	28.0	5.1	13.7	38.1	13.3	25.9
Philippines	1993	3.2	2.8	3.0	2.7	2.7	2.7
Singapore	2000	48.8	23.0	33.5	6.5	7.7	7.1

number of world countries reporting to the World Health Organisation (2003) for the most recent year available.

The higher rate of suicide in older age is observed between both male and female genders, with elderly males completing suicide at a rate that is almost universally higher than that for females (De Leo, 1999). In general, the male-female ratio of suicide increases with age, from approximately 3:1 in young people up to 12:1 among those over the age of 85 (De Leo, 1997). However, the gender ratio differs somewhat between countries. In Anglo-Saxon nations (e.g., New Zealand, Canada, Australia, and also Scotland and Ireland), the male-female ratio is typically 5–7 times higher in men in both young and old age groups. On the contrary, Latin nations have experienced a lower male-female ratio of suicide in younger age (approximately 3:1), which increases to a higher ratio in older age (e.g., 6:1 in Portugal, 4:1 in Italy and Spain, and 5:1 in Belgium and France) (De Leo, 1997). This phenomenon, however, does not extend itself to every nation that may be of Latin or Anglo-Saxon descent (De Leo, 1999).

In Asian countries, greater rates of suicide have been observed across genders among older as opposed to younger age groups, with elderly/youth ratios as high as 8.7 in Japan, 7.3 in Hong Kong and 5.9 in Singapore (Pritchard & Baldwin, 2002). In particular, women of Asian nations exhibit significantly higher rates of suicide in older age compared to women residing in Anglo-Saxon countries (Pritchard & Baldwin, 2002). More recent evidence also shows a disproportionate number of women aged 75 years and older in rural China at a heightened risk of completing suicide compared to women in English-speaking countries (Qin & Mortensen, 2001; Pritchard & Baldwin, 2002). In younger ages groups (15–44 years), suicide rates among females exceed those for males of the same age bracket. Furthermore, a significantly lesser proportion of females who die by suicide in China may be suffering from depression or other mental illness at the time of death (Brown, 1997). This state of affairs presents a gender difference that is not only unobservable anywhere else in the world, but strongly suggests that the socio-cultural climate of Asian nations may innately foster fatal suicidal outcomes among women.

Non-Fatal Suicidal Behaviour

In older age, suicidal behaviours (attempts and ideations) are less frequently reported. With respect to age, attempted and completed suicide incidence rates exhibit opposing tendencies: whilst the incidence of suicide rises as age increases, attempted suicide tends to decrease reaching lowest levels among the elderly (De Leo & Diekstra, 1990). The ratio of attempts and completions in late-life has been approximated as 4:1 versus somewhere between 8:1 and 15:1 for the population in general and 200:1 for the young (McIntosh et al., 1994). Furthermore, as age increases, the difference in suicide attempt rates between sexes tends to converge considerably (McIntosh et al., 1994).

The WHO/EURO Multi-Centre Study on Suicidal Behaviour has provided invaluable data on attempted suicide (and to a lesser extent, suicide) in both a multinational and regional context. The Multi-Centre study, undertaken between 1989 and 1993 in 16 centres from 13 European countries, found that individuals aged 65 years and older are less likely to engage in non-fatal suicidal behaviour compared to younger groups. Of a sample consisting of 22,665 attempted suicides, older-aged individuals accounted for only 9% compared to a rate of 50% among the 15–34 year age group. The study found that as non-fatal suicidal behaviour decreased with increasing age, suicide rates rose. The ratio between fatal and non-fatal behaviours was 1:2, with only a limited tendency for older aged subjects to repeat self-destructive acts (De Leo et al., 2001). Moreover, suicide attempts were four times less frequent among elderly women than young women, while the elderly/young ratio in males was 1 to 3 (Schmidtke et al., 1996). Longitudinal investigations of older-aged suicide attempters indicate that between 3.6% (Chiu et al., 1996) and 11.1% (De Leo et al., 2002a) make further attempts, and between 5.5% (Chiu et al., 1996) and 12.7% (De Leo et al., 2002a) complete suicide.

In general, older people seem to exhibit a similar frequency of suicidal thoughts as the younger population (Paykel et al., 1974). In a study of individuals aged 65 years and over, only a small percentage (3.1%) of elderly individuals felt the actual wish to die in the month prior to being interviewed (Kirby et al., 1997). Death thoughts and suicidal ideation have been reported to be present in the elderly population at frequencies of 15.9% and 2.3% respectively, whereby the "oldest old" (85 years and over) and women are most affected (Scocco et al., 2001a). Notwithstanding, these indications may underestimate of the true prevalence of death thoughts and suicidal ideation among the elderly due to the subjective nature in which they are reported, the potential for recall bias, and the unwillingness of individuals, particularly men, to disclose such feelings.

Socio-Cultural Aspects of Suicide in Late-Life

The international trend depicted by epidemiological observations has lead to speculation that social and cultural factors contribute to high numbers of completed suicide in late-life. Variations in religion, ethnicity, socio-economic status, social systems, and types of health and mental health care have provided important links to understanding and predicting suicidal behaviour.

Religious views on suicide differ across cultures and may play a part in the rates of suicide in particular countries. Most religions condemn suicide. For example, the religious values of the Hadith faith explicitly forbids a Muslim from praying for death, and the standards of the Holy Koran of Islam protests that it is God who has given life and he alone is entitled to take it (Morgan & Laungani, 2002). The Orthodox doctrine embraced in Greece holds theological sanctions against suicide, such as the burying of suicide victims outside hallowed ground (Neeleman et al.,

Table 2 Comparison of main religions in world countries typified by lowest and highest rates of suicide in late-life (75 years+), for the most recent year available.

Country	Main religion	Suicide rate per 100,000* (75+ years)	Year
	Highest rates of suicide (> 40 per 100,000)		
Austria	Roman Catholic	45.5	2000
Bulgaria	Bulgarian Orthodox	56.4	1999
China (selected mainland)	Taoist	72.8	1998
China (mainland, selected rural)	Taoist	129.1	1998
China (Hong Kong)	Taoist	44.2	1999
Croatia	Roman Catholic	58.1	2000
Cuba	Roman Catholic	68.0	1996
Estonia	Evangelical Lutheran	59.8	1999
France	Roman Catholic	41.4	1998
Hungary	Roman Catholic	81.8	2000
Japan	Shinto and Buddhist	43.4	1999
Latvia	Lutheran	51.8	2000
Lithuania	Roman Catholic	42.6	2000
Republic of Korea	Buddhist, Confucianism, Christian	48.1	2000
Russian Fed.	Russian Orthodox	44.6	1998
Slovenia	Roman Catholic	45.2	1999
Switzerland	Roman Catholic, Protestant	43.5	1996
Yugoslavia	Orthodox, Muslim	57.3	1990
	Lowest rates of suicide (< 6.5 per 100,000)		
Albania	Muslim	4.4	1998
Azerbaijan	Muslim	2.5	2000
Costa Rica	Roman Catholic	3.7	1995
Ecuador	Roman Catholic	5.2	1995
Egypt	Muslim	0.2	1987
Greece	Greek Orthodox	6.3	1998
Iran	Muslim	1.1	1991
Peru	Roman Catholic	1.3	1989
Philippines	Roman Catholic	3.0	1993
Thailand	Buddhist	5.0	1994

*Suicide rates (per 100,000) obtained from World Health Organisation, 2003.

1997). In contrast, attitudes in Japan contest that to take one's own life, as long as it is, culturally speaking, for a good reason, can manifest utmost self-control, a taking in hand not merely of life's affairs but of one's own destiny (Watanabe, 2001). Other religious views on suicide however are ambiguous. For example, the Buddhist stance expressly forbids suicide in Chinese scriptures, yet self-immolation or self-sacrifice based on religious motivations is honourable in China and other far-eastern countries (Morgan & Laungani, 2002). Table 2 summarises the major religions that predominate cultures whose rates of suicide are among the lowest (< 6.5 per 100,000) compared to the highest rates (> 40 per 100,000) in the world.

One may speculate then, that suicides among cultures where major religious beliefs assert theological sanctions against suicide are correspondingly lower in comparison to rates higher in societies that honour, romanticize or beautify death by suicide. This conjecture has been supported to a certain extent by Durkheim (1897/1951), who argued that Catholic countries had lower suicide rates than Protestant countries, partly attributable to greater commitments to the extended family and traditional religious beliefs (Bhatia et al., 1987; Neeleman et al., 1997; Stack 1992). Moreover, a number of studies suggest lower suicide rates in countries with less social or religious tolerance of suicide (Pescosolido & Georgianna 1989; Neeleman & Persaud 1995; Neeleman et al., 1997).

Church membership (Breault 1986) may protect against suicide, and regular church attendance may reduce the risk of suicide (Stack, 1992) by up to four times (Comstock & Partridge, 1972). Participation in religious activities may also reduce the odds of suicide among individuals aged 50 years and older (Nisbet et al., 2000). Of relevance, older persons who practice their faith have frequently lower rates of depression, alcoholism, and hopelessness (Koenig, 1994), all prominent risk factors for suicidal behaviour (Rifai et al., 1994). However, the propensity for religious affiliations to benefit suicide rates may only operate according to gender. Older-aged women tend to be more religious than men, attend church more, and have lower suicide rates (Weaver & Koenig, 1996). Therefore the results of many studies may be confounding where the gender difference of religiosity has not been taken into account when investigating the correlation of suicidal behaviour in religious compared to non-religious elderly.

Societal changes and the breakdown in traditional family structure may contribute to the increase in suicide in late-life also in non-Latin countries. For example, Hong Kong and Turkey have endured changes to family structure as a result of industrialisation and the westernisation of society. Markedly in these cultures, the family is considered as the basic social unit. However, over time, the traditional extended family structure has somewhat been replaced by the concept of nuclear family, which has contributed to social alienation and the loosening of family ties, resulting in isolation for elderly individuals (Sayil & Aydemir, 2001). The higher rate of suicide in older age in Asian nations contradicts the accustomed belief that the elderly are well looked after by the younger generation. This view was put forth by Yip et al.. (1998) when it was proposed that while the younger generation struggle to overcome economic pressure or pressure to become westernised, clashing expectations between the two generations may render the elderly, most of whom are emotionally and financially dependent on the young, with a sense of disappointment and loneliness. Increasing migration and the tendency not to live with parents in Hong Kong and Taiwan also leave more elderly people on their own, with limited government support, particularly for sickness and physical handicaps (Yip, 1996). Better welfare and social systems for the elderly in Western countries may explain the higher rate of suicide among the elderly in Asia (Cheng & Lee, 2000).

In many nations, there has been a thrust towards earlier retirement for older individuals, sourced by lifetime superannuation funds. This has stemmed from the increased numbers of elderly and the consequent increase in government expenditure required to provide adequate care and support of older individuals. For example, in Hong Kong, the greater loss of lives due to suicide among the elderly (30 per 100,000, 1997) compared to the general population (12 per 100,000, 1997) may be affected by inadequate governmental provision of pension support and medical and health services (Yip & Chi, 2001). On the contrary, the decline in suicide in late-life in Anglo-Saxon nations may be attributed, in part, to developments in elderly political and social activism, improved social services, changing attitudes towards retirement, increased economic security and improved psychiatric care (De Leo, 1998).

A number of studies have found that immigrants tend to preserve particular aspects of suicidality that are typical of their country of origin. For example, Lester (1994) observed similar epidemiological features of suicide to country of origin among Asian immigrants to America. Specifically, a lower male/female suicide ratio and the more frequent use of hanging methods rather than firearms compared to Caucasian and African Americans. Research conducted in the United Kingdom and Australia also demonstrates this phenomenon (Raleigh & Balarajan 1992; Burvill, 1995). In Australia during the period 1979–1990 (Burvill, 1995), it was shown that migrants aged 65 years and older had suicide rates that were overall higher than in their country of origin. Similar findings have been found among older-aged immigrants to Hong Kong, whereby approximately 80% of elderly suicides studied were immigrants from Mainland China where suicide rates are very high (Yip et al., 2000). Other evidence also suggests that immigrant-ethnic groups with strong levels of community cohesiveness and low rates of suicide in the country of origin may maintain their low suicidality when substantial acculturation occurs: thereafter, the greater the degree of social assimilation among immigrant-ethnic groups, the greater the suicide rate (Trovato, 1986).

Characteristics of Suicidal Behaviour in Late-Life

Whether suicidal behaviour among adults in late-life exists along a continuum ranging from death wishes, suicidal ideation and planning to suicide attempt and completed suicide, is somewhat unclear. The suicidal continuum theory was originally proposed and investigated by Paykel and colleagues (1974) among a representative sample of the general population (18 years and older) and did not characterise the prevalence of the phenomenon according to age. To date, only one study (Scocco & De Leo, 2002) has investigated the phenomenon among an older-aged population (aged 65 years and over). The study was based on cases of attempted and completed suicide obtained from a data bank maintained by the World Health Organisation Collaborating Centre for Research and Training in Suicide Prevention in Padua, Italy. This study found that the prevalence of suicidality decreases from those of an emotional/ideational nature to most extreme behaviour in older age (Scocco & De Leo, 2002).

A high suicidal intent associated with attempted suicide in older age contrasts with the more heterogeneous nature of attempted suicide in younger age groups, where motivations other than ending life are more likely to underlie the act (Harwood & Jacoby, 2000). In a study conducted in the United Kingdom, it was found that an older person's wish to die is a significant predictor of suicide equal in magnitude to depression (Dewey et al., 1993). Moreover, this concept has been observed in the WHO/EURO Multi-Centre Study (De Leo et al., 2001) and other studies (Merrill & Owens, 1990; Salib et al., 2001), where it was confirmed that the characteristics of elderly individuals who attempt suicide might not overlap with those who complete suicide. Further evidence suggests that, among those who attempt suicide in late-life, the act is often highly premeditated (Frierson, 1991). Hence, a suicide attempt in older age often lays claim to a failed suicide.

Corresponding with this notion is the use of more violent means of suicide compared with younger age bands, albeit with some cultural differences. Suicide methods typically employed in older age include hanging (particularly in men), firearms (particularly in the USA, but also in Australia and Finland), drug overdose (particularly in women with benzodiazepines), jumping from high places (e.g., in Asian metropolitan cities like Hong Kong and Singapore), suffocation (Harwood & Jacoby, 2000), and self-poisoning with agricultural organophosphates (e.g., in Sri Lanka; Ganesvaran et al., 1984).

The Risk of Suicide in Late-Life

Fatal Suicidal Behaviour

Demographic Factors

Despite the considerable variation in rates of suicide between countries, international trends contend that suicides among individuals 65 years and older are the highest rates of any age group, and are completed predominantly by males (De Leo, 1999). Moreover, a steep rise in the rate for older, white men continues to increase even after age 80 (Turvey et al., 2002).

Lower socio-economic status may be associated with suicide in late-life. In a study of suicide rates among the elderly white male population in the United States,

McCall (1991) found that the suicide rate had benefited from growing societal affluence, represented as the reduction in the percentage of elderly persons living below the poverty line, improved health care availability (Medicare enrolment and doctors pro capita), and increased financial protection provided by social security. Farber (1965) suggested that the introduction of the social security programme (Old Age Pensioner Program) in the USA has reduced the likelihood of suicide among the elderly by relieving economic distress.

Psychopathological Factors

Psychopathology is the most important risk factor for suicide in late-life, where approximately 75% of all elderly suicide victims suffer from some sort of psychiatric disorder at the time of their death (Conwell, 1997). Affective disorders are the most common psychopathological diagnosis observed among suicides in older age (Clark & Clark, 1993; Carney et al., 1994; Henriksson et al., 1995; Conwell et al., 1996; Waern et al., 2002a), and such disorders represent a powerful independent risk factor for suicide in older adults (Conwell et al., 2002). Conwell and colleagues (1991) found that 67% of a sample of suicides were committed by individuals aged 50 years and over with a diagnosis of major depression. Furthermore, 83% of those in the sample with a diagnosis of major depression were aged 65 years and over (44% of individuals aged over 60 in a research sample investigated by Henriksson et al., 1995). A significant number of elderly with dysthymia, minor depression, (Waern et al., 2002b) and amidst a first episode of major unipolar depression (Barraclough, 1971; Conwell, 1994; Waern et al., 2002b), also complete suicide. Unremitting hopelessness after recovery from a depressive episode can also pose a risk for older adults (Szanto et al., 2002).

Schizophrenia has been reported in approximately 6–17% of elderly suicide deaths – a proportion that is notably higher than that observed in the general population (0.1%) (Shah & De, 1998). To a lesser extent, anxiety disorders in older age may present an associated high suicide risk (Waern et al., 2002a), especially in the case of anxiety-depressive syndrome (De Leo, 1997; Shah & De, 1998). Personality disorders may also be associated with suicidal thoughts and behaviours among elderly individuals (Harwood et al., 2001); however, the condition is more frequently encountered in young suicidal individuals (Heinriksson et al., 1995).

Alcohol abuse has been reported in 3–44% of suicides in late-life – a prevalence that is higher than the general population of the same age (Shah & De, 1998). A concurrent alcohol abuse and depressive disorder may also present a specific risk for suicide in late-life, and the onset of depression subsequent to a period of alcohol abuse may, in turn, complicate several other psychiatric conditions, including bipolar disorder, schizophrenia, anxiety disorders and personality disorders (McIntosh et al., 1994). However, it is not clearly understood whether alcohol abuse results in

Table 3 Risk factors for suicide in late-life.

Demographic factors	Male Caucasian Lower socio economic status
Psychopathologic factors	Depressive disorder Depressive symptomatology Schizophrenia or paraphrenia Alcohol abuse disorder Personality disorder Co-morbid depressive/alcohol abuse disorders Co-morbid depressive/anxiety disorders Psychiatric hospital admission within previous year Previous suicide attempts
Physical illness	Physical illness (acute, chronic, painful) Fear of illness Co-morbid physical illness/depressive disorder Co-morbid physical illness/alcohol abuse disorder
Personality traits	Strong and frustrated need to be active and independent Hostility Hopelessness and helplessness Lower openness to experience Inability to tolerate changes Inability to verbally express psychological pain Loss of control Dependency on others
Life conditions and events	Widowed, single, divorced Family conflict Loneliness, despair, loss of social ties Cumulative recent losses Death of spouse Loss of relatives, friends, pets Unresolved grief and bereavement Parental loss early in life Abrupt, complete and involuntary retirement Inadequate income Loss of physical and mental capabilities

the experience of depression, or whether alcohol is used as a mechanism to cope with symptoms of depression among the elderly (McIntosh et al., 1994).

Personality Traits

Certain pre-existing personality traits are often associated with an increased suicide risk in late-life, however, suicide in older persons with personality difficulties is rare without a co-existent psychiatric illness (Harwood et al., 2001). In late-life, women may possess personality characteristics that protect against suicide, such as a greater capacity to adjust to changes, a greater preservation of social networks, a greater self-sufficiency in daily activities, and a stronger commitment to their children and grandchildren (Canetto, 1992). Personality features associated with suicidal behaviour, particularly among men, take in account a strong, frustrated need to be active and independent (Murphy & Wetzel, 1990), a hostile persona (Scocco et al., 2001a; Scocco et al., 2001b), anancastic (obsessional) and anxious traits, cognitive rigidity, hopelessness and helplessness, and lower openness to experience (Harwood et al., 2001). A lack of adaptability and ability to cope with change (Harwood et al., 2001), inability to verbally express psychological pain, inability to form close relationships (Canetto, 1992) and loss of control and dependency on others also contribute to an increased risk of suicide (Canetto, 1992).

Previous Suicide Attempts

Attempted suicide is a strong predictive factor for completed suicide in late-life (De Leo & Scocco, 2000), where suicide attempts by individuals in this age band are reported in approximately 15% of cases who die by suicide (Kjolseth et al., 2002). Higher rates of completed suicide following one or more previous attempts are found in older age, compared with younger groups (Gardner et al., 1964). Suicide attempts in this age bracket may take place at least one year prior to completing suicide, and individuals with a history of suicidal behaviour may be more likely to employ the same suicide method used in an attempt to complete suicide (Salib et al., 2001). Risk factors associated with completed suicide in late-life among those who make attempts include living alone, physical illness, psychiatric illness, high suicidal intent in the attempt (Merrill & Owens, 1990), death of father during childhood, the desire to express despair to others, presence of an adjustment reaction and problems with anti-depressants (De Leo et al., 2002a).

Physical Illness

At all ages, physical illness has been identified as a stressor in suicide attempts (Hawton & Fagg, 1988; Stenager & Stenager, 1998) and suicidal ideation (Skoog et al., 1996; Scocco et al., 2001a), but more so among the older aged. The experience of a physical illness is also common among elderly people who take their life, compared to younger individuals (Dorpat et al., 1968; Miller, 1979). However the impact of physical illness upon suicidal behaviour is not completely understood due to the fact that the majority of the elderly population experience a physical illness and only a small minority actually complete suicide. It is only rare that physical illness is considered to be a precipitating factor for suicide in older age.

The influence of other factors, primarily depressive pathologies and other psychiatric conditions (e.g., substance abuse), may relegate physical illness to the place of a secondary contributing factor. Co-morbid depressive and somatic syndromes have in fact been found in most elderly suicidal people, be they characterised by suicide ideation, suicide attempt or suicide (Heinriksson et al., 1995; Skoog et al., 1996; De Leo, 1999).

Few controlled studies have considered the association between suicide and physical illness in the elderly. Conwell et al. (2000) reported the presence of serious physical illness in 56% of a sample of individuals aged 60 years and older who committed suicide following recent contact with a primary care facility, compared with 16% of a control group. Waern et al. (2002a) found that both serious physical illness and high overall burden of illness are stronger risk factors for suicide in older-aged men compared to women. Among the illnesses independently associated with an increased risk of suicide in the elderly are visual impairment, neurological disorders and malignant diseases (Waern et al., 2002a), particularly cancer (Harris & Barraclough, 1994).

Life Conditions and Events

In late-life, particularly after the age of 75 years, the concentration of more unfavourable life circumstances may contribute to an elevated rate of suicide (Scocco & De Leo, 2002). The decline in physical health, lower degree of autonomy and more frequent losses can precipitate suicide in the elderly. However, these changes are common in older age, and it is not entirely clear why some individuals are better equipped to cope than others.

It has been suggested that what differentiates a suicidal reaction to a loss from a non-suicidal one is the frequency and timing of these experiences (Slater & Depue, 1981). Hence, some individuals may be unable to resolve grief prior to the experience of another loss. Unresolved grief has been identified in 13–44 percent of cases of attempted suicide, chiefly owing to death of the spouse (Draper, 1994; Schmid et al., 1994). Suicide as a consequence of acute grief is considered rare, and occasionally the death of a pet is implicated (Draper, 1994). Bereavement is very frequently represented as a stressful life event for elderly persons, and particularly for men, especially when the death of a spouse is sudden (McIntosh et al., 1994). The first 6 months of bereavement may present the greatest risk for suicide (McIntosh et al., 1994).

Widowhood may increase the risk of completed suicide (De Leo et al., 2001) and suicide attempts (Polewka et al., 2002) in late-life, particularly among men. Widows who die by suicide are more likely to do so within the first 4 years of widowhood than thereafter, and whilst accessing psychiatric treatment (Duberstein et al., 1998). A history of early loss of or separation from parents may also indirectly increase the likelihood of suicide among widows, moderated by long-standing personality and attachment vulnerabilities, and precipitated by intervening events, such as spouse loss (Duberstein et al., 1998). Previous psychiatric vulnerabilities, a history of substance abuse (Duberstein et al., 1998), and episodes of major depression (Byrne & Raphael, 1999) among recently widowed older persons may also contribute to heightened suicidal behaviour. Single and divorced elderly males are also over-represented among those who suicide (De Leo et al., 2001). Hence, marriage may be a protective factor for suicide in older-aged males, demonstrated by lower rates of suicide among married men reported in Asia (Yip et al., 1998), England and Wales (Kelly & Bunting, 1998; Harwood et al., 2000) and the USA (Li, 1995).

Living situation and accommodation is another important facet to consider. Earlier studies have found a higher correlation between suicide and living alone in the old than in the young population (Sainsbury, 1955), and in the general community (Waern et al., 2002b). Between 24 and 60 percent of elderly people who complete suicide live alone (Draper, 1996) and the percentage of elderly suicide attempters who live alone increases with age (Merril & Owens, 1990). However, other factors were found to influence the outcome of suicide among elderly individuals, such as recent isolation following bereavements and loss, and that suicide only occurred as a result of an intervening physical or psychiatric disorder (Waern et al., 2002b). An association between increased isolation and elderly suicide has not been found when compared to younger victims of suicide (Draper, 1996). That is, living alone is not necessarily synonymous with social isolation, and social isolation and diminished capacity for social interaction is not commonly found in elderly suicides (Conwell et al., 1990; Clark, 1993).

Suicide is relatively rare in nursing homes (Osgood et al., 1991). However, the anticipation of, or a recent nursing home placement, has been considered to be a precipitating factor, particularly among those elderly who were married at the time of their suicide (Loebel et al., 1991). Older-aged individuals who have been living in nursing homes for a substantial amount of time may show high levels of suicidal ideation and depression, but are less likely suicide attempters (Schmid et al., 1994).

The inevitability of retirement can create emotional disruption in late-life. In general, studies have found that retirement per se does not constitute an important risk factor for suicide unless it is abrupt and involuntary, particularly in the case of "young-old" men (McIntosh et al., 1994). The first month after retirement may present a particularly high risk of suicide (Delisle, 1992).

Elderly Subjects Who Attempt Suicide

The majority of older-aged subjects who attempt suicide are aged between 65–74 years of age, with sharp declines after the age of 75 in the United Kingdom (Pierce, 1987), and after 85 in Hong Kong (Chiu et al., 1996). In elderly subjects, the risk of attempted suicide is augmented 10-fold by the diagnosis of a mood disorder (Beautrais, 2002). As well as this, an existing mood disorder following a suicide attempt has been documented in 69% (Scocco et al., 1999) and 80% (Lyness et al., 1992) of elderly subjects

60 years and older. Also, among patients with an affective disorder, the presence of an attempt is significantly associated with a later age of onset of major depression (Lyness et al., 1992).

A number of other factors that may increase the likelihood of a suicide attempt in older age include a past history of mental health treatment and at-

Table 4 Personal characteristics of elderly subjects who attempt suicide.

– Diagnosis of any mental disorder, particularly mood disorder
– Previous and/or current mental health treatment
– Previous history of attempted suicide
– Limited social interaction
– Recent relationship stress
– Chronic relationship problems
– Recent financial stress
– History of childhood adversity
– Concerns of being burden on others
– Tensions with caregivers

tempted suicide, limited social interaction, recent relationship and financial stresses, and a history of childhood adversity (which may contribute to enduring vulnerability to the development of mood disorders and suicidal behaviour) (Beautrais, 2002). Recent suicide attempts in late-life may also be associated with chronic relationship problems, concerns about being a burden on others, and tensions with caregivers (Zweig & Hinrichsen, 1993; Draper, 1994).

Repeated suicidal behaviour in older age may be associated with a number of factors. The death of the father in childhood (De Leo et al., 2002a) may be implicated, where the ability to cope with difficulties in youth and adulthood taper in older age when the ensuing dependence seems to present an insuperable obstacle (Erikson, 1963; Clark, 1993). Elderly at risk of further self-harm are also likely to be in contact with psychiatric services and to be suffering from persistent depression (Hepple & Quinton, 1997). Extreme rates of suicidal ideation (96.4%) in the week following hospitalisation for a suicide attempt have been observed among the elderly, and, in 11% of cases, hospitalisation may invoke a further suicide attempt (Yang et al., 2001).

Suicidal Ideation

Suicidal ideation is common among medically ill elderly inpatients (Shah et al., 2000). In a study conducted in Berlin, Germany (Barnow & Linden, 2001), more than 80% of a sample of persons aged 70 years and older who were entertaining thoughts of suicide were suffering from acute psychiatric disorders at the time. Suicidal ideation among the elderly has been associated with a diagnosis of depressive disorder (Jorm et al., 1995; Skoog et al., 1996; Forsell et al., 1997; Bartels et al., 2002), the presence of depressive symptomatology (Jorm et al., 1995), anxiety (Scocco et al., 2001a, 2001b) and hostility (Scocco et al., 2001a, 2001b). Bartels and colleagues (2002) found that among elderly primary care patients, suicidal ideation was highly prevalent among those with a diagnosis of depression (including co-occurring at-risk alcohol use or anxiety disorder), and was associated with increased inpatient hospitalisations and outpatient medical visits and greater medical co-morbidity compared with patients with no suicidal ideation (Bartles et al., 2002). Other specific evidence on elderly inpatients suggests that among those who are moderately to severely depressed, self-destructive acts are strongly correlated with feelings of anger and hostility rather than with depression itself (Yesavage, 1983).

The wish to die or the manifestation of suicidal behaviour in the elderly has also been correlated with the use of psychotropic drugs (Skoog et al., 1996; Forsell et al., 1997), widowhood or being separated/divorced (Henriksson et al., 1995; Draper, 1996; Skoog et al., 1996), institutionalisation (Jorm et al., 1995; Forsell et al., 1997), physical disability, pain, visual and hearing impairment, and unmarried status (Jorm et al., 1995; Forsell et al., 1997).

In late-life, suicidal ideation is often sustained over long periods of time. However, elderly persons with suicidal thoughts are often unwilling to communicate their intent (De Leo et al., 2001), particularly elderly men who are much more reluctant to verbalize their inner feelings compared to females of the same age (Haste et al., 1998). Hence, suicide in the elderly may often be preceded by suicidal ideation that is hidden or disguised (Scocco & De Leo, 2002). Consequently, general practitioners are only able to detect suicidal feelings in a minority of cases.

It has been reported that approximately 10–20% of the elderly are in a depressive state, which is considered to be of a clinically significant level (Blazer & Williams, 1980; Lindesay et al., 1989). This level ranges from about 10% for older persons living independently in the community to about 25% for those with chronic illness, especially persons with ischemic heart disease, stroke, cancer, chronic lung disease, arthritis, Alzheimer's disease and Parkinson's disease (Jones & Yang, 1985; Borson et al., 1986; Blazer, 1989a; Oxman et al., 1990; Callahan et al., 1994 Beekman et al., 1995; Borson, 1995). Yet, a considerably greater proportion of the elderly present depressive symptomatology that do not fulfil the criteria for a DSM diagnosis (Blazer, 1989b; Newman & Bland, 1989; Kessler et al., 1992; Girling et al., 1995). Often only one in six elderly patients affected by depression are diagnosed and treated appropriately by primary care physicians (National Institutes of Health, 1992). In a study of suicides among older-aged individuals, only 8% of cases with a diagnosed depressive disorder had received adequate anti-depressive medication prior to death (Pitkala et al., 2000).

In older age, individuals tend to complain of somatic symptoms, which make them, and others, including physicians, overlook depressive symptoms (Takahashi et al., 1995). Geriatric depression can and frequently does amplify physical symptoms; however, many elderly patients may deny psychological symptoms of depression or reject the diagnosis due to the stigma attached to it. The effects of stigma on acceptance of the diagnosis seem particularly significant among men (Reynolds & Kupfer, 1999).

Settings for Suicide Prevention in Late-Life

Primary Health Care

A high proportion, approximately 90%, of elderly individuals who suicide consult with a general practitioner (GP) in the three months prior to death, and 50% within one week (Vasilas & Morgan, 1994), while only 13% access psychiatric care in a lifetime (Conwell et al., 1990). Moreover, only a minority of older adults with psychiatric disorders access mental health services, preferring to visit their primary care physician instead (Goldstrom et al., 1987). Recent evidence derived from the WHO/EURO Multi-Centre Study of Suicidal Behaviour, Part II (Repetition-Prediction) has found that because requests for help are most frequently addressed to relatives and GPs, elderly patients might be fairly open about their suicidality should the topic be approached by a physician (De Leo et al., 2002a).

In the primary care setting, the detection of depression among older-aged patients, albeit slight, ought indicate to the physician to proceed with inquiry into suicidality. A suicide risk assessment is a vital component when investigating patient suicidality, yet many physicians lack sufficient knowledge about suicide (Rockwell & O'Brian, 1973). In a study conducted in Vienna, Ritter and colleagues (2002) utilized a random sample of two hundred GPs and found that GPs tended to have a sufficient knowledge of suicidality and its management, as well as an awareness of risk groups, particularly regarding the suicide risk of depressed persons. However, GPs tended to underestimate the suicide risk among alcoholics, and, in general, found it difficult to assess suicide risk as a result of inadequate training in suicide prevention.

Rutz and colleagues (1992) conducted a study in Gotland, Sweden between 1984–1986 to determine whether education of primary care physicians can improve treatment of depression and reduce suicide rates. After completing the training programme, primary care physicians were more likely to prescribe anti-depressants and less likely to prescribe anxiolytics. Accordingly, the rate of hospital admission for depression and the suicide rate decreased during the study. However, the decrease in suicides was reflected mostly by a decrease in suicides among women with depression (Rihmer et al., 1995). The suicide rate rose two years after the completion of the study. However, due to the small number of suicides observed, it is difficult to distinguish whether or not the rise and fall was spontaneous or occurred as a response to the intervention per se (Szanto et al., 2002).

The number of active mental health professionals may also impact upon suicide rates. For example, the suicide rate in Hungary, which is more than 2-fold the rate observed in some countries, has been negatively associated with the rate of diagnosed depression and the number of working psychiatrists (Rihmer et al., 1995). Other findings indicate that Nevada and Montana, which have the highest suicide rates in the USA, also possess the least number of active psychiatrists, psychologists, social workers and psychiatric nurses (American Association of Suicidology, 2000). Hence, the availability of trained professionals may indirectly impact upon suicide rates.

Despite the potential for intervention with depressed patients and consistent findings that indicate that elderly patients, even the very old, respond to anti-depressant medication (Reynolds et al., 1993), physicians have encountered numerous challenges in detecting suicidal ideations and depressive syndromes. Firstly, older-aged individuals and their family members may attribute depressive symptoms and suicidal ideation to the ageing process, see depression as a "normal" aspect of aging, and as an expectable "side effect" of physical illness (Pearson & Brown, 2000). Secondly, older depressed adults are less likely to accept dysphoric mood as a symptom (Gallo et al., 1994), and in particular, older men are less likely to report depressive symptoms (Allen-Burge et al., 1994). Thirdly, it has been suggested that primary care physicians tend to spend less time with older patients and focus on physical problems to the exclusion of mental morbidity (German et al., 1985). In some cases, physicians deliberately avoid diagnosing a mood disorder, even when recognized, to avoid stigmatising the patient as well as reimbursement problems (Rost et al., 1994). Discussing depressive symptoms and enquiring about suicidal ideation in the primary care setting increases the length of physician-patient contact (Badger et al., 1994), and time-limited office visits are perceived to be a barrier to effective depression treatment (Banazak, 1996).

Psychiatric Health Care

The treatment of depressive symptoms may be an important component in preventing suicide in late life. To date, the majority of research undertaken has investigated the efficacy of anti-depressant agents, and, to a lesser extent, mood stabilisers, particularly lithium. Currently, selective serotonin reuptake inhibitors (SSRIs) are the most favourable treatment for depression in later life, mostly attributable to a lesser tendency to produce impinging side effects and a greater safety in relation to overdose.

Regardless of class, anti-depressants lead to improvement of depressive symptomatology in approximately 60–70% of elderly patients, in whom the placebo response rate is 30–40% (Schneider, 1996). In mixed age groups, maintenance anti-depressant drug treatment has proven more efficacious than placebo (Frank et al., 1990; Bondareff et al., 2000; Keller et al., 2000).

A delayed onset of clinical anti-depressant activity, between four and five weeks, however, represents a period of prolonged suffering and disability, potentially reducing compliance, not infrequently shifting therapy from pharmacotherapy to electro-convulsive therapy, and increasing the risk for suicide and suicidal behaviour (Reynolds & Kupfer, 1999). Therefore the need for strategies that accelerate the treatment response and improve the early recognition of patients who are not responding to anti-depressant treatment would be an important advance (Reynolds & Kupfer, 1999).

Controlled trials of suicidal behaviour among patients treated with lithium have not yet been conducted in older-aged samples. In younger groups (Schou, 2000), in patients with major mood disorders suicide attempts may be reduced 6–15 fold and completed suicide 3–17 fold, compared to patients not prescribed lithium (Schou, 2000). Lithium might reduce suicidality by controlling aggressive behaviour (Fava & Rosenbaum, 1999), increase treatment compliance (Szanto et al., 2002) and reduce the long-term risk of recurrent depression and mixed states (Tondo et al., 1997).

Although a number of studies show a close association between long-term lithium treatment and lowered mortality and reduced suicidal behaviour, these findings do not prove definitively that lithium has an anti-suicidal action.

Symptomatologic benefits of electro-convulsive therapy (ECT) have been documented in patient samples of major depressive disorder (American Psychiatric Association, 2000). ECT is used extensively among severely depressed elderly patients with co-morbid medical conditions or poor tolerance of psychotropic medications (Mulsant & Sweeney, 1997). ECT has been found to be a safe and efficient intervention for depressed patients with cardiovascular disease (Zielinski et al., 1993) and stroke (Murray et al., 1986), and for physically ill elderly patients (Hay, 1989). It is well tolerated even among the very old (Tew et al., 1999).

ECT may exert a profound short-term beneficial effect on suicidality; however, limited evidence supports a long-term positive effect on suicide rates (Prudic & Sackeim, 1999), and there is no current evidence that supports its ability to specifically prevent suicidal behaviours in late-life.

Interpersonal psychotherapy, cognitive-behavioural therapy, problem-solving therapy and, perhaps, psychodynamic approaches may be as effective as anti-depressant drugs in the acute treatment of elderly outpatients with mild to moderate non-psychotic depression. Moreover, cognitive therapy has also been used successfully to treat suicidal persons (Beck et al., 1979, Beck & Weishaar, 1990), including the elderly. However, in the treatment of suicidal patients, the often-combined use of psychotherapeutic and pharmacological interventions, and the associated interaction between the two, render the evaluation of the impact from those treatments often indistinguishable. As a consequence, investigative efforts have been unable to delineate the extent to which psychosocial interventions contribute to reduce suicidal behaviours in old age.

The Religious/Spiritual Setting

In many cultures and societies, clergy are sought by older-aged individuals for counselling in crisis situations, such as personal illness or injury, death of spouse, death of a close family member, divorce or marital separation, change in health of a family member or the death of a close friend (Fairchild, 1980). Depression is either or very nearly the most frequent presenting problem among people seeking the help of clergy (Abramczyk, 1981; Ingram & Lowe, 1989). Clergy play a particularly vital role for older-aged individuals in rural or small community settings where mental health services are less common and faith communities often function as the community counselling resource (Rowles, 1986). The higher rate of depression (Parmelee et al., 1989) and suicidal ideation (Lindsey & Murphy, 1989) documented among residents of nursing homes may warrant intervention at this level, in the wake of appropriate training for pastors in suicide risk assessment and the efficient linkage with mental health services.

However, investigations have demonstrated that clergy often have inadequate skills to recognise suicide lethality (Holmes & Howard 1980; Domino 1985; Pieper & Garrison 1992). In a review of literature involving the referral patterns among clergy over a 20-years time span, it was found that less than 10% of individuals who sought the assistance of clergy for psychological problems were then referred to mental health specialists. By the same token, mental health specialists very seldom make referrals to clergy or other religious resources (Meylink & Gorsuch, 1987).

Although the great majority of clergy receive some training in counselling (Weaver, 1995) – albeit not specific to suicidality in older age – very few mental health professionals receive training in religious issues or spirituality, and mental health professionals may be more inclined to "medicalise" or "psychologise" the significant existential/spiritual issues that a suicidal crisis presents (Weaver & Koenig, 1996). An alliance between the mental health and religious sectors in assisting psychological concerns and suicidality is likely to occur only after the first step of purging attitudinal barriers, fears and concerns about establishing collaborative links is achieved.

The Community Setting

Only a small proportion of callers to agencies such as the Samaritans are elderly and the aged are under-represented in the clientele of suicide prevention programs and general mental health facilities (McIntosh et al., 1994). Many older-aged individuals do not receive adequate information about the nature of community-based services and programs and as a result, harbour beliefs that services of these types are "not meant for the elderly," are "costly" and "not credible" (McIntosh et al., 1994). Irrespective of the potential that isolation and poor social support, so common in late-life, can have in inducing suicidal ideation, these factors reduce the opportunity for expressing or communicating suicidality (De Leo & Scocco, 2000).

Relatives are among the most frequently sought for help by older-aged individuals (De Leo et al., 2002a). The mobilisation of relatives and friends to monitor the emotional and psychological health status of older-aged individuals may assist in preventing suicidal ideations from progressing towards action. This strategy may not only increase social contact with older persons, but may also contribute to enhancing the chances of discovery and assistance in the event of a suicide attempt for elderly who live on their own.

Relatives may also be more effective than primary care physician in detecting suicidality among older-aged individuals. Waern et al. (1999) examined the suicidal feelings and behaviours of 85 elderly deaths by suicide, as noted by a doctor and relatives during the year preceding death. Relatives were more proficient in detecting suicidal feelings during the year before death (72.9%), particularly those of female subjects, compared to a doctor (38.4%). In only 9.6% of cases, a doctor recorded suicidal feelings during the final consultation with the person before suicide.

The use of telecommunications has proven to effectively reduce the expected rate of suicide in an elderly population of Veneto, Italy (De Leo et al., 2002b). The Tele-Help-TeleCheck service was implemented in 1988 to provide twice-weekly telephone support and emergency response for up to 20, 000 individuals. During the long-term follow up, suicide rates among older-aged individuals were lower among TeleHelp-TeleCheck users than among comparable general community members. Possibly, suicidality among this age group was reduced because the service addressed suicide risk factors, and provided older individuals with a sense of connectedness (De Leo et al., 1995). However, evidence from this experience was much stronger in the case of females than male subjects, suggesting that verbalisation of psychological suffering may result much more effectively with female subjects (De Leo et al., 2002b).

Conclusion

Ageism works against research and outreach efforts, and suicides in older age may occur as a result of a gross overestimation of the ability of individuals to cope with major life events, losses or threatening conditions in the light of seemingly resilient former efforts made earlier in their lives. Suicide in older age may be wedged between two conflicting forces: the societal suggestion that internal struggle and depression and suicidality should be suppressed and dealt with on one's own; and that elderly individuals must come forth and access mental health services, verbally express their anguish and live. Hence to a certain extent, efforts to prevent suicide in old age will only operate in vain if they are implemented in societies where social stigma and ill perceptions towards older age, and the acceptance of internal harbouring of depression and suicidality in late-life still exist.

Empirical evidence does not convincingly support the efficacy of interventions that have been devised thus far to prevent suicidal outcomes among the elderly. However, value may be placed in the controlled investigation of the efficacy of com-

bined psychotherapeutic and anti-depressant interventions, as well as trialling lithium in highly suicidal older-aged samples. Particular attention should also be afforded to the inclusion of treatments such as electro-convulsive therapy, to prevent
suicidal outcomes during the initial phase of onset of clinical anti-depressant activity.

The fact that no direct evidence from trials exists to definitively prove that the
treatment of depression reduces the suicide rate in late-life is most likely to be reflected in the limited ability of primary care professionals to detect depressive symptomatology and suicidal ideation. Hence, in the absence of adequate anti-depressant
treatment, many depressed suicidal elderly may take their own life.

Contrary to some existing modes in primary health care, the obligation to opti-
mise patient health, increase life quality, and prevent premature death by suicide
ought to outweigh the cost-effectiveness and time required to investigate about suicidality. There is no evidence that specifically investigating the presence of suicidal
ideation may increase the risk of subsequent suicidal behaviour. On the contrary,
just one (direct) qustions could help save a life. Needless to say, an increase in the
availability of active mental health professionals, such as psychiatrists, psychologists, social workers and psychiatric nurses, may also contribute to reducing suicide
rates among older-aged patients.

Suicide in late-life should also be prevented within communities. Contending
community attitudes toward ageism may be addressed through large-scale media-
based education programmes, mobilising and skilling family and friends in risk
factor identification and assessment pertinent to suicide in late-life, as well as the
possible contribution of telemonitoring.

References

Allen-Burge, R., Storandt, M., Kinscherf, D. A., & Rubin, E. H. (1994). Sex differences in the
   sensitivity of two self-report depression scales in older depressed inpatients. *Psychology and
   Aging, 9*, 443–445.

Abramczyk, L. W. (1981). The counselling function of pastors: A study in practice and preparation. *Journal of Psychology and Theology, 9*, 257–265.

American Association of Suicidology. (2000). Is there a connection between state suicide rates
   and the availability of mental health professionals [abstract]. *News Link, 26*, 7.

American Psychiatric Association. (2000). *Practice guideline for the treatment of psychiatric
   disorders, compendium*. Washington, DC: Author.

Badger, L. W., De Gruy, F. V., Hartman, J., Plant, M. A., Leeper, J., Ficken, R., Maxwell, A., Rand,
   E., Anderson, R., & Templeton, B. (1994). Psychosocial interest, medical interviews, and
   the recognition of depression. *Archives of Family Medicine, 3*, 899–907.

Banazak, D. A. (1996). Late-life depression in primary care: how well are we doing? *Journal of
   General Internal Medicine, 11*, 163–167.

Barnow, S., & Linden, M. (2001). Do old persons wish to die? Suicidal tendencies and weariness of life in old age. Results of the Berlin Aging Study (BASE). *Fortschritte der Neurologie Psychiatrie, 119,* 33–36.

Barraclough, B. M. (1971). Suicide in the elderly. In D. W. Kay & A. Walk (Eds.), *Recent developments in psychogeriatrics* (pp. 87–97). Ashford: Headley Bros.

Bartels, S. J., Coakley, E., Oxman, T. E., Constantino, G., Oslin, D., Chen, H., Zubritsky, C., Cheal, K., Durai, U. N., Gallo, J. J., Llorente, M., & Sanchez, H. (2002). Suicidal and death ideation in older primary care patients with depression, anxiety, and at-risk alcohol use. *American Journal of Geriatric Psychiatry, 10,* 417–427.

Beautrais, A. L. (2002). A case control study of suicide and attempted suicide in older adults. *Suicide and Life Threatening Behavior, 32,* 1–9.

Beck, A. T., Rush, A. J., & Shaw, B. F. (1979). *Cognitive therapy of depression: A treatment manual.* New York: Guildford.

Beck, A. T., & Weishaar, M. E. (1990). Suicide risk assessment and prediction. *Crisis, 11,* 22–30.

Beekman, A. T., Deeg, D. J., van Tilburg, T., Smit, J. H., Hooijer, C., & van Tilburg, W. (1995). Major and minor depression in later life: a study of prevalence and risk factors. *Journal of Affective Disorders, 36,* 65–75.

Bhatia, S. C., Khan, M. H., & Mediratta, R. P. (1987). High-risk suicide factors across cultures. *International Journal of Social Psychiatry, 33,* 226–236.

Blazer, D. (1989a). Depression in the elderly. *New England Journal of Medicine, 320,* 164–166.

Blazer, D. (1989b). The epidemiology of depression in late life. *International Journal of Geriatric Psychiatry, 22,* 35–52.

Blazer, D., & Williams, C. D. (1980). Epidemiology of dysphoria and depression in an elderly population. *American Journal of Psychiatry, 137,* 439–444.

Bondareff, W., Alpert, M., Friedhoff, A. J., Richter, E. M., Clary, C. M., & Batzar, E. (2000). Comparison of sertraline and nortriptyline in the treatment of major depressive disorder in late life. *American Journal of Psychiatry, 157,* 729–736.

Borson, S. (1995). Psychiatric Problems In The Medically Ill Elderly. In H. I. Kaplan & B. J. Sadock (Eds.), *Comprehensive textbook of psychiatry* (6th ed., p. 2586). Baltimore: Williams & Wilkins.

Borson, S., Barnes, R. A., Kukull, W. A., Okimoto, J. T., Veith, R. C., Inui, T. S., Carter, W., & Raskind, M. A. (1986). Symptomatic depression in elderly medical outpatients, I: Prevalence, demography, and health service utilization. *Journal of the American Geriatrics Society, 34,* 341–347.

Breault, K. D. (1986). Suicide in America: a test of Durkheim's theory of religious and family integration, 1933–1980. *American Journal of Sociology, 92,* 628–656.

Brooke, E., & Atkinson, M. (1974). Ascertainment Of Death From Suicide. In E. M. Breeks (Ed.), *Suicide and attempted suicide.* Geneva: World Health Organisation.

Brown, P. (1997). No way out. *New Scientist, 153,* 34–37.

Burvill, P. W. (1995). Suicide in the multiethnic elderly population of Australia, 1979–1990. *International Psychogeriatrics, 7,* 319–333.

Byrne, G. J., & Raphael, B. (1999). Depressive symptoms and depressive episodes in recently widowed older men. *International Psychogeriatrics, 11,* 67–74.

Callahan, C. M., Hui, S. L., Nienaber, N. A., Musick, B. S., & Tierney, W. M. (1994). Longitudinal study of depression and health services use among elderly primary care patients. *Journal of the American Geriatrics Society, 42,* 833–838.

Canetto, S. S. (1992). Gender and suicide in the elderly. *Suicide and Life Threatening Behavior, 22,* 80–97.

Carney, S., Rich, C., Burke, P., & Fowler, R. C. (1994). Suicide over 60: The San Diego study. *Journal of the American Geriatrics Society, 42*, 174–180.

Cheng, A. T., & Lee, C. S. (2000). Suicide in Asia and the Far East. In K. Hawton & K. van Heeringen (Eds.), *The International handbook of suicide and attempted suicide* (pp. 29–48). New York: Wiley.

Chiu, H. F., Lam, L. C., Pang, A. H., Leung, C. M., & Wong, C. K. (1996). Attempted suicide by Chinese elderly in Hong Kong. *General Hospital Psychiatry, 18*, 444–447.

Clark, D. C. (1993). Narcissistic crisis of aging and suicidal despair. *Suicide and Life Threatening Behavior, 23*, 21–26.

Clark, D., & Clark, S. (1993). Suicide among the elderly. In K. Bohme, R. Freytag, C. Vachtler & H. Wedler (Eds.), *Suicidal behaviour: The state of the art. Proceedings of the XVI Congress of the International Association for Suicide Prevention* (pp. 161–164). Regensburg, Germany: Roderer.

Comstock, G. W., Partridge, K. B. (1972). Church attendance and health. *Journal of Chronic Diseases, 25*, 665–672.

Conwell, Y. (1992). Suicide in the elderly. *Crisis, 13*, 6–8.

Conwell, Y. (1994). Suicide in elderly patients. In L. S. Schneider, C. F. Reynolds, B. D. Lebowitz & A. J. Friedhoff (Eds.), *Diagnosis and treatment of depression in late life.* Washington: American Psychiatric Press.

Conwell, Y. (1997). Management of suicidal behavior in the elderly. *The Psychiatric Clinics of North America, 20*, 667–683.

Conwell, Y., Duberstein, P. R., & Caine, E. D. (2002). Risk factors for suicide in later life. *Biological Psychiatry, 52*, 193–204.

Conwell, Y., Duberstein, P. R., Cox, C., Herrmann, J. H., Forbes, N. T., & Caine, E. D. (1996). Relationships of age and axis I diagnoses in victims of completed suicide: A psychological autopsy study. *American Journal of Psychiatry, 153*, 1001–1008.

Conwell, Y., Lyness, J. M., Duberstein, P., Cox, C., Seidlitz, L., DiGiorgio, A., & Caine, E. D. (2000). Completed suicide among older patients in primary care practices: a controlled study. *Journal of the American Geriatrics Society, 48*, 23–29.

Conwell, Y., Olsen, K., Caine, E. D., & Flannery, C. (1991). Suicide in later life: Psychological autopsy findings. *International Psychogeriatrics, 3*, 59–66.

Conwell, Y., Rotenberg, M., & Caine, E. D. (1990). Completed suicide at age 50 and over. *Journal of the American Geriatrics Society, 38*, 640–644.

De Leo, D. (1997). I comportamenti suicidari negli anziani: fattori demografici, psicosociali, malattie croniche. [Suicidal behaviour in the elderly: Demographic, psychosocial, and chronic illness-related factors]. *Italian Journal of Suicidology, 9*, 277–290.

De Leo, D. (1998). Is suicide prediction in old age really easier? *Crisis, 19*, 60–61.

De Leo, D. (1999). Cultural issues in suicide and old age. *Crisis, 17*, 147–148.

De Leo, D., Carollo, G., & Dello Buono, M. (1995). Lower suicide rates associated with a Tele-Help/Tele-Check service for the elderly at home. *American Journal of Psychiatry, 152*, 632–634.

De Leo, D., Dello Buono, M., & Dwyer, J. (2002b). Suicide among the elderly: The long-term impact of a telephone support and assessment intervention in northern Italy. *British Journal of Psychiatry, 181*, 226–229.

De Leo, D., & Diekstra, R. F. (1990). *Depression and suicide in late life.* Toronto/Bern: Hogrefe & Huber.

De Leo, D., & Scocco, P. (2000). Treatment and prevention of suicidal behaviour in the elderly.

In K. Hawton & K. van Heeringen (Eds.), *The international handbook of suicide and attempted suicide* (pp. 555–570). New York: Wiley.

De Leo, D., Padoani, W., Lönnqvist, J., Kerkhof, A. J., Bille-Brahe, U., Michel, K., Salander-Renberg, E., Schmidtke, A., Wasserman, D., Caon, F., & Scocco, P. (2002a). Repetition of suicidal behaviour in elderly Europeans: A prospective longitudinal study. *Journal of Affective Disorders, 72,* 291–295.

De Leo, D., Padoani, W., Scocco, P., Lie, D., Bille-Brahe, U., Arensman, E., Hjelmeland, H., Crepet, P., Haring, C., Hawton, K., Lönnqvist, J., Michel, K., Pommereau, X., Querejeta, I., Phillipe, J., Salander-Renberg, E., Schmidtke, A., Fricke, S., Weinacker, B., Tamesvary, B., Wasserman, D., & Faria, S. (2001). Attempted and completed suicide in older subjects: Results from the WHO/EURO Multicentre Study of Suicidal Behaviour. *International Journal of Geriatric Psychiatry, 16,* 300–310.

Delisle, I. (1992). Suicide at the age of retirement. *Canadian Journal of Nursing, 88,* 39–41.

Dewey, M. E., Davidson, I. A., & Copeland, J. R. M. (1993). Expressed wish to die and mortality in older people: A community replication. *Age and Ageing, 22,* 109–113.

Diekstra, R. F. W., & Gulbinat, W. (1993). The epidemiology of suicidal behaviour: A review of three continents. *WHO Statistical Quarterly, 46,* 52–68.

Domino, G. (1985). Clergy's attitudes toward suicide and recognition of suicide lethality. *Death Studies, 9,* 187–199.

Dorpat, T. L., Anderson, W. F., & Ripley, N. S. (1968). The relationship of physical illness to suicide. In H. L. Resnik (Ed.), *Suicidal behaviours* (pp. 209–219). Boston: Little Brown.

Draper, B. (1994). Suicidal behaviour in the elderly. *International Journal of Geriatric Psychiatry, 8,* 655–661.

Draper, B. (1996). Attempted suicide in old age. *International Journal of Geriatric Psychiatry, 11,* 577–587.

Duberstein, P. R., Conwell, Y., & Cox, C. (1998). Suicide in widowed persons. A psychological autopsy comparison of recently and remotely bereaved older subjects. *American Journal of Geriatric Psychiatry, 6,* 328–334.

Durkheim, E. (1897/1951) *Suicide: A sociological study.* Glencoe, IL: Free Press.

Erikson, E. H. (1963). *Childhood and society* (2nd ed.). New York: Norton.

Fairchild, R. W. (1980). *Finding hope again: A pastor's guide to counseling depressed persons.* New York: Harper & Row.

Farber, M. L. (1965). Suicide and welfare state. *Mental Hygiene, 49,* 371–373.

Farmer, R. T. (1988). Assessing the epidemiology of suicide and parasuicide. *British Journal of Psychiatry, 153,* 16–20.

Fava, M., & Rosenbaum, J. F. (1999). Anger attacks in patients with depression. *Journal of Clinical Psychiatry, 60* (Suppl. 15), 21–24.

Forsell, Y., Jorm, A. F., & Winblad, B. (1997). Suicidal thoughts and associated factors in an elderly population. *Acta Psychiatrica Scandinavica, 95,* 108–111.

Frank, E., Kupfer, D. J., Perel, J. M., Cornes, C., Jarrett, D. B., Mallinger, A. G., Thase, M. E., McEachran, A. B., & Grochocinski, V. J. (1990). Three-year outcomes for maintenance therapies in recurrent depression. *Archives of General Psychiatry, 47,* 1093–1099.

Frierson, R. L. (1991). Suicide attempts by the old and the very old. *Archives of Internal Medicine, 151,* 141–144.

Gallo, J. J., Anthony, J. C., & Muthén, B. G. (1994). Age differences in the symptoms of depression: A latent trait analysis. *Journal of Gerontology: Psychological Sciences, 49,* 251–264.

Ganesvaran, T., Subramaniam, S., & Mahadevan, K. (1984). Suicide in a northern town in Sri Lanka. *Acta Psychiatrica Scandinavica, 69,* 420–425.

Gardner, E. A., Bohn, A., & Mack, M. (1964). Suicide and psychiatric care in the ageing. *Archives of General Psychiatry, 10*, 547–553.

German, P. S., Shapiro, S., & Skinner, E. A. (1985). Mental health of the elderly: Use of health and mental health services. *Journal of the American Geriatrics Society, 33*, 246–252.

Girling, D. M., Barkley, C., Paykel, E. S., Gehlhaar, E., Brayne, C., Gill, C., Mathewson, D., & Huppert, F. A. (1995). The prevalence of depression in a cohort of the very elderly. *Journal of Affective Disorders, 34*, 319–329.

Goldstrom, I. D., Burns, B. J., Kessler, L. G., Feuerberg, M. A., Larson, D. B., Miller, N. E., & Cromer, W. J. (1987). Mental health services use by elderly adults in a primary care setting. *Journal of Gerontology, 42*, 147–53.

Gulbinat, W. (1995). The epidemiology of suicide in old age. In R. F. Diekstra, W. Gulbinat, I. Kienhorst & D. De Leo (Eds.), *Preventive strategies on suicide.* Leiden: WHO–EJ Brill.

Hasegawa, K., Finkel, S. I., & Bergerner, M. (1992). Late life suicide. *International Psychogeriatrics, 4*, 163.

Harris, E., & Barraclough, B. (1994). Suicide as an outcome for medical disorders. *Medicine, 73*, 281–296.

Harwood, D., Hawton, K., Hope, T., & Jacoby, R. (2001). Psychiatric disorder and personality factors associated with suicide in older people: A descriptive and case-control study. *International Journal of Geriatric Psychiatry, 16*, 155–165.

Harwood, D., Hawton, K., Hope, T., & Jacoby, R. (2000). Suicide in older people: Mode of death demographic factors, and medical contact before death. *International Journal of Geriatric Psychiatry, 15*, 736–743.

Harwood, D., & Jacoby, R. (2000). Suicidal behaviour among the elderly. In K. Hawton & K. van Heeringen (Eds.), *The international handbook of suicide and attempted suicide* (pp. 275–292). West Sussex: Wiley.

Haste, F., Charlton, J., & Jenkins, R. (1998). Potential for suicide prevention in primary care? *British Journal of General Practice, 48*, 1759–1763.

Hawton, K., & Fagg, J. (1988). Suicide and other causes of death following attempted suicide. *British Journal of Psychiatry, 152*, 359–366.

Hay, D. P. (1989). Electroconvulsive therapy in the medically ill elderly. *Convulsive Therapy, 5*, 8–16.

Henriksson, M. M., Marttunen, M. J., Isometsa, E. T., Heikkinen, M. E., Aro, H. M., Kuoppasalmi, K. I., & Lönnqvist, J. K. (1995). Mental disorders in elderly suicide. *International Journal of Psychogeriatrics, 7*, 275–286.

Hepple, J., & Quinton, C. (1997). One hundred cases of attempted suicide in the elderly. *British Journal of Psychiatry, 171*, 42–46.

Holmes, C. B., & Howard, M. E. (1980). Recognition of suicide lethality factors by physicians, mental health professionals, ministers, and college students. *Journal of Consulting and Clinical Psychology, 48*, 383–387.

Ingram, B. L., & Lowe, D. (1989). Counseling activities and referral practices of rabbis. *Journal of Psychology and Judaism, 13*, 133–148.

Jones, B. E., & Yang, T. Z. (1985). The efferent projections from the reticular formation and the locus coeruleus studied by anterograde and retrograde axonal transport in the rat. *Journal of Comparative Neurology, 242*, 56–92.

Jorm, A. F., Henderson, A. S., Scott, R., Korten, A. E., Chirstensen, H., & Mackinnon, AJ. (1995). Factors associated with the wish to die in elderly people. *Age and Ageing, 24*, 389–392.

Keller, M. B., McCullough, J. P., Klein, D. N., Arnow, B., Dunner, D. L., Gelenberg, A. J., Markowitz, J. C., Nemeroff, C. B., Russell, J. M., Thase, M. E., Trivedi, M. H., & Zajecka, J. (2000). A comparison of nefazodone, the cognitive behavioral-analysis system of psychotherapy, and their combination for the treatment of chronic depression. *New England Journal of Medicine, 342,* 1462–1470.

Kelly, S., & Bunting, J. (1998). Trends in suicide in England and Wales, 1982–1996. *Population Trends, 92,* 29–41.

Kessler, R. C., Foster, C., Webster, P. S., & House, J. S. (1992). The relationship between age and depressive symptoms in two national surveys. *Psychology and Aging, 7,* 119–126.

Kirby, M., Bruce, I., Radic, A., Coakley, D., & Lawlor, B. A. (1997). Hopelessness and suicidal feelings among the community dwelling elderly in Dublin. *Irish Journal of Psychological Medicine, 14,* 124–127.

Kishi, Y., Robinson, R. G., & Kosier, J. T. (1996a). Suicidal plans in patients with acute stroke. *Journal of Nervous and Mental Disease, 284,* 274–280.

Kishi, Y., Robinson, R. G., & Kosier, J. T. (1996b) Suicidal plans in patients with strokes: Comparison between acute-onset and delayed-onset suicidal plans. *International Psychogeriatrics, 8,* 623–634.

Kjolseth, I., Ekeberg, O., & Teige, B. (2002). Suicide among the elderly in Norway. *Tidsskrift Nor Laegeforen, 122,* 1457–1461.

Koenig, H. G. (1994). *Aging and God.* New York: Haworth Press.

Lester, D. (1994). Suicide in immigrant groups as a function of their proportion in the country. *Perceptual and Motor Skills, 79,* 994.

Lester, D. (2001). Suicide among the elderly in the world: Covariation with psychological and socio-economic factors. In D. De Leo (Ed.), *Suicide and euthanasia in older adults: A transcultural journey* (pp. 1–20). Göttingen: Hogrefe & Huber.

Li, G. (1995). The interaction effect of bereavement and sex on the risk of suicide in the elderly: An historical cohort study. *Social Science and Medicine, 40,* 825–828.

Lindesay, J., Briggs, K., & Murphy, E. (1989). The Guy's/Age Concern survey: Prevalence rates of cognitive impairment, depression and anxiety in an urban elderly community. *British Journal of Psychiatry, 155,* 317–329.

Lindsey, J., & Murphy, E. (1989). Dementia, depression and subsequent institutionalization: The effects of home support. *International Journal of Geriatric Psychiatry, 4,* 3–9.

Loebel, J. P., Loebel, J. S., Dager, S. R., Centerwall, B. S., & Reay, D. T. (1991). Anticipation of nursing home placement may be a precipitant of suicide among elderly. *Journal of the American Geriatrics Society, 39,* 407–408.

Lyness, J. M., Conwell, Y., & Nelson, J. C. (1992). Suicide attempts in elderly psychiatric inpatients. *Journal of the American Geriatrics Society, 40,* 320–324.

McCall, P. L. (1991). Adolescent and elderly white male suicide trends: Evidence of changing well-being? *Journal of Gerontology, 46,* S43–51.

McIntosh, J. L., Santos, J. F., & Hubbard, R. W. (1994). *Elderly suicide research, theory and treatment.* Washington, DC: American Psychological Association.

Merrill, J., & Owens, J. (1990). Age and attempted suicide. *Acta Psychiatrica Scandinavica, 82,* 385–388.

Meylink, W., & Gorsuch, R. (1987). Relationship between clergy and psychologists: The empirical data. *Journal of Psychology and Christianity, 7,* 56–72.

Miller, M. (1979). *Suicide after sixty.* New York: Springer-Verlag.

Morgan, J., & Laungani, P. (2002). *Death and bereavement around the world, Vol. 1.* Amityville, NY: Baywood.

Mulsant, B. H., & Sweeney, J. A. (1997). Electroconvulsive therapy. In P. D. Nussbaum (Ed.), *The handbook of neuropsychology and aging* (pp. 508–514). New York: Plenum.

Murphy, G. E., & Wetzel, R. D. (1990). The lifetime risk of suicide in alcoholism. *Archives of General Psychiatry, 47,* 383–392.

Murray, G. B., Shea, V., & Conn, D. K. (1986). Electroconvulsive therapy for poststroke depression. *Journal of Clinical Psychiatry, 47,* 258–260.

National Institutes of Health Consensus Conference: diagnosis and treatment of depression in late life. (1992). *Journal of the American Medical Association, 268,* 1018–1024.

Neeleman, J., Halpern, D., Leon, D., & Lewis, G. (1997). Tolerance of suicide, religion and suicide rates: An ecological and individual level study in 19 Western countries. *Psychological Medicine, 27,* 1165–1171.

Neeleman, J., & Persaud, R. (1995). Why do psychiatrists neglect religion? *British Journal of Medical Psychology, 68,* 169–178.

Nelson, F. L., & Farberow, N. L. (1980). Indirect self-destructive behaviour in the elderly nursing home patient. *Journal of Gerontology, 35,* 949–957.

Newman, S. C., & Bland, R. C. (1989). Estimating the morbidity risk of illness from survey data. *American Journal of Epidemiology, 129,* 430–438.

Nisbet, P. A., Duberstein, P. R., Conwell, Y., & Seidlitz, L. (2000). The effect of participation in religious activities on suicide versus natural death in adults 50 and older. *Journal of Nervous and Mental Disease, 188,* 543–6

Osgood, N. J., Brant, B. A., & Lipman, A. (1991). *Suicide among the elderly in long term care facilities.* New York: Greenwood Press.

Oxman, T. E., Barrett, J. E., Barrett, J., & Gerber, P. (1990). Symptomatology of late-life minor depression among primary care patients. *Psychosomatics, 31,* 174–180.

Parmelee, P. A., Katz, I. R., & Lawton, M. P. (1989). Depression among institutionalized aged: assessment and prevalence estimation. *Journal of Gerontology, 44,* M22–M29.

Paykel, E. S., Myers, J. K., Lindenthal, J. J., & Tanner, J. (1974). Suicidal feelings in the general population: A prevalence study. *British Journal of Psychiatry, 124,* 460–469.

Pearson, J. L., & Brown, G. K. (2000). Suicide prevention in late life: Directions for science and practice. *Clinical Psychology Review,* 20:685–705.

Pescosolido, B. A., & Georgianna, S. (1989). Durkheim, suicide, and religion: Toward a network theory of suicide. *American Sociological Review, 54,* 33–48.

Pieper, H. G., & Garrison, T. (1992). Knowledge of social aspects of aging among pastors. *Journal of Religious Gerontology, 8,* 89–105.

Pierce, D. (1987). Deliberate self-harm in the elderly. *International Journal of Geriatric Psychiatry, 2,* 105–110.

Pitkala, K., Isometsa, E. T., Henriksson, M. M., & Lönnqvist, J. K. (2000). Elderly suicide in Finland. *International Psychogeriatrics, 12,* 209–220.

Polewka, A., Kroch, S., Chrostek Maj, J., Pach, J., & Zieba, A. (2002). Suicide attempts by self-poisoning among the elderly. *Przeglad Lekec, 59,* 291–4

Pritchard, C., & Baldwin, D. S. (2002). Elderly suicide rates in Asian and English-speaking countries. *Acta Psychiatrica Scandinavica, 105,* 271–275.

Prudic, J., & Sackeim, H. A. (1999). Electroconvulsive therapy and suicide risk. *Journal of Clinical Psychiatry, 60* (Suppl. 2), 104–110.

Qin, P., & Mortensen, P. B. (2001). Specific characteristics of suicide in China. *Acta Psychiatrica Scandinavica, 103,* 117–121.

Raleigh, V. S., & Balarajan, R. (1992). Suicide levels and trends among immigrants in England and Wales. *Health Trends, 24,* 91–94.

Reynolds, C. F., & Kupfer, D. J. (1999). Depression and aging: A look to the future. *Psychiatric Services, 50*, 1167–1172.

Reynolds, C. F. 3rd, Lebowitz, B. D., & Schneider, L. S. (1993). The NIH consensus development conference on the diagnosis and treatment of depression in late life: An overview. *Psychopharmacology Bulletin, 29*, 83–85.

Rihmer, Z., Rutz, W., & Pihlgren, H. (1995). Depression and suicide on Gotland: An intensive study of all suicides before and after a depression-training program for general practitioners. *Journal of Affective Disorders, 35*, 147–152.

Rifai, A. H., George, C. J., Stack, J. A., Mann, J. J., & Reynolds, C. F. (1994). Hopelessness in suicide attempters after acute treatment of major depression in later life. *American Journal of Psychiatry, 151*, 1687–1689.

Ritter, K., Stompe, T., Voracek, M., & Etzersdorfer, E. (2002). Suicide risk-related knowledge and attitudes of general practitioners. *Wiener Klinische Wochenschrift, 114*, 685–90.

Robins, L. N., & Kulbok, P. A. (1988). Epidemiologic studies in suicide. *Review of Psychiatry, 7*, 289–306.

Rockwell, D. A., & O'Brien, W. (1973). Physicians' knowledge and attitudes about suicide. *Journal of the American Medical Association, 225*, 1347–1349.

Rost, K., Smith, G., Matthews, D., & Guise, B. (1994). The deliberate misdiagnosis of major depression in primary care. *Archives of Family Medicine, 3*, 333–337.

Rowles, G. D. (1986). The rural elderly and the church. *Journal of Religion and Aging, 2*, 79–98.

Rutz, W., von Knorring, L., & Walinder, J. (1992). Long-term effects of an educational program for general practitioners given by the Swedish Committee for the Prevention and Treatment of Depression. *Acta Psychiatrica Scandinavica, 85*, 83–8.

Sainsbury, P. (1955). *Suicide in London.* Maudsley Monographs N1. London: Chapmen Hill.

Sainsbury, P., & Jekins, J. S. (1982). The accuracy of officially reported suicide statistics for purposes of epidemiological research. *Journal of Epidemiology and Community Health, 36*, 43–48.

Salib, E., Tadros, G., & Cawley, S. (2001). History of deliberate self harm may predict methods of fatal self harm in the elderly. *Medicine, Science and the Law, 41*, 107–110.

Sayil, I., & Aydemir, C. (2001). Elderly people and suicide in Turkey. In D. De Leo (Ed.), *Suicide and euthanasia in older adults: A transcultural journey* (pp. 89–95). Göttingen: Hogrefe & Huber.

Schmid, H., Manjee, K., & Shah, T. (1994). On the distinction of suicide ideation versus attempt in elderly psychiatric inpatients. *Gerontology, 34*, 332–339.

Schmidtke, A., Bille-Brahe, U., DeLeo, D., Kerkhof, A., Bjerke, T., Crepet, P., Haring, C., Hawton, K., Lönnqvist, J., Michel, K., Pommereau, X., Querejeta, I., Phillipe, I., Salander-Renberg, E., Temesvary, B., Wasserman, D., Fricke, S., Weinacker, B., & Sampaio-Faria, J. G. (1996). Attempted suicide in Europe: Rates, trends and sociodemographic characteristics of suicide attempters during the period 1989–1992. Results of the WHO/EURO Multicentre Study on Parasuicide. *Acta Psychiatrica Scandinavica, 93*, 237–338.

Schneider, L. S. (1996). Pharmacologic considerations in the treatment of late-life depression. *American Journal of Geriatric Psychiatry, 4* (4 Suppl. 1), S51–65.

Schou, M. (2000). Suicidal behavior and prophylactic lithium treatment of major mood disorders: A review of reviews. *Suicide and Life Threatening Behavior, 30*, 289–293.

Scocco, P., & De Leo, D. (2002). One-year prevalence of death thoughts, suicide ideation and behaviours in an elderly population. *International Journal of Geriatric Psychiatry, 17*, 842–846.

Scocco, P., De Leo, D., & Marietta, P. (1999). Mood disorders and parasuicide. *Italian Journal of Psychiatry and Behavioral Sciences, 8*, 85–89.

Scocco, P., Meneghel, G., Caon, F., Dello Buono, M., & De Leo, D. (2001a). Death ideation and its correlates: Survey of an over-65-year population. *Journal of Nervous and Mental Disease, 189*, 210–218.

Scocco, P., Meneghel, G., Dello Buno, M., & De Leo, D. (2001b). Hostility as a feature of suicidal ideators. *Psychological Reports, 88*, 863–868.

Seidlitz, L., Duberstein, P. R., Cox, C., & Conwell, Y. (1995). Attitudes of older people toward suicide and assisted suicide: an analysis of Gallup Poll findings. *Journal of the American Geriatric Society, 43*, 993–8.

Shah, A. K., & De, T. (1998). Suicide and the elderly. *International Journal of Psychiatry in Clinical Practice, 2*, 3–17.

Shah, A., Hoxey, K., & Mayadunne, V. (2000). Suicidal ideation in acutely medically ill elderly inpatients: Prevalence, correlates and longitudinal stability. *International Journal of Geriatric Psychiatry, 15*, 162–169.

Shaw, S., & Sims, A. (1984). A survey of unexpected deaths among psychiatric patients. *British Journal of Psychiatry, 145*, 473–476.

Simpson, J. C. (1988). Mortality studies in schizophrenia. In M. T. Tsuang & J. C. Simpson (Eds.), *Handbook of schizophrenia, Vol. 3: Nosology, epidemiology and genetics.* New York: Elsevier.

Skoog, I., Aevarsson, O., Beskow, J., Larsson, L., Palsson, S., Waern, M., Landahl, S., & Ostling, S. (1996). Suicidal feelings in a population sample of non-demented 85-year-olds. *American Journal of Psychiatry, 153*, 1015–1020.

Slater, J., & Depue, R. (1981). The contribution of environmental events and social support to serious suicide attempts in primary depressive disorder. *Journal of Abnormal Psychology, 40*, 275–285.

Stack, S. (1992). Marriage, family, religion and suicide. In R. W. Maris (Ed.), *Assessment and prediction of suicide* (pp. 540–553). New York: Guilford.

Steinberg, M., Donald, K., Clark, M. J., & Tyman. R. (1997). Towards successful ageing in the twenty-first century. In M. Lupton & J. M. Najman (Eds.), *Sociology of health and illness: Australian readings* (2nd ed., pp. 186–216). Singapore: Superskill Graphics Pty Ltd.

Stenager, E. N., & Stenager, E. (1998). *Disease, pain and suicidal behaviour.* London: Hamworth Medical Press.

Szanto, K., Gildengers, A., Mulsant, B. H., Brown, G., Alexopoulos, G. S., & Reynolds, C. F. 3rd. (2002). Identification of suicidal ideation and prevention of suicidal behaviour in the elderly. *Drugs and Aging, 19*, 11–24.

Takahashi, Y., Hirasawa, H., Koyama, K., Asakawa, O., Kido, M., Onose, H., Udagawa, M., Ishikawa, Y., & Uno, M. (1995). Suicide and aging in Japan: An examination of treated elderly suicide attempters. *International Psychogeriatrics, 7*, 239–251.

Tew, J. D., Mulsant, B. H., Haskett, R. F., Prudic, J., Thase, M. E., Crowe, R. R., Dolata, D., Begley, A. E., Reynolds, C. F. 3rd, & Sackeim, H. A. (1999). Acute efficacy of ECT in the treatment of major depression in the old-old. *American Journal of Psychiatry, 156*, 1865–1870.

Tondo, L., Jamison, K. R., & Baldessarini, R. J. (1997). Effect of lithium maintenance on suicidal behavior in major mood disorders. *Annals of the New York Academy of Sciences, 836*, 339–351.

Tsuang, M. T., & Simpson, J. C. (1985). Mortality studies in psychiatry: Should they stop or proceed? *Archives of General Psychiatry, 42*, 98–103.

Trovato, F. (1986). A time series analysis of international immigration and suicide mortality in Canada. *International Journal of Social Psychiatry, 32*, 38–46.

Turvey, C. L., Conwell, Y., Jones, M. P., Phillips, C., Simonsick, E., Pearson, J. L., & Wallace, R. (2002). Risk factors for late-life suicide: a prospective community-based study. *American Journal of Geriatric Psychiatry, 10*, 398–406.

Vasilas, C. A., & Morgan, H. G. (1994). Elderly suicides' contact with their general practitioner before death. *Journal of the American Geriatrics Society, 9*, 1008–1009.

Waern, M., Beskow, J., Runeson, B., & Skoog, I. (1999). Suicidal feelings in the last year of life in elderly people who commit suicide. *The Lancet, 354*, 917–918.

Waern, M., Rubenowitz, E., Runeson, B., Skoog, I., Wilhelmson, K., & Allebeck, P. (2002a). Burden of illness and suicide in elderly people: Case-control study. *British Medical Journal, 324*, 1335.

Waern, M., Runeson, B. S., & Allebeck, P. et al. (2002b) Mental disorder in elderly suicides: A case-control study. *American Journal of Psychiatry 159*, 450–455.

Watanabe, N. (2001). An investigation into resilience and suicide in Japan's elderly. In D. De Leo (Ed.), *Suicide and euthanasia in older adults: A transcultural journey* (pp. 97–116). Göttingen: Hogrefe & Huber.

Weaver, A. J. (1995). Has there been a failure to prepare and support parish-based clergy in their role as front-line community mental health workers? A review. *Journal of Pastoral Care, 49*, 129–149.

Weaver, A. J., & Koenig, H. G. (1996). Elderly suicide, mental health professionals, and the clergy: A need for clinical collaboration, training, and research. *Death Studies, 20*, 495–508.

World Health Organisation. (2003). *Country report.* Available at http://www5.who.int/mental_health/main.cfm?p = 0000000515. Accessed 05/02/03.

Yang, C. H., Tsai, S. J., Chang, J. W., & Hwang, J. P. (2001). Characteristics of Chinese suicide attempters admitted to a geropsychiatric unit. *International Journal of Geriatric Psychiatry, 16*, 1033–1036.

Yesavage, J. A. (1983). Direct and indirect hostility and self-destructive behaviour by hospitalised depressives. *Acta Psychiatrica Scandinavica, 68*, 345–350.

Yip, P. S. F. (1996). Suicides in Hong Kong, Taiwan and Beijing. *British Journal of Psychiatry, 169*, 495–500.

Yip, P. S., Callanan, C., & Yuen, H. P. (2000). Urban/rural and gender differentials in suicide rates: East and West. *Journal of Affective Disorders, 57*, 99–106.

Yip, P. S., & Chi, I. (2001). Suicidal behaviour in the hong kong elderly. In D. De Leo (Ed.), *Suicide and euthanasia in older adults: A transcultural journey* (pp. 97–116). Göttingen: Hogrefe & Huber.

Yip, P. S., Chi, I., & Yu, K. K. (1998). An epidemiological profile of elderly suicides in Hong Kong. *International Journal of Geriatric Psychiatry, 13*, 631–637.

Zielinski, R. J., Roose, S. P., Devanand, D. P., Woodring, S., & Sackeim, H. A. (1993). Cardiovascular complications of ECT in depressed patients with cardiac disease. *American Journal of Psychiatry, 150*, 904–909.

Zweig, R. A., & Hinrichsen, G. A. (1993). Factors associated with suicide attempts by depressed older adults: A prospective study. *American Journal of Psychiatry, 150*, 1687–1692.

Chapter 19
Immigrants and Attempted Suicide in Europe

Halise Devrimci-Özguven[1], Isik Sayil[1], Bora Baskak[1]
and Unni Bille-Brahe[2]

[1]Ankara University, Turkey, [2]Suicide Research Centre, Odense, Denmark

Introduction

During recent decades, the number of immigrants, especially from the Far and the Middle East, and Africa, has increased markedly in most European countries, and, in addition, an increasing migration is taking place between the countries. The integration of such an increasing number of foreigners may be a difficult process, and the cost of this process may be high for many immigrants. In their new country, the immigrants and their descendants have to adapt to new norms, values and lifestyles that often are very different from those in force in their home country. Some will consider this a natural process, while others will have difficulties in changing their ethno-cultural identity, and the acculturation process may lead to loss of identity, resulting in feelings of impotence, anger and loneliness (Berry, 1992; Antonowsky, 1993; Molina, et al., 1994; Marsella, et al., 1996).

Several researchers have studied the relationship between immigration and suicidal behaviour, but with different results. After the previous huge waves of immigration that took place during the 1950s and 1960s, researchers such as Sainsbury and Barraclough (1968), Sainsbury (1973), and Withlock (1971) concluded that the rates of suicide among various groups of immigrants correlated with the rates in their home country. It should be noted, however, that in the 1950s and 1960s, most migration went from the "old" to the "new" world, that is, from, e.g., the European countries to Australia and New Zealand or to USA and Canada; while in later years, the direction of migration has changed, the main flow now going from politically unstable or less developed countries to the more stable and affluent parts of the world. This means that the characteristics of the immigrants – and of both their countries of origin and their new countries – have changed. Accordingly, the integration processes that the immigrants are going through today are quite different from those facing the immigrants of the 1950s and 1960s, and a more recent study indicates that the rates of suicide among immigrants now are approaching the rates of their new country (Kliever & Ward, 1988).

Several studies have indicated that there are positive correlations between immigration and suicidal behaviour (Lester, 1972; Stack, 1981; Kliever & Ward, 1988; Ambrumova & Postovalova, 1991; Varnik & Wasserman, 1992; Hovey & King, 1996; Patel & Gaw, 1996; Johansson, 1997; Sorenson & Golding, 1998; Ponizovsky, 1999), while others did not find any unambiguous relationship (Bille-Brahe, 2000; Burvill, et al., 1982; Lester, 1989; Ferradanol, 1997; Pavlovic & Marusic, 2001).

The material collected by the WHO/EURO Multi-Centre Study on Suicidal Behaviour (Platt, et al., 1992; Kerkhof, et al., 1994) includes information on suicide attempters from various European areas, and it provides us with the opportunity to study some of the basic socio-demographic and social characteristics of immigrant versus non-immigrant attempters. The aim of this chapter is to try and see whether there are differences between the two groups in the frequencies in parameters that are commonly seen as risk factors for suicidal behaviour.

The monitoring form used by the Multi-Centre Study does not include one specific question regarding immigrant status, but by employing the following three parameters: 1) the place (country) of the suicide attempt, 2) the attempter's nationality and 3) the attempter's country of birth, the suicide attempters can be divided in two groups, namely 1st generation immigrants and non-immigrants. It has to be noted that, as we do not have any information on the number of immigrants in the various total populations, our data can only show the percentage of the suicide attempters being immigrants, and not the rates of attempted suicide among immigrants.

It is also important to keep in mind that the term "immigrant" refers to very different groups of people, such as guest workers, people who look for a new life in more affluent societies, people who migrate for political or religious reasons, and refugees escaping from torture, war or disaster, and also that there might be marked cultural differences both between the areas under study and between the various ethnical groups.

In all, the material includes 35,076 suicide attempters from 18 European areas under study.

However, in several cases, information on the various social characteristics were not available. The number of missing data varies from centre to centre and from item to item, but apparently there were no systematic patterns in the various frequencies of missing data, and cases with missing values therefore have been deleted from the analyses. In order to compare the socio-demographic characteristics of immigrant and non-immigrant suicide attempters, we used Student's t tests for continuous variables and chi-square tests for transient variables.

Results

The distribution of suicide attempts by the immigration status in the various areas under study is shown in Table 1. The table indicates huge differences between the centres ($p < .000$). In Tallinn, more than half (53%) and in Stockholm one fifth (21.6%) of the suicide attempts were carried out by immigrants, while in Emilia Romagna, Pecs and Szeged, the percentages were about zero. It should be noted that the high numbers of immigrant suicide attempters in Tallin and in Stockholm can probably be explained by historical factors: close to 40% of those defined as immigrants in Tallinn are Russians (close to one third of the total Estonian population is Russian), and 43% of those in Stockholm come from Finland, the two countries having had strong political, administrative and economical ties for centuries (Bille-Brahe, 1999). Also the French data indicate that recent history has played a role; more than 50% of the immigrant group come from the Northern part of Africa, especially from Algeria. For the rest, there seems to be a tendency that, especially in Northern Europe, a greater part of the immigrant group come from Turkey, the Middle East and Vietnam.

The differences between the centres were significant for both men and women, but the various centres differed somewhat as to the distribution on gender. In Gent, Helsinki, Odense, Padova and Stockholm, there was (in contrast to the non-immigrant group) an disproportionate number of women among the immigrant attempters, while in the other centres there was an excess of men.

In general, the immigrant suicide attempters were younger than the non-immigrant attempters; the mean age being 33.7 ± 13.66 years for the immigrants and 37.7 ± 15.27 years for the non-immigrants ($F = 43.94, p > .000$).

Table 2 shows the distribution on the methods used by immigrants and non-immigrants. In respectively 18 (0.7%) and 660 (2.1%) of the cases, information on the method used was missing. There were significant differences between immigrants and non-immigrants as to their choice of method, but, in both groups, the most commonly used method was self-poisoning, especially by psychotropic agents, and, in both groups, self-poisoning was more common among women than among men. Cutting or stabbing was the next most often used method – especially among male immigrants, where close to one third had chosen this method.

In more than half of the total cases under study, one or more suicide attempts had been carried out prior to the index attempt (see Table 3). Non-immigrants seem to be significantly more likely to be repeaters than immigrants, but we have to be aware that there are huge differences between the areas under study. In Ankara, Guipuzcoa and Padova, previous attempts were actually more common among immigrants than among non-immigrants, and only in Leiden, Sør-Trøndelag and Würzburg were previous attempts significantly more common among the non-immigrants than among the immigrants ($p < .05, p < .05, p < .01$, respectively).

When it comes to the various social characteristics, there seems to be a similar

Table 1 Attempted suicide (events) by immigrant status, gender, and area under study (%).

Centre	Immigrants			Non-immigrants			Unknown/missing data			Total (N)		
	Male N=990	Female N=1510	Total N=2500	Male N=13135	Female N=18648	Total N=31786	Male N=335	Female N=458	Total N=790	Male	Female	Total
Ankara (1998–2001)	1.2	0.9	1.0	98.8	99.1	99.0	–	–	–	84	228	312
Bern (1989–1990)(1993–1998)	13.0	11.0	11.8	86.2	87.9	88.2	0.8	1.0	0.9	660	1053	1713
Bordeux (1989)	10.7	9.6	10.0	88.8	89.5	90.0	0.5	0.8	0.7	374	841	1215
Emilia Romagna (1989–1994)	–	–	–	30.2	69.8	100	–	–	–	288	666	954
Gent (1996–1999)	5.3	7.0	6.2	93.3	90.4	93.6	1.4	2.6	0.2	808	1005	1813
Guizpuzcoa (1989–1991)	4.5	3.5	3.9	95.5	96.5	96.1	–	–	–	89	141	230
Helsinki (1989–1994)	0.4	0.6	0.5	99.5	99.4	99.5	0.1	–	0.04	2057	2040	4097
Leiden (1989–1992)	6.8	6.4	6.6	91.4	91.0	93.3	1.8	2.5	2.2	279	513	792
Ljubljana (1995–1999)	6.2	4.5	5.4	93.8	99.5	94.6	–	–	–	468	485	953
Odense (1989–1999)	2.1	2.9	2.6	96.5	95.0	97.4	1.5	1.5	1.5	3678	4623	8301
Padova (1989–1996)	2.0	2.7	2.5	97.7	96.7	97.5	0.03	0.5	0.04	396	732	1128
Pecs (1997–1999)	–	0.5	0.3	100	99.5	99.7	–	–	–	255	428	683
Sør-Trøndelag (1989–1999)	1.5	1.2	1.3	98.5	98.8	98.7	–	–	–	1471	2053	3524
Stockholm (1989–1998)	20.6	22.2	21.6	66.2	67.5	75.6	13.2	10.3	11.3	1312	2339	3651
Szeged (1989–1991)	0.2	0.2	0.2	99.8	99.8	100	–	–	–	508	659	1167
Tallinn (1995–1996)	49.9	47.9	53.3	38.6	47.5	46.7	11.5	4.6	8.1	503	478	981
Umeå (1989–1995)	10.1	9.8	9.9	89.1	90.1	90.1	–	0.1	0.1	643	1337	1980
Würzburg (1989–1999)	11.2	10.7	6.9	84.7	83.1	88.5	4.1	6.2	5.4	587	995	1582
All	6.8	7.3	7.1	90.8	90.4	90.6	2.3	2.2	2.2	14460	20616	35076

Total: $\chi^2 = 5366.09, p < .000$, Men: $\chi^2 = 2671.66, p < .000$, Women: $\chi^2 = 2741.19, p < .000$

Table 2 Suicide attempts (events) by immigrant status, gender and method used (%).

	Men N=984	Women N=1496	Total N=2480	Men N=12799	Women N=18324	Total N=31123
Other drugs	17.0	27.7	23.5	15.5	19.2	17.7
Hanging	4.2	1.4	2.5	3.1	1.3	2.1
Moving vehicle	1.9	0.9	1.3	1.3	0.5	0.8
Alcohol	1.2	1.1	1.1	1.6	1.1	1.3

χ^2: 173.85, $p \leq .000$

Table 3 Attempted suicide (events) by immigrant status, the frequency of previous attempt(s), and area under study (%).

	Immigrants			Non-immigrants		
Centre	Previous attempt(s) N=987	No previous attempt N=903	Total (N) N=1890	Previous attempt(s) N=14831	No previous attempt N=9412	Total (N) N=24243
Ankara	33.3	66.7	3	23.3	75.1	309
Bern	57.4	42.6	136	61.3	38.7	1130
Bordeux	43.8	56.2	121	47.5	52.5	1071
Emilia Romagna	–	–	–	48.0	52.0	700
Gent	42.9	57.1	56	53.4	46.6	761
Guizpuzcoa	77.8	22.2	9	49.3	50.7	213
Helsinki	62.5	37.5	16	69.4	30.6	2970
Leiden	38.0	62.0	50	58.5	41.5	680
Ljubljana	45.7	54.3	46	44.6	55.4	749
Odense	71.7	28.3	106	78.7	21.3	4934
Padova	58.8	41.2	17	49.2	50.8	731
Pecs	–	100	2	50.5	49.5	681
Sør-Trøndelag	44.1	55.9	34	61.7	38.3	2886
Stockholm	55.3	44.7	739	62.6	37.4	2299
Szeged	–	–	–	35.3	64.7	1157
Tallinn	38.0	62.0	229	41.5	58.5	200
Umeå	68.5	31.5	178	68.6	31.4	1645
Würzburg	37.2	62.8	148	43.4	56.7	1132
All	52.2	47.8	100%	61.2	38.8	100%

$\chi^2 = 58.84$, $p \leq 0.000$

Table 4 Attempted suicide (events) by immigrant status, household composition and area under study (%).

Centre	Immigrants			Non-immigrants		
	Living alone N=456	Living with someone N=1533	Total (N) N=1989	Living alone N=6855	Living with someone N=14750	Total (N) N=21605
Ankara	–	100	3	2.0	98.0	300
Bern	21.0	79.0	124	29.5	70.5	485
Bordeux	–	100	114	–	100	1040
Emilia Romagna	–	–	–	12.8	87.2	531
Gent	18.5	81.5	81	26.1	73.9	1039
Guizpuzcoa	–	100	9	4.2	95.8	213
Helsinki	47.1	52.9	17	56.8	43.2	2610
Leiden	25.0	75.0	52	26.7	71.9	708
Ljubljana	10.6	89.4	47	14.8	85.2	764
Odense	19.0	81.0	121	34.8	65.2	4005
Padova	16.7	83.3	18	14.6	85.4	767
Pecs	–	100	2	10.4	89.6	681
Sør-Trøndelag	18.9	81.1	37	31.4	68.6	1726
Stockholm	29.2	70.8	774	42.0	58.0	2393
Szeged	–	–	–	33.6	66.4	1160
Tallinn	16.0	84.0	231	11.7	88.3	196
Umeå	37.1	64.9	191	40.7	59.2	1721
Würzburg	15.5	84.5	168	26.6	73.4	1266
All	22.9	77.1	100%	31.7	68.3	100%

$\chi^2 = 65.99, p \leq .000$

pattern. Generally, there are significant differences between the immigrant suicide attempters and the non-immigrant attempters, but when it comes to the various areas under study, the distributions on various parameters sometimes vary to a great extent.

Table 4 shows, perhaps somewhat unexpectedly, that, in most cases under study, the immigrant attempters were more seldom living alone compared to non-immigrant attempters, and only in Padova and Tallinn were more of the immigrant than of the non-immigrant attempters living alone.

Table 5 shows that in spite of the fact that immigrant attempters in general were younger than the non-immigrant attempters, more immigrant attempters than

Table 5 Attempted suicide (events) by immigrant status and civil status (%).

Civil status	Immigrants N=2,056	Non-immigrants N=24,716	Total N=26,748
Never married	39.6	41.8	11157
Widowed	3.4	5.4	1402
Divorced/Separated	20.9	20.8	5571
Married/legal cohabitation	36.0	31.9	8626

Table 6 Attempted suicide (events) by immigrant status, address change and area under study (%).

Centre	Immigrants			Non-immigrant		
	Did Not change N=1,177	Changed N=365	Total (N) N=1542	Did not change N=14894	Changed N=3591	Total (N) N=18485
Ankara	100	–	3	91.6	8.4	299
Bern	74.7	25.1	99	76.1	23.9	393
Bordeux	78.5	21.5	121	76.5	23.5	1081
Gent	81.9	18.1	83	88.4	11.6	1145
Guizpuzcoa	100	–	9	94.5	5.5	217
Helsinki	42.9	57.1	7	73.2	26.8	1185
Leiden	83.7	16.3	49	86.4	13.6	693
Odense	73.3	26.7	105	78.4	21.6	3899
Padova	92.3	7.7	13	88.4	11.6	623
Pecs	100	–	2	81.9	18.1	681
Sør-Trøndelag	42.9	57.1	35	72.9	27.1	2499
Stockholm	80.2	19.8	717	86.0	14.0	2264
Szeged	–	–	–	94.4	5.5	1116
Umeå	65.0	35.0	143	70.7	29.3	1208
Würzburg	70.5	29.5	156	81.7	18.3	1182
All	76.3	23.7	100%	80.6	19.4	100%

$\chi^2 = 16.17, p \leq .000$

non-immigrant attempters were married. It is also interesting to note that one fifth of both the immigrants and the non-immigrants were divorced or separated.

In most areas under study, the majority of both immigrant and non-immigrant suicide attempters had not been moving during the last year. Exceptions were in Helsinki and in Sør-Trøndelag, where significantly more immigrant attempters than non-immigrant attempters had changed address (Table 6).

Table 7 Attempted suicide (events) by level of education and area under study (%).

Centre	Immigrants				Non-immigrants			
	Low N=722	Mid N=831	High N=177	Total (N) N=1730	Low N=9043	Mid N=7803	High N=2345	Total (N) N= 19191
Ankara	33.3	66.7	–	3	28.2	62.6	8.9	305
Bern	68.5	20.7	10.9	92	79.7	8.1	12.2	418
Bordeux	–	91.7	8.3	121	–	91.1	8.9	1085
Emilia Romagna	–	–	–	–	70.6	21.3	8.1	521
Gent	30.8	66.7	2.6	78	28.1	54.5	17.4	1062
Guizpuzcoa	44.4	44.4	11.1	9	42.0	50.7	7.2	207
Helsinki	50.0	25.0	25.0	8	49.7	40.1	10.2	2487
Leiden	46.9	37.5	15.6	32	57.0	27.5	15.6	597
Ljubljana	66.7	31.3	2.1	48	42.2	48.2	9.6	678
Odense	29.1	54.5	16.4	55	44.7	43.5	11.9	1742
Padova	66.7	20.0	13.3	15	65.4	28.8	5.8	702
Pecs	–	50.0	50.0	2	53.4	40.5	6.1	676
Sør-Trøndelag	41.4	20.7	37.9	29	47.8	31.9	20.3	2402
Stockholm	50.2	40.9	8.9	677	41.0	48.4	10.6	2109
Szeged	–	–	–	–	65.5	22.5	12.0	1161
Tallinn	4.7	88.9	6.4	235	5.8	82.6	11.6	207
Umeå	55.3	34.6	10.1	188	58.3	34.9	6.8	1680
Würzburg	62.3	16.7	21.0	138	56.3	23.1	20.6	1152
All	41.7	48.0	10.2	100%	47.1	40.7	12.2	100%

$\chi^2 = 35.984, p \leq .000$

In general, fewer immigrant than non-immigrant attempters had a lower level of education and more middle, but, as can be seen from Table 7, there were marked differences between the areas under study.

Finally, the economical activity for immigrant and non-immigrant attempters is shown in Table 8. Quite surprisingly, more immigrant than non-immigrant attempters were economically active and employed, and the frequency of unemployment was almost the same in the two groups. Again, however, there were marked differences between the areas under study, both regarding the level of economical activity in general and regarding the differences between the two groups.

As mentioned in the introduction, factors like being divorced, living alone, having previously attempted suicide, having a low level of education and being unemployed are known to be risk factors for suicidal behaviour. Based on the information available on these parameters, a risk score, ranking from 0 to 6, was therefore constructed. The average risk score turned out to be surprisingly low, ranging from less

Table 8 Attempted suicide (events) by economic status and area under study (%).

Centre	Immigrants				Non-immigrants			
	A N=904	B N=367	C N=879	Total (N) N=2150	A N=8681	B N=3951	C N=11345	Total (N) N= 23977
Ankara	–	66.7	33.3	3	26.5	15.8	57.7	298
Bern	62.1	4.9	33.0	103	50.7	4.9	44.5	452
Bordeux	44.7	17.5	37.7	114	37.0	19.7	43.3	1028
Gent	21.7	30.1	48.2	83	31.4	23.3	45.3	1129
Guizpuzcoa	33.3	55.6	11.1	9	30.8	24.2	45.0	211
Helsinki	29.4	17.6	52.9	17	46.0	16.3	38.0	3406
Leiden	38.8	28.6	32.7	49	30.2	33.1	36.7	673
Ljubljana	20.0	50.0	30.0	50	31.8	26.0	48.2	785
Odense	15.2	23.2	61.6	112	17.5	20.2	62.3	4593
Padova	43.6	18.8	37.4	16	35.2	17.8	47.0	776
Pecs	–	50.0	50.0	2	34.1	22.2	43.8	681
Sør-Trøndelag	28.2	12.8	59.0	39	30.1	18.9	51.0	2513
Stockholm	44.5	20.0	35.5	755	47.8	13.4	38.9	2337
Szeged	–	–	–	–	59.5	3.3	37.2	1164
Tallinn	50.2	6.9	42.9	448	47.4	8.8	43.8	388
Umeå	38.1	12.2	49.7	189	44.6	6.8	48.6	1692
Würzburg	41.0	17.4	41.6	161	44.4	11.9	43.7	1270
All	42.0	17.1	40.9	100%	36.2	16.5	47.3	100%

A = Economically active employed, B = Economically active unemployed, C = Economically inactive
$\chi^2 = 36.216, p \leq .000$

than 1 for both groups in Pecs, to 3 and 2, respectively, in Helsinki. In general, the scores were somewhat lower among the immigrants than the non-immigrants, but the difference was significant only in the Leiden area.

Discussion

The immigrants in the areas under study may have left their home country for very different reasons, and they may be very differently prepared to meet the challenge of integrating in their new country. However, while our material may include both the affluent businessman, who immigrated to Italy primarily to be able to enjoy the "dolce vita," and the uneducated man from a village in Somalia, who want to immigrate to any European country, it seems that the majority come from countries that are very different from their new country with regards to religion and lifestyles.

Table 9 Total risk score (X) by immigrant status and centres.

Centre	Immigrants		Non-immigrants			
	X ± ss	N	X ± ss	N	F	p
Ankara	1.33 ± 1.53	3	0.86 ± 0.92	285	1.39	0.38
Bern	1.89 ± 1.04	56	2.16 ± 1.13	287	0.85	0.10
Bordeux	1.06 ± 0.87	110	1.09 ± 0.93	973	1.66	0.78
Gent	1.69 ± 1.33	45	1.69 ± 1.24	511	0.25	0.98
Guizpuzcoa	1.89 ± 1.05	9	1.44 ± 1.09	200	0.21	0.23
Helsinki	3.00 ± 1.58	5	2.49 ± 1.23	907	0.33	0.36
Leiden	1.73 ± 0.79	30	2.14 ± 1.27	552	10.14	0.01
Odense	1.96 ± 1.39	24	2.31 ± 1.26	1112	0.31	0.18
Padova	1.92 ± 0.90	12	1.78 ± 1.12	544	2.41	0.68
Pecs	0.50 ± 0.71	2	1.80 ± 1.18	676	0.81	0.12
Sør-Trøndelag	1.95 ± 0.84	22	2.28 ± 1.29	1344	8.26	0.08
Stockholm	2.03 ± 1.20	615	2.01 ± 1.17	1922	0.16	0.74
Szeged	–	–	1.84 ± 1.08	1099	–	–
Umeå	2.30 ± 1.11	132	2.24 ± 1.16	1086	1.11	0.56
Würzburg	1.81 ± 1.17	119	1.78 ± 1.16	937	0.02	0.80
All	1.92 ± 1.19	1184	1.96 ± 1.23	12435	3.67	0.25

Many of these will want to constitute or become part of one particular ethnic group, so that their ethno-cultural identity will continue to refer to the traditional culture of their home country and they themselves will tend to adhere to the norms and values and (not at least) to the religion and the life styles held in force by their particular ethnic group (Marsella, personal communication). On one hand, this may be very supportive to the individual; on the other, it may be a severe hindrance to successful integration, and thus in the end make the life of the immigrant and his family very difficult.

Of the more than 35,000 registered suicide attempters in our material, about 7% were defined as 1st generation immigrants. Although we do not have any estimates of the frequency of attempted suicide among immigrants in general (due to the lack of information on the total number of immigrants in the various areas under study), the percentage seems to be rather high, especially when considering that according to the religion in force in many of these ethnic groups, suicidal behaviour is strictly forbidden.

Other unexpected results refer to the various characteristics of the immigrant and the non-immigrant suicide attempters. It has not been the aim of this study to discuss per se the importance of risk factors, such as being divorced, living alone, etc., but when comparing our data with the frequencies of some of factors in the total population in the various areas under study, it turns out that the percentages for being, e.g., divorced or living alone are markedly higher in our material (Bille-Brahe, 1999). However, rather unexpectedly, the results showed that the immigrant suicide attempters had a relatively higher economic status and a higher level of education than the non-immigrant attempters. Fewer of the immigrants were living alone and more were married at the time of the index attempt, and those having a history of previous suicide attempt(s) were more frequently non-immigrant than immigrant attempters. It is, however, interesting to note, that, while there are differences between the areas on all the parameters, there are in general only small differences between the immigrant and the non-immigrant groups – and when it comes to the total risk score (Table 9), in 7 out of 15 centres, the immigrants actually had a lower risk score than the non-immigrants.

Summing up, rather unexpectedly, our results indicate that, in general, risk factors such as divorce, unemployment, etc. are less frequent among immigrant than among non-immigrant suicide attempters. However, taking into considerations the many limitations of the study and the at times huge variations between the areas under study, more studies in the field are definitely needed.

References

Antonovsky, A. (1993). Complexity, conflict, chaos, coherence, coercion and civility. *Social Science and Medicine, 37*, 969–974.

Ambrumova, A. G., & Postovalova, L. I. (1991). *The social-psychological factors in formation of suicidal behavior: Methodical review*. Moscow: Ministry of Health of Russia.

Berry, J. W., Poortinga, Y. H., Segall, M. H., & Dasen, P. R. (1992). *Cross-cultural psychology: Research and applications*. New York: Cambridge University Press.

Bille-Brahe, U., Schmidtke, A., Kerkhof, A. J., De Leo, D., Lönnqvist, J., Platt, S., & Sampaio Faria, J. (1995). Background and introduction to the WHO/EURO Multicentre Study on Parasuicide. *Crisis, 16*, 72–84.

Bille-Brahe, U. (1999). *WHO/EURO Multicentre Study on Parasuicide. Facts and figures* (2nd ed.). Copenhagen: World Health Organisation.

Bille-Brahe, U. (2000). *Selvmordsadfærd blandt indvandrere og deres efterkommere* [Suicidal behaviour among 1st and 2nd generation immigrants]. Odense: Centre for Suicidological Research.

Burvill, P. W., Woodings, T. L., Stenhouse, N. S., & McCall, M. G. (1982) Suicide during 1961–1970 migrants in Australia *Psychological Medicine, 12*, 295–308.

Ferrada-Noli, M. (1997). A cross-cultural breakdown of Swedish suicide. *Acta Psychiatrica Scandinavica, 96*, 108–111.

Hovey, J. D., & King, C. A. (1996). Acculturative stress, depression, and suicidal ideation among immigrant and second generation Latino adolescents. *Journal of the American Academy of Child and Adolescent Psychiatry, 3*, 1183–1192

Johansson, L. M., Sundquist, J., Johansson, S. E., Bergman, B., Qvist, J., & Traskman-Bendz, L. (1997). Suicide among foreign-born minorities and native Swedes: An epidemiological follow-up study of a defined population. *Social Science and Medicine, 44*, 181–187.

Kliewer, E. V., & Ward, R. H. (1988). Convergence of suicide rates to those in the destination country. *American Journal of Epidemiology, 127,* 640–653.

Lester, D. (1972). Migration and suicide. *Medical Journal of Australia, 1,* 941–942.

Lester, D. (1989). Immigration and rates of personal violence (suicide and homicide). *Psychological Reports, 65*(3), 1298.

Marsella, A. J., Friedman, M. J., Gerrity, E. T., & Scurfield, R. M. (1996). *Ethnocultural aspects of posttraumatic stress disorder.* Washington, DC: American Psychological Association.

Molina, C., Zambrana, R. E., & Aguirre-Molina, M. (1994). The influence of culture, class, and environment on health care. In C. Molina & M. Aguirre-Molina (Eds.), *Latino health in the US: A growing challenge.* Washington, DC: American Public Health Association.

Patel, S. P., & Gaw, A. C. (1996). Suicide among immigrants from the Indian subcontinent: A review. *Psychiatry Services, 47,* 517–521.

Pavlovic, E., & Marusic, A. (2001). Suicide in Croatia and in Croatian immigrant groups in Australia and Slovenia. *Croatian Medical Journal, 42,* 669–672.

Platt, S., Bille-Brahe, U., Kerkhof, A., Schmidtke, A., Bjerke, T., Crepet, P., De Leo, D., Haring, C., Lönnqvist, J., Michel, K., Philippe, A., Pommereau, X., Querejeta, I., Salander-Renberg, E., Temesvary, B., Wasserman, D., & Sampaio Faria, J. (1992). Parasuicide in Europe: The WHO/EURO Multicentre Study on Parasuicide, I: Introduction and preliminary analysis for 1989. *Acta Psychiatrica Scandinavica, 85,* 97–104.

Ponizovsky, A. M., & Ritsner, M. S. (1999). Suicide ideation among recent immigrants to Israel from the former Soviet Union: An epidemiological survey of prevalence and risk factors. *Suicide and Life-Threatening Behavior, 29,* 376–392.

Sainsbury, P., Barraclough, B. (1968). Differences between suicide rates. *Nature, 220,* 1252.

Sainsbury, P. (1973). Suicide: Opinions and facts. *Proceedings of the Royal Society of Medicine, 66,* 579–587.

Sorenson, S. B., & Golding, J. M. (1988). Prevalence of suicide attempts in a Mexican-American population: Prevention implications of immigration and cultural issues. *Suicide and Life-Threatening Behavior, 18,* 322–333.

Stack, S. (1981). The effect of immigration on suicide: A cross-national analysis. *Basic and Applied Social Psychology, 2,* 205–218.

Varnik, A., & Wasserman, D. (1992). Suicides in the former Soviet republics. *Acta Psychiatrica Scandinavica, 86,* 76–78.

Whitlock, F. A. (1971). Migration and suicide. *Medical Journal of Australia, 11,* 840.

Part 5

Clinical Aspects in Non-Fatal Suicidal Behaviour

Chapter 20
Contacts with Health Care Facilities Prior to Suicide Attempts

Sándor Fekete[1], Peter Osváth[1] and Konrad Michel[2]

[1]*Department of Psychiatry, University of Pecs, Hungary,* [2]*Department of Psychiatry, University of Bern, Switzerland*

Suicidal behaviour is a considerable public health problem. It is one of the most tragic events in human life, causing a serious problem among relatives and friends as well as imposing a great economic burden on the whole of society. Recent major epidemiological studies reveal that about 3–5% of the general population have made a suicide attempt and almost one-fifth have reported suicidal ideation at some time in their lives. Both attempted suicide and mental disorders are important risk factors for later suicide. The vast majority of the suicide attempters had contact with health care facilities during the 12 months before the index attempt or had received psychiatric inpatient or outpatient treatment (Appleby et al., 1999; Suominen et al., 2002), providing an opportunity to prevent suicidal behaviour. However, Suominen and co-workers (2002) found that half of them were without a treatment contact during the final 30 days before the index attempt.

According to Appleby et al. (1999), around a quarter of people who commit suicide have been in contact with mental health services in the year before death. Of these cases, 16% are psychiatric inpatients and 24% have been discharged from inpatient care in the previous three months. Suicide in former inpatients occurs most commonly in the week after discharge. Non-compliance with treatment and loss of contact with services are common before suicide. The findings suggest a range of measures which could improve suicide prevention by mental health services, including measures to increase compliance with treatment, prevent loss of contact with services, and reduce access to large quantities of psychotropic drugs. Most psychiatric patients who commit suicide are not regarded as being at high immediate risk at their final contact with mental health services. Better suicide prevention may therefore need changes to services for all patients rather than specific initiatives for those known to be at highest risk. Of those patients who commit suicide, about 80% or more had permanent contact with a general practitioner and/or other a medical specialist within a few months preceding their death, many of them visited GPs within a few weeks or one month before the act (Pirkis & Burgess, 1988; Appleby et al., 1999; Hawton et al., 1999; Andersen et al., 2000). In a psychological autopsy study of 571 suicides in Finland, in which a health care professional had been contacted prior to suicide, it was investigated whether the intent to commit suicide was communicated and discussed during the visit before the act (Isometsa et al., 1995). Of all suicides, 41% were reported to have had their last contact with a health care professional within the 4 weeks prior to death. The authors found that, at the occasion of the last visit, the issue of suicide had been discussed in 22% of the cases (in psychiatric outpatients 39%, in general practice 11% and in other specialties 6%). Eighteen percent of those who had contacted a physician had done so on the day of committing suicide, yet even then the issue of suicide was discussed in only 21% of these cases.

With regard to attempted suicide, the situation is very similar. A significant part of attempters have contacted a doctor before parasuicide (Volk-Wasserman, 1987; Runeson & Wasserman, 1994; Stenager & Jensen, 1994; Magoz-Gurpide et al., 1999; Suominen et al., 2002; Osváth et al., 2003). More than one third of these patients were found to have visited a medical specialist within one week before the attempt (Hawton & Blackstock, 1976). An increase in the frequency of visits to general practitioners prior to suicide and attempted suicide has been demonstrated (Appleby et al., 1999; Michel et al., 1997). So, theoretically, there should be large scope for preventive interventions by medical professionals.

Many studies demonstrate that 84–98% of suicide attempters have Axis I mental disorder at the time of attempt, and the most frequent diagnosis is major depression (56–77%) (Beautrais et al., 1996; Suominen et al., 1996; Ferreira de Castro et al., 1998; Balazs et al., 2000). Therefore, recognizing and treating depression has special importance during the last medical contact. However, patients may find it difficult to talk to their physician about emotional problems, because they may be ashamed or fear stigmatization, and may therefore choose to stay on safe ground by presenting physical problems only (Lin et al., 1989). When asked in retrospect about the reason for the last visit before attempting suicide, about 50% of the patients from patient samples in Bern as well as in Stockholm indicated physical reasons only (Michel et al., 1997).

One question arising from these findings is if factors related to the organisation of a health care system, such as the funding of medical services or the availability of primary health care providers, influence help-seeking behaviour. In Europe, different health care systems are in operation. Furthermore, in Europe there are striking national differences in the rates of attempted suicide (Platt et al., 1992), as well as in the characteristics of suicide attempters (Grootenhuis et al., 1994). In order to develop preventive measures, specific national and cultural factors should be taken into consideration. For example, it is possible that the help-seeking behaviour of people in suicidal crises differs according to the type of health care provision. In a comparison between Bern and Stockholm, it was found that in Bern more patients had seen their GP regularly, more had talked about their suicidal thoughts and fewer had been prescribed psychotropic medication at the last visit before attempting suicide (Michel et al., 1997).

In our study we compared patterns of contact with GPs made by suicide attempters prior to the attempt, in Pecs (Hungary) and Bern (Switzerland), and related the findings to differences in health care provision in the two countries. The health care systems are very different in the two countries and cities. In Switzerland, GPs and specialists working in private practice provide outpatient treatment. Hungary has a public health care system, and the private sector is very small and is not supported by health insurance companies.

The two catchment areas differ in the rates of parasuicide: Bern has lower rates of suicide attempts (129/100,000 in males and 177/100,000 in females) than Pecs (196/100,000 in males and 321/100,000 in females).

Methods

This investigation was part of the WHO/EURO Multi-Centre Study on Suicidal Behaviour. The method of data collection has been described by Platt et al. (1992), Kerkhof et al. (1993) and Schmidtke et al (1996). An important aspect of this study is that the data have been collected in a standardised way and were based on geographically defined catchment areas, which allows direct comparison of the results.

Study Population

Samples of suicide attempters interviewed in Bern and Pecs were part of medically treated suicide attempters recorded by the monitoring part of the WHO/EURO Study. Data were collected from all general and psychiatric hospital units within geographically defined catchment areas comprising populations of 301,000 (Bern) and 190,000 (Pecs). The subjects of our comparative study were suicide attempters, admitted consecutively, aged > 15 years, and living either in Pecs ($n = 101$) or in Bern ($n = 66$).

In Bern, 119 patients out of 327 attempters, aged > 15 and admitted to hospital were asked during 1990 by a member of the research team to participate in a structured interview (see below). The other patients could not be contacted either because they were discharged before they were reported ($n = 102$) or because of other reasons such as language problems or disturbed state of mind. Out of the 119 patients, a further 53 interviews could not be accomplished because patients refused ($n = 38$), or because of other reasons ($n = 15$), leaving altogether 66 suicide attempters with a completed interview, which represent 20% of all known suicide attempters in the catchment area. A comparison with the total number of suicide attempters registered during the investigation year ($N = 327$) showed no significant differences in age and sex distribution, civil status, living situation (alone, with family, etc.) and employment status. The only difference found was in the educational background: the sample reached a higher level of schooling ($\chi^2 = 17.58$, $df = 3$, $p < .001$).

In Pecs, in the same manner, 101 hospitalised patients agreed to participate in the study, representing 31% of those treated in the hospital during the period of the study. Of the 325 attempters who were admitted after parasuicide, 199 could not be contacted because they were discharged before the interview. A further 25 interviews could not be conducted because the patients refused to participate ($n = 5$) or for other reasons ($n = 20$). A comparison of the patients who were interviewed and those who were not revealed no significant differences in age, sex, marital and employment status or level of education.

Interviewing Instruments

Information about contacts with medical agencies prior to attempting suicide was collected as part of a comprehensive interview schedule (European Parasuicide Study Interview Schedule, EPSIS I, Kerkhof et al., 1993). This interview schedule had been carefully translated and back-translated from English into the languages of the centres participating in the study. The content of the schedules was derived from existing empirical research findings and theoretically based hypotheses about predictors of suicidal behaviour. The EPSIS consists of a number of observer-rated and self-rated instruments covering (in addition to medical and sociodemographic information) constructs such as social integration, social support, motives for parasuicide, life events, depression and hopelessness. The interview includes some questions about connections with health care systems (e.g., frequency of contacts, date and events of last visit, previous psychiatric treatment). All the interviewers had been trained in the correct use of this interview. The information presented here was collected in a semi-structured way and later coded accordingly. Descriptive statistics, Chi-square test and Fisher exact test were performed using the procedures available in SPSS for Windows 7.5.

Results

Characteristics of Study Population

Table 1 shows the basic characteristics of the two samples. The Pecs sample has slightly more females and a slightly lower mean age, but the differences are not significant. The Pecs sample has a lower percentage of single persons and a higher

Table 1 Characteristics of the samples.

Characteristics	Bern (*N* = 66)		Pecs (*N* = 101)	
	n	%	*N*	%
Male	29	44	38	32.7
Female	37	56	63	62.4
Sex ratio (male/female)	0.78		0.60	
Mean age (years)				
Male	38.5		33.4	
Female	38.8		36	
Marital status				
Single	29	43.9	32	31.7
Married	19	28.8	37	36.6
Widowed	3	4.5	5	5
Divorced	11	16.7	17	16.8
Separated	4	6.1	10	9.9
Number of children*				
None	34	43.9	30	29.7
1	10	15.2	29	28.7
2	13	19.7	33	32.7
3	6	9.1	6	5.9
4+	3	4.5	3	3
Not applicable	5	7.6	–	–
Employment status				
Employed full-time	25	37.9	40	39.6
Employed part-time*	9	13.6	4	4
Temporarily sick	1	1.5	2	2
Unemployed*	1	1.5	20	19.8
Student	7	10.6	7	6.9
Disabled	13	19.7	11	10.9
Retired*	5	7.6	9	8.9
Housewife/homemaker	4	6.1	4	4
Other	1	1.5	4	4
Previous parasuicide*				
None	38	57.6	38	37.6
1	15	22.7	25	24.8
2+	13	19.7	38	37.6

*$p < .05$

percentage of married and separated persons. A higher percentage of subjects in Pecs has one or more children (70.3 vs 56.1 χ^2 = 16.532, df = 6, p < .05). Some differences were found in the employment status of attempters in the two areas. In the Pecs sample, there are more unemployed, retired people and fewer students (χ^2 = 19.574, df = 9, p < .05).

In the Pecs sample, more patients had made previous suicide attempts (62.4% vs 42.4% χ^2 = 7.760, df = 2, p < .05). In Bern, more violent methods (hanging, shooting, drowning, jumping, explosion) (15.5% vs 1.5%) were used. In Pecs, poisoning was more frequent (78.7% vs 56.7%, χ^2 = 27.837, df = 7, p = 0).

Significant differences in the prevalence of mental disorders (according to ICD 10) were found in the two sample (χ^2 = 57.830, df = 9, p < .0001). In 97% of the cases in Pecs and 70% in Bern, at least one Axis I diagnosis was made. Adjustment disorder was the most common diagnosis (51% in Pecs, 35% in Bern). In Pecs, more depressive (19% vs 16%) and anxiety (4% vs 0%) disorders, and fewer substance abuse (11% vs 25%) and psychotic disorders (2% vs 10%) were found. Personality disorders were diagnosed almost in the same proportion in the two cities (Pecs: 12.5%, Bern: 13.5%).

Before the suicide attempt, a few more attempters regularly took anxiolytics/hypnotics (55% vs 52%), antidepressants (24% vs 23%), and antipsychotics (8% vs 5%) in Bern than Pecs. More Hungarian patients (46% vs 36%) took the anxiolytics/hypnotics in higher doses in the week before the attempt, while more Swiss attempters (56% vs 39%) increased the dose of antidepressants at that time.

Contacts with GPs

Patients were asked how many times they had visited their GP in the past 12 months. There were no substantial differences in the frequency of visits throughout the previous year. In the Pecs sample, 16.8% had no contact with GPs (Bern 13%); 42.6% had 1–3 contacts (Bern: 45%); and 40.6% over 4 (Bern 42%). In Pecs, 20.2% of subjects who had contacted their GPs in the previous week, and 10.6% of subjects in Bern visited their GP within the last week before the suicide attempt and 29.8% vs 35.1% within one month. Thus in Pecs significantly more patients visited a GP in the week before the attempt than in Bern (χ^2 = 12.527, df = 6, p < .05), while in Bern more attempters visited GPs within the previous month.

Almost two thirds of the patients in both cities (63.1% in Pecs, and 59.6% in Bern) said they had gone to see their doctor solely because of physical symptoms. Hungarian patients more often indicated psychological reasons only (27.4% vs 17.5%), while more patients in Bern visited their doctor because of both physical and psychological symptoms (22.8% vs 9.5%).

Almost the same proportion of the patients who contacted GPs before the parasuicidal act had suicidal ideation (21 patients in Pecs, 25%, and 17 in Bern, 29.8%).

However, of those patients who had suicidal ideation, 6 subjects (28%) in Pecs and 8 subjects (47%) in Bern said that they mentioned it to their doctor explicitly or vaguely (χ^2 = 10.896, df = 4, p < .05). The majority of patients were prescribed medication (84.5% in Pecs, 75% in Bern), and, of those subjects, 40% in Pecs but only 28% in Bern used these drugs for self-poisoning.

Previous Psychiatric Treatment

Almost the same proportion of patients reported previous psychiatric in-patient treatment (42% in Pecs and 38% in Bern). A history of two or more previous admissions was more frequent in the Pecs sample (24.7% vs19.7%). Hungarian patients more frequently attended psychiatric outpatient clinics (62% vs27%), while in Bern a much higher proportion of attempters were treated by private psychiatrists and psychologists (62% vs 9%, χ^2 = 63.034, df = 2, p = 0). In Bern more patients had attended a consultation service for alcohol or drug problems (14% vs 7%, χ^2 = 29.644, df = 2, p = 0).

Discussion

The objective of our study was to investigate whether differences in the provision of health care could possibly influence the help-seeking behaviour of parasuicidal patients. We compared the patterns of contact of suicide attempters with their GPs in Pecs with those in Bern. Although the numbers of cases are relatively small, both patient samples are representative of the total number of medical treated suicide attempters living in the catchment areas. To ensure consistent data collection, both patient samples were interviewed by trained interviewers using the same semi-structured interview schedule (EPSIS I.). The patient samples are directly comparable because they are based on catchment areas and not on admissions to an institution.

Patients in Pecs were slightly younger than those in Bern, and the ratio of males to females in Pecs was lower. The samples did not differ significantly with regard to social characteristics and marital status.

There was little difference in the proportion of patients visiting their GPs throughout the year. However, twice as many Hungarian patients went to see their GP in the last week before the suicide attempt than Swiss patients, while few more attempters visited GPs in the previous month in Bern. Almost the same proportion of these patients reported suicidal ideation, but only more than one quarter of patients in Pecs and half of the patients in Bern talked about their suicidal thoughts during the last visit to the GP. Of those who had contacted a GP within a month, in the Hungarian sample more patients were prescribed medication, and more used these drugs for self-poisoning. In the Swiss sample, more patients took antidepressants in a bigger dose in the period before their attempt. This fact may refer to the better diagnosis and treatment of depression in Bern.

The higher number of visits during the week before the suicide attempt suggests that this was an expression of help seeking, which, however, did not prevent these patients from attempting suicide. The relatively lower percentage of patients seeing their GP in the week before the attempt in Bern is difficult to interpret. It may be that patients sought help earlier (as, indeed, within a month prior to the attempt more patients saw their GP in Bern) or, theoretically, one could imagine that due to the GP visits less people attempted suicide. However, this would be a bold interpretation of the data. What we do not know is how many patients in both samples visited their GPs for similar reasons, but did not attempt or commit suicide. Obviously, the patients in our samples represent only a proportion of all patients that can be considered at risk for attempting or committing suicide, although we do not know what the total number is.

The samples were comparable in terms of previous psychiatric treatment, although in the Pecs sample there were more previous admissions. Patients in Pecs more frequently had attended a psychiatric outpatient clinic, while in Bern a higher proportion of subjects were treated by a private psychiatrist or psychologist.

One of the factors determining the role of GPs could be the availability of GP services ($n = 23$) and time. In Bern, there are 710 patients per practice for the population aged > 15 years, while in Pecs the number of patients per GP practice amounts to 1700. It is not surprising, therefore, that in Bern attempters mention their suicidal thoughts more often. Apart from the higher number of GPs, it is likely that the private medical care system in Switzerland encourages a more personal patient-doctor relationship. In Pecs, large numbers of patients belong to one doctor, and, for this reason, the visits tend to be very short, formal and impersonal. Mostly there is no possibility to develop a more closer and personal relationship with GPs. That a relatively high percentage of patients (higher in Pecs) use their prescribed drugs for an overdose suggests that the drugs were often prescribed in lieu of a psychotherapeutic relationship, which is time consuming and may not be practical in a health care system with crowded outpatient clinics.

Obviously, with the drastically higher number of patients per GP in Pecs, it is to be expected that there is limited time for patients and GPs to engage in a therapeutic relationship. In crisis situations patients visit their GPs, but, because of difficulties in communicating suicidal intent, they are not able to ask for help and doctors do not recognise the pre-suicidal situation and therefore cannot give emotional or psychological support to them. On the other hand, psychiatric out-patient services are provided by a much higher number of psychiatrists in Bern than in Pecs. In Bern, the number of psychiatrists per 100,000 inhabitants is nearly double to that of Pecs (43/100,000 vs 23/100,000). Furthermore, as a consequence of differences in mental health care systems, patients are treated mostly in out-patient clinics in Pecs, while Swiss attempters prefer private psychiatrists, who can provide better circumstances for the treatment (more time availability, closer and more personal doctor-patient relationship, etc.)

We should consider that only a small proportion of all attempters (6% and 12% respectively) mentioned their suicidal thoughts to their doctor. This also proves that there is, generally, a real problem in getting people to communicate their intent. People with suicidal thoughts hardly talk about them. We should also mention, as a limiting factor of our study, that suicide attempts are not always planned a week or a month before the act. Sometimes these are impulsive reactions, especially in the case of personality disorders (in our samples the proportion of personality disorders was a little bit more than 10% in both cities).

To summarise, we found substantial differences in the time and events of last contact with GP between the Pecs and Bern samples of suicide attempters, which may refer to different problems in help-seeking behaviour. No causal inferences can be made, but it is likely that the differences are related to the higher number of practising GPs and a more personal and consistent patient-doctor relationship in Bern. The rate of attempted suicide as well as the repetition rate of suicide attempts was higher in the Pecs sample – which again may partly be related to the health care system in Pecs. We believe that a consistent and personal relationship with a medical helper or system (e.g., GP as gatekeeper) facilitates the communication of suicidal ideation. However, the recognition of risk of suicide is associated with knowledge about and attitudes towards suicide and the role of the physician in suicide prevention (Domino & Swain, 1985). A better understanding of suicidal behaviour is likely to improve the communication and the therapeutic relationship with the suicidal patient. Arato et al (1988) demonstrated that 63% of Hungarian suicide victims suffered form a major depressive disorder. Thus, training GPs on depression (Rutz et al., 1992; Lepine et al., 1997; Rihmer, 1997), suicidal behaviour and communication would significantly increase their competence and effectiveness in the diagnosis and treatment of depression and pre-suicidal crisis. The study by Rutz et al (1992) proved that this strategy has a potentially preventative effect.

However, we know that consultation rates and help seeking patterns in men are consistently lower than in women in the case of emotional problems and depressive symptoms. Empirical evidence shows that low treatment rates for men cannot be explained by better health, but must be attributed to a discrepancy between perception of need and help-seeking behaviour. It is argued that social norms of traditional masculinity make help seeking more difficult, because of the inhibition of emotional expressiveness influencing symptom perception of depression (the "male depression" syndrome). Consequently, we should pay attention to this factor, too, in addition to all other medical and social factors that presently constitute known barriers to help seeking.

In conclusion, contact with health services before the act is common among those who attempt suicide. This is a necessary but not sufficient condition for clinicians to intervene. More work is needed to determine whether these people show characteristic patterns of care and particular risk factors that would enable a targeted approach to be developed to assist clinicians in detecting and managing these patients. Suicide prevention efforts involving primary care may be most effective in preventing suicide among older adults and possibly women (Luoma et al., 2002). It is likely that a consistent and personal relationship with a medical helper or system (e.g., GP as gatekeeper) facilitates the communication of suicidal ideation. Our results suggest that this effect may partly depend on the characteristics of the health care system.

References

Andersen, U. A., Andersen, M., Rosholm, J. U., & Gram, L. F. (2000). Contacts to the health care system prior to suicide: A comprehensive analysis using registers for general and psychiatric hospital admissions, contacts to general practitioners and practising specialists and drug prescriptions. *Acta Psychiatrica Scandinavica, 102,* 126–134.

Appleby, L. Shaw, J., Amos, T., McDonnell, R., Harris, C., McCann, K., Kiernan, K., Davies, S., Bickley, H., & Parsons, R. (1999). Suicide within 12 months of contact with mental health services: National clinical survey. *British Medical Journal, 318,* 1235–1239.

Arató, M., Demeter, E., Rihmer, Z., & Somogyi, E. (1988). Retrospective psychiatric assessment of 200 suicides in Budapest. *Acta Psychiatrica Scandinavica, 77,* 454–456.

Balasz, J., Bitter, I., Lecrubier, Y., Csiszer, N., & Ostorharics, G (2000). Prevalence of subthreshold forms of psychiatric disorders in persons making suicide attempts in Hungary. *European Psychiatry, 15,* 354–361.

Beautrais, A., Joyce, P., Mulder, R., Fergusson, D., Deavoll, B., & Nightingale, S. (1996). Prevalence and co-morbidity of mental disorders in persons making serious suicide attempts: A case-control study. *American Journal of Psychiatry, 153,* 1009–1014.

Domino, G., & Swain, B. J. (1985). Recognition of suicide lethality and attitudes toward suicide in mental health professionals. *OMEGA, 16,* 301–308.

Ferreira de Castro, E., Cunha, M. A., Pimenta, F., & Costa, I. (1998). Parasuicide and mental disorders. *Acta Psychiatrica Scandinavica, 97,* 25–31.

Grootenhuis, M., Hawton, K., Van Rooijen, L., & Fagg, J. (1994). Attempted suicide in Oxford and Utrecht. *British Journal of Psychiatry, 165,* 73–78.

Hawton, K., & Blackstock, E. (1976). General practice aspects of self-poisoning and self-injury. *Psychological Medicine, 6,* 571–575.

Hawton, K., Houston, K., & Shepperd, R. (1999). Suicide in young people: Study of 174 cases, aged under 25 years, based on coroner's and medical records. *British Journal of Psychiatry, 175,* 271–274.

Isometsa, E. T., Heikkinen, M. E., Marttunen, M. J., Henriksson, M. M., Aro, H. M., & Lönnqvist, J. K. (1995). The last appointment before suicide: Is suicide intent communicated? *American Journal of Psychiatry, 152,* 919–922.

Kerkhof, A., Bernasco, W., Bille-Brahe, U., & Schmidtke, A. (1993). European Parasuicide Study Interview Schedule (EPSIS I). In U. Bille-Brahe et al (Eds.), *Facts and figures* (pp. 53–118). Copenhagen: WHO/EUR/ICP/PSF 018.

Lepine, J.-P., Gastpar, M., Mendlewicz, J., & Tylee, A. (1997). Depression in the community: The first pan-European study DEPRES (Depression Research in European Society), *International Clinical Psychopharmacology, 12,* 19–29.

Lin, E. H. B., von Korff, M., & Wagner, E.H (1989). Identifying suicide potential in primary care. *Journal of General Internal Medicine, 4*, 1–6.

Luoma, J. B., Martin, C. E., & Pearson, J. L. (2002). Contact with mental health and primary care providers before suicide: A review of the evidence. *American Journal of Psychiatry, 159*, 909–916

Magoz-Gurpide, A., Baca-Garcia, E., & Diaz-Sarastre, C. (1999). Attempted suicide and previous contact with health system. *Actas Espanola de Psiquiatria, 27*, 329–333.

Michel, K., Runeson, B., Valach, I., & Wasserman, D. (1997). Contacts of suicide attempters with GPs prior to the venet: A comparison between Stockholm and Bern. *Acta Psychiatrica Scandinavica 95*, 94–99.

Osváth, P., Michel, K., & Fekete, S. (2003). Contact with health care services before suicide attempt in Bern and in Pecs. *International Journal of Psychiatry in Clinical Practice, 7*, 3–8

Pirkis, J., & Burgess, P. (1998). Suicide and recency of health care contacts. *British Journal of Psychiatry, 173*, 462–474.

Platt, S., Bille-Brahe, U, Kerkhof, A., Schmidtke, A., Bjerke, T., Crepet, P., De Leo, D., Haring, C., Lönnqvist, J., Michel, K.. Pommereau, X., Querejeta, I., Phillipe, I., Salander-Renberg, E., Temesvary, B., & Wasserman, D. (1992). Parasuicide in Europe: The WHO/EURO Multicentre Study on Parasuicide, I: Introduction and preliminary analysis for 1989. *Acta Psychiatrica Scandinavica, 85*, 97–104.

Rihmer, Z. (1997). Recognition of depression and prevention of suicide: the role of general practitioners and general physicians. *International Journal of Psychiatry in Clinical Practice, 1*, 131–134.

Rihmer, Z., Rutz, W., & Barsi, J. (1993). Suicide rate, prevalence of diagnosed depression and prevalence of working physicians in Hungary. *Acta Psychiatrica Scandinavica, 88*, 391–394.

Runeson, B., & Wasserman, D. (1994). Management of suicide attempters: What are the routines and the cost? *Acta Psychiatrica Scandinavica, 90*, 222–228.

Rutz, W., von Knorring, L., & Walinder, J. (1992). Long-term effects of an educational program for general practitioners given by the Swedish Committee for the Prevention and Treatment of Depression. *Acta Psychiatrica Scandinavica, 85*, 83–88.

Schmidtke, A., Bille-Brahe, U, DeLeo, D., Kerkhof, A., Bjerke, T., Crepet, P., Haring, C., Hawton, K., Lönnqvist, J., Michel, K., Pommereau, X., Querejeta, I., Phillipe, I., Salander-Renberg, E., Temesvary, B., Wasserman, D., Fricke, S., Weinacker, B., & Sampaio-Faria, J. G. (1996). Attempted suicide in Europe. Rates, trends and sociodemographic characteristics of suicide attempters 1989–1992. Results of the WHO/EURO Multicentre Study on Parasuicide. *Acta Psychiatrica Scandinavica, 93*, 327–338.

Stenager, E. N., & Jensen, K. (1994). Attempted suicide and contact with the primary health authorities. *Acta Psychiatrica Scandinavica, 90*, 109–113.

Suominen, K., Isometsa, E., Ostamo, A., & Lönnqvist, J. (2002). Health care contacts before and after attempted suicide. *Social Psychiatry and Psychiatric Epidemiology, 37*, 89–94.

Suominen, K., Henriksson, M., Suokas, J., Isometsa, E., Ostamo, A., & Lönnqvist, J. (1996). Mental disorders and co-morbidity in attempted suicide. *Acta Psychiatrica Scandinavica, 94*, 234–240.

Wolk-Wasserman, D. (1987). Contacts of suicidal neurotic and prepsychotic/psychotic patients and their significant others with public care institutions before the suicide attempts. *Acta Psychiatrica Scandinavica, 75*, 358–372.

Chapter 21
Suicide Attempters, Health Care Systems and the Quality of Treatments

Unni Bille-Brahe[1] and Cordula Löhr[2]

[1]*Suicide Research Centre, Odense, Denmark,* [2]*Department of Clinical Psychology, University of Würzburg, Germany*

Introduction

When plans were made for the WHO/Euro Multi-Centre Study on Parasuicide (later to be renamed WHO/Euro Multi-Centre Study on Suicidal Behaviour), it was agreed that the project should cover two areas of research, namely, the *Monitoring Study* and the *Repetition-Prediction Study* (Kerkhof et al., 1994), but it was also underlined that it should aim at enhancing an awareness of the problem of suicide and encouraging suicidological research, in general, and prevention throughout Europe.

In this, the intentions of the Multi-Centre Study were supported by the fact that, already in 1987, a set of *Guiding Principles for Development of Social Welfare Policies and Programs in the Near Future* had been endorsed at an UN Interregional Consultation of Social Welfare Ministers, and, in the same year, a *Formulation and Implementation of Comprehensive National Strategies for Prevention of Suicidal Behaviours and the Provision of Supportive and Rehabilitative Services to Persons at Risk and to Other Affected Persons* was worked out (UN & WHO, 1993; UN, 1996),

Taken literally, the request for "national strategies" as yet has been met with only moderate success, as only relatively few countries have implemented nation-covering strategies for the prevention of suicide. On the other hand, in most European countries there is by now an increasing awareness of the problem of suicide, and also an increasing number of activities in the field of suicide prevention. Many of these activities target persons who have attempted suicide, and focus is – as underlined in, e.g., the national plans being worked out in the Scandinavian countries (Finland 1987, Norway 1994, Sweden 1995, Denmark 1998) – on the importance of being able to offer qualified treatment and aftercare to all suicidal persons.

The aim of this paper is to give an overview of the procedure of offering treatment and aftercare to suicide attempters in the various areas under study. The descriptions are based on information from the WHO publication *Facts and Figures* (Bille-Brahe et al., 1993; 1999) and data from the *Monitoring Study* and from the *Repetition-Prediction Study*. The WHO/Euro Multi-Centre Study does not provide us with any information as to what type of treatment – that is, whether the patients are offered, e.g., psychopharmacological treatment, psychotherapy, cognitive therapy or other treatment, neither was it ever intended to carry out general evaluations of the various treatments. Data from the Repetition-Prediction Study give us, however, the opportunity to study the quality of the treatment from the user's point of view – that is, how the suicide attempter him/herself experienced the treatment he/she had been offered.

An Overview of Praxis Followed in the Various Areas

In the publications *Facts and Figures* (Bille-Brahe et al., 1993, 1999), which are based on reports from the individual centre participating in the Multi-Centre Study, data on demographic, socio-economic, psychosocial, and health and health care characteristics of the area under study are presented, and the pathways of suicide attempters through the health care system described.

In most of the areas under study, the main gateway to the immediate treatment after the attempt is the emergency unit at a (nearby) general or university hospital. In some areas, however, the GP will be the first person to be contacted, and, in a few areas, a special ambulance service will be the first caretaker.

The information provided by the various centres about the next steps on the pathway is rather rare, but differences in routines are indicated. One centre may report that up to 50% of all attempters usually leave hospital immediately after first aid, another that 80% are referred to a hospital bed. The reports indicate, however, that in most cases, the suicide attempter will at least be assessed by a psychiatrist. Interesting differences were found, including that in the Turkish area under study, the assessment includes a police report, in Slovenia an assessment by a psychiatrist is obligatory, and that in the Israel area all suicide attempters have to stay in hospital for 24 hours.

Finally, there are huge differences as to the question of aftercare, and also many centres report that offers exist, but there are problems with compliance. The failure to comply with referral to outpatient aftercare is a well-documented problem, and several strategies to enhance compliance have been discussed (e.g., van Heeringen, 1992; van Heeringen et al., 1995). It should be noted though that, even if aftercare is accepted, compliance may also be a question of distance and the availability of transport; some of the areas under study cover more than 55,000 km^2, while others cover less than 50 km^2, with the population densities varying between 11,000 and 5 inhabitants per km^2.

Referrals after the Initial Treatment

The Monitoring Study gives more detailed and comparable information on referrals recommended after the initial treatment of the suicide attempters. During the first period of registration (1989–1993), 17,110 cases were registered in 12 centres; during the second (1994–1998) 17,261 in 14 centres, i.e., in all 34,371 cases of suicide attempts. All cases were registered according to the same definition and case finding criteria, and identical monitoring schedules were used (Kerkhof et al., 1994).

Generally, in about a quarter of the cases, the attempter left the hospital after the initial treatment had been completed (28% of the male and 22% of the female attempters in the first period, 25% and 21%, respectively, in the second). There were, however, huge differences between the areas under study. In Padua, Stockholm, Umeå, Szeged, Ljubljana and Pecs, about 90% of both male and female attempters were recommended further treatment, and in Würzburg this was the case for the female attempters during the first period. In contrast, in Odense about half of the attempters left the hospital after the initial treatment, while the rest of the centres reported percentages varying between 10 and 38%. In some centres, the pattern changed significantly from the one period to the other. In Stockholm, the male attempters were more often recommended inpatient treatment during the second period, while in Sør-Trøndelag and Würzburg, fewer female attempters were now recommended further treatment. In Padua and Würzburg, too, more female attempters went home after the initial treatment without any further recommendation, while in Helsinki, Oxford and Stockholm, more female attempters were recommended further treatment.

There were significant differences between the genders, but again the pattern was not the same in all areas. During the first period, only in Helsinki, Sør-Trøndelag and Umeå did more men than women leave the hospital without any recommendation for further treatment, while during the second period this was the case in Helsinki, Sør-Trøndelag and in and Würzburg. In contrast, in Odense and Tallin, more women than men went home without any further recommendation.

Results from the *Repetition-Prediction Study* (EPSIS) provide us with more detailed information on referrals and also about how the suicide attempters themselves evaluate the treatment they received. Of the centres participating in the Multi-Centre Study, 8 centres, namely Bern (Switzerland), Helsinki (Finland), Leiden (The Netherlands), Odense (Denmark), Padua (Italy), Sør-Trøndelag (Norway), and Stockholm and Umeå (Sweden), have carried out both the first and the second wave of the European Parasuicide Study Intervention Schedule (EPSIS I and EPSIS II) (Kerkhof et al., 1993 a, 1993b.).

In total, 1,269 EPSIS I and 601 EPSIS II interviews were completed, yielding an average follow-up percentage of 55. To check the representativeness of the group of attempters completing the follow-up interview, test were carried out on differences between this group ($n = 601$) and the drop-outs ($n = 468$) with regard to age, gender, methods, previous suicide attempts, and previous psychiatric treatment. The results showed that, as far as pooled data was concerned, there were no significant differences between the two groups on any of these variables. With two (minor) exceptions, this was also the case at the individual centres: in Helsinki, there was an excess of attempters who had attempted suicide previous to the index attempt (i.e., the attempt that included the person in the study) in the EPSIS II group, and, in Leiden, there were significant differences between the two groups regarding previous psychiatric treatment. This was, however, mainly due to differences in missing values (4% in the EPSIS II group, 26% among the drop-outs). It therefore seems reasonable to conclude that the EPSIS II group constitutes a representative sample of the whole interviewed population.

Finally, some basic characteristics of the suicide attempters interviewed during the *Repetition-Prediction Study* were compared with the corresponding figures from the *Monitoring Study* on all attempters registered in 1990 (Bille-Brahe et al., 1996). On the average, men were underrepresented in the groups of interviewed attempters compared to the total population of registered suicide attempters. Self-poisoning was more frequent in the interview group, while fewer had used one method only. There were no significant differences between the two groups as far as age and previous attempts were concerned. It has to be kept in mind, however, that at times there might be significant differences between the centres, and, consequently, conclusions based on pooled data have to be drawn with care. The following analyses are based on information from EPSIS I and EPSIS II interviews with a total of 601 suicide attempters.

On the average, approximately two thirds (72%) of the suicide attempters interviewed had arrived at the emergency ward at a general hospital, while 11% had been admitted directly to an internal medical ward and 9% to a psychiatric ward. However, the procedure followed when referring suicide attempters to treatment differed markedly between the centres as known from both *Facts and Figures* and the *Monitoring Study*. In Helsinki and in Stockholm, the majority (94%, 93%) was first seen at an emergency ward, while in Padua very few (3%) and in Sør-Trøndelag none were admitted to hospital via the emergency ward, but instead went directly to an internal medical ward.

After the initial treatment, more than one third (34%) went home (which is more than shown by the information from *Facts and Figures* and by the data from the *Monitoring Study*), while 11% and 19%, respectively, were transferred to in-

Table 1 First transferral after the initial treatment after the index attempt (%).

Centre	Intensive ward	Intern. Med.	Surgical ward	Psychiat. ward	Other wards	Going home	Total *N*
Bern	–	8	2	27	–	63	48
Helsinki	2	35	3	23	5	32	115
Leiden	6	1	–	41	2	51	106
Odense	35	3	–	38	9	15	92
Padova	–	–	–	14	3	83	35
Stockholm	17	44	2	29	8	1	133
Sør Trøndelag	–	–	–	13	–	87	23
Umeå	10	12	–	29	8	41	49
All	11	19	1	30	5	34	601

tensive care or to an internal medical ward, and close to one third (30%) to a psychiatric ward.

On average, more than a third (34%) stayed in hospital for only 24 hours, 37% were discharged within one week, 11% within two weeks, while 12% stayed for a longer period of time. In Odense, Stockholm and Umeå, 19%, 20%, and 22%, respectively, stayed for a longer period of time, while in Helsinki the percentage staying for 1 day or less was much higher than the average, namely 68% versus 34%.

On average, 20% of the attempters were transferred to other wards once or twice before being discharged. These transferrals took place particularly in Odense, Stockholm and Umeå, and most were to a psychiatric ward. In the end, 62% of those who did not go home after the initial treatment received in-patient treatment at a psychiatric ward before leaving the hospital.

When leaving the hospital, 472 attempters (79%) were referred to some kind of aftercare service.

Of these, 28% were referred to inpatient treatment and 72% to some kind of outpatient treatment. Of the 72% that were referred to out-patient care, about half (51%) was referred to out-patient treatment by a psychiatrist, while close to one third (31%) was referred to some "other health programme" (e.g., treatment for alcohol abuse). It should be noted that one person could be referred to more than one type of aftercare.

The referral practices, however, differed significantly between the areas under study. For instance, in Berne, Helsinki and Sør-Trøndelag, more than 40% were referred to in-patient treatment at a psychiatric hospital, while in Stockholm and Padua only 6% and 15%, respectively, were referred to in-patient treatment. On the other hand, referrals to out-patient treatment by a psychiatrist were more frequent in Leiden and especially in Padua, where 52% and 65%, respectively, of all patients referred to aftercare treatment (out- and in-patients) were referred to outpatient treatment by a psychiatrist. On the contrary, in Sør-Trøndelag and in Umeå, none

Table 2 Length of stay at hospital after index attempt (%).

Centre	1 day or less	2–7 days	8–14 days	14 days – 3 months	More than 3 months	NA	Total *N*
Bern	23	44	13	6	2	12	48
Helsinki	68	25	2	1	–	4	115
Leiden	38	38	9	3	–	12	106
Odense	23	23	32	15	4	3	92
Padova	9	71	6	9	–	6	35
Stockholm	32	42	6	10	10	1	133
Sør Trøndelag	39	57	–	–	–	4	23
Umeå	6	39	18	20	2	14	49
All	34	37	11	9	3	6	601

or very few were referred to a psychiatrist. In Sør-Trøndelag, many attempters (43%) were referred to a psychologist, but it has to be remembered that the figures for Sør-Trøndelag are very small indeed. At most centres, rather few were referred to the local GP or family doctor – an exception was in Stockholm, where close to one fifth (19%) of all referrals were to the GP.

The Patient's View on the Treatment Received

The Initial Treatment Received in Connection with the Index Attempt

During the EPSIS II interview, all patients were asked in detail about how they had experienced the immediate treatment they had received in connection with the index attempt. Thirty-one percent had, however, only vague memories from the stay at the hospital, and 8% had none at all. The attempters' assessment of their stay, as shown in Tables 3 and 4, therefore, has to be taken with some reservation.

On average, the attempters were rather satisfied with the somatic/medical aspects of the treatment they had received during their stay at the hospital, although there were, as seen from Table 3, significant differences between the centres with regard to the degree of satisfaction.

The attempters were also rather satisfied with the psychosocial aspects of their treatment, but to a far less degree than when medical aspects were concerned. While on average only 7% were directly dissatisfied with the medical aspects, 24% were dissatisfied with the psychosocial aspect of the treatment. Correspondingly, 60% versus 47% were satisfied with the medical and the psychosocial aspects, respectively. In general, the suicide attempters in Sør-Trøndelag were the least satisfied with

Table 3 The attempters' assessment of the somatic/medical aspects of the treatment received at hospital after the index attempt (%).

Centre	Very bad	Bad	Neither bad nor good	Good	Very good	NA	Total N
Bern	8	–	8	28	25	21	48
Helsinki	1	5	17	48	17	12	115
Leiden	–	3	30	48	6	13	106
Odense	7	4	15	23	38	13	92
Padova	–	3	11	66	14	6	35
Stockholm	2	8	17	53	5	15	133
Sør Trøndelag	13	4	44	22	9	8	23
Umeå	4	2	22	49	8	14	49
All	3	4	20	45	15	13	601

Table 4 The attempters' assessment of the psychosocial aspects of of the treatment received at hospital after the index attempt (%).

Centre	Very bad	Bad	Neither bad nor good	Good	Very good	NA	Total N
Bern	4	15	10	27	17	27	48
Helsinki	6	13	17	39	12	12	115
Leiden	5	13	24	39	10	9	106
Odense	19	15	15	11	33	8	92
Padua	9	6	23	40	14	9	35
Stockholm	7	23	20	33	4	13	133
Sør Trøndelag	22	17	9	30	9	13	23
Umeå	10	6	18	33	25	8	49
All	9	15	18	32	15	12	601

the treatment, while the attempters in Padova were the least dissatisfied. It is noteworthy that in all areas under study, the attempters were more critical when it came to the psychosocial than to the medical/somatic aspects of the initial treatment after the index attempt.

Aftercare In-Patient Treatment

Information on in-patient aftercare treatment contain many missing values, but it seems that close to two thirds were admitted for treatment within a month after the

Table 5 The inpatients' view on the aftercare treatment (%).

Centre	Very bad	Bad	Neither bad nor good	Good	Very good	Total N
Bern	–	17	17	17	50	18
Helsinki	3	13	26	40	18	38
Leiden	–	19	44	38	–	16
Odense	–	24	28	12	36	25
Padua	–	33	33	33	–	3
Stockholm	17	17	50	17	–	6
Sør Trøndelag	–	33	–	67	–	3
Umeå	14	29	–	29	29	7
All	3	19	27	28	23	116

discharge from the hospital, and close to a half of them stayed for approximately one month.

In the following, cases with missing values have been deleted from the material. The in-patients' view on the aftercare treatment was elucidated by a 12-item questionnaire, yielding values from 12 to 60 (see note).

In general, inpatients were rather satisfied with their aftercare treatment. There were no significant differences between the centres; on average half of the patients (51%) found the treatment good or very good, while 21% were definitely dissatisfied. There was no significant correlation between the in-patients' satisfaction with the medical/somatic aspects of the treatment they had received after the index attempt and their level of satisfaction with the aftercare treatment, while the correlation with the evaluation of the psychosocial aspects of the treatment was highly significant ($p < .005$).

Aftercare Out-Patient Treatment

Information on the out-patients' view on the aftercare was obtained via an 8-itemed questionnaire (see note). Of the 299 attempters who were referred to some form of out-patient treatment other than GP, 17 (6%) did not make use of the referral. Of the rest, only 249 persons were able to tell us when they had made the first contact and how long they had been in treatment. More than half of them (58%) had made the first contact immediately or at least within the first month, while close to one fifth (18%) had made their first contact only after 6 months. It should be noted that in some areas there would be waiting lists for out-patient treatment (e.g., in Odense, it usually takes about six months to get an appointment with a psychiatrist or a psychologist). On average, 20 contacts were made, ranging from 1 to more than 60

Table 6 The out-patients' view on the treatment (%).

Centre	Very bad	Bad	Neither bad nor good	Good	Very good	Total N
Bern	13	–	31	19	38	16
Helsinki	2	9	21	35	33	43
Leiden	4	10	16	48	22	50
Odense	2	12	7	23	56	43
Padua	17	6	6	56	17	18
Stockholm	7	16	29	33	16	58
Sør Trøndelag	–	–	25	50	25	4
Umeå	12	6	6	53	24	17
All	6	10	18	37	29	249

within the follow-up year. Fifty percent had had up to 14 contacts, the average length of the contacts being ≤ of an hour (range 10 min.–4 hours). Of the 39 attempters referred to the GP/family doctor, 8 made contact within a week after discharge and two thirds within the first month. Four persons did not contact their GP at all, and five of the attempters had seen their GP only once during the follow-up year.

In general, the outpatients were more satisfied with the treatment they had received than the inpatients; only 16% found it bad or very bad. There were, however, significant differences between the areas as to the degree of satisfaction. Especially in Padua and in Stockholm, and to some extent in Umeå, a relatively large proportion of the attempters was directly dissatisfied with the treatment they had received. On the other hand, both in Padua and in Umeå, many of the attempters were also highly satisfied.

The level of satisfaction with the aftercare treatment of the outpatients did not correlate with what they felt about the medical/somatic aspects of the treatment they had received while staying in hospital after the index attempt, but again, when the psychosocial aspects were considered, there was were a significant correlation ($p < .05$). The small number of attempters being referred to their GP makes analyses of data distributed by centres rather meaningless, but it seems that, in general, data from the individual data are close to the pooled data. On the whole, of the 39 attempters who had been referred to their GP, about half of them (51%) judged contact as good or very good, 5 (13%) bad or very bad, and one fifth (20%) said it had been neither good nor bad (15% missing values or no contact).

Satisfaction with the Treatment and the Risk of Repetition

The majority of the interviewed suicide attempters were repeaters; only 41% had not made any attempt previous to the index attempt. The number of previous attempts varied from one (by 24%) to 20 or more (by 2.5%). Close to one third of those who had previously made an attempt had made 4 or more. Only 54% of those having previously made suicide attempt(s) had received treatment after the attempt(s).

Interestingly, there were, in general, no significant differences between the areas regarding the frequencies of first-evers and repeaters.

The following tables show the correlations between the satisfaction with the treatment offered and the frequency of repetition. The tables show that there were no differences between first-evers and repeaters with regard to their view on the medical/somatic aspects and the treatment immediately after the index attempt.

Apparently, the level of satisfaction with the psychosocial aspects of the treatment at the hospital did not have any influence on the frequency of repetition after the index attempt either – the level of satisfaction was more or less the same for those who had

Table 7 Suicide attempters by repetition.

Centre	Only index attempt	Attempts before index	Attempts after index	Attempts before and after index	NA	Total
Bern	24	18	1	4	1	48
Helsinki	34	39	10	30	2	115
Leiden	36	26	4	39	1	106
Odense	13	17	4	13	45	92
Padua	20	9	3	2	1	35
Stockholm	58	52	4	17	2	133
Sør Trøndelag	9	7	2	5	0	23
Umeå	14	14	5	15	1	49
All	208	182	33	125	52	601

Table 8 The attempters' view on the somatic/medical aspects of the treatment received at the hospital after the index attempt by recidivism.

	Only index	Only before index	Only after index	Before and after index
(Very) good	53.6	52.7	48.1	50.0
Neither good nor bad	18.7	21.2	14.8	25.0
(Very) bad	27.6	26.1	37.0	25.0

Table 9 The attempters' view on the psychosocial aspects of the treatment received at the hospital after the index attempt by recidivism.

	Only index	Only before index	Only after index	Before and after index
(Very) good	69.1	68.9	77.8	66.1
Neither good nor bad	21.1	21.9	18.5	27.8
(Very) bad	9.8	9.3	3.7	6.1

Table 10 Out-patients' view on the aftercare treatment by recidivism.

	Only index	Only before index	Only after index	Before and after Index
(Very) good	60.2	64.3	75.0	76.9
Neither good nor bad	20.4	18.4	8.3	15.4
(Very) bad	19.3	17.2	16.7	7.7

Table 11 In-patients' view on the aftercare treatment by recidivism.

	Only index	Only before index	Only after index	Before and after index
(Very) good	68.6	40.0	62.5	45.5
Neither good nor bad	14.3	40	25	24.2
(Very) bad	17.1	20	12.5	30.3

repeated the attempt during the follow-up period and those who had not – and this was the case in all areas. Although the level of satisfaction was lower than with medical/somatic aspects, it is noteworthy that more than two thirds of those who had repeated after the index attempt said that the treatment had been good or very good.

There were no significant relationship between the level of satisfaction with the outpatient aftercare and repetition of suicide attempts, and this was the case whether the analyses were based on polled data or on data from the individual centres. Only 9% of the 62 outpatients who had repeated the attempt during the follow-up period were not satisfied, and more than three quarters of the "heavy" repeaters said that the treatment had been good or very good. In fact, these repeaters, having attempted suicide both prior to the index attempt and after, were the most satisfied of all with the treatment they had received as outpatients.

Compared with the outpatients, the relationship was as far as the inpatients were concerned, to some degree reversed: 29% of the repeaters and only 18% of those who had not repeated the attempt after the index attempt were dissatisfied with the treatment they had received. That means that 53% of the non-repeaters and 48% of the repeaters viewed the treatment as good or very good.

Discussion and Conclusion

Prevention of suicide behaviour has been on the agenda for years now in most western countries, and numerous treatment and aftercare programmes for suicide attempters have been tried out. Our knowledge on the usual procedures and praxis, and of interventions offered through Europe has, however, been scarce. Results from the Multi-Centre Study have shown that – perhaps as expected – treatment routines of suicide attempters vary to a great extent in the various European areas under study. In particular, there were marked differences in the use of psychiatric treatment between inpatients or outpatients. In general, however, in most areas under study, suicide attempters were usually assessed by a psychiatrist, and the majority would, at some point – either during their stay at hospital after the index attempt or during the aftercare – receive psychiatric treatment. In a few areas, offers of aftercare were scarce or non-existent, and several centres reported problems with compliance.

Unexpected was perhaps the attempters overall satisfaction with the treatment they had received. There were some differences between the areas as to the level of satisfaction, but in general, relatively few of the attempters were directly dissatisfied with the treatment they had received, be it during their stay at hospital after the index attempt or during aftercare as an out- or inpatient. In fact, the results indicate an apparent paradox: *the better or more satisfactory the treatment seemed to the attempters, the higher the risk of recidivism.*

There may, of course, be several reasons for this: in some cases the motive behind the repeated attempt might have been a more or less unconscious wish or need to re-live the feeling of getting attention and being taken care of. This may especially be the case when the suicide attempter, after the index attempt, has experienced a 2–3 hours long interview, having the full attention of a health care person.

Another explanation could be that the treatment was experienced as "good" only because it had not included the painful probing sometimes necessary to uncover the attempter's real problems and thereby enabling him/herself to try and solve these problems, or at least cope with them in a more expedient way.

Recent overviews of studies aiming at measuring the effects of various treatments and programmes have shown that, in general, beneficial effects are not easy to prove (Dew et al., 1987; Hawton et al., 1998; Streiner & Adams, 1987; van de Sande, 1997). The main obstacle seems to be the construction of valid and comparable measures of the treatment outcome. The result from our analyses based on data from the WHO/Euro Multi-Centre Study of the apparent inverse relationship between how the attempters had experienced the treatment they had received and the pattern of repetition, strongly indicates that using the patient's satisfaction as a measure of treatment outcome does not solve our problem.

Appendix

During the EPSIS II interview, all persons were asked the following 8 questions about the treatment they had received during their stay in hospital after the index attempt and during aftercare:
- Did you and the mental health care professional (MHCP) (in case of admission to a psychiatric hospital, the doctor who treated you) discuss the fact that you had taken too many pills/injured yourself, and the motives or reason you had to do it?
- Was the MHCP able to show understanding for you and your problems?
- How did the treatment link up with you problems?
- Did you feel that you and your problems were taken seriously?
- Did you feel at ease during the talk/admission ?
- Did the MHCP have an open attitude towards criticism?
- Did you feel that the MHCP paid enough attention to you and your problems?
- If family or friends of yours should have the same problems as you have had, could you recommend them to ask for help at the same MHCP/ same place?

In addition, inpatients were asked the following four questions:
- Was the nursing staff able to show understanding for you and your problems?
- What did you think of the contact you had with you fellow patients?
- What do you think about your privacy?
- What did you think about the atmosphere on the hospital/ward?

References

Bille-Brahe, U. (Ed.). (1999). *Facts and figures* (2nd ed.). Copenhagen: WHO European Regional Office.

Bille-Brahe, U., Kerkhof, A., De Leo, D., Schmidtke, A. et al. (1996). A repetition-prediction study on European parasuicide populations. Part II of the WHO/Euro Multi-Centre Study on Parasuicide in Cooperation with the EC Concerted Action on Attempted Suicide. *Crisis, 17,* 22–31.

Dew, M. A., Bromet, E. J., & Brent, D. (1987). A quantitative literature review of the effectiveness of suicide prevention centres. *Journal of Consulting and Clinical Psychology, 55,* 239–244.

Hawton, K., Arensman, E., Townsend, E. et al. (1998). Deliberate self harm: Systematic review of efficacy of psychological and pharmacological treatments in preventing repetition. *British Medical Journal, 317,* 441–447.

Kerkhof, A., Bernasco, W., Bille-Brahe, U., Platt, S., & Schmidtke, A. (1993a). A European Parasuicide Interview Schedule (EPSIS I, version 5.1). In U. Bille-Brahe (Ed.), *Facts and figures.* Copenhagen: WHO European Region Office.

Kerkhof, A., van Egmond, M., Bille-Brahe, U., & Schmidtke, A. (1993b). A European Parasuicide Interview Schedule (EPSIS II, version 3.2.). In U. Bille-Brahe (Ed.), *Facts and figures.* Copenhagen: WHO European Region Office.

Kerkhof, A., Schmidtke, A., Bille-Brahe, U., De Leo, D., & Lönnqvist, J. (1994). *Attempted suicide in Europe. Findings from the Multicentre Study on Parasuicide by the WHO Regional Office for Europe.* Leiden: DSWO Press.

Streiner, D. L., & Adam, K. S. (1987). The effectiveness of suicide prevention programmes: A methodological perspective. *Suicide & Life Threatening Behavior, 17,* 93–106.

UN & WHO. (1996). *Formulation and implementation of comprehensive national strategies for prevention of suicidal behaviours and the provision of supportive and rehabilitative services to persons at risk and other affected person* (working paper 1992). New York: Author.

Van der Sande, R., Buskens, E., Allart, E., van der Graaf et al. (1997). Psychosocial intervention following suicide attempt: A systematic review of treatment interventions. *Acta Psychiatrica Scandinavica, 96,* 43–50.

Van Heeringen, C. (1992). The management of non-compliance with outpatient aftercare in suicide attempts. A review. *Italian Journal of Suicidology, 2*(2), 79–83.

Van Heeringen, C, Jannes, S., Buylart, W. et al. (1995). The management of non-compliance with referral to outpatient aftercare among attempted suicide patients: A controlled intervention study. *Psychological Medicine, 25,* 963–970.

List of Contributors

Arensman E.
National Suicide Research Foundation
1 Perrott Avenue, College Road
IRL Cork
Ireland

Audenaert K.
Department of Psychiatry
University Hospital
De Pintelaan 185
B-9000 Gent
Belgium

Baskak B.
Department of Psychiatry
Medical School of Ankara University
Dikimevi
06590 Ankara
Turkey

Bertolote J. M.
World Health Organisation
Geneva
Switzerland

Bille-Brahe U.
Strandgade 46
DK-5683 Haarby
Denmark

Burgis S.
Australian Institute for Suicide Research
and Prevention
Mt Gravatt Campus
Griffith University
4111 Brisbane, Queensland
Australia

Chopin E.
Department of Clinical Psychology
Vrije Universiteit Amsterdam
De Boelelaan 1109
NL-1081 Amsterdam
The Netherlands

Corcoran P.
National Suicide Research Foundation
1 Perrott Avenue, College Road
IRL Cork
Ireland

De Leo D.
Australian Institute for Suicide Research
and Prevention
Mt Gravatt Campus
Griffith University
4111 Brisbane, Queensland
Australia

Devrimci-Özguven H.
Department of Psychiatry
Medical School of Ankara University
Dikimevi
06590 Ankara
Turkey

Fekete S.
Department of Psychiatry
University of Pécs
H-7623 Pécs
Hungary

Hawgood J.
Australian Institute for Suicide Research
and Prevention
Mt Gravatt Campus
Griffith University
4111 Brisbane, Queensland
Australia

Hawton K.
Centre for Suicide Research
Deptartment of Psychiatry
University of Oxford
Warneford Hospital Headington
Oxford OX3 7 JX
United Kingdom

Hjelmeland H.
Department of Psychology
Norwegian University of Science
and Technology
NO-7491 Trondheim
Norway

Jensen B.
Suicide Research Centre
Sondergade 17
DK-5000 Odense C
Denmark

Jessen G.
Suicide Research Centre
Sondergade 17
DK-5000 Odense C
Denmark

Keeley H. S.
National Suicide Research Foundation
1 Perrott Avenue, College Road
IRL Cork
Ireland

Kerkhof A.
Department of Clinical Psychology
Vrije Universiteit Amsterdam
De Boelelaan 1109
NL-1081 Amsterdam
The Netherlands

Lindgren S.
Department of Psychiatry
Umeå University
S-90187 Umeå
Sweden

Löhr C.
Department of Clinical Psychology
Clinic for Psychiatry and Psychotherapy
University of Würzburg
Fuechsleinstrasse 15
D-97080 Würzburg
Germany

Michel K.
Universitäre Psychiatrische Dienste (UPD)
Murtenstrasse 21
CH-3010 Bern
Switzerland

Österberg I.
Department of Psychiatry
Umeå University
S-90187 Umeå
Sweden

Osváth P.
Szeged M.J.V.Ö.Kórház
Pszichiatriai és Addiktológiai Osztály
Kálvária sgt.57
H-6725 Szeged
Hungary

Portzky G
Department of Psychiatry
University Hospital
De Pintelaan 185
B-9000 Gent
Belgium

Rutz W.
Regional Adviser
World Health Organization (WHO)
Regional Office for Europe
8 Scherfigsvejj
DK-2100 Copenhagen
Denmark

Salander-Renberg E.
Department of Psychiatry
Umeå University
S-90187 Umeå
Sweden

Sayil I.
Department of Psychiatry
Medical School of Ankara University
Dikimevi
06590 Ankara
Turkey

Schmidtke A.
Departme nt of Clinical Psychology
Clinic for Psychiatry and Psychotherapy
University of Würzburg
Fuechsleinstrasse 15
D-97080 Würzburg
Germany

Spathonis K.
Australian Institute for Suicide Research
and Prevention
Mt Gravatt Campus
Griffith University
4111 Brisbane, Queensland
Australia

Van Heeringen C.
Department of Psychiatry
University Hospital
De Pintelaan 185
B-9000 Gent
Belgium